THE POLITICAL ECOLOGY OF FORESTRY
IN BURMA, 1824-1994

To my Parents

RAYMOND L. BRYANT

The Political Ecology
of Forestry in Burma
1824-1994

UNIVERSITY OF HAWAI'I PRESS
HONOLULU

Published in North America by
University of Hawai'i Press
2840 Kolowalu Street
Honolulu, Hawai'i 96822

First published in the United Kingdom by
C. Hurst & Co. (Publishers) Ltd.
38 King Street,
London WC2E 8JZ, England

Printed in India by Thomson Press (India) Ltd.

Library of Congress Cataloging-in-Publication Data

Bryant, Raymond, 1953-
    The political ecology of forestry in Burma, 1824-1994 / Raymond L.
    Bryant
       p.   cm.
    Based on author's thesis
    Includes bibliographical references (p.   ) and index.
    ISBN 0-8248-1909-8
    1. Forest policy—Burma—History. —   2. Forests and forestry —
Political aspects—Burma–History.   3. Forest management—Burma—
History.   I. Title.
SD657.B93B78   1997
333. 75: 09591—dc 20   96-30877
                                                 CIP

PREFACE AND ACKNOWLEDGEMENTS

This study examines forest politics in Burma by addressing the question: 'What were the political consequences of the advent of a forest service in 1856 on forest access and conflict?' To answer it, three notions were differentiated: forests as a contested resource, the Forest Department as a resource manager, and conflicting perceptions of forest use. In turn, these notions serve as the analytical framework.

The book examines Burmese forest politics between 1824 and 1994, but focuses on the period 1856-1942 when the main patterns of state forest control and popular resistance were established. Given this colonial focus, research centred on a reading of colonial reports, journals, and proceedings. Providing a detailed record of forest management in British Burma, most of these documents are located at the India Office Library and Records in London. Especially valuable were the annual reports of the Forest Department (1856-1940), the India and Burma Forest Proceedings (1864-1924), the *Indian Forester* (1876-1954), the European Manuscript collection, and the Burma Office Files (1938-47). A comprehensive collection of Burma Working Plans (1885-1951) at the Indian Institute in Oxford, as well as other forestry materials located at the Oxford Forestry Institute, provided a valuable source of material on the post-1923 period. Legislative Council proceedings (Burma and India), general colonial documents (i.e. gazetteers) and secondary sources at the School of Oriental and African Studies and the University of London libraries were used to round out coverage of the colonial era.

Several problems associated with the use of colonial forest records merit comment. First, colonial sources often overlook or fail to capture the breadth and scale of everyday forms of peasant resistance. As Scott notes, the logic of such resistance is 'to leave few traces in the wake of its passage . . . [which] eliminates much of the documentary evidence that might convince social scientists and historians that real politics was taking place.'[1] If this is a general and inescapable drawback, it must not be overstated. As this book shows, the colonial state was not always internally united. Many civil officials opposed the

---

[1] James C. Scott, *Domination and the Arts of Resistance: Hidden Transcripts*, New Haven, 1990, p. 200.

expansion of Forest Department powers by drawing attention to the social effects (including peasant unrest) of forest restrictions.

Colonial forestry accounts have an additional drawback in so far as records are often highly technical. For non-foresters, there is, then, a problem of interpretation – understanding scientific reports in order to glean their political meaning. Yet, such an endeavour is essential. To understand how the Forest Department asserted control over diverse groups is also to appreciate the scientific dimensions of social and ecological control.

In seeking to understand developments in the postcolonial era, the problem of interpretation is compounded by the well-known difficulties associated with undertaking research in Burma since 1962. To be sure, those difficulties have eased somewhat in the 1990s as the State Law and Order Restoration Council (SLORC) has moved (albeit gradually) to end Burma's international isolation. However, research is still hindered by a relative paucity of available and reliable official data, restrictions on travel in the country, and by the general political climate of uncertainty and fear that yet characterizes Burma. Nonetheless, research conducted in Burma in July and August 1994 permitted the acquisition of a range of hitherto unavailable documents and was the occasion for an extensive series of interviews with officials in the Ministry of Forestry. Additional research was conducted in Thailand with non-government organizations involved with Burma as well as with forest officials and political leaders of the Karen National Union government. This research provides a basis for understanding the main developments of postcolonial Burmese forest politics.

If this book examines forest politics in Burma, it situates that investigation in a theoretical and comparative perspective. Chapter 1 introduces the analytical framework in the context of a discussion of political ecology that encompasses the role of the state, peasant resistance, bureaucratic politics and perceptions of resource use in forest access and conflict. In contrast, Chapter 8 compares and contrasts the Burmese experience with that of Indonesia, India and Thailand in order to emphasize the regional significance of trends in forest politics and management since the mid-nineteenth century. In this manner, the book links an analysis of forest politics in Burma with broader theoretical and comparative questions.

This study has benefited from the assistance and insights of many people and institutions in England, Burma and Thailand. The book is based largely on a Ph.D. dissertation addressing forest politics in colonial

Burma, undertaken at the School of Oriental and African Studies (SOAS) between September 1989 and March 1993. Financial support for this research was provided by the Committee of Vice-Chancellors and Principals of the Universities of the United Kingdom (under the Overseas Research Students Awards Scheme) and the School of Oriental and African Studies. Subsequent research on postcolonial Burmese forest politics was associated with fieldwork in Burma and Thailand in July-August 1994 which was supported by the School of Humanities at King's College London.

My time at SOAS was highly rewarding, and the research on which this book is based has been strengthened by the insights and practical help of (among others) Richard Boyd, Michael Heller, David Taylor, Ian Brown, Jonathan Rigg, Anna Allott, John Okell, Catherine Lawrence, Helen Cordell, Elizabeth O'Donnell, Tin Maung Maung Than and Duncan McCargo. I owe a big debt to Philip Stott for his enthusiastic support of my work in general. The assistance of Robert Taylor merits special recognition. Not only did he supervise my dissertation at SOAS, but he also assisted me subsequently in obtaining the necessary permission to conduct research in Burma in 1994. His assistance throughout this research is gratefully acknowledged.

At the British Library and India Office Library and Records, Patricia Herbert, Andrew Griffin and other staff provided guidance, as did Jasmin Howse at the Oxford Forestry Institute, and the staff of the Indian Institute (University of Oxford), Guildhall Library (London), and MacMillan Forestry Library (University of British Columbia). My thanks also to James Manor, Mike Parnwell, Phil Hirsch, Larry Lohmann, Glen Hill, Kate Geary, Robert Maule, Marlene Buchy, Mahesh Rangarajan, Marcus Colchester, Richard Gayer and Ann Usher for their general assistance.

An earlier version of Chapter 6 was published as 'Fighting over the Forests: Political Reform, Peasant Resistance and the Transformation of Forest Management in Late Colonial Burma', *Journal of Commonwealth and Comparative Politics* 32 (July 1994), pp. 244-60; parts of chapters 2 and 3 appeared originally together as 'From Laissez-faire to Scientific Forestry: Forest Management in Early Colonial Burma, 1826-85', *Forest and Conservation History* 38 (October 1994), pp. 160-70. They are reprinted here with the permission of the publishers.

My research on postcolonial Burmese forestry in Burma and Thailand could not have been conducted without the help of many individuals. In Thailand, Witoon Permpongsacharoen and the staff of the Foundation for Ecological Recovery were generous with their time and ideas; their assistance in providing contacts with officials in the Karen National

Union (KNU) government is also gratefully acknowledged. The willingness of the latter to speak to me during a difficult time in the KNU's struggle with Rangoon is most appreciated.

In Burma, many individuals took time out from their work to explain contemporary Burmese forestry to me both in the field and in Rangoon. To all of these individuals I owe a debt of gratitude. U Thaw Kaung and other library staff ensured that my time at the Universities Central Library in Rangoon and at the Forest Research Institute Library in Yezin was well spent. I am especially indebted, however, to U Myat Thin, U Ye Myint, U Aung Din and U Aung Zeya for their practical help in facilitating my research in the country, and for their patience and helpful responses to my unending series of questions and requests. For much of my time in Burma, I was accompanied by U Aung Zeya, and could not have wished for a more helpful, interesting and genial companion.

The writing of this book has benefited from the general encouragement and advice of my colleagues in the Department of Geography at King's College London. I am particularly grateful to Keith Hoggart, Linda Newson and Geoff Wilson for providing constructive feedback on theoretical and empirical questions associated with this book. Roma Beaumont and Gordon Brown in the department prepared the maps used in the book. Michael Dwyer has been a patient and supportive editor. Finally, thanks are due to my family and friends, to Noreen Davey for her support and encouragement in England, and above all to my parents without whose support the book would not have been possible.

King's College London   RAYMOND L. BRYANT
November 1996

CONTENTS

MAPS

TABLES

GLOSSARY

Baho	Central (as in the Central Administration during the Japanese occupation).
Begar	Compulsory labour (India).
Bobabaing	Ancestral lands; used by peasants and traders as a means to circumvent colonial restrictions on cutch production.
Chao	Hereditary local rulers in north-west Siam (see also *Sawbwa*).
Compound	To inflict an on-the-spot fine for a violation of the forest rules.
Cutch	Water extract of the sha tree used for tanning and dyeing purposes in the nineteenth and early twentieth centuries.
Disforest	To clear a reserve of forest cover in order to facilitate permanent cultivation.
Do Bama Asiayon	'We Burmese' Association; 1930s political group of youth and students.
Fire-trace	An area of varying width on which vegetation is cut and burned so as to facilitate the protection from fire of a designated area.
Fituris	Small localized uprisings (India).
Girdling	Method of killing a tree by removing a ring of bark and sapwood around its base; used as a means to regulate the extraction of teak.
Improvement fellings	Silvicultural system involving selective tree removal in order to facilitate the growth of teak and other commercial species.
Jhum	Shifting cultivation (India). See also *taungya*.
Kyo-waing	Reserved Forest.
Mahout	Timber elephant manager; occupation popular with the Karen in southern Burma.
Myo-ok	Township officer under British rule.

Myo-wun	Provincial governors appointed by the Burmese monarchy.
Nat	Animistic beings or spirits thought to control most aspects of human life.
Pongyi kyaung	Monastery; Buddhist school.
Pyidawtha	Literally 'happy and prosperous royal land'. The name given to a national development plan of the U Nu government in the early 1950s.
Pya Ley Pya	'Four Cuts'; the name given to the Burmese army's counter-insurgency campaign against the country's insurgent groups.
Rokkasoe	Guardian spirit of the trees in Burmese Buddhism.
Sanad	Treaty (as between the British government and the Shan Sawbwa).
Satyagraha	Popular revolt (India).
Sawbwa	Hereditary local rulers in the Shan States.
Sit-tans	Precolonial administrative records.
Taungya	Dry hill cultivation by shifting cultivators.
Taungya forestry	Reforestation method whereby shifting cultivators plant teak and other tree species in their taungya.
Teak selection system	Harvesting based on selective teak extraction.
Thakin	Literally 'master'. A self-designation of Burmese nationalists during the 1930s.
Thu-gyi	Headman (usually of a village).
Tumpang sari	Reforestation scheme (Indonesia); see also taungya forestry.
Uniform system	Timber extraction by clear felling followed by natural regeneration.
Working plan	Document detailing timber extraction and regeneration operations in a forest reserve or division.
Wunthanu athin	Village nationalist organizations of the 1920s and 1930s.
Ya-thit	Undersized teak log.
Yoma	Range of hills.

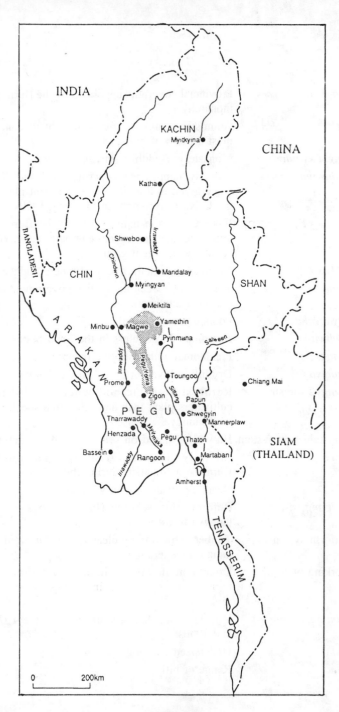

BURMA

xiv

Part I. INTRODUCTION

1

CONTESTING THE RESOURCE

The history of Burma's forests is a study in paradox. No other country in the world has been so closely identified in the popular imagination with its forests. Yet the political processes that have governed the fate of those forests are even today scarcely understood. This book addresses this paradox through an analysis of the politics of forest management in Burma between 1824 and 1994.

Before British rule, Burma's forests were already well known as a result of the country's lucrative teak trade. Indeed, growing British interest in Burma in the early nineteenth century was partly linked to the quest for teak. During colonial rule, the association of Burma with its forests (especially its teak forests) was strengthened such that by the twentieth century Burma was 'the land of teak'. Books about Burma written in colonial times by anthropologists, missionaries, travel writers or colonial officials invariably featured some reference to the country's forests.[1] This identification of Burma with its forests intensified following the Second World War and Burmese independence in January 1948, and was heavily tinged with nostalgia over Burma's role in the British Empire and in the war with Japan. The link between Burma, forests and 'adventure' was reflected in post-war travel accounts and the autobiographies of British employees of the European timber firms.[2] In recent years, the degradation of Burma's forests has symbolized to some the repressive nature of the ruling military regime known as the State Law and Order Restoration Council

---

[1] H.I. Marshall, *The Karen Peoples of Burma: A Study in Anthropology and Ethnography,* Columbus, 1922; D.M. Smeaton, *The Loyal Karens of Burma,* London, 1887; Max Ferrars and Bertha Ferrars, *Burma,* London, 1900; R. Talbot Kelly, *Burma: Painted and Described,* London, 1912; George Orwell, *Burmese Days,* Harmondsworth, 1987 (1934).

[2] Ethel Mannin, *Land of the Crested Lion: A journey through Modern Burma,* London, 1953; Norman Lewis, *Golden Earth: Travels in Burma,* London, 1952; J.H. Williams, *Elephant Bill,* London, 1950; J.H. Williams, *Bandoola,* London, 1953.

1

(SLORC).[3] Light-hearted or serious, all of these accounts have reinforced the association of Burma with its forests.

Yet this association is fraught with political significance. From precolonial times to the present day, the forests have been an integral element in warfare – a refuge for retreating forces and an obstacle to advancing armies. However, an alternative political significance is linked to the view that forests are also a resource to be exploited. It is through incorporation in human activities that the forests acquire their main significance.

About this Book

Forest use can only be fully understood in relation to the political processes which condition forest access. In contrast to popular and official accounts that have hitherto glorified Burma's forests, therefore, this book explores how Burma's forests have been incorporated into the political process, and how such incorporation, in turn, has been ripe with political and ecological meaning.

In doing so, the study emphasizes the central role of the state in shaping forest use and management in Burma. Although not the only arbiter of forest access and use, the state has nevertheless been at the heart of this process. However, the state's role as a resource manager has been widely contested by non-state actors, and has been the source of divisions within the state itself. Thus, the study of forest politics in Burma must also explore political conflict engendered by state forestry policies.

The genesis of modern forest politics in Burma can be traced back to the period 1856-1942 when patterns of state forest control and popular resistance were first elaborated. Although important political and economic developments affecting the forest sector have occurred since independence in 1948, these developments have not substantially altered the dynamic of control and resistance established during the colonial era.

For these reasons, the book focuses on the role of the colonial state in elaborating forest management practices that have conditioned forest politics well into the postcolonial era. Specifically, it analyzes how the colonial Forest Department sought to control forest activities, and the ways in which others fought such control. Guided by the

---

[3] Martin Smith, *Ethnic Groups in Burma*, London, 1994; Martin Smith, *Paradise Lost? The Suppression of Environmental Rights and Freedom of Expression in Burma*, London. 1994; Kate Geary, *The Role of Thailand in Forest Destruction along the Thai-Burma Border, 1988-1993*, Bangkok, 1994.

tenets of scientific forestry, colonial forest officials mapped, enumerated and valued the forests in the promotion of long-term commercial timber production. In doing so, they acquired a detailed understanding of how peasants, timber traders and shifting cultivators used those forests. Such knowledge was used to regulate extraction, increase revenue and promote conservation. The Forest Department thus attempted to rationalize forest use in order to further diverse political, economic and ecological objectives. But it did so in a context of British rule that privileged imperial interests over local concerns.

This process had far-reaching implications for state and society. The creation of reserved forests, and complex rules regarding their access and use, the emergence of a prosperous timber industry, and a sizable forest bureaucracy, heralded major changed in the way that forests were used. These changes encountered widespread popular opposition, and earned the forest official notoriety. The extent of that notoriety was in itself suggestive of the importance of the changes in the forest sector.

It is therefore remarkable that these changes have received so little attention. Several authors address aspects of the subject but few provide detailed accounts. None adequately treat the politics of colonial forest management.[4] In contrast, general analyses focus on issues such as agrarian development and nationalism to the neglect of forest-related change.[5] The absence of work on colonial forest politics is matched by an equally noticeable dearth of material addressing post-colonial forestry issues. The few works that broach the subject typically only do so in the context of a critique of the poor human rights record of the Burmese state since 1988.[6]

In this book we address this lacuna by examining how the Forest Department transformed forest access and use in colonial Burma, and the ways in which the colonial legacy is reflected in postcolonial Burmese forest politics. The study also situates the Burmese experience in comparative perspective in order to highlight how that

[4] Maria Serena I. Diokno, 'British Firms and the Economy of Burma, with Special Reference to the Rice and Teak Industries, 1917-1937', Unpubd. Ph.D. thesis, University of London, 1983; A.W. MacGillivray, 'Forest Use and Conflict in Burma 1750-1990 Unpubd. M.Sc. thesis, University of London. 1990; F.T. Morehead, *The Forests of Burma*, London, 1944; E.P. Stebbing, *The Forests of India*, London, 1922-6, vols I-III.

[5] G.E. Harvey, *British Rule in Burma, 1824-1942*, London, 1946; J.S. Furnivall, *Colonial Policy and Practice: A Comparative Study of Burma and Netherlands India*, New York, 1956 (1948); John F. Cady, *A History of Modern Burma*, Ithaca, 1958; see also Robert H. Taylor, *An Undeveloped State: The Study of Modern Burma's Politics*, Centre of Southeast Asian Studies Working Paper No. 28, Melbourne, 1983 in which an extensive literature review fails to mention forestry issues.

[6] Smith, *Ethnic Group in Burma; Paradise Lost?*

experience is similar to, or different from, the experiences of other Asian countries.

It is logical to begin this study of Burmese forest politics with the events of 1856. In that year, Burma's Forest Department was created, and the government of India (Burma was a part of the British Indian empire from 1824 to 1937) ordered the scientific management of Burma's forests in aid of long-term commercial timber production. To appreciate the significance of these events, it is first necessary to examine forest politics in early colonial Burma. Chapter 2 thus examines pre-scientific forestry (1824-55) to show how a system of *laissez-faire* forestry predominated. However, widespread overharvesting led to calls for state intervention which in an altered imperial context became feasible politically.

Chapter 3 considers the political implications of the advent of scientific forestry during the years 1856-81. A professional forest service was established, but this administrative change had far-reaching implications for the ways in which the state was internally organized and for relations between the state and non-state forest users. Chapters 4 and 5 trace the efforts of the Forest Department to rationalize forest use in the late nineteenth and early twentieth century. During the era of expansion (1881-1901), the subject of Chapter 4, forest management was extended to new territories and activities, and was marked by the rapid development of a network of reserved forests. Chapter 5 relates that during the era of consolidation (1902-22) these reserves were the principal focus of Forest Department forest politics, and as shown in Chapter 6, the links between forest management, nationalism and the political process were then tightly woven.

Chapter 7 explores Burmese forest politics from independence in 1948 to 1994. It examines how the quest to restore order in the forests in the face of multiple insurgencies shaped forest management, but notes how that the SLORC has formally abandoned socialism, yet in the mid-1990s it was unclear whether recent changes in the forestry sector represented a new direction in Burmese forest politics. Chapter 8 then situates forest politics in colonial and postcolonial Burma in a wider context by comparing the Burmese experience with that of Indonesia, India and Thailand – three Asian countries which arguably have the strongest historical and contemporary relevance to the Burmese situation.

Political Ecology and the State

This study of Burmese forest politics adopts a political ecology perspective. Political ecology is an inquiry into the political sources, conditions and ramifications of environmental change. As Blaikie and Brookfield note:

> The phrase 'political ecology' combines the concerns of ecology and broadly defined political economy. Together this encompasses the constantly shifting dialectic between society and landbased resources, and also within classes and groups within society itself.[7]

Embracing different social and ecological scales, political ecology addresses several inter-related research areas.[8] First, research into the contextual sources of environmental change examines the general ecological impacts of the state, interstate relations and global capitalism. In a world of increasing political and economic inter-dependence, these topics signal the growing social and ecological influence of national and international forces. A second research area investigates the location-specific aspects of ecological change. By studying conflict over access to environmental resources, scholars gain insights into how contextual actors impinge on specific socio-ecological relationships. Such research also documents the resistance of poor peasants and shifting cultivators as they fight for their livelihoods. A third research area assesses the effects of environmental change on socio-economic and political relationships. To what extent are environmental costs borne by disadvantaged groups, and how does this unequal burden affect existing inequalities? Further, and as discussion of peasant militancy in twentieth century colonial Burma will illustrate, unequal exposure to environmental change may lead to political confrontation. This research thus highlights that the impact of environmental change is rarely neutral and may reinforce prevailing inequalities.

A key theme in political ecology relates to tropical forest change. Third World deforestation has been a ubiquitous phenomenon since the nineteenth century as forests have been logged or converted to agriculture.[9] This trend transformed forest access and use, but the creation of eucalyptus plantations illustrates that reforestation also

[7] Piers Blaikie and Harold Brookfield, *Land Degradation and Society,* London, 1987, p.17; see also Piers Blaikie, *The Political Economy of Soil Erosion in Developing Countries,* London, 1985; Stephen G. Bunker, *Underdeveloping the Amazon: Extraction, Unequal Exchange, and the Failure of the Modern State,* Urbana, 1985.

[8] Raymond L. Bryant, 'Political Ecology: An Emerging Research Agenda in Third World Studies *Political Geography* 11 (January 1992), pp. 12-36; see also Richard Peet and Michael Watts. 'Development Theory and Environment in an Age of Market Triumphalism *Economic Geography* 69 (July 1993), pp. 238-42.

[9] Richard P. Tucker and J.F. Richards (eds), *Global Deforestation and the Nineteenth-Century World Economy,* Durham, 1983; John F. Richards and Richard P. Tucker (eds), *World Deforestation in the Twentieth Century,* Durham, 1988.

resonates with political and ecological meaning.[10] That tropical forests are a focus of attention is hardly surprising. These forests are a popular source of timber and non-timber products, and thus are integral to rural subsistence. They also provide essential ecological services regulating the hydrological and nutrient cycles. Tropical forests are the focus too of a global timber trade.[11] Finally, they are places to which 'surplus' populations may be exported, thereby obviating the need for land reform in central agricultural areas.[12]

The state has played a key role in tropical forest change. The human ability to manipulate the forests predates the development of the modern state, but the organizational characteristics that have enabled that institution to flourish have also served to enhance social control over the environment. Two characteristics in particular make the state such a powerful source of environmental change.

The first characteristic concerns the state's role as a facilitator of economic development. That role has varied historically and spatially, but only the state has been in a position to provide the physical, financial and social infrastructure essential to capital accumulation.[13] The state is involved in the provision of public goods – common currency, defence, education, health care – which the private sector cannot provide or does so only imperfectly. A second characteristic centres on the autonomous capabilities of the state. The state is not simply an agent of capital, but has its own sources of power that derive from the state's unique socio-spatial position at the intersection of the domestic political order and the interstate system. This distinctive position ensures that the state has its own political, economic and strategic interests that are not always synonymous with capital accumulation.[14]

[10] Larry Lohmann, 'Freedom to Plant: Indonesia and Thailand in a Globalizing Pulp and Paper Industry' in M.J.G. Parnwell and R.L. Bryant (eds), *Environmental Change in South-East Asia: People, Politics and Sustainable Development*, London, 1996, pp. 23-48

[11] Ooi Jin Bee, 'The Tropical Rain Forest: Patterns of Exploitation and Trade' *Singapore Journal of Tropical Geography* 11 (December 1990), pp. 177-42

[12] Larry Lohmann. 'Land, Power and Forest Colonization in Thailand' *Global Ecology and Biogeography Letters* 3 (July-November 1993), pp. 180-91

[13] R.J. Johnston, *Environmental Problems: Nature, Economy and State* London, 1989, chap. 5; Dietrich Rueschemeyer and Peter B. Evans, 'The State and Economic Transformation: Toward an Analysis of the Conditions Underlying Effective Intervention' in Peter B. Evans, Dietrich Rueschemeyer and Theda Skocpol (eds), *Bringing the State Back In*, Cambridge, 1985, pp. 44-77.

[14] Theda Skocpol, 'Bringing the State Back In: Strategies of Analysis in Current Research' in Peter B. Evans, Dietrich Rueschemeyer and Theda Skocpol (eds), *Bringing the State Back In*, Cambridge, 1985, pp. 3-37; Michael Mann, 'The Autonomous Power of the State: Its Origins, Mechanisms and Results' in John A. Hall (ed.), *States in History,*

Both the state's relationship to capitalism and the development of its own distinctive interests have been increasingly important factors in human-environmental interaction. With colonialism, this type of state came to dominate such interaction in the Third World too. Strengthened in the nineteenth century by such technological advances as the steamboat, machine gun and quinine, the colonial state initiated a process of change that redefined existing practices.[15] Economies were monetized, communications networks elaborated, international economic linkages expanded, new export crops grown, state-peasant relations regularized, and human expectations altered. Social transformation was accompanied by environmental permutation: changes in forest cover and type, the extension of agricultural production, modified soil conditions and increased pollution.

These changes were predicated on the use of new techniques of control and power. The colonial state used such means as the census, map, and museum to imagine 'the nature of the human beings it ruled, the geography of its domain, and the legitimacy of its ancestry'.[16] This process of imagining was most pervasive in those forested areas in which central authority was most tenuous. As the colonial state defined those forests, it also transformed them. What was 'progress', after all, if not the steady accumulation of knowledge in aid of more 'efficient' forest land-use?

In pursuit of such progress, the colonial state drew upon scientific forestry practices from Germany and France. Scientific forestry was a management system designed to promote long-term commercial timber production as a transition from pre-industrial forests to industrial tree plantation was made.[17] As transplanted to Burma (and elsewhere in Asia), scientific forestry was imbued with a strong ecological element. Throughout the colonial period, officials debated the links between the forests and local water supply, stream flow, rainfall and climate change.[18] Although couched in ecological terms, these

---

Oxford, 1986, pp. 109-36; Andrew Hurrell, 'A Crisis of Ecological Viability? Global Environmental Change and the Nation State', *Political Studies* 42 (1994), pp. 146-65.

[15] Daniel R. Headrick, *The Tools of Empire: Technology and European Imperialism in the Nineteenth Century,* Oxford, 1981, pp. 205-6. On the importance of the state in colonial India,see David Arnold and Ramachandra Guha (eds), *Nature, Culture, Imperialism: Essays on the Environmental History of South Asia,* Delhi, 1995.

[16] Benedict Anderson, *Imagined Communities: Reflections on the Origin and Spread of Nationalism,* rev. edn, London, 1991, pp. 163-4.

[17] Alexander S. Mather, *Global Forest Resources,* London, 1990.

[18] Richard Grove, 'Conserving Eden: The (European) East India Companies and their Environmental Policies on St. Helena, Mauritius and in Western India, 1660 to 1854', *Comparative Studies in Society and History 35* (April 1993), pp. 318-51.

debates resonated with political meaning. Ecology and politics were often conjoined to discredit indigenous practices while providing a powerful justification for the extension of state forest control.

The interlinked nature of political and ecological issues and problems is thus central to political ecology, as it is to this book. Specifically, the study traces the development of state control over Burma's forests focusing mainly on the colonial era. In doing so, however, such development is always related to one or more of three themes that run through the entire book. The argument is that forest politics in Burma needs to be understood in relation to at least three key notions: (1) forests as a contested resource, (2) the Forest Department as a resource manager, and (3) conflicting perceptions of forest use. As they are central to this analysis, each theme is summarized as part of a consideration of the wider literature.

Forests as a Contested Resource

The British transformed but did not create conflict over forest access in Burma. The monarchical state attempted to regulate and tax diverse forest users, not mainly teak traders as often assumed; and, forest users fought such control. In populated and settled areas, forest produce was not a 'free gift of nature'.[19]

If anything, early colonial rule relaxed access restrictions imposed by the monarchical state. Influenced by contemporary principles of economic liberalism, and preoccupied with the need to control a hostile population in an unfamiliar territory, British officials at first had neither the inclination nor the resources to regulate forest use systematically. Yet by the mid-nineteenth century British rule was beginning to have a major impact on Burma's forests.

The deforestation of the deltaic rainforests in the late nineteenth century is one type of forest change prompted by colonial rule.[20] This study is predominantly concerned, however, with another type of forest transformation that pertains to modified patterns of access and use in those regions retained as 'forest lands'.[21] The colonial state increased revenue and control in these areas not by eliminating

---

[19] J.S. Furnivall, 'Land as a Free Gift of Nature', *Economic Journal* 19 (1909), pp. 552-62.

[20] Michael Adas, 'Colonization, Commercial Agriculture, and the Destruction of the Deltaic Rainforests of British Burma in the Late Nineteenth Century' in Richard P. Tucker and J.F. Richards (eds), *Global Deforestation and the Nineteenth-Century World Economy*, Durham, 1983, pp. 95-110.

[21] See Appendix for a brief description of the main forest types (and commercial species therein) of Burma.

forest, but rather by the systematic investigation and retention of forest cover. These two types of forest change were interrelated: deforestation in the Irrawaddy delta affected conflict over residual forests, while altered access and use in the latter influenced patterns of deforestation in the former.

Forest conflict was not static. Under the impetus of practices introduced by the British, Burma's forests were modified, as were patterns of forest use and conflict. How forest produce was attained, what was considered legal appropriation, the manner in which 'traditional' practices were invoked to resist or enforce regulation, and the ways in which shifting forest use reflected relative scarcity and a quest to 'outflank' restrictions, varied by time and place, but are the essence of forest politics in colonial Burma. Shifting cultivators, peasants and timber traders challenged the regulation of their activities, and in doing so, ensured that forests remained a contested resource throughout the colonial period.

Conflict over forest access continued in postcolonial Burma. However, that conflict has changed somewhat in light of altered political and economic conditions. In central areas, the state has sought to protect reserved forests for long-term commercial forestry, and has encountered opposition from local forest users. In the border areas, conflict has centred on the Burmese state's attempts to wrench control of the timber trade from insurgent forces.

In pursuing the theme of forests as a contested resource, this book draws upon a burgeoning literature on conflict over access. This literature is premised on the assumption that poor peasants and other politically marginal groups resist the predations of political and economic elites. By eschewing reductionism, it explores the complexity of human interaction; as Giddens notes, 'all power relations, or relations of autonomy and dependence, are reciprocal: however wide the asymmetrical distribution of resources involved, all power relations manifest autonomy and dependence "in both directions"'.[22]

Much of the conflict integral to peasant-elite interaction is characterized by what Scott has termed 'everyday forms of peasant resistance'.[23] Everyday resistance is the antithesis of a peasant rebellion. whereas the latter is overt and collective, the former is covert and often individual, and while peasant rebellion directly challenges prevailing political and economic norms, everyday resistance does so but indirectly, and always on the sly. It is precisely this anonymity which

[22] Anthony Giddens, *Central Problems in Social Theory: Action, Structure and Contradiction in Social Analysis*, London, 1979, p. 149.

[23] James C. Scott, *Weapons of the Weak: Everyday Forms of Peasant Resistance*, New Haven, 1985.

is, paradoxically, its greatest strength, and yet, gravest weakness Everyday resistance may ultimately undermine a detested political-economic order. But, it will only do so in the long-term, if at all. There are no guarantees, moreover, as to the desirability of the order that takes its place.

Everyday resistance thus focuses attention on 'the weapons of the weak', and is a concept that is used to explain what colonial and postcolonial states alike have termed forest 'crime': theft of forest products, arson, trespass and illicit grazing.[24] Such resistance was ubiquitous in colonial Burma as peasants attempted to undermine access restrictions, and it has persisted (albeit unevenly depending on the extent of state authority) in postcolonial times as well.

Resistance in Burma has also encompassed what Adas calls 'avoidance protest'.[25] Under certain conditions, protest is manifested more dramatically than everyday resistance through the transfer of peasant services to a new patron, sectarian withdrawal, or flight to a new territory. These elaborate forms of protest are usually an act of desperation that reflect the failure of everyday resistance 'to hold elite exactions at a tolerable level'.[26] In part, the decision reflects the social structure and economic practices of the oppressed groups – for example, shifting cultivators may be more disposed to flight than settled agriculturists in well established villages. Yet flight in general is contingent on low population density, a refuge territory or a relatively weak state.

Scholars have used the concepts of everyday resistance and avoidance protest to explain peasant resistance to state forest control. Guha, for example, examines the impact of scientific forestry on forest politics in colonial and postcolonial India.[27] British intervention in the country disrupted local practices, and provoked resistance that culminated in incendiarism and labour strikes in 1921. Such protest was a potent challenge to the colonial state – a challenge maintained in postcolonial times by the Chipko movement.

---

[24] Ramachandra Guha, 'Saboteurs in the Forest: Colonialism and Peasant Resistance in the Indian Himalaya' in Forrest D. Colburn (ed.), *Everyday Forms of Peasant Resistance,* London, 1989, pp. 64-92; Ramachandra Guha and Madhav Gadgil, 'State Forestry and Social Conflict in British India', *Past and Present* 123 (May 1989), pp. 141-77.

[25] Michael Adas, 'From Avoidance to Confrontation: Peasant Protest in Precolonial and Colonial Southeast Asia', *Comparative Studies in Society and History* 23 (April 1981), pp. 217-47.

[26] Michael Adas, 'From Footdragging to Flight: The Evasive History of Peasant Avoidance Protest in South and South-east Asia', *Journal of Peasant Studies* 13 (January 1986), p.69.

[27] Ramachandra Guha, *The Unquiet Woods: Ecological Change and Peasant Resistance in the Himalaya,* Delhi, 1989.

Peluso documents how access to Java's teak forests has been restricted by Dutch and Indonesian rulers.[28] This assertion of state control over land, labour, species and ideology gave rise to analogous forms of popular resistance: clandestine farming in state forests, labour stikes or migration, counter-appropriation or sabotage of key species, and counter-ideologies of communal ownership and resistance. This process of state control and peasant resistance has left a legacy of forester – villager antagonism, rural poverty and forest degradation in Java.

The studies by Guha and Peluso emphasize everyday resistance over more dramatic types of avoidance protest. In many cases, flight was not a realistic option in densely populated regions of India and Java in late colonial and postcolonial times.[29] In comparison, outside the Dry Zone and Irrawaddy delta, Burma has been sparsely populated. Even in the twentieth century, a range of avoidance options, including flight, have been a means of resistance.

This book thus explores how various forest users have resisted state forest control in Burma, and how that resistance has been modified to meet changing political, economic and ecological conditions. To fully understand forest politics, however, the role of the state, and specifically the Forest Department, must be evaluated.

The Forest Department as a Resource Manager

The Forest Department in Burma has been steeped in controversy since its creation in 1856 Whereas colonial forest officials saw themselves as impartial stewards of the country's forests who balanced short-term public needs with long-term national requirements, critics saw only unnecessary restrictions on popular access or commercial development. While the former believed that they promoted efficient forest exploitation, and in the process, contributed revenue for essential social services, the latter alleged that such efficiency only favoured European firms at the expense of Burmese traders. In contrast, whereas European firms in the nineteenth century were highly critical of the Forest Department, by the early twentieth century they were generally supportive of management practices that were to their advantage.

These views serve to illustrate the importance of the Forest Department as a resource manager in colonial times. It sustained that role by drawing on the colonial state's 'continuous administrative, legal, bureaucratic and coercive systems' to enforce its will and modify

---

[28] Nancy Lee Peluso, *Rich Forests, Poor People: Resource Control and Resistance in Java*, Berkeley, 1992.

[29] *Ibid.*, p. 23; Guha,*Unquiet Woods*, pp. 143-7.

forest activity.[30] In the process, the role of the Forest Department came to be contested as much as the forests themselves.

Since 1948 the Forest Department has struggled to re-assert a central role for itself as a resource manager. Yet a key theme in postcolonial forest politics in Burma has been the relative weakness of the Forest Department (left with forest conservation duties) in relation to the State Timber Board (responsible for timber extraction, milling and marketing). Ironically, the quest to introduce socialism into the forestry sector after independence resulted in a shift of power away from the Forest Department and towards the State Timber Board. Whether the policy changes recently introduced by the SLORC to give greater weight to forest-conservation issues will strengthen the position of the Forest Department remains to be seen. The vicissitudes of bureaucratic politics aside, however, the postcolonial era has been marked by an assertion of centralized forest control by the state in militarily secure areas.

The state is described generally in the literature primarily as the instigator of ecological degradation. In an African context, for example, state intervention designed to enhance water availability in drought-prone areas or to convert pastoralists to settled agriculture is often linked to soil erosion and social conflict.[31] Other writers explore the state's contribution to tropical deforestation. Repetto and Gillis, for example, document the credit and other inducements that encourage forest removal in South-East Asia and the Brazilian Amazon.[32] These studies highlight 'an inherent, continuing potential for conflict between the state's role as developer and as protector and steward of the natural environment on which its existence ultimately depends.'[33]

Such ambiguity has characterized resource management in Burma. British rule encouraged clearance of the deltaic rainforests to promote agriculture, but also led to the creation of a Forest Department dedicated to the rigorous protection of selected commercial forests. The notoriety of forest officials noted earlier did not derive from policies that encouraged deforestation. Rather, such notoriety reflected their efforts to discourage deforestation. Colonial forest officials thus sought to

---

[30] Alfred Stephan cited in Skocpol, 'Bringing the State Back In', p. 7.

[31] P.E. Peters, 'Struggles over Water, Struggles over Meaning: Water and the State in Botswana', *Africa* 54 (1984), pp. 29-49; Michael M. Horowitz, 'Ideology, Policy, and Praxis in Pastoral Livestock Development' in Michael M. Horowitz and T.M. Painter (eds), *Anthropology and Rural Development in West Africa,* Boulder, CO, 1986, pp. 251-72.

[32] Robert Repetto and Malcolm Gillis (eds), *Public Policies and the Misuse of Forest Resources,* Cambridge, 1988.

[33] K.J. Walker, 'The State in Environmental Management: The Ecological Dimension', *Political Studies* 37 (March 1989), p. 32.

uphold the state's stewardship role. Since 1948, Burmese forest officials have pursued a similar goal, most recently in the campaign to afforest the Dry Zone. However, this is occurring against the backdrop of state-sanctioned deforestation elsewhere in the country.

In promoting state stewardship of the natural environment, forest officials have been embroiled in conflict with officials in charge of contiguous policy areas who are motivated by different interests. What Furnivall termed 'departmentalism' was an almost inevitable by-product of the way that the colonial state in Burma was structured.[34] As the British rationalized and expanded state activities, they organized them along functional lines. Unlike in Dutch-ruled Java, however, these specialist services were not grouped in large departments with the result that 'none of these [specialist] officials saw life whole and, by reason of frequent transfers, none of them saw it steadily.'[35] The separation of forest management from civil administration in 1856 was part of a process of bureaucratic growth and differentiation in the nineteenth and twentieth centuries that led to bureaucratic conflict. Following independence, conflict centred on the struggle between the State Timber Board and the Forest Department.

Discussion of bureaucratic growth, differentiation and conflict raises the important issue of the 'corporate cohesiveness' of the state.[36] Earlier, the role of the state was considered as if it were a single actor. Here, it is appropriate to emphasize the internal complexity of the state, and the political significance of the fact that although the state may be an 'actor', it is also a 'set of institutions',

To view the state as a unitary actor is to assume that policy formulation and implementation are basically the same. The bureaucracy is the ultimate expression of rationalization and efficiency: 'the fully developed bureaucratic apparatus compares with other organisations exactly as does the machine with the non-mechanical modes of production.'[37] In this Weberian ideal-type, 'the civil servant is an automaton, an infinitively pliable administrative chameleon.'[38]

In practice, this ideal is not attained.[39] Thus, to understand policy

---

[34] Furnivall, *Colonial Policy and Practice.* pp. 40-1, 72-3, 77, 240.

[35] *Ibid.,* p. 77.

[36] Rueschemeyer and Evans. 'The State and Economic Transformation', p. 60

[37] Max Weber, *Economy and Society,* edited by Guenther Roth and Claus Wittich, New York, 1968, vol. III, p.973.

[38] Patrick Dunleavy and Brendan O'Leary, *Theories of the State: The Politics of Liberal Democracy,* New York, 1987, p.170.

[39] As even Weber recognized, see *Economy and Society,* vol. I, p. 225, and vol. III, p. 991. Nevertheless, Weber tended to emphasize the machine-like quality of the bureaucracy

implementation requires that attention be given to bureaucratic practices. Yet the literature has been relatively weak in this regard – pluralist scholars view such practices as mere manifestations of societal relations, whereas state-centred theorists devalue bureaucratic politics in favour of broader state-society interactions.[40] Recently, scholars have begun to reassess Weberian notions of the 'rational bureaucrat' and the apolitical bureaucracy. This has been expressed through explorations of how contemporary states combine modern rational-legal techniques with pre-modern authority structures.[41] Research has also questioned whether it is always in a bureaucrat's self-interest to budget-maximize; there may be other, more efficacious forms of individual and collective empowerment.[42] Such research highlights the complex political nature of much bureaucratic interaction.[43]

The point here is not that states should be treated 'simply as disconnected collections of competing agencies'.[44] Rather, addressing bureaucratic politics as part of a broader analysis of state activities is merely to recognize that power is contested within state structures just as it is in other realms of political interaction. The precise nature of bureaucratic politics is highly variable, and depends on agency development and structure, the presence or absence of administrative coordinating mechanisms, individual ambitions and perceptions, and the definition of formal responsibilities.

In Burma, bureaucratic politics arising from the interaction of forest and civil official was a key aspect of forest politics in colonial times. As forestry and agriculture were interconnected subjects, cooperation between forest and civil officials was essential. Yet such cooperation was tempered by programmatic and perceptual differences. Civil administrators feared the elaboration of a forestry management that

---

(e.g. vol. III, pp. 987-90).

[40] On pluralist accounts, see Skocpol, 'Bringing the State Back In', p. 4. This article also illustrates how bureaucratic politics is not a central concern of state-centred research.

[41] For example, Michael Heller, 'The Politics of Telecommunications Policy in Mexico', unpubl. D.Phil. thesis, University of Sussex, 1990; see also Bernard S. Silberman, *Cages of Reason: The Rise of the Rational State in France, Japan, the United States and Great Britain,* Chicago, 1993, who argues that the bureaucratic state developed in the first place for reasons linked not to efficiency but to conditions of political uncertainty.

[42] Patrick Dunleavy, *Democracy, Bureaucracy and Public Choice: Economic Explanations in Political Science,* London, 1991, p. 174.

[43] Bill Jenkins and Andrew Gray, 'Bureaucratic Politics and Power: Developments in the Study of Bureaucracy', *Political Studies* 31 (June 1983), pp. 177-93.

[44] Peter B. Evans, Dietrich Rueschemeyer and Theda Skocpol, 'On the Road Toward a More Adequate Understanding of the State' in Peter Evans, Dietrich Rueschemeyer and Theda Skocpol (eds), *Bringing the State Back in,* Cambridge, 1985, p. 360.

would limit their power to regulate agriculture . Forest officials lamented the predisposition of civil officials to advocate deforestation wherever permanent agriculture was considered feasible. These differences reflected the fact that forest officials saw themselves as 'stewards' of the forest, while civil officials were the people's 'guardians'.[45] The need for specialized training reinforced this division by reducing inter-departmental movement and encouraging departmental insularity.

To understand the Forest Department's role as a resource manager, it is therefore necessary to be clear about its position within a functionally defined bureaucratic context. Yet colonial rule was also significant for its attempt to territorialize political control over people and resources within 'Burma', a process with important implications for the role of the Forest Department as a resource manager. This attempt had two distinct but interrelated elements.

To begin with, the British sought to define political control in terms of 'inside/outside' – that is, it sought to define state control clearly and permanently in terms of what was both within and without its legal jurisdiction.[46] Such action reflected a European conception of political power, and of the institution of the state itself. This conception was at odds with existing practices in Burma (and South-East Asia generally) where political power declined gradually as one moved away from the capital, and where a precolonial state was 'typically defined not by its perimeter, but by its centre'.[47] Frontiers between political entities were typically imprecise and in constant flux.[48] Colonial rule changed all that. Fuzzy frontiers were replaced by carefully defined borders sanctioned by international law (itself a European creation). Fixed borders permitted the state to conduct resource management with greater confidence in 'its' territory than was hitherto the case. In 'peripheral' areas rich in forest and mineral resources, the state no longer need fear that its actions might precipitate inter-state conflict due to contested ownership.

Yet the colonial state's assertion of territorial political control over people and resources was heavily contested by non-state groups, and was never co-terminous with the formal borders of the Burmese na-

---

[45] B. Ribbentrop, *Forestry in British India,* Calcutta, 1990, p. 146; B.H. Baden-Powell, *The Forest System of British Burma,* Calcutta, 1873, p. 45.

[46] R.B.J. Walker, *Inside/outside: International Relations as Political Theory,*Cambridge, 1993.

[47] Benedict Anderson, *Language and Power: Exploring Political Cultures in Indonesia,* Ithaca, 1990, p. 41; see also Victor B. Lieberman, *Burmese Administrative Cycles: Anarchy and Conquest, c. 1580-1760,* Princeton, 1984.

[48] E.R Leach, 'The Frontiers of "Burma" ', *Comparative Studies in Society and History* 3 (1960), pp. 49-68.

tion-state. Indeed, during times of political unrest, territorialization was even reversed – that is, groups in civil society captured control over people and resources from the state. However, this process was especially evident following independence when communist and ethnic insurgents overran much of the country. Not surprisingly. since 1948 a central concern of Burmese forest officials has been the 're-territorialization' of state forest control in Burma.

The colonial state also attempted to territorialize political control through the 'territorialization of national space'.[49] Here the focus was purely 'domestic' in that the colonial state sought to develop a national profile of the people and resources under its formal jurisdiction as part of an attempt to enhance political control and commercial activity. This desire was not new since precolonial states had long sought similar information. What was new was the ability of the colonial state to compile such a profile. This was only partly associated with superior military force – rather, an array of seemingly innocuous new techniques of political control (e.g. census, maps) dramatically enhanced the state's ability to meet its objectives.

These techniques were utilized in the legal and spatial definition of 'reserved forests' – forests claimed by the state in Burma for commercial production, and in which accordingly only limited popular access was permitted. Just as maps abstractly, and boundary markers physically, established inside/outside in relation to different national territories, so too maps and physical symbols (e.g. rock mounds, masonry pillars) were used to distinguish inside/outside but this time in relation to state and non-state territories. These internal markers of territoriality were essential to forest use and politics (as were external markers), and were often the subject of ferocious contestation. The postcolonial state has inherited the colonial interest in, and conflict associated with, this internal territoriality.

To understand Burmese forest politics, then, is to consider how the functionally-defined Forest Department was organized in relation to other departments, and how it sought to assert territorial political control as part of its management goals. Such an understanding also requires an appreciation of how other forest users resisted state control. Yet forest politics was also a struggle of ideas over what constituted appropriate forest use.

---

[49] Peter Vandergeest and Nancy Lee Peluso, 'Territorialization and State Power in Thailand', *Theory and Society* 24 (1995), pp. 385-426. For an exploration of the links between Thai nationhood, territoriality and national identity, see Thongchai Winichakul, *Siam Mapped: A History of the Geo-Body of a Nation,* Honolulu, 1994.

Conflicting Perceptions of Forest Use

The conquest of Burma in the nineteenth century led to its incorporation in the world's largest empire headed by its most industrialized nation. British rule transformed Burma through the introduction of new ideas of social and environmental practice: *laissez-faire,* scientific forestry, rationalization, the bureaucratic state and nationalism. Following independence, and largely in reaction to colonial rule, Burma's leaders promoted socialism, albeit adapted to the Burmese cultural context. In the 1990s, the SLORC has sought to gradually integrate Burma into the global capitalist economy, but associated with this move has been official promotion of forest management premised on sustainable development.

Burma's forests have borne witness to the power of these assorted ideas, one way of classifying forest politics in colonial Burma is by the ideas that characterized a period – *laissez-faire* forestry in the early years and scientific forestry after 1856. More importantly, these ideas altered perceptions of forest use with dramatic effect. Under the influence of *laissez-faire* ideas, colonial officials nurtured a thriving timber industry in Tenasserim, but at the cost of extensive over-harvesting.[50] From 1856, new ideas (and personnel) were imported from Europe to prevent similar degradation in Pegu's teak forests. The means chosen to promote scientific forestry, the functionally-defined Forest Department, itself manifested a new way of thinking.

The idea of *laissez-faire* was associated with economic liberalism, a doctrine popular with Britain's leaders and intellectuals in the late eighteenth and early nineteenth century. Economic liberalism promoted free trade, comparative advantage, and a limited state. As proposed by Adam Smith, and subsequently refined by such British writers as Ricardo, Torrens, and Mill, economic liberalism promised a simple path to 'the wealth of nations'.[51] If states removed barriers to trade, economic growth would result through an international division of labour that placed a premium on the optimal allocation of human and natural resources. Through the timely provision of public goods, the state would play an essential, if clearly supportive role.

Such views shaped early colonial forest management in Burma.

---

[50] The Tenasserim experience is a useful corrective to the recent overgeneralized claim that in British India, 'the cherished Victorian notion of *laissez-faire* [was] an ecological myth and an economic fantasy'; see David Arnold and Ramachandra Guha, 'Introduction: Themes and Issues in the Environmental History of south Asia', in Arnold and Guha (eds), *Nature, Culture, Imperialism,* p. 10. In British Burma this claim is true, but only after 1856.

[51] Adam Smith, *An Inquiry into the Nature and Causes of the Wealth of Nations,* edited by R.H. Campbell and A.S. Skinner, Oxford, 1976 (1776), vols I-II.

But *laissez-faire* forestry never went unchallenged. After 1856, moreover, a new 'scientific' approach based on state intervention was adopted. Scientific forestry was first developed in Germany and France, and called for selective harvesting and planting to ensure future timber supplies.[52] Under this system, the fate of the forest was not entrusted to Smith's 'unseen hand of the market', but rather was guaranteed through strict rules – the highly 'visible' hand of the forest official. Those rules also tended to undermine existing patterns of popular access and use. As forest officials promoted commercial woods, they eliminated 'worthless' species that were often of considerable local use-value. Scientific forestry was thus a system premised on long-term commercial timber production 'designed to reorder both nature and customary use in its own image.'[53]

The growing influence of scientific forestry coincided with the rise of the bureaucratic state in colonial Burma. With its emphasis on regulation, enumeration and calculation, it is not difficult to see why scientific forestry was so well suited to the outlook of the country's new Leviathan.[54] Both were predicated on the principle of rationalization, understood here in the Weberian sense of 'formal rationalization'.[55] The latter may simply be considered as a dynamic process whose 'implicit ultimate value' is one of control: 'control over nature through scientific and technological rationalization', and 'control over humans through rational-legal domination'; formal rationalization is not about revolutionary change, but rather consists of 'controlled change' in order to strengthen mastery, and 'render it deeper, more comprehensive, more subtle, and more legitimate.'[56] Such was the ultimate goal of scientific forest management in colonial Burma.

With its adoption, forest officials became more critical of 'unscientific' indigenous practices. Peasants and timber traders were criticized for

---

[52] Franz Heske, *German Forestry,* New Haven, 1938; Dietrich Brandis, *Indian Forestry*, Woking, 1897, pp. 6-7; Robert K. Winters, *The Forest and Man*, New York, 1974, pp. 275-7.

[53] Guha, *Unquiet Woods,* p. 59. For a critique of scientific forestry, see Madhav Gadgil and Ramachandra Guha, *This Fissured Land: An Ecological History of India,* Delhi, pp. 207-14.

[54] However, the relationship between imperial science and colonial rule was not necessarily always a harmonious one, see David Gilmartin, 'Scientific Empire and Imperial Science: Colonialism and Irrigation Technology in the Indus Basin', *Journal of Asian Studies* 53 (August 1994), pp. 1127-49.

[55] Weber, *Economy and Society,*vol. I, pp. 85-6, 223-6; vol. III, pp. 973-5, 987-9; see also Raymond Murphy, *Social Closure: The Theory of Monopolization and Exclusion,* Oxford, 1988, pp. 196-9.

[56] Murphy, *Social Closure,* pp. 218-9

being 'wasteful', but shifting cultivators were condemned even more vigorously. The latter stood accused of perpetrating massive deforestation and other ecological crimes.[57] British assessments of the superiority of scientific forestry over indigenous methods were decidedly paternalistic, if not racist. As one British official in Burma remarked: 'the paternity of the State in the welfare of its children is surely manifested by restricting the unthrifty methods of a few for the benefit of the many.'[58] Modern, abstract (mathematical) and industrial, scientific forestry was seen as yet another example of how European skill and ingenuity would save the natives from themselves. Given the importance of Burma's forests, this burden was a 'White Man's Burden' indeed.[59]

Ecological thinking was integral to the critique of indigenous practices. Whereas the British considered themselves to be 'good' ecologists, the Burmese were viewed as being ecologically disruptive. This perceptual dichotomy was not unique to colonial Burma, or for that matter, to forestry. In Africa, for example, indigenous practices were criticized by colonial officials. Such criticism was then used to justify state intervention through agricultural improvement and soil conservation programmes.[60] In Burma, the Forest Department followed a similar procedure to assert control over a widening territory and range of activities. Indeed, the stewardship ethos noted earlier was based on the claim to superior ecological credentials.

The Burmese challenged that claim.[61] 'Traditional' forest practices

---

[57] Richard H. Grove, 'Colonial Conservation, Ecological Hegemony and Popular Resistance: Towards a Global Synthesis' in John M. MacKenzie (ed.), *Imperialism and the Natural World*, Manchester, 1990, p. 23; Mahesh Rangarajan, 'Imperial Agendas and India's Forests: The Early History of Indian Forestry, 1800-1878', *Indian Economic and Social History Review* 31 (April-June 1994), pp. 157-8. However, not all colonial officials shared this antipathy to shifting cultivators, see Sarah Jewitt, 'Europe's "Others"? Forestry Policy and Practices in Colonial and Postcolonial India', *Environment and Planning D: Society and Space* 13 (1995), pp. 67-90.

[58] *Burma Forest Proceedings* (March 1902), p.5. The links between science, technology, and ideologies of Western control are explored in Michael Adas, *Machines as the Measure of Men: Science, Technology, and Ideologies of Western Dominance*, Ithaca, 1989.

[59] The ethos of the White Man's Burden was part of a much wider 'Orientalist' discourse. The classic account is Edward Said, *Orientalism*, London, 1978, but see also Jewitt, 'Europe's "Others"'. For an early critique of colonialism in Burma, see Orwell, *Burmese Days*.

[60] Paul Richards, *Indigenous Agricultural Revolution: Ecology and Food Production in West Africa*, London, 1985; David Anderson and Richard Grove (eds), *Conservation in Africa: People, Parks, Priorities,* Cambridge, 1987. Jenny Elliott, 'Environmental Degradation, Soil Conservation and the Colonial and Post-colonial State in Rhodesia/Zimbabwe', in Chris Dixon and Michael J. Hefferman (eds), *Colonialism and Development in the Contemporary World,* London, 1991, pp. 72-91.

[61] In this book, 'Burmese' and 'Burman' are used interchangeably; 'Burma' rather than

were asserted through everyday resistance and avoidance protest. After the First World War, the rise of nationalism in Burma provided another means of attacking imperial scientific forestry. In a context of partial self-rule, the combination of peasant resistance and nationalist agitation was a formidable challenge to the Forest Department's efforts to rationalize forest activity in the imperial interest. A central objective of the book is to assess that challenge as it explores those links between perceptions, interests, access and conflict that are the essence of forest politics in colonial Burma.

Following independence, new ideas about how to organize forest use became influential. The quest to transform Burma into a socialist country was important in this regard, especially after the military coup of March 1962 brought General Ne Win to power. State socialism has often been held to be responsible for highly destructive environmental management policies in the Third World.[62] In Burma, the destructive impact of state socialism on the forestry sector was partially limited by economic autarky in the 1960s and early 1970s (as well as by the lack of central control over peripheral parts of the country), but was a contributory factor in the accelerating deforestation of the late 1970s and 1980s.

Since 1988, socialism has been formally abandoned in Burma in favour of a gradual opening to the global capitalist system. Yet in response to international criticism of widespread deforestation associated with logging, the SLORC has moved to reform forestry management as part of a formal commitment to sustainable development. Especially since the Earth Summit held in Rio de Janeiro in June 1992, the concept of sustainable development has been at the heart of international development discourse. However, it is clear that the implementation of this intellectually problematic concept will be exceedingly difficult politically.[63] In the Burmese context, the ultimate impact of the concept on forest politics is thus yet to be determined.

'Myanmar' is used throughout to denote the country.

[62] Martin W. Lewis. *Green Delusions: Am Environmentalist Critique of Radical Environmentalism*, Durham, 1992, pp. 163-6; Vaclav Smil, *The Bad Earth: Environmental Degradation in China*, Armonk 1984; Melane Beresford and Lyn Fraser, 'Political Economy of the Environment in Vietnam', *Journal of Contemporary Asia* 22 (January 1992), pp. 3-19.

[63] Michael Redclift, *Sustainable Development: Exploring the Contradictions*, London, 1987; W.M. Adams, *Green Development: Environment and Sustainability in the Third World*, London, 1990; Stephen R. Dovers and John W. Handmer, 'Contradictions in Sustainability', *Environmental Conservation 20* (Autumn 1993), pp. 217-22; Eduardo Silva, 'Thinking Politically about Sustainable Development in the Tropical Forests of Latin America', *Development and Change 25* (October 1994), pp. 697-721.

Contesting the Resource

As this chapter has suggested, Burmese forest management has not been peaceable. Adopting conflict as a central theme takes issue with traditional accounts that extol the virtues of forest 'progress', and which imply that Burma's forests were above politics in the colonial era.[64] Forest management was indeed political, as forest users, including the state, contested resource access and use. Further, such politically-driven forest management has continued since 1948.

Three themes in this study address the issue of forest politics in colonial and postcolonial Burma. The first theme concerns the contested nature of the forest resource, and explores how diverse forest users have resisted the imposition of state forest control. The second theme examines the complexities of such control through an evaluation of the Forest Department's role as a resource manager, and how that role has been conditioned by broader political and institutional forces. The third theme, which is about conflicting perceptions of forest use, describes how state forest control has changed as new ideas of social and environmental practice have been introduced, and how popular resistance has been based, in turn, on the assertion of 'traditional' practices that have often been articulated as modern nationalist demands. Forest politics can thus be seen to be a dynamic of control and resistance rooted in different perceptions of 'appropriate' forest use.

But, as usage of the term 'resource' with reference to Burma's forests highlights, those forests have been conceived of in a particular way. Rarely, for example, have the forests been valued for themselves. Rather, they have been valued for how they could be used to promote human welfare, and in the case of certain ecological arguments, overall well-being. Their utility has resided precisely in their incorporation in human activity.

It fell to the Forest Department to regulate this process of incorporation. As a resource manager, it has been in the business of making choices – where, when, how, or even if, the forests are to be exploited. In making these decisions, the Forest Department has inevitably been engaging in politics. The next chapter will show how forest management in the early colonial period helped determine the nature of forest politics in Burma well into the twentieth century.

[64] E.P. Stebbing, 'The Teak Forests of Burma', *Nature 160* (13 December 1947), pp. 818-20; Stebbing, *Forests of India*, vols I-III; J. Nisbet, *Burma under British Rule and Before*, Westminster, 1901, vol. II, chap. 3; C.W. Scott, 'Forestry in Burma', *Journal Oxford University Forest Society*, 3rd series 1 (1946), pp. 24-34.

Part II

FROM LAISSEZ-FAIRE TO SCIENTIFIC FORESTRY

2

PRE-SCIENTIFIC FORESTRY, 1824-1855

After the first Anglo-Burmese war (1824-6), the British transformed the newly acquired territory of Tenasserim from an economic backwater into a major regional centre. A prosperous timber and shipbuilding industry developed at the principal town of Moulmein based on exploitation of local teak forest. Yet, despite the fact that such exploitation was characterized by widespread overharvesting and conflict, colonial officials were slow to intervene to regulate the trade.

This chapter describes this situation, But these same *laissez-faire* practices in Tenasserim's forests ultimately led to state intervention in the mid-1850s. Such intervention, and its implications for forest users, is the subject of later chapters, but here the concern is to explore the bases of such intervention.

Between 1829 and 1857, private firms in Tenasserim were essentially free to extract teak as they wished. Forest rules were few in number, and limited in scope. In any case, they were ineffectual in the absence of a forest service entrusted with their enforcement. But this state of affairs, which is here termed *laissez-faire* forestry, never went unchallenged. Throughout this period, government officials and scientists warned of the consequences of unfettered timber extraction. By the 1850s, the depletion of Tenasserim's teak forests made state intervention seem the only realistic option if the teak forests of Pegu, annexed after the second Anglo-Burmese war (1852), were to avoid a similar fate. More importantly, in an altered imperial context, the assertion of state forest control at last became politically feasible.

Laissez-faire Forestry in Tenasserim

The depletion of Tenasserim's teak forests had a major impact on the development of forest policy in colonial Burma. Among forest officials, this event was a reminder of the dangers associated with the abdication of the state's stewardship role. As with any event that is mythologized, however, early colonial forest practice was deprived of much of its original complexity. That *laissez-faire* forestry resulted in extensive overharvesting is well known. Less well understood are the political and economic conditions that produced this outcome, and the reasons why an alternative system was not adopted.

Burma's reputation as a major source of teak was known to the British in the eighteenth century, but it was only in the early nineteenth century that obtaining access to Burmese teak became an urgent imperial priority. The reasons for growing British interest in Burma's teak forests at this time were related to the depletion of suitable forests in Britain and the British colonies as well as the disruption of timber supplies from the Baltic states as a result of the Anglo-French struggle in Europe around the turn of the century. With a large naval fleet whose combined tonnage in 1809 exceeded four million tons, Britain's need for alternative supplies was great, and attention initially centred on the teak forests of Malabar in southern India.[1] A versatile timber, teak was especially sought for construction of naval vessels. Indeed, teak proved superior to oak for shipbuilding, for unlike the latter, teak contained an oil which prevented metal corrosion.[2] However, such was the demand for teak that the Malabar forests were largely depleted of quality teak by the 1820s.[3] Yet, teak from the other major known source, monarchical Burma, was in erratic supply.[4] In this context, then, the acquisition of the Tenasserim teak forests in 1826 was crucial to wider British imperial interests.

---

[1] Mahesh Rangarajan, 'Imperial Agendas and India's Forests: The Early History of Indian Forestry, 1800-1878', *Indian Economic and Social History Review* 31 (April-June 1994), pp. 154-5.

[2] J. Nisbet, *Burma Under British Rule and Before,* Westminster, 1901, vol. II, p. 47; Robert Greenhalgh Albion, *Forests and Sea Power: The Timber Problem of the Royal Navy 1652-1862,* Cambridge, Mass., 1926, pp. 35-6, 365-8. On naval shipbuilding in Britain at this time see N.D.G. James, *A History of English Forestry,* Oxford, 1981, pp. 139-60.

[3] B. Ribbentrop, *Forestry in British India,* Calcutta, 1900, pp. 64-6

[4] The point here is not that Burma's rulers discouraged teak exports – indeed, they were on the rise at this time, see Victor Lieberman, 'Secular Trends in Burmese Economic History, c. 1350-1830, and their Implications for State Formation', *Modern Asian Studies* 25 (February 1991), pp. 14-15; B.R. Pearn, *A History of Rangoon,* 1939, pp. 70-2. Rather, political and economic conditions in Burma were such that the annual teak supply was

The British sent Nathaniel Wallich, the Danish-born physician and Superintendent of the Calcutta Botanical Garden, forthwith to report on whether the belief that Tenasserim's teak forests were 'not ample but of very superior quality' was correct. Wallich was delighted to confirm in 1827 that 'in point of timber forests they stand altogether unrivalled', thereby prompting the government of India to order Tenasserim's first commissioner, Anthony Maingy, to retain the forests on the government's behalf.[5] For the next two years, those forests were worked by government monopoly. In December 1827, Maingy reported that a supply of timber had been collected at Tavoy and Mergui 'equal to load a vessel of 6 or 700 tons burthen' that required shipment to Bengal.[6] Five months later, 511 teak logs valued at six thousand rupees were shipped from Tavoy to Calcutta to meet military, and other public purposes, as well as to test the Calcutta market. However, this experiment flopped as the consignment sold at a loss of 250 rupees.[7]

In 1829 the government ended its teak monopoly. Powerful timber merchants pressured senior officials in Calcutta and London, and in 1828 they may have colluded to defraud the government of revenue at the sale of state timber just noted.[8] These merchants had anticipated less regulation under British rule than they had experienced under the Burmese state, and were consequently furious at the prospect of permanent state intervention.[9] Further, a precedent had recently been set in Malabar where the abolition of the post of Conservator of Forests in 1823 was partly in response to pressure from timber traders.[10]

Yet to attribute the advent of *laissez-faire* forestry in Tenasserim simply to pressure from the business lobby would be to neglect the significance of debates about the issue going on within the colonial state itself. In effect, the government was divided on the issue of

---

not reliable. see Oliver B. Pollack, *Empires in Collision: Anglo-Burmese Relations in the Mid-Nineteenth Century,* Westport, CT, 1979, pp. 54-5.

[5] E.P. Stebbing, *The Forests of India,* London, 1922, vol. I, pp. 125, 135.

[6] *Selected Correspondence of Letters Issued from and Received in the Office of the commissioner, Tenasserim Division for the Years 1825-26 to 1842-43,* Rangoon, 1916, p. 71.

[7] W.R. Baillie (ed.), 'Summary of Papers Relating to the Tenasserim Forests', *Selections from the Records of the Bengal Government* 9 (1852), p. 81.

[8] Stebbing, *Forests of India,* vol. I, p. 141.

[9] J.S. Furnivall, 'The Fashioning of Leviathan: The Beginnings of British Rule in Burma', *Journal of the Burma Research Society* 29 (April 1939), pp. 3-137, reprint edited by Gehan Wijeyewardene, Canberra, 1991, p. 71.

[10] Ribbentrop, *Forestry in British India,* pp. 64-6.

the teak monopoly between those advocating state intervention and those favouring free trade. The arguments of the interventionists are examined later in this chapter. Here, however, the position of their opponents in government is discussed.

In this regard, the timber merchants found a powerful ally in commissioner Maingy, who advocated a system of quasi-regulated private extraction.[11] He argued that private firms should be free to extract teak subject to payment of a duty of 10 or 15 percent upon the value of the timber. Maingy further believed that a flat duty on each tree cut combined with a regulation confiscating all timber cut under specified dimensions would be sufficient guard against overharvesting.[12] The Commissioner saw this plan as a reasonable compromise between the legitimate claims of the state and the demands of the timber industry. The former would be remunerated for the use of its forests while the latter extracted timber, and still the teak forests would be preserved.

However, the decision to end the government teak monopoly reflected the influence of broader imperial ideas about the proper role of the state and private sector in economic life. Maingy was not the only colonial official who believed in private enterprise. As a representative of the British empire, he was influenced, as were many others, by intellectual trends of the day. The doctrine of economic liberalism was highly influential in the early nineteenth century, befitting Britain's status as the world's preeminent power. Adam Smith's *The Wealth of Nations* had been published just fifty-three years prior to Tenasserim's forests being thrown open to free enterprise in 1829, and David Ricardo's *The Principles of Political Economy and Taxation* had been out only twelve years.[13] If, as Smith argued, the sovereign had only three essential duties – defense, justice, and certain public works and institutions for 'facilitating the commerce of society and the instruction of the peoples' – then as the Crown's representative in Tenasserim, and with support from Calcutta and London, Maingy's task was to implement this vision of a limited state.[14]

The decision to end the monopoly was thus not, as Stebbing

---

[11] A similar role was played by Governor of Bombay Thomas Munro with regard to the Malabar forests in the early 1820s, see Rangarajan, 'Imperial Agendas', p, 156.

[12] *Selected Correspondence*, pp. 71-2.

[13] Adam Smith, *An Inquiry into the Nature and Causes of the Wealth of Nations*, edited by R.H. Campbell and A.S. Skinner, Oxford, 1976 (1776), vols I-II; David Ricardo, *The Principles of Political Economy and Taxation*, London, 1821 (1817).

[14] Smith, *Wealth of Nations*, vol. II, p. 723; Robert H. Taylor, *The State in Burma*, London, 1987, pp. 83, 108.

implies, largely the work of Maingy.[15] It is highly improbable that senior officials in Calcutta and London would have agreed to the abandonment of a potentially lucrative monopoly simply as a result of a minor loss at a first timber sale. Rather, the loss was more likely a convenient pretext for the government to extricate itself from a politically difficult situation. As in the case of the Malabar forests, it was under pressure from a timber industry that could associate its unimpeded access to the forests with a broader campaign for free trade and limited government involvement in the economy. In an empire that produced the likes of Smith and Ricardo, those who promoted a teak monopoly were fighting an uphill battle in the early nineteenth century.

This point is an important one. Various scholars have shown how imperial perceptions of forests in the colonies were conditioned by attitudes towards nature formed in the domesticated and largely tree-less British landscape.[16] Transferred to the colonies, these attitudes encouraged the view that forest clearance was synonymous with progress. The discussion here raises a different though related point. Imperial attitudes towards the forest were also conditioned by attitudes about political and economic organization, which in turn affected human-environmental interaction. Thus, it is only when the political and economic temper of the times is recognized that it is possible to understand why *laissez-faire* forestry should have persisted in Tenasserim for so long after Maingy had left the Province, and despite the best efforts of a succession of opponents to have it ended. It was only after 1850, and in an altered imperial context, that interventionist ideas became influential.

The triumph of economic liberal ideas in 1829 led to the introduction of *laissez-faire* practices that quickly transformed Tenasserim's teak forests. Private traders flocked to the area, and Moulmein became an important timber and shipbuilding town. By 1833, teak exports to India reached 7,309 tons, three large teak vessels had been built, and three more were under construction. To encourage this development, Maingy urged his superiors to impose a duty on teak imported from monarchical Burma to Calcutta. [17] Extraction increased in the main teak forests located to the south and east of Moulmein along the

---

[15] Stebbing, *Forests of India,* Vol. I, pp. 140-2.

[16] Rangarajan, 'Imperial Agendas', pp. 152-3; Geoff A. Wilson, *The Urge to Clear the 'Bush': A Study of Native Forest Clearance on Farms in the Catlins District of New Zealand, 1861-1990,* Christchurch, 1992.

[17] *Selected Correspondence*, pp. 98-9.

Ataran river, but as Table 2.1 suggests, by the late 1840s the best tracts had been exhausted. Activity then moved to adjoining territories under the rule of Shan and Karenni chieftains, and drained by the Salween River.

As noted later in this chapter, the number of harvested trees was much greater than suggested by the data in this table. The figure of 137,947 trees is an estimate derived from the total amount of timber officially reported at Moulmein. As a result, it does not include the substantial amount of timber illicitly logged and exported from Tenasserim.

Table 2.1. TEAK TIMBER FROM THE ATARAN FORESTS, 1829-1858

	Trees harvested	% of total harvest
1829-April 1841	77,704	56.3
May 1841-April 1847	44,269	32.1
May 1847-April 1853	11,682	8.5
May 1853-April 1858	4,292	3.1
Total	137,947	100.0

Source: Adapted from D. Brandis, 'Report on the Attaran Forests for the Year 1860', *Selections from the Records of the Government of India (Foreign Department)* 32 (1861), p. 139.

Yet table 2.1 is primarily of interest here for another reason. By charting the cycle of extraction in the Ataran forest, it gives some indication of the movement of the timber frontier across a major teak forest. Thus, between 1829 and 1841 forest work was on the increase, with annual extraction averaging 6,500 trees. During the period 1841-7, production peaked at about 7,400 trees, before dropping to under 2,000 trees per annum in 1847-53. After 1853, fewer than 1,000 trees per year were being removed, indicating that, under *laissez-faire* conditions, the Ataran forest had been cleared of marketable teak in under thirty years.

Much of the timber was exported to Europe and India to be used for shipbuilding or other purposes. A considerable proportion was also used locally. Thus by 1852 shipbuilders at Moulmein had produced more than one hundred ships with an aggregate tonnage of thirty thousand. Many timber merchants prospered, especially those who were affiliated with the large Calcutta firms and who enjoyed influence in government circles.[18]

This record of growth seemed to vindicate economic liberals like

---

[18] Pollack, *Empires in Collision*, p. 46; J.S. Furnivall, *Colonial Policy and Practice: A Comparative Study of Burma and Netherlands India*, New York, 1956, p. 45.

Maingy. A small and nondescript village had been replaced by a prosperous lumber town and Tenasserim's forests had become a valuable economic resource. It seemed a textbook example of the benefits of free trade, comparative advantage, and limited state involvement.

In theory the government controlled timber extraction. It could revoke licenses if traders failed to abide by basic rules. Those rules stipulated that traders must keep the government informed of their operations and that trees with a girth of less than four feet could not be felled.[19] Timber was also subject to a 15 percent duty and could be requisitioned by the government. This arrangement was designed to meet the government's financial and military needs while permitting the freest possible exploitation. But as Stebbing observes:

> With an adequate supervising staff these rules might have been effective and a check to ruthless exploitation. When the size of the country is taken into account, the absence of a trained staff and the ignorance appertaining to the forests themselves, which were unsurveyed, the above rules were counsels of perfection quite unrealisable.[20]

A small establishment comprised of local people was created in 1833 to ensure that traders 'fell the teak trees fairly and do no unnecessary damage to the forests.' However, this token force proved itself incapable of regulating timber extraction in Tenasserim.[21]

Government policy had a disastrous effect on the forests. It effectively sanctioned unfettered private teak extraction while the system of short-term leases (revokable at any time) simultaneously discouraged private traders from recognizing any long-term interest in the forests. As the value of teak increased, traders maximized profits and yields by adopting a cut-and-run strategy.[22] Unlike in later years, many of these traders were individuals of little substance.

Table 2.2 gives only a partial glimpse of teak extraction, but highlights nevertheless that non-Europeans were responsible for at least 65 per cent of the timber harvested in 1841. Contemporary records typically fail to note the specific circumstances of these non-Europeans. However, 18 per cent of the total was extracted from the 'Thoung yeen' (Thaungyin) valley by Karens who enjoyed 'the

---

[19] License holders were also technically liable for the activities of their workers. For example, see the license of Shoay Byee, 4 June 1833, reprinted in H. Leeds to Secretary to the Chief Commissioner, 10 May 1865, *India Forest Proceedings,* November 1866, p. 350.

[20] Stebbing, *Forests of India,* vol. I, p. 142.

[21] *Selected Correspondence,* p. 99; Baillie, 'Summary of Papers', p. 83.

[22] B.O Binns, *Amherst District Gazetteer,* Rangoon, 1935, p. 49. The East India Company acknowledged this problem in 1842, see A. Bogle to C. Beadon, 30 November 1855, quoted in Brandis, 'Attaran Forests', p. 9.

first right to the produce of their own forests' in return for the payment of taxes.[23] Karen participation in the teak trade extended well beyond the Thaungyin valley and they were in particular demand as elephant *mahouts* (or riders).[24]

Table 2.2. TEAK EXTRACTED FROM TENASSERIM'S
FORESTS BY AGENCY, 1841

	Trees harvested	% of total harvest
Cockerell and Co.	2,156	23.8
Shaik Abdullah	398	4.4
Captain Clarke	194	2.1
Mr Darwood	135	1.5
Mr Fox	322	3.6
Mr Richardson	301	3.3
Thoung Yeen[a]	1,641	18.1
Weingo	412	4.6
Mr Munrell	66	0.7
Gyne Lyne Boey	675	7.4
Pandon Salween	824	9.1
Native Grants	1,945	21.4
Total	9,069	100.0

[a] 'Thoung Yeen' refers to timber extracted in the Thaungyin valley by Karen villagers.

Source: Selected Correspondence of Letters issued from and received in the Office of the Commissioner, Tenasserim Division for the years 1825-26 to 1842-43, Rangoon, 1916, p. 280.

Non-Europeans predominated in teak extraction, but Europeans controlled the marketing arrangements. The relationship between the latter who 'sat in Moulmein counting profits' and indigenous traders varied.[25] Europeans contracted 'natives' to extract a specified number of trees from the forest, the latter being allowed to retain for their own

[23] D. Brandis, 'Progress Report of the Forests of the Tenasserim and Martaban Provinces for 1858-9 and 1859-60', *Selections from the Records of the Government of India (Foreign Department)* 29 (1861), p. 20, Karen worked the Lower Thaungyin forests until 1904 and the Upper Thaungyin forests until 1911 as government contractors. Thereafter, the forests were transferred to Steel Brothers, see A.E. Ross, *Working Plan for Lower Thaungyin Working Circle*, Rangoon, 1909, p. 14; W. Lawton, *Working Plan for Upper Thaungyin Working Circle*, Rangoon, 1918, p. 11.

[24] Baillie, 'Summary of Papers', pp. 129-31; Charles F. Keyes, 'The Karen in Thai History and the History of the Karen in Thailand' in Charles F. Keyes (ed.), *Ethnic Adaptation and Identity: The Karen on the Thai Frontier with Burma*, Philadelphia, 1979, p. 46.

[25] Pollack, *Empires in Collision*, p. 46; Furnivall, *Colonial Policy and Practice*, p. 45.

use or sale one-half of the consignment. However, European merchants also paid advances to Burmese workers to extract trees at a specified rate for each, leaving it to the discretion of those workers as to the total number of trees extracted.[26]

Irrespective of their nationality, timber traders were scarcely troubled by government regulation. Busy establishing British control in the newly conquered territory, and in any event unlikely to find fault with the *laissez-faire* system he had fought so hard to introduce, Commissioner Maingy and other colonial officials took little action to determine whether license holders obeyed the rules. In some cases such inaction had ominous roots: as competition for the remaining forests intensified, corruption and bribery flourished.[27]

Local officials generally considered selective deforestation a small price to pay for economic development. Thus, the first two commissioners of Tenasserim, Maingy (1825-33) and Edmund Blundell (1833-43), each requested a lowering of the timber duty to facilitate teak extraction and shipbuilding. In rejecting these requests, the government of India noted that the 'thriving condition of the trade' was the 'best evidence' that the duty was not too high.[28]

As the trade thrived, revenue stagnated. Although teak represented as much as 50 per cent of total exports by value, between 1829 and 1841 it yielded 192,590 rupees (an average 16,049 rupees per year).[29] In 1839, when as much as three-quarters of the timber may have escaped paying duty, the state earned more revenue from the hire of Indian convicts than from the forest.[30] Taking the economy of Tenasserim as a whole, the British may have been 'more effective in taxing the land and people than the precolonial state had been', but this was probably not so in the case of the teak trade.[31]

As the extent of overharvesting became known, the government of India introduced stricter rules in 1841. It increased the minimum girth of harvestable trees from four feet to six feet and required licensees to plant five trees for every one extracted. The government designated the Executive Engineer of Moulmein as the province's first Superintendent of Forests. Under this more regulated regime,

---

[26] *Selected Correspondence,* p. 198.

[27] Pollack, *Empires in Collision,* p. 46; Binns, *Amherst District Gazetteer,* p. 50.

[28] *Selected Correspondence,* pp. 103, 246-7. Blundell subsequently changed his position on the duty question.

[29] Brandis, 'Attaran Forests', p. 140.

[30] Furnivall, *Colonial Policy and Practice,* pp. 45-6.

[31] Taylor. *State in Burma,* p. 90.

timber revenue increased to 133,481 rupees in the first three years (nearly 45,000 rupees per year).[32]

These measures acknowledged the problem, but did not provide the political and economic resources to resolve it. With only a small establishment and many other duties, the new Superintendent was unable to supervise forest work effectively. As a result, forest rules continued to be subject to what Commissioner Henry Durand called in 1846 'the most gross neglect and the most barefaced violation'.[33] One indication of the Government's continued reluctance to intervene was its treatment of the 'revocable' timber license. Between 1829 and 1846 it did not revoke even one license, and in 1846 when Superintendent Guthrie attempted a revocation, business-owners' outrage prompted the government in India to discountenance the move. Indeed, 'large sums were paid for the transfer of the licenses, showing the feeling of security that was placed in them.'[34]

If the government was reluctant to intervene in the teak trade, it was largely powerless to regulate non-teak forest use. With only a small staff to control a large territory, the British were dependent on village leaders (*thu-gyi*) who inevitably under-reported local resources, thereby denying revenue to the state. As Blundell noted in 1840, forest products

> .... do not belong to any individuals in particular and are collected by those who choose to resort to the forests for them and who are supposed to give in an account of the quantity so collected, on which the duty is levied, but as we have no means of checking such statements, most of the duty is of course avoided and the amount collected small.[35]

In lieu of posting officials in the forest to enforce the duty, Blundell had little option but to remit the tax.

Colonial officials were similarly ill-placed to regulate shifting cultivation. Shifting cultivators of mainly Karen ethnic origin cut an annual hill clearing (*taungya*) in which they grew subsistence and cash crops. The Karen were long-standing participants in the regional economy, and paid tribute in kind to the local Burmese Governor.

---

[32] Baillie, 'Summary of Papers', p. 128.

[33] Cited in Pollack, *Empires in Collision*, p. 49.

[34] H. Falconer, 'Report on the Teak Forests of the Tenasserim Provinces', *Selections from the Records of the Bengal Government* 9 (1852), p. 36. Two Calcutta-based firms (Cockerell and Company; Mackay and Company) liable to lose out as a result of Guthrie's actions led the business campaign. These companies' leases were restored upon the orders of the Deputy Governor of Bengal; Guthrie then resigned in protest, see Stebbing, *Forests of India*, vol. I, pp. 177-86.

[35] *Selected Correspondence*, p.193.

The British converted that tribute to a money payment which was 'much more convenient' to the government 'if not to the Karens'.[36] First levied at the annual rate of fifteen rupees per family, it was subsequently reduced by more than 50 percent. However, Blundell rejected its total abolition, arguing that

> ... by so doing we should rather afford a premium to their continuance in their wild and unsettled habits than encourage their settlement into regular villages when they would come under the operation of other taxes. A judicious reduction would, I think, have a better tendency to encourage settled habits among them, while to encourage immigration, new arrivals among them may be declared free of tax for periods of 3 or 5 years.[37]

As with his predecessor, Commissioner Blundell wanted to convert shifting cultivators into sedentary farmers. In doing so, he revealed the concerns of a civil administrator; shifting cultivators were condemned because they were difficult to tax and control. However, shifting cultivators were criticized by other officials for allegedly destroying vast forests, a criticism which was part of a broader critique of *laissez-faire* forestry.

Challenging Laissez-Faire

A succession of officials argued that unfettered private extraction would lead inevitably to the depletion of Tenasserim's teak forests. Shifting cultivation was also seen as a major problem. State intervention was required if the forest were to be protected from the depredations of both loggers and shifting cultivators.

As early as 1827, Wallich warned of the ecological perils or *laissez-faire*. As a government physician and botanist, he held views diametrically opposed to those of Commissioner Maingy. With other medical surgeons in India, Wallich opposed destruction of the Empire's largely unexplored forests.[38] Whereas Maingy saw only an under-utilized resource, Wallich noted the biotic diversity; while the Commissioner enthused about apparently limitless forests, the Superintendent raised the spectre of a timber famine. Reporting to the government's local political agent, Archibald Campbell, Wallich argued:

---

[36] Furnivall, 'Fashioning of Leviathan', p.138; *Selected Correspondence,* pp. 18-19; Brandis, 'Attaran Forests', pp. 119-20.

[37] *Selected Correspondence* p. 193.

[38] Richard Grove, 'Conserving Eden: The (European) East India Companies and their Environmental Policies on St. Helena, Mauritius and in Western India, 1600 to 1854', *Comparative Studies in Society and History* 35 (April 1993), pp. 339-40.

No forest exists which can with propriety be called inexhaustible – at least that is liable to constant and extensive demands for timber. The quantity of teak used for public purposes, both Military and Naval, is so great, and it will go on increasing to so great an extent in proportion as new sources of supplies are opened, that the Martaban Forests, ample as they are, would soon be impoverished, unless they were placed under a vigilant and strict superintendence, their supplies regulated with economy, and their extent gradually augmented. I hope I take a correct view of the case, if I consider all the teak forests which grow in these Provinces as the exclusive property of the State, applicable only on public use, and not to be interfered with by any private individual whatever. Unless this principle be acted upon from the very outset, I will venture to predict that private enterprise will very soon render fruitless all endeavours to perpetuate the supplies for the public service, and one of the principal and most certain sources of revenue will thus be irrecoverably lost.[39]

Quoted approvingly in subsequent years by Burma's imperial forest historians,[40] Wallich's statement summarized succinctly the interventionist position – namely, that without state intervention, Tenasserim's teak forests would be destroyed by private enterprise.

Events in Tenasserim soon confirmed Wallich's warning. After less than a decade of *laissez-faire*, widespread overharvesting led the government to send the scientist John Helfer to investigate. Helfer reported in 1838 that Tenasserim's developing timber trade was leading to the extermination of the teak forests. Agreeing with Wallich, he called on the state to intervene to stop the destruction. Helfer also criticized indigenous practices, condemning as an archaic and highly destructive form of agriculture the shifting cultivation that the hill Karen of southeast Burma practised.[41]

Helfer's findings convinced Blundell of the need for state intervention. An erstwhile supporter of *laissez-faire*, the Commissioner now urged his superiors to introduce measures to halt overharvesting.[42] The government of India responded by appointing Captain Tremenheere as Tenasserim's first Superintendent of Forests in 1841.

This appointment was an important first step in the promotion

---

[39] Baillie, 'Summary of Papers', pp. 76-7. Wallich later reiterated the interventionist argument before a British parliamentary committee in 1831, see Grove, 'Conserving Eden', p. 340.

[40] Brandis, 'Attaran Forests', p. 73; Stebbing, *Forests of India*, vol. I, p. 136; Ribbentrop, *Forestry in British India*, pp. 69-70; F.T. Morehead, *The Forests of Burma*, London, 1944, p. 21.

[41] Cited in Baillie, 'Summary of Papers', p. 90; John William Helfer, 'Third Report on Tenasserim', *Journal of the Bengal Asiatic Society* 8 (December 1839), p. 985.

[42] *Selected Correspondence*, p. 163; Stebbing, *Forests of India*, vol. I, p. 148.

of a colonial forest policy. However, its importance did not lie in any immediate effect on harvesting since *laissez-faire* practices persisted in Tenasserim until 1857. Rather, Tremenheere's appointment was important because it provided for the first time in colonial Burma an institutional base from which to challenge unfettered private extraction. Tremenheere and his immediate successors in Tenasserim lacked training, staff and political influence to alter the status quo. Yet they used their official mandate to publicize the rule-breaking and overharvesting that was integral to *laissez-faire*.

Frustrated by their lack of influence over the teak trade, the superintendents therefore turned their attention to a weaker foe: the hill Karen. The propensity of these cultivators to clear fields in teak forests earned them official displeasure because 'they prefer spots where young Teak abounds to any other, the soil being generally richer and well elevated.'[43] In 1848, Superintendent T. Latter went so far as to claim that shifting cultivators, not timber traders, were the 'greatest cause' of teak destruction locally.[44]

In contrast, others believed that the Karen could be reformed. Commissioner Durand claimed that British rule would make them 'the best conservators of forests which the British Government could employ'. It was suggested that the Karen in the Thaungyin valley should even receive legal title to local forests. As Superintendent Guthrie noted, this move would tend to 'fix and increase the Karen population' along the strategic Siamese border at the same time encouraging them to protect teak trees. Further, timber 'could be purchased from them at as low a rate as it could be worked by hired labour.'[45] The East India Company's Court of Directors rejected this idea in 1849, however, opposing the recognition of any non-state right to the teak forests. In doing so, the directors affirmed the status quo; the colonial state owned the forests, the timber merchants exploited the forests, and the forests would continue to be degraded.

In the same year, however, the government once more solicited scientific advice, sending Hugh Falconer, the Superintendent of the Calcutta Botanical Garden to inspect Tenasserim's forests. Falconer's report documented what Wallich, Helfer, and successive superintendents predicted: *laissez-faire* practices had ruined the forests. Licensees were not establishing plantations as the law required even though they

---

[43] Deputy Superintendent Maling cited in Baillie, 'Summary of Papers', p. 131.

[44] *Ibid.,* p. 154. Shifting cultivators were also a 'softer target' than timber traders in southern India around this time, see Rangarajan, 'Imperial Agendas,' p. 157.

[45] Baillie, 'Summary of Papers', pp. 127-8, 132, 135.

were 'fully aware of the impending exhaustion of their grants'; he mused:

> If such have been the results of the past, when the forests were covered with abundance of valuable Teak timber, what reasonable grounds are there for expecting adequate measures of renewal from the grantees, now that they are bared?[46]

Yet in tacit recognition of the power of the timber lobby, Falconer did not recommend a government teak monopoly, but rather urged that licensees be subjected to stricter regulation.

Even these recommendations were not heeded by the government in India. When Tenasserim's forests finally came under a regular system of forest management in 1857, only the most inaccessible areas remained untouched. Annual extraction from the Ataran forests was less than one thousand trees.[47] Table 2.3 gives some idea of the extent of overharvesting during the *laissez-faire* era.

Table 2.3. TEAK OVERHARVESTING IN
THE ATARAN FORESTS, 1827-1858

	Average annual no.	*Total no.*
Trees removed	5,529	171,400[a]
Sustainable level	3,270	101,370[b]
Difference (Overharvest)	2,259	70,030

[a] Based on the estimated number of stumps in the forest in 1858.
[b] As calculated by Brandis.

Source: D. Brandis, 'Report on the Attaran Forests for the year 1860', *Selections from the Records of the Government of India (Foreign Department)*, 32 (1861), pp. 97-99. First-class trees only, defined as 6 feet in girth or larger.

No complete record exists of overharvesting in Tenasserim, but data collected by Brandis in 1858 provides an indication of the scale of the problem. By counting the number of stumps in a sample area, Brandis was able to extrapolate that, for the Ataran forests as a whole, 171,400 first-class trees were harvested between 1827 and 1858 – 70,030 trees more than the estimated 'sustainable' amount. However, the overharvest was even greater in practice than this discrepancy indicates. Brandis only counted the stumps of first-class trees, that is, trees 6 feet in girth and larger. But, as noted, the official minimum girth until 1841 was 4 feet – a rule which was, in any event, ignored by traders practising a cut-and-run strategy.

The most telling indication of the depletion of Tenasserim's forests

---

[46] Falconer, 'Teak Forests', pp. 36-7.
[47] Brandis, 'Attaran Forests', p. 100.

was to be seen in the shift in logging out of the Province – by 1855, for instance, most Ataran leases had been abandoned by their owners.[48] By the mid-nineteenth century, teak extraction centred on two regions: the mountainous Salween watershed separating Burma from Siam that was controlled by local rulers (*Chao*); and the low-lying Pegu hills (*yoma*) between the Irrawaddy and Sittang valleys of southern Burma.[49] In the latter, timber traders anticipated new opportunities and a system of *laissez-faire* practices as a British victory in the second Anglo-Burmese war (1852) liberated more of Burma's great teak wealth from monarchical rule.

When Legacies Meet: Forestry in Pegu, 1852-1855

Yet state intervention marked the subsequent development of the Pegu teak forests, a different course from that which had occurred in the Tenasserim forests. The Tenasserim experience, the growing influence of scientific advisers, and the consolidation of empire all contributed to a political context conducive to change.

Pegu's annexation coincided with the publication of two important documents critical of a *laissez-faire* approach to forestry management. Falconer's report in January 1851 recorded the depletion of Tenasserim's teak forests, and the government subsequently published it along with other papers pertaining to that issue. About the same time a report by leading surgeons of the East India Company warned that unregulated timber extraction in India (and elsewhere) would cause social and ecological disaster on a regional and even global scale. As Richard Grove observes, these warnings were published at a time when official anxiety over human induced ecological change gave scientists some public influence.[50]

Broader political and economic trends reinforced the impact of these reports. By the middle of the nineteenth century, the British Indian empire was beginning to coalesce, as manifested notably in the transition from East India Company to direct British government rule. Colonialism entered a new and more aggressive phase. This change was illustrated in the British attitude towards Burma. Following

---

[48] A. Bogle to C. Beadon, 30 November 1855, cited in *ibid.*, p. 25.

[49] On teak extraction along the Burma-Siam border, see Banasopit Mekvichai, 'The Teak Industry in North Thailand: The Role of a Natural-Resource-Based Export Economy in Regional Development', unpubl. Ph.D. thesis, Cornell University, 1988, chap. 3.

[50] Grove, 'Conserving Eden', p. 350; see also C.A. Bayly, *Indian Society and the Making of the British Empire,* New Cambridge History of India, Cambridge, 1988, vol. II, part I, p. 140.

the first Anglo-Burmese war, British officials considered returning 'unprofitable' Tenasserim to the Burmese monarchy – deliberations that were not repeated upon the annexation of Pegu in 1852.[51]

As the idea of empire took hold, attention turned to systematic development. There was perhaps no more vigorous an exponent of such development than Lord Dalhousie, the Governor General of India in the early 1850s. Dalhousie promoted the railway, the telegraph, and a unified postal system for the Indian sub-continent.[52] Equally important, however, he promoted a modern system of forest management. As Chapter 3 shows, Dalhousie appointed Dietrich Brandis as Pegu's Superintendent of Forests in 1856; he also wrote the 'Minute on Forest Policy of 1855' which signalled 'the dawn of scientific forestry' in the British Indian empire.[53] Unlike many of his predecessors, Dalhousie saw utility in state intervention, and it was in Pegu that an organized system of imperial forest management first developed.

Altered imperial circumstances facilitated a new approach to forest issues, but Burma's unique social and ecological conditions had also to be taken into account. In drawing the border at the end of the second Anglo-Burmese war, the British included as much of the teak-bearing Pegu Yoma as possible.[54] In doing so, colonial officials also inherited a complex tradition of indigenous forest management. That tradition was an important, if subsequently under-rated influence on forest policy in colonial Burma.

Between 1852 and 1855, the government introduced preliminary measures to regulate Pegu's teak forest. On 26 September 1853, the government declared those forests state property and prohibited unauthorized teak extraction in keeping with precolonial precedent. The status of teak as a royal tree was thereby affirmed. Shortly thereafter, Pegu's first Superintendent of Forest and predecessor to Brandis, the British physician John McClelland, examined the teak bearing Pegu Yoma. In two reports published in 1855, McClelland provided a first account of those forests.[55] These reports were remarkably

---

[51] Pollack, *Empires in Collision*, pp. 41-2; D.G.E. Hall, *A History of South-East Asia*, 4th edn, London, 1981, pp. 644-6.

[52] Michael Adas, *Machines as the Measure of Men: Science, Technology, and Ideologies of Western Dominance*, Ithaca, 1989, p. 225.

[53] Stebbing, *Forests of India*, vol. I, pp. 256-60. Dalhousie's keen interest in forest matters was linked to his close association with Joseph D. Hooker, see Grove, 'Conserving Eden', p. 348.

[54] Pollack, *Empires in Collision*, p. 109; Hall, *History of South-East Asia* p. 652; David Joel Steinberg et al., *In Search of Southeast Asia: A Modern History*, rev. edn, Sydney, 1987, p. 107.

[55] J. McClelland, 'Report on the Sitang and other Teak Forests of Pegu' and 'Report

similar to Wallich's earlier report on Tenasserim's forests. Both men documented the incidence of teak and warned of the perils of unregulated private extraction. Echoing Wallich's original warning, McClelland predicted that 'if we fail in the comparatively simple duty of preserving the old forests, we can scarcely hope to succeed in the more difficult task of creating new ones.'[56]

McClelland emphasized that many of Pegu's accessible forests had already been cut, and traders were felling undersized trees. Faced with such evidence, he concluded that indigenous forest management in Pegu was non-existent. Large landlords in conjunction with Rangoon merchants employed workers seasonally to drag timber from forest to stream (from where it was floated to market). When supplies in one area were exhausted, loggers simply moved to a new forest. In McClelland's view, this business was not part of the regular industry of the country. There were no professional foresters or woodcutters who earned an income solely from forest work; hence no one could be 'thrown out of accustomed employment or be in any way injuriously affected by any alteration in the forest laws of rules.[57] The British were thus as free in Pegu as they were in Tenasserim to manage the forests as they saw fit without disrupting indigenous practices.

McClelland's denial of precolonial forest management in Pegu was part of a broader colonial conviction that the Burmese were incapable of managing their own forests. Whereas in Tenasserim they had 'under-exploited' a valuable asset, in Pegu the Burmese were guilty of overharvesting the teak forests. To later generations of British forest officials, Burmese incompetence in forestry was axiomatic.

Yet McClelland's claim that precolonial forestry was non-existent in Pegu did not square with the evidence gathered by other colonial officials. A report by Robert Abreu, McClelland's own assistant, for example, observed that as teak was a royal tree in monarchical Burma, woodcutters were required to pay an annual axe tax for the privilege of working the forest.[58] All timber left in the forest at the end of each year reverted to the state. As Pegu's first Commissioner Arthur Phayre noted, the role of the village *thu-gyi* was crucial for this individual authorized teak extraction locally in return for a fee paid on each tree felled.

---

on the Southern Forests of Pegu' both in *Selections from the Records of the Government of India (Foreign Department)* 9 (1855).

[56] McClelland, 'Southern Forests', p. 21.

[57] Cited in Stebbing, *Forests of India,* vol. I, p. 249.

[58] Robert Abreu, 'Report on the Lhine, Phoungyee, and Zamayee Teak Forests', *Selections from the Records of the Government of India (Foreign Department)* 9 (1855), pp. 43-4.

Teak trees were to them in fact a property held in virtue of their offices, and a number of the inhabitants of each circle were generally interested in the killing of the trees and sometimes in the dragging of them. This consideration will show at once the great obstacles which have to be overcome in preserving the forest, since an important privilege of the Thoogyees has, under the British Government, been abrogated.[59]

Phayre did not suggest that precolonial practices were sustainable. Rather, he recognized what McClelland overlooked: the existence of a system of forest regulation and control in monarchical Burma.

Such a system not only existed, but was also an important, if underrated influence on colonial forest policy itself. Patterns of forest control and extraction techniques established in monarchical times were often perpetuated under British rule. Thus, contrary to the Eurocentric notion that technology transfer was a one-way process from Europe to the colonies, technology sometimes 'flowed in reverse'. Such was the case in the forestry sector as techniques of timber extraction and regulation were passed from the Burmese to the Europeans.[60]

This is not surprising since Burmese involvement in the teak trade long predated that of the Europeans. From at least the seventeenth century, southern Burma exported locally built teak ships, and 111 square-rigged vessels of European model representing an aggregate tonnage of thirty-five thousand were constructed in Rangoon between 1786 and 1824 alone.[61] A booming shipbuilding industry attracted labourers from around the region, and in the late eighteenth century they earned some twenty *kyats* for every hundred teak logs sawn into planks.[62]

The precolonial state played a central role in the teak trade. Burma's rulers developed a complex regulatory system designed to maximize revenue and control. This system appears to have had two major components.[63] First, revenue and customs posts along the principal river and cart routes were used to regulate and tax trade in commercial

[59] A. Phayre to J. McClelland, 20 March 1855, in *ibid,* p. 182.

[60] Khin Maung Kyi, 'Western Enterprise and Economic Development in Burma',*Journal of the Burma Research Society* 53 (June 1970), p. 44. On Eurocentric notions of technology transfer generally, see Adas, *Machines as the Measure of Men.*

[61] Pearn, *History of Rangoon,* p. 71; see also Victor B. Lieberman, *Burmese Administrative Cycles: Anarchy and Conquest,* c.1580-1760, Princeton, 1984, pp. 119-20; Morehead, *Forests of Burma,* p. 19.

[62] Htin Aung, *Epistles Written on the Eve of the Anglo-Burmese War,* The Hague, 1968, pp. 10-11.

[63] Precolonial forestry has yet to be the subject of systematic research. Thus the discussion here is necessarily tentative.

goods including teak. For internal commerce, land (*te*) and water (*hseik*) toll stations served this purpose, whereas customs posts (*kin*) enabled Burmese rulers to control capital-district, inter-district and international trade. These posts were 'a means of monitoring centrally the flow of manpower and other resources in a way no other institution could in such a diffuse administrative system.[64] As teak was most easily transported by river, revenue and customs posts were an effective method of control.

The precolonial state also attempted to regulate teak extraction from the forest itself. A technique of killing commercially mature trees known as girdling (or ring barking) was central to this endeavour:

> Girdling consists in cutting through the bark and sapwood till the darker-coloured heartwood is entered about an inch below the surface. The effect of this operation is to check the possibility of sap rising from the root system. Deprived of food supplies the leaves wither and the tree dies. A process of natural seasoning on the stock them follows... the seasoned stem being ready for felling and extraction in two years or more.[65]

This process facilitated dragging and floating operations such that girdled teak was easier to extract from the forest than green teak. However, teak girdling was also a useful means of state control.[66] By funnelling timber into the river network, it limited the number of routes by which teak could be transported to market, thereby easing the task of control and taxation. Timber arriving at revenue stations could be checked to see if, when, and where it had been girdled (according to marks required by law to be placed on logs at the time of girdling). In the case of the more valuable forests, specially appointed forest guards made dry season inspections of the forest.[67]

This system did not prevent illicit extraction. Burma's forest were too large, and the administrative capacity too small, to achieve complete control. Further, teak used locally was habitually extracted by land with the aid of buffaloes, and could be taken from the forest while

---

[64] Taylor, *The State in Burma*, p. 44; see also William J. Koenig, *The Burmese Polity, 1752-1819: Politics, Administration, and Social Organization in the Early Kon-baung periods,* Ann Arbor, 1990, p. 56.

[65] Nisbet, *Burma under British Rule,* vol. II, p. 52.

[66] The origins of girdling in monarchical Burma are unclear. Brandis believed the practice to have been in force 'ever since Teak has been exported on a large scale', Government of India, Public Works Department, *Seasoning of Timber by Girdling previous to Felling,* London, 1868, p. 29.

[67] J.S. Vorley and C.H. Thompson, *Working Plan for Magwe Forest Division, 1927-28 to 1957-58,* Rangoon, 1928, vol. I, p. 24.

still green. Although *thu-gyi* controlled this trade, the extent to which the Burmese monarchy derived benefit from such extraction depended on the power of the ruler in relation to regional and local leaders. Yet, the vicissitudes of political control and teak extraction aside, girdling was in principal an effective defence against illegal extraction.[68]

The precolonial state also developed rules governing the use of non-teak forest products. Precolonial revenue records (*sit-tans*), for example, reveal that a range of timber and non-timber forest products were taxed.[69] *Thu-gyi* and other local officials collected the taxes, retaining a percentage of the revenue for their services. Taxes varied from place to place depending on local forest use, patron-client relations, and the relative power of the central state.[70] In an administratively diffuse system, the revenue received by the monarch was invariably much less than that collected at the village level. As with other forms of surplus, forest revenue was subject to competing local, regional and central claims. In addition, low population density, unoccupied lands, and the relatively weak coercive powers of the state facilitated peasant avoidance of punitive taxation.

Precolonial forestry thus developed as a means to tax and control forest use. Its overall effectiveness from the state's viewpoint is to be seen in the fact that the British continued or later revived many indigenous forms of forest control. Colonial forest officials thus affirmed the royal monopoly on teak, and regulated extraction through the technique of girdling. They monitored and taxed the flow of timber at revenue stations located along the main river routes. Other forest products were also taxed as the administrative capacity of the colonial Forest Department increased. However, diverse forest users resisted the exactions of the colonial state as they denied the demands of its predecessor. A central objective of this book, then, is to examine how control over forest activities grew under the British, and the manner in which resistance was modified to meet a more powerful state presence in the forest.

The British borrowed techniques of resource control from the Burmese, but the impetus for state intervention derived largely from the early colonial experience with forest management in Burma. The depletion of Tenasserim's teak forests illustrated the pitfalls of *laissez-faire* forestry, and in an altered imperial context, it became possible

---

[68] Nisbet, *Burma under British Rule*, vol. II, p. 52; *Progress Report on Forest Administration in British Burma*, 1863-4, pp. 60-1.

[69] Frank N. Trager and William J. Koenig, *Burmese Sit-tans 1764-1826: Records of Rural Life and Administration*, Tucson, AZ, 1979.

[70] This variability is illustrated in the Hanthawadi and Taungngo land rolls of southern Burma reprinted in *ibid.*

to experiment with new management techniques premised on state intervention.

The Tenasserim experience demonstrated, above all, the need for a forest department empowered to manage the forest resource on a long-term basis. The appointment of a part-time Superintendent notwithstanding, forest management in Tenasserim was characterized by the absence of state authority in the forest: forest rules were ignored, even on occasion by state officials themselves. Conflict in the teak forests was thus not about resistance to these rules. Rather, it reflected a struggle between timber traders for control of a rapidly diminishing resource under anarchic conditions. However, such conflict, and associated forest depletion, was an almost inevitable by-product of a system of unfettered private enterprise.

The colonial state's response to the events in Tenasserim is the subject of succeeding chapters of this book. The Burma Forest Department was created in 1856 under the direction of Dietrich Brandis, and was given extensive powers to regulate forest use. As the next chapter shows, however, the transition from *laissez-faire* to scientific forestry in the mid-nineteenth century provoked much conflict. Timber traders, peasants, and shifting cultivators all resisted the imposition of state forest control. In the process, a dynamic of control and resistance was established that was to characterize Burmese forest politics into the twentieth century.

3

SCIENTIFIC FORESTRY: CONTROL AND RESISTANCE, 1856-1881

The basic pattern of forest administration in colonial Burma was established during the twenty-five year period that began with Brandis's arrival in Pegu in 1856 and ended with the passage of the Burma Forest Act in 1881. The previous chapter explained how *laissez-faire* forestry in Tenasserim was predicated on unfettered private enterprise. Subsequent chapters examine the political ramifications of the elaboration of state forest control and popular reaction to such control in the late nineteenth and twentieth centuries. In contrast, the aim of this chapter is to explore the transition from *laissez-faire* practices to a scientific forestry premised on state intervention. At the heart of such intervention was the Forest Department – created in 1856 to assert control over forest users as part of an attempt to manage Burma's commercial forests scientifically.

Control

The literature on colonial forest politics examines the impact of scientific forestry on state-civil society relations, but in doing so has tended to neglect changes occurring within the state itself. The effect of scientific forestry on peasants, shifting cultivators and timber traders is an important subject addressed in this chapter. Yet, such an understanding is incomplete without first appreciating how the advent of scientific forestry prompted significant changes in the bureaucratic and legal behaviour of the colonial state.

Creating a Forest Department.   The Forest Department's creation was part and parcel of the establishment of a functionally-defined state in Burma in the nineteenth century.[1] In the natural resources sector, various departments were set up specializing in the management of a given resource (i.e. forestry, agriculture, mining), and whose aim

---

[1] Robert H. Taylor, *The State in Burma,* London, 1987, chap. 2.

was to maximize commercial production. As part of this process, specialized professional training was required for entry to service in these departments. As chapter 1 noted, bureaucratic conflict was an almost inevitable by-product of this process.

In effect, a basic disjuncture developed between the way in which the colonial state organized its administration of natural resources and the spatial distribution and characteristics of those resources: the 'political-administrative world' did not coincide neatly with the 'real resource world'. This chapter explores some of the implications of this disjuncture by analyzing the bureaucratic politics associated with forest-civil official relations as well as efforts to codify scientific forestry in law. First, however, the creation of the Forest Department itself requires consideration. The Forest Department was established in 1856 so as to permit the introduction of scientific forest management in the Pegu teak forests. As Chapter 2 noted, those forests were already partially depleted at the time of the British conquest in 1852. With only a small staff to control the forests, Superintendent McClelland was thereafter unable to stop illegal practices which flourished in the unsettled conditions followed the second Anglo-Burmese war. Further, differences between McClelland and the Commissioner Arthur Phayre over the extent of forest regulation led to the former's resignation and the intervention of Lord Dalhousie in his 'Minute on Forest Policy' in August 1855.

Dalhousie's Minute is noteworthy for its strong criticism of private enterprise. The perpetuation of *laissez-faire* practices in Pegu would deprive the government of 'the full value' of its forests and would not 'ensure those traders a supply of timber who want it most, unless they happen to be great capitalists and speculators in timber'.[2] Noting the adverse impact of the latter on Tenasserim's forests, Dalhousie urged that big timber merchants be bypassed in favour of small-scale local contractors who would extract teak on the state's behalf.

Dalhousie's Minute ordered the Forest Department to implement state controlled teak extraction in Pegu. This task was entrusted upon McClelland's resignation in 1855 to Dietrich Brandis, a German botanist-turned forester who left a lecturing post in botany at the University of Bonn for the opportunity to be Superintendent of Forests in a region with some of the most botanically diverse forests on earth.[3]

---

[2] The minute was contained in C. Beadon, Secretary, Government of India, to Commissioner, Pegu, 3 August 1855, *Selections from the Records of the Government of India (Foreign Department)* 9 (1855), p. 76.

[3] On Brandis, see Herbert Hesmer, 'Dietrich Brandis and Forestry in Burma', trans. E and D. von Bendemann, *Guardian* (Rangoon), 25 (April 1978), pp. 33-4; Gifford Pinchot, 'Sir Dietrich Brandis', *Indian Forester 35* (August 1909), pp. 468-80.

Brandis started work in a climate of political, economic, and ecological uncertainty. Little was known about Pegu's forests, and the characteristics of the teak tree, making estimation of the annual allowable cut largely guesswork at first. On the political front, annexation of Pegu put Britain in control of a Burmese population whose allegiance was suspect.[4] Moreover, the colonial state shared a border with a truncated but still independent Burma in turmoil after the British defeated it a second time. While the threat of a Burmese invasion was remote, the border area was nevertheless subject to unrest, mirroring the vicissitudes of Anglo-Burmese relations and Burmese court politics.[5] To forest officials, such uncertainty was particularly troubling because most of Pegu's valuable forests were near the frontier. The border bisected the teak-bearing Pegu Yoma. Brandis also faced the economic uncertainties associated with creating a new department during a time of change and crisis. Preoccupied with the Indian Mutiny (1857-8), the government of India devoted only limited resources to the Burma Forest Department. Yet the department was expected to generate an economic surplus for the imperial treasury. Timber merchants inevitably pointed out the limited nature of that initial surplus and pressed the government to relinquish control of the forests.

Forest rules first proclaimed in Pegu in October 1856 provided a framework within which the Forest Department could operate. These rules were revised (and extended to Tenasserim) in 1859, and later incorporated in India-wide legislation (1865).[6] Forest rules were a mechanism to transform the state's nominal ownership of the teak forest into an actively exercised proprietorial right. The rules prohibited unauthorized felling of teak, but also constrained non-teak timber extraction in teak areas. Shifting cultivators were subject to special

[4] Robert H. Taylor, *The State in Burma,* London 1987, pp. 116-7, 156-7; John F. Cady, *A History of Modern Burma,* Ithaca, 1958, pp. 89-90, 94; J.A. Mills, 'Burmese Peasant Response to British Provincial Rule 1852-1885' in D.B. Miller (ed.), *Peasants and Politics: Grass Roots Reaction to Change in Asia,* London, 1979, pp. 77-104.

[5] R.R Langham-Carter, 'Burmese Rule on the Toungoo Frontier', *Journal of the Burma Research Society* 27 (1937) pp. 15-32; Albert Fytche, 'Narrative of the Mission to Mandalay in 1867', *Selections from the Records of the Government of India (Foreign Department) 63 (1868): pp. 21-2; Cady, History of Modern Burma,* p. 63.

[6] The following discussion is based on 'Rules for Preserving the Forests in Pegu (1856)' in D. Brandis, 'Report on the Teak Forests of Pegu for 1856', *Selections from the Records of the Government of India (Foreign Department)* 28 (1860), pp. 62-5; see also D. Brandis, *Rules for the Administration of Forests in the Province of Pegu,* Rangoon, 1859; 'British Burma Forest Rules of 1865' in D. Brandis, *Memorandum on the Forest Legislation proposed for British India other than the Presidencies of Madras and Bombay,* Simla, 1875, pp. 53-7. Arakan's forests were of limited commercial importance and were administered by civil officials until the end of the nineteenth century, A.H.M. Barrington, *Forest Administration in the Arakan Forest Division,* Rangoon, 1918.

control. They were prohibited from cutting taungya in areas containing more than fifty teak trees, large or small, seedlings included, without Department approval. The infringement of any of these rules could result in a 200-rupees fine or six months' imprisonment.

At first these rules had minimal impact. In theory, forest administration was based on a three-tiered structure in which subordinates patrolled districts, assistants managed divisions, and the Superintendent was responsible for general matters. In practice Brandis experienced difficulty in finding recruits for the superior service and relied instead on civil officials in several divisions.[7] However, these officials provided only a general supervision from the towns. As a result, administration was practically synonymous with the actions of untrained and poorly paid Burmese subordinates. In 1858-59, the subordinate staff in Pegu consisted of 56 individuals, 8 of whom earned between 15 and 40 rupees per month, but with the rest on 10 rupees per month.[8] Under these conditions, fraud and indolence were rife. Locally hired, these men were ideally placed to profit from their posts – through the illegal sale of timber, for example. Yet they also did much useful work, and the principal difficulty was illness: in 1859-60, four out of eight men in the eastern Prome forests alone died while on duty.[9]

As early as 1858, Brandis sought trained foresters from Germany to establish the Forest Department on a professional basis. This initiative failed, but he was nevertheless able to hire sufficient assistants from the civil and military service to ensure that by the time of his departure for India in 1862 the Forest Department was established on a viable basis. Under the direction of non-foresters Henry Leeds and William Seaton, the department expanded gradually thereafter in the 1860s.

Yet the need for trained foresters grew in the measure that forest administration became more complex. Developments in India confirmed that need. The creation of the Indian Forest Department (1864) and the passage of the Indian Forest Act (1865) illustrated the government of India's growing interest in forest management. It thus became imperative that forest policy in Burma be implemented by professionals.[10] To this end, Brandis obtained the approval of Lord Cranborne, Secretary of State for India in 1865, to recruit two German foresters, and

[7] D. Brandis, 'Report on the Pegu Teak Forests for 1858-59', *Selections from the Records of the Government of India (Foreign Department)* 31 (1861), p. 14; D. Brandis, 'Report on the Pegu Teak Forests for 1859-60' in *ibid.*, pp. 90-1

[8] Brandis, 'Report for 1858-59', p. 15.

[9] Brandis, 'Report for 1859-60', p. 90

[10] Government of India, Public Works Department (PWD), to Secretary of State for India, 19 September 1868, *India Forest Letters* (henceforth *IFL*), no. 10 of 1868.

while on European furlough he selected William Schlich and Berthold Ribbentrop.[11] As in Dutch-ruled Java, British officials in India were hindered by the backwardness of forestry in their native country, and had little choice but to turn to Germany for assistance.[12]

Brandis also arranged for the training of English candidates for the Indian forest service in France and Germany since at that time there were no forest schools in Britain. Seven candidates commenced study in Europe in 1867 and two years later the first graduates arrived in India. Ninety-five men were trained in this manner by 1886, including a number of foresters who later gained prominence in Burma.[13] A national forest school was finally opened in England at Coopers Hill (Surrey) in 1885 where students undertook a three-year course of study in scientific forestry. By the early twentieth century, forestry was taught at Oxford (1905), Cambridge (1913) and Edinburgh (1915). These developments represented a recognition by the British Government of the need to employ trained men so as 'to guard against the ruin of one of the most important sources of national wealth, if the care of the forests were left to ignorant persons.'[14]

Arrival of a growing number of professional foresters in British Burma helped to stabilize the Forest Department. Staff turnover due to transfers, death, resignation or dismissal was high prior to 1870, and administrative continuity suffered. Recruits from Europe to fill new posts formed the basis of more established forest service thereafter (Table 3.1).

A trebling in the size of the superior service between 1861 and 1885 permitted the extension of state forest control. To facilitate such control, European recruits were also now required to undergo Burmese language training.[15]

[11] Secretary of State for India to Governor General of India, 14 September 1866, *Selections from Dispatches to India* (henceforth *SDI*), 1866, p. 56. D. Brandis to H. Merivale, Under-Secretary of State for India, 23 October 1866, *India Forest Proceedings* (henceforth *IFP*), March 1867, p. 81; Government of India (PWD) to Secretary of State for India, 11 April 1867, *IFL* no. 10 of 1867.

[12] D. Brandis, *Indian Forestry*, Woking, 1897, pp. 6-11, 21; R.S. Troup, 'Forestry in India', *Calcutta Review* 273 (July 1913), p. 305, 312; Peter Boomgaard, 'Forest Management and Exploitation in Colonial Java, 1677-1897', *Forest and Conservation History* 36 (January 1992), p. 11.

[13] B. Ribbentrop, *Forestry in British India*, Calcutta, 1900, p. 227; W.F. Perree, 'Indian Forest Administration', *Asiatic Review 23* (April 1927), p. 251; Robert K. Winters, *The Forest and Man*, New York, 1974, p. 281.

[14] Parliamentary Return on Forest Conservancy, Part I, India, 1871, p. 404, cited in Brandis, *Indian Forestry*, p. 49; see also Secretary of State for India to Governor General of India, 15 November 1867, *SDI* (1867), pp. 126-7; Secretary of State for India to Governor General of India, 6 October 1869, *SDI* (1869), p. 152.

[15] Resolution, Government of India, Department Revenue, Agriculture and Commerce

Table 3.1. GROWTH OF THE SUPERIOR SERVICE, 1861-1885

Position	1861	1874	1885[a]
Conservator	1	1	2
Deputy Conservator	3	3	12
Assistant Conservator	3	11	7
Total	7	15	21

[a] Burma and the Andaman Islands.

Source: W. Seaton, 'Report on the Conservancy and Management of the Forests of British Burma', Government of India, *Copy of Enclosures of Forests Despatch from the Government of India* 14 (1874), pp. 4, 6; B. Ribbentrop, *Forestry in British India*, Calcutta, 1900, p. 81.

Yet new recruitment procedures effectively barred Burmese from entering the superior service. A racial division of labour was instituted that only began to break down in the late colonial period. If the 'superior' staff included German and Dutch officials, Burmese foresters were confined to the 'subordinate' service.[16]

To be sure, an Imperial Forest School for the training of indigenous students as Rangers and Sub-Assistant Conservators was created at Dehra Dun in India in 1878. However, there was virtually no prospect of promotion from these positions. A parallel education system was thereby established: British candidates were educated in Europe for senior posts, and Indian and Burmese recruits were trained at Dehra Dun for subordinate positions. As E.C. Buck, Secretary to the government of India, noted in 1888: 'At present, there does not exist in India the means of training men so as to qualify them for direct appointment to the Upper Controlling [i.e. Superior] Staff.'[17]

A *de facto* division also developed amongst Burmese forest officials

---

(DRAC), 6 February 1877, *IFP* (February 1877), p. 31; *Indian Forester* 4 (January 1879), pp. 298-315; Government of India, *Code of Instructions for the conduct of Office Business and for the Regulation of Accounts in the Forest Department,* Calcutta,1886, pp. 16, 20.

[16] In theory, Burmese could become an Assistant Conservator after completing five years' service as a Sub-Assistant Conservator. However, promotion was then only possible if trained European recruits were unavailable, Government of India, *Code of Instructions,* p. 8. Ironically, the Burmese forester Poh Oh had attained the rank of Assistant Conservator before 1870, Government of India (PWD) to Chief Commissioner, 14 June 1869, *IFP* (August 1869), p. 201; *Progress Report on Forest Administration in British Burma* (henceforth *RFA*), 1872-73, pp. 12, 48.

[17] E.C. Buck to Revenue and Agriculture Department circ. 9F, 2 June 1888, *Burma forest Proceedings* (henceforth *BFP*) (June 1888), p. 7. The school's location in India also deterred Burmese students, and it was not until 1899 that a vernacular forest school was established in Burma. See J. Nisbet, *Burma under British Rule and Before,* Westminster, 1901, vol. I, p. 247; Anon., 'The New Burma Forest School at Pyinmana,' *Indian Forester* 37 (August 1911), pp. 421-4; R.S. Wilkie, *Yamethin District Gazetteer,* Rangoon, 1934, pp. 87-8.

themselves. Comprised of Rangers and Sub-Assistant Conservators, the 'executive' service supervised the work of Foresters and Forest Guards (the 'local' service). Although men were promoted from local to executive service, particularly in the early years, the expansion of the Forest Department in the late nineteenth century led to a hardening of the boundaries between the two services. Whereas Foresters and Forest Guards were generally illiterate local men, Rangers and Sub-Assistant Conservators were literate and received special training. The latter were predominantly townsfolk – the sons of merchants and government officials – but better educated youth of large villages also gained executive rank.[18]

Forest officials were thus differentiated by education, experience, class and race. Foresters and Forest Guards protected local forests, Rangers and Sub-Assistant Conservators undertook reservation, extraction and regeneration work, and superior staff supervised subordinates. The chain of command was not always so straightforward in practice due to illness, unfilled positions and the relative economic importance of a forest division. In general, the less important the division, the greater the delegation of responsibility.

Yet one of the distinctive features of the Forest Department by the early 1880s was an organizational structure premised on the European-Burmese divide. Barred from senior posts, the Burmese earned a reputation for dishonesty and indolence. They failed to perform assigned duties, fabricated reports, defrauded the government of revenue, and extorted money from forest offenders.[19] Even long-standing employees would 'suddenly submit to the temptation to misappropriate revenue or accept bribes'.[20] Such conduct was often attributed to the 'inferior' class of person employed by the Department, but colonial officials acknowledged that unhealthy work conditions and poor pay were also to blame. Ineffectual efforts to address this problem – notably through a modest pay increase in 1876 meant that low paid Burmese foresters were a perennial source of trouble for colonial officials.[21]

Paradoxically, a department that was unable to pay its junior staff

---

[18] Anon., 'Burma Forest School,' p. 421.

[19] *RFA* (Pegu), 1876-7, p. 10; *RFA* (Pegu), 1882-3, p. 8; *RFA* (Pegu), 1883-4, pp. 47-8.

[20] *RFA* (Pegu), 1880-1, p.24. Assistant Conservator Poh Oh was a case in point. Despite years of 'exemplary' service, he was dismissed in 1875 for involvement in illicit girdling, Conservator Ribbentrop to Secretary, Chief Commissioner, 6 September 1875, *IFP* (December 1875); A. Fraser, Secretary, Chief Commissioner, to Secretary, Government of India (PWD), 5 June 1869, *IFP* (September 1869), p. 334.

[21] *RFA*, 1872-3, p. 48; B.H. Baden-Powell, *The Forest System of British Burma*, Calcutta, 1873, p. 44; D. Brandis, *Suggestions regarding Forest Administration in British Burma*, Calcutta, 1876, p. 20.

a wage on par with that of even the lowest paid unskilled labourer was also a highly lucrative source of revenue for the colonial state. However, forest revenue was the subject of much inter-governmental bargaining. Revenue accrued at first entirely to the government of India, and the budget of the Burma Forest Department was framed in India.[22] Forest administration was also directed from Calcutta under the successive control of the Foreign, Public Works, Revenue and Agriculture, and Home Departments.[23] It was in this context of central control that the Indian Forest Department was created, and Brandis appointed the first Inspector-General of Forests, in 1864.

Financial and administrative power began to be decentralized in the 1870s as an incentive to provincial governments to increase revenue and curb expenditures. Under the provincial contract system, the government of Burma was granted a share in selected heads of revenue. In terms of forest revenue, that share was set at one-sixth in 1878, but four years later, was raised to one-half – a ratio not changed until the early twentieth century. [24] As the government of Burma gained a direct financial interest in forest revenue, the Burma Forest Act (1881) delegated immediate control of the Department to the Chief Commissioner. [25] If operational control rested in Burma, the broad parameters of forest administration, including the appointment and pay of the superior staff, continued to be determined in India and England.[26]

These new arrangements encouraged greater continuity in Burma's superior service. A separate Burma List was established on which promotions were based and transfers to other provinces below the rank of Conservator were discouraged. If Burma continued as a 'nursery' for India's Conservators and Inspector-Generals,[27] it nevertheless became

---

[22] Shein, Myint Myint Thant and Tin Tin Sein, 'Provincial Contract System of British Indian Empire, in Relation to Burma – A Case of Fiscal Exploitation', *Journal of the Burma Research Society* 52 (December 1969), p. 3; Ribbentrop, *Forestry in British India*, p. 135.

[23] Government of India (PWD), circular no. 4, 22 March 1864, *IFP* (May 1864), pp. 125-7.

[24] Shein, *Burma's Transport and Foreign Trade, 1885-1914*, Rangoon, 1964, p. 201. The government of Burma assumed control over forest revenue in 1911.

[25] *Burma Forest Act 1881*, Rangoon, 1884, nos. 5, 29, 31 35, 37; Brandis, *Indian Forestry*, p. 46.

[26] Government of India, *Code of Instructions*, pp. 2-6; B.H. Baden-Powell, *A Manual of Jurisprudence for Forest Officers*, Calcutta, 1882, p. 409; Ribbentrop, *Forestry in British India*, p. 137.

[27] Anon., 'Promotion in the Forest Department', *Indian Forester* 15 (January 1889), pp. 9-10. Seven of the first ten Inspectors-General served originally in Burma.

standard for forest officials to spend most, if not all of their professional lives in the country. By the turn of the century, the Forest Department had been transformed from a small group of untrained civil and military officials into a large professional organization.[28] As the Forest Department grew, however, it came into conflict with civil officials apprehensive over its increasing power.

Bureaucratic Politics. Forest policy was never devised in isolation from other political and economic objectives. Rather, the social and economic importance of Burma's forest ensured that civil officials took an active hand in their management. Subsequent chapters examine the implications of this situation for specific policy issues. Here, the concern is to describe the general relationship between civil and forest officials as it developed in the year immediately following the creation of the Forest Department.

After 1856, forest and civil matters came to be considered as distinct but interrelated policy areas. Before that date, forest issued had been treated as an integral part of civil administration. Chapter 2 noted , for instance, the engineer Captain Tremenheere brought in forest rules in his capacity as Tenasserim's first Superintendent of Forests in 1841. In the economically peripheral Arakan forests, the Commissioner restricted extraction of *pyinkado* (Burmese ironwood) in 1863, and retained full control over forest matters until 1902.[29]

In contrast, forest officials swiftly asserted control over Pegu's teak forest. In doing so, they impinged on civil administration in two ways. First, in so far as forests had been an exclusively civil matter, the advent of the Forest Department entailed a transfer of authority that was much resented. Hitherto, the civil official held 'sole control of all lands in his district, and the unoccupied lands were his chief means of conferring patronage'.[30] The arrival of the forest official ended such autonomy.

Secondly, Forest Department activities affected purely civil matters.

---

[28] One indication of this change is to be found in the increasingly detailed and standardized procedure which forest officials were required to follow in their daily work. See Burma Forest Department, *Departmental Instructions for Forest Officers in Burma,* Rangoon, 1919.

[29] W. S. Oliphant, Assistant Secretary, Chief Commissioner to Secretary, Government of India (PWD), 24 November 1863, *IFP* (May 1864), pp. 57-64; Barrington, *Forest Administration in the Arakan Forest Division*; E.P. Stebbing, 'A Note on the Forests of Arakan', *Indian Forester* 27 (February, April-May 1901), p. 67.

[30] C.F. Amery, 'On the Relation Between District and Forest Officers', *Indian Forester* (January 1876), p. 295.

Of particular concern to civil officials was the impact of forestry on agriculture. Expanding paddy cultivation in Pegu was a top priority of government after 1852, and the amount of forest converted to agriculture became 'the recognised measure of a district [civil] officer's capability and tact'.[31] Forests were also needed for the manufacture of carts, boats and implements essential to the agrarian economy; restrictions on forest access might impede such development.

The potential for bureaucratic conflict depended in part on the relative economic importance of the forest compared with alternative land uses. Forest officials by and large acquiesced in the conversion of deltaic forest to permanent cultivation. In contrast, they severely restricted access to the Pegu Yoma's teak forests, but civil officials rarely questioned this move. Yet this image of forest officials controlling the hills as civil officials regulated the plains is misleading.[32] Just as teak, and other commercially important forests spilled on to the plains surrounding the Pegu Yoma, inviting the attention of forest officials, so too the growth of the domestic forest sector in conjunction with agrarian development prompted a keen civil interest in the hill economy. Civil and forest interests could not be compartmentalized in these areas, but were part of a seamless web of agrarian and forest concerns.

It was the interlaced nature of those concerns that made cooperation as essential as it was problematic. Civil officials acknowledged that deforestation in Lower Burma was leading to a growing scarcity of forest products. Yet, they were reluctant to introduce measures that might limit the general prosperity associated with nineteenth-century agrarian development.[33] Civil officials were also unwilling to surrender to forest officials the additional powers that extension of forest rules in the plains forests inevitably implied.[34] Conversely, most forest officials recognized the principle that agrarian development took precedence over forest conservancy in suitable areas. Yet, such development was often associated with the destruction of residual forests

---

[31] *Ibid.*; see also Michael Adas, 'Colonization, Commercial Agriculture, and the Destruction of the Deltaic Rainforests of British Burma in the late Nineteenth Century', in Richard P. Tucker and J.F. Richards (eds.), *Global Deforestation and the Nineteenth-Century World Economy*, Durham, NC, 1983, pp. 104-5.

[32] Alexander L. Howard, 'The Forests and Timbers of Burma', *Journal of the East India Association* (n.s.) 15 (1924), p. 142.

[33] Ashley Eden, 'The Reorganization of the Forest System of British Burma', Government of India, *Copy of Enclosures*, p. 5; *RFA*, 1873-74, p. 11.

[34] W.C. Plant, Deputy commissioner, Myanoung, to Commissioner, Pegu, 12 February 1870, *IFP* (August 1870), pp. 507-8; E.M. Ryan, Deputy Commissioner, Amherst, to Commissioner, Tenasserim, 9 October 1871, *IFP* (June 1872), p. 320.

as land clearance led to unchecked timber extraction. The problem confronting civil and forest officials was, therefore, a complex one: to allow agricultural expansion in selected areas, but not so as to damage the residual forest.

If accelerating deforestation made the need for rational decision-making more pressing, the expansion of civil and forest administration in the 1860s and 1870s encouraged the articulation of narrow department perspectives. The gulf between these perspectives was nowhere more evident than over the question of reserved forests. Under the Burma Forest Rules (1865),[35] civil and forest officials were instructed to cooperate in the demarcation of forest tracts. A forest official inspected the tract and prepared a report that was submitted to the Deputy Commissioner for comment. The report was then forwarded through the Commissioner to the Conservator who in turn attached further remarks, before it was submitted to the Chief Commissioner for final orders.

The fate of the proposal often rested with the Deputy Commissioner. If this individual did not object to the proposed reserve, he could prohibit forest clearance pending the Chief Commissioner's decision. In practice, the Deputy Commissioner often opposed reservation, and could delay or even halt the proceedings.[36] Forest officials denounced such obstructionism, and the lack of concern many civil officials showed for forest conservancy.[37] But civil officials resisted forest reservation because they feared an erosion of their powers by a Forest Department which, 'by its demands for absolute authority over the forests, has provoked the District Officials to the support of forest rights as against the Department.'[38]

Lacunae in the Forest Rules reinforced these fears. The Rules did not provide for popular access to reserves, based as they were on the assumption that it was possible 'from the great mass of excess forest and waste, to set apart reserves, to be at the absolute disposal of the State, without interfering with the rights of the people.'[39] This assumption was probably ill-founded even in the 1850s. Subsequently, it became completely untenable as hundreds of thousands

[35] Drawn up under the India Forest Act (1865), D. Brandis, *Memorandum,* p. 57.

[36] Resolution, Chief Commissioner, 10 May 1870, *IFP* (October 1870), pp. 704-5; W. Seaton, Conservator, to Secretary, Chief Commissioner, 18 November 1871, *IFP* (June 1872), p. 322; A.O. Hume, Secretary, Government of India, to Chief Commissioner, 14 September 1872, *IFP* (September 1872), p. 593.

[37] Amery, 'Relation', pp. 294-8; B.H. Baden-Powell, 'Forest Conservancy in Its Popular Aspect,' *Indian forester* 2 (July 1876), pp. 8-9.

[38] Anon., 'A Few Notes on "Suggestions Regarding Forest Administration in British Burma" by D. Brandis', *Indian Forester* 2 (October 1876), p. 191.

[39] Brandis, *Suggestions,* p. 15.

of migrants cleared Lower Burma's forests. As a result, when faced with the prospect of outright land alienation, civil officials resisted typically the creation of reserves. The Forest Rules were also defective in that they made no provision for forest conservancy outside 'Government Forests'.[40] This omission led to the notification of much of British Burma under this heading. A vast area was thereby incorporated that was never intended for regulation.[41] Yet the legal definition of many low-lying areas as Government Forest reinforced the fears of civil officials of a land grab by the Forest Department.

Resolution of policy differences within the Forest Department around 1870 increased the likelihood of bureaucratic conflict. The Department had been divided over how to guarantee future teak supplies. Whereas one group led by Conservator Leeds promoted plantations, another group under Inspector-General Brandis's direction favoured reservation of the best tracts 'to be converted gradually into more or less compact Teak Forests'.[42] In 1869 the latter prevailed with the government of India and Leeds was replaced as Conservator by men (such as Seaton and Ribbentrop) who accepted the new policy. Although plantations continued to expand, reservation became the Forest Department's main method to ensure long-term teak production.[43]

Civil officials persistently hindered such work especially when it involved populated areas. As Conservator Ribbentrop reported in 1875, proposed fuel reserves 'which have been made from time to time have been annulled or ordered to be revised' which he attributed to a 'disinclination, on the part of the Civil authorities, to consent to the reservation of areas, in the midst of populated parts.'[44] Civil officials also held up reservation on a technicality. In the Thayetmyo region in 1877-8, for example, they objected to proposals because 'the prescribed procedure had not been fully carried out'.[45]

Foot-dragging also extended to other areas. This chapter later examines

---

[40] D. Brandis, 'Memorandum on revision of Act VII of 1865', in *IFP* (December 1868), appendix; A. Fraser, Secretary, Chief Commissioner, to Secretary, Government of India (PWD), 11 April 1870, *IFP* (August 1870), p. 503.

[41] B.H. Baden-Powell, 'On the Defects of the Existing Forest Law (Act VII of 1865) and Proposals for a New Forest Act', in B.H. Baden-Powell and J.S. Gamble (eds), *Report of the Proceedings of the Forest Conference, 1873-74*, Calcutta, 1874, p. 13.

[42] *RFA*, 1865-6, pp. 45-6; *RFA*, 1866-7, p. 8; Secretary of State for India to Governor General of India, 16 July 1868, *SDI* (1868), p. 109.

[43] Brandis, *Suggestions*, p. 1; Secretary of State for India to Governor General of India, 8 June 1871, *SDI* (1871), p. 115; Secretary of State for India to Governor General of India, 19 November 1874, *SDI* (1874), p. 90

[44] *RFA* 1874-5, pp. 7, 9-10; see also *RFA*, 1873-4, pp. 2-4.

[45] *RFA* (Pegu), 1877-8, p. 5.

peasant resistance to Forest Department efforts to regulate non-teak forest use. However, such opposition was strengthened by the actions of civil officials who also often objected to these restrictions. At the centre of the regulation of non-teak forest use was a permit system in which forest and civil officials shared control of the distribution of free and trade permits. Forest officials also required the Deputy Commissioner's approval before illegal wood could be confiscated.[46] Yet in 1878 the Chief Commissioner felt the need to issue revised rules to correct the 'misapprehensions' of civil officials who were 'putting too liberal an interpretation on the scope and applicability of free permits,'[47] Differences between civil and forest officials over this issue persisted. Two years later, for example, Seaton complained that civil officials in Toungoo division had increased the number of free permits issued by nearly one-third in just one year without satisfactory justification.[48]

The bureaucratic politics of the permit system highlights not only another instance of conflict between forest and civil officials, but also the tacit complicity that occasionally occurred between colonizer and colonized in the circumvention of colonial law. The great heterogeneity of colonial officaldom is increasingly recognized in the literature.[49] Less well known are the ways in which such diversity led to official actions that breached the intent, if not the letter, of colonial law.

With the fiscal and legal changes of 1878-82, the Forest Department came under the direct control of the Chief Commissioner. An attempt was then made to improve inter-departmental relations by partially integrating civil and forest administration.[50] Beginning in 1880, the divisional forest official became the assistant of the Deputy Commissioner, retaining a direct link with the Conservator on professional matters. The Deputy Commissioner submitted all forest correspondence to the conservator, but was otherwise answerable only to the Com-

---

[46] B. Ribbentrop. 'Special Report on the Working of the Revenue Notifications nos. 33 and 34 of 8 March 1876', in *RFA*, 1876-7. pp. 33-4; Nisbet, *Burma under British Rule*, vol. II, p. 57.

[47] Resolution, *RFA*, 1877-8, pp. 3-4.

[48] *RFA* , 1879-80, pp. 32-3.

[49] Sarah Jewitt, 'Europe's "Others"? Forestry Policy and Practices in colonial and Postcolonial India', *Environment and Planning D: Society and Space* 13 (1995), pp. 67-90; Ann Laura Stoler, 'Rethinking Colonial Categories: European Communities and the Boundaries of Rule', *Comparative Studies in Society and History*, 31 (January 1989), pp. 134-61.

[50] This move was encouraged by London, Secretary of State for India to Governor General of India, 15 January 1880, *IFP* (March 1880), p. 127.

missioner. As with the latter, the Conservator was responsible to the Chief Commissioner who had final say on operational matters. Thus, the relationship between the Conservator and the Chief Commissioner set the general tone of forest management, as the interaction of divisional forest officials and Deputy Commissioners established the complexion of local forest administration.

These changes clarified forest-civil relations but did not eliminate bureaucratic conflict. Forest and civil officials continued to dispute control in a number of policy areas. The partial integration of forest and civil administration nevertheless promoted greater cooperation, and this, in turn, facilitated forest reservation in the late nineteenth and early twentieth century. However, central to the reservation campaign was a clarification of forestry law, and specifically the thorny issue of how forest rights were to be treated in law.

Forestry and the Law.   Forest politics in colonial Burma was all about the determination of forest access according to the law. As a result, the manner in which rights were legally defined had a direct impact on the nature of state forest control. Yet this process was not straightforward, and during the 1870s colonial officials throughout British India debated basic principles that shaped forest politics for the remainder of colonial rule. These debates were part of a process of legislative reform that culminated in the India Forest Act (1878), the Burma Forest Act (1881) and the Madras Forest Act (1882). The issues that they addressed were crucial to the millions of people in the British-Indian empire who were reliant on the forests.

The impetus behind these debates was the need for new legislation to replace the inadequate Indian Forest Act (1865). In 1868, and again in 1869, Brandis circulated a draft forest bill to the provincial governments but a consensus was not achieved.[51] In 1873, a conference of foresters at Allahabad in northern India examined the issue further.[52] In 1875, Brandis prepared a memorandum on forest legislation that formed the basis of the India Forest Act (1878), but Burma was the subject of special reports by Baden-Powell (in 1873) and Brandis (in 1876).[53]

Burma's unique position in imperial forestry led directly to the Burma Forest Act of 1881. Such legislation recognized Burma's distinctive social and ecological conditions. The 1881 Act catered above

[51] Government of India (DRAC) to Secretary of State for India, 28 September 1876, *IFL* no. 30 of 1876.

[52] B.H. Baden-Powell and J.S. Gamble (eds), *Report of the Proceedings of the Forest Conference, 1873-74,* Calcutta, 1874.

[53] Baden-Powell, *Forest System;* Brandis, *Suggestions.* On India as a whole see Brandis, *Memorandum.*

all to the special administrative requirements associated with management of the Province's teak forest. Without a doubt, those forests
were the jewel in the crown of Indian forestry, and revenue derived
from their exploitation formed the largest share of the imperial forest
surplus. Between 1889-90 and 1894-5, for example, the annual net
revenue of Burma's forest amounted to 3,308,000 rupees or 45 per
cent of the British-Indian total.[54] The government of India was thus
only too aware of the need to tailor legislation to Burmese needs
in order to maximize efficient resource extraction.

Yet the 1878 Act and the 1881 Act were both concerned with
the question of forest rights. Each aimed to distinguish state from
societal claims as a precursor to large-scale commercial exploitation
of state forests. Determination of rights and forest reservation were
linked: 'the acquisition of more extensive rights by Government within
the demarcated area, against concessions made outside its limits to
the surrounding population.'[55]

It was the precise nature of that link that was debated in the
1870s. With reference to India, Guha has suggested that three positions
emerged on this issue:

> The first, which we call *annexationist* held out for nothing less than
> *total* state control over all forest areas. The second, which one can call
> *pragmatic,* argued in favour of state management of ecologically
> sensitive and strategically valuable forests, allowing other areas to
> remain under communal systems of management. The third position
> (a mirror image of the first), we call *populist.* It completely rejected
> state intervention, holding that tribals and peasants must exercise
> sovereign rights over woodland.[56]

Elements of all three positions appeared in the Burmese debate, but
the Province's distinctive socio-economic and ecological conditions
ensured that the debate would take a different course from that taking
place in India.

Most evidently, the economic importance of Burma's teak forest
was a powerful incentive for their intensive management. Although
quality teak was found elsewhere Burma was its principal source
in European demand.[57] Yet its incidence in the country posed special

---

[54] Brandis, *Indian Forestry,* p. 42. In 1869-70, net revenue was 39 per cent of the
British-Indian total, Government of India (PWD), circ. no. 5f, 11 March 1871, *IFP* (March
1871).

[55] Brandis, *Memorandum,* p. 10.

[56] Ramachandra Guha, 'An Early Environmental Debate: The Making of the 1878 Forest
Act', *Indian Economic and Social History Review* 27 (1990), pp. 67-8.

[57] P.L. Simmonds, 'The Teak Forests of India and the East, and Our British Imports of

management problems. Native to the mixed evergreen and deciduous forest, teak is found scattered below an elevation of three thousand feet and in areas with a rainfall of 60-130 inches per year.[58] Even in 'teak forest' the tree rarely comprises more than 12 percent of total forest cover. The diffuse nature of teak increased extraction and administration costs, and prompted forest officials to advocate extensive reservation.

Social factors also contributed to a distinctively Burmese debate. The debate took place at a time when the development of an export-oriented agrarian economy was in full swing in Lower Burma. In only a matter of decades, a 'plural society' emerged divided by language, religion, culture and history.[59] What is important here is less the precise nature of that society than the fact of its impermanence; it was the antithesis of a 'traditional' society. The lack of a traditional society in late nineteenth-century Lower Burma was in marked contrast to many areas of India, and this had important implications for the direction of the debate in Burma.

A brief comparison with the situation in Madras Presidency illustrates the point. It was no coincidence that the Madras government was 'the most articulate spokesman for village interests in the controversy around the 1878 Act' for it ruled a densely populated territory with a long tradition of communal forest ownership.[60] In this setting, civil opposition to the new legislation flourished, and combined jealousy of the Forest Department, fear of popular discontent, and apprehension that restriction of customary forest access would destabilize the agrarian economy. In contrast, and to the extent that it had ever previously existed, traditional communal forest ownership in Lower Burma was eliminated by the influx of Burmese and Indian migrants who transformed large forested areas into paddy fields. As noted, this did not stop civil officials from resisting the assertion of Forest Department control. Yet, in Lower Burma's plural society, their defence of traditional access lacked authenticity, and may partly explain why the populist position was relatively unimportant in Burma.[61]

Teak', *Journal of the Society of Arts* 33 (February 1885), pp. 345-55; R.S. Troup, *The Silviculture of Indian Trees,* Oxford, 1921, vol. II, pp. 699-700.

[58] D.J. Atkinson, 'Forests and Forestry in Burma', *Journal of the Royal Society of Arts* 96 (1948), pp.483-4; and Appendix.

[59] J.S. Furnivall, *Colonial Policy and Practice: A Comparative Study of Burma and Netherlands India,* New York, 1956, pp. 303-12.

[60] Guha, '1878 Forest Act', p. 69.

[61] In 1871, one Deputy Commissioner condemned the restriction of free forest access enjoyed by villagers throughout the colonial era and for 'countless ages before', but lamely concluded that if these villagers were to be excluded from selected areas, they

Rather, the annexationist and pragmatic positions, as championed by Baden-Powell and Brandis respectively, formed the focus of attention. In 1873, Baden-Powell set out his plan for Burmese forestry predicated on extensive reservation and severely restricted popular access.[62] An extensive network of reserves would protect watersheds for climatic purposes, curtail shifting cultivation, generate revenue, and 'religiously preserve' existing teak supplies. The Pegu Yoma, and much of the surrounding plains forests, were implicated in Baden-Powell's scheme, reflecting the author's uncompromising belief in absolute state forest control. That belief was also manifested in proposed limits to popular forest access. Baden-Powell claimed that all land not under actual cultivation belonged to the state, access to which was a privilege and not a legal right.[63] There were 'no such things as forest *rights,* properly so called, held by individuals or communities over any forest in British Burma'; rather, the state was the 'unrestricted owner' of the forest and all that it contained.[64] Rights only existed therefore where expressly admitted in land settlements; otherwise, forest access was a privilege that could be modified or withdrawn by the state at any time.[65]

Baden-Powell's proposal appealed to some foresters but predictably angered civil officials. Thus, Secretary to the Government of India A. O. Hume rejected a system in which popular forest access would be severely curtailed.[66] Not only would such a system be impossible to enforce, Hume also believed that it would exacerbate state-peasant relations. Civil officials in Burma echoed Hume's condemnation of Baden-Powell's plan.[67]

Responding to these criticisms, Brandis outlined an alternative system in 1876 based on one class of reserves encompassing all teak tracts that merited long-term management. Civil officials would enforce basic rules elsewhere to protect selected species and regulate the

---

should receive compensation. See A.G. Duff, Deputy Commissioner, Shwegyin, to Commissioner, Tenasserim, 23 September 1871, *IFP* (June 1872), p. 317.

[62] Baden-Powell, *Forest System.*

[63] Guha, '1878 Forest Act', p. 68.

[64] Baden-Powell, *Forest System,* p. 50.

[65] This argument is based on two linked assumptions. First, that in precolonial times, the sovereign owned all land not explicitly alienated. Second, by right of conquest, the British inherited that ancient right. See Guha, '1878 Forest Act', pp. 68-9; Baden-Powell, *Manual of Jurisprudence,* pp. 44-5, 48, 55-6, 62-3.

[66] A.O. Hume to Chief Commissioner, 28 July 1874, Government of India, *Copy of Enclosures,* pp. 2-3. The British Government confirmed Hume's decision, see Secretary of State for India to Governor General of India, 19 November 1874, *SDI* (1874), p. 90.

[67] Ribbentrop, 'Special Report', p. 23.

timber trade. However, few restrictions would be placed on popular access in these latter forests.[68]

Unlike Baden-Powell, Brandis insisted that customary forest access by settled agriculturists was a right and not a privilege. Such liberality reflected Brandis' belief that reservation for teak extraction would not 'in any way' interfere with 'the present requirements of the agricultural population'.[69] The same could not be said about shifting cultivators who practiced extensive agriculture in the heart of teak forests. Brandis was adamant that shifting cultivation did not constitute a right: the Forest Department was free to take up 'all valuable forest tracts, provided no actual settlements are included ... deserted *toungyas* ... may be taken up without prejudice to any one.'[70]

The 1881 Act followed the 1878 Act but with important modifications. The former prescribed one class of reserves in which only rights explicitly recognized were permitted. Unauthorized access was forbidden, and damage to the forests was subject to a 500-rupees fine, six months imprisonment, or both. Going beyond the Indian legislation, the 1881 Act restricted *taungya* within reserves and emphasized that shifting cultivation was not a right. The primary goal in non-reserved forests was to protect reserved species and regulate trade. The Forest Department had considerable power in these forests to regulate economic activities. Avoiding the legal ambiguities of the 1878 Act, the Burma legislation also made no specific provision for popular rights in unreserved forests – an omission that increased the Forest Department's flexibility over rights to these forests as it reserved residual teak tracts.[71]

The 1881 Act combined elements of the pragmatic and annexationist positions. The rights of settled agriculturists in the vicinity of reserves were selectively acknowledged, but those of shifting cultivators were formally denied. Brandis's proposal for the creation of one class of reserves was sanctioned, but the Act did not specify the ultimate extent of reservation. It expedited the assertion of Forest Department control, but did not place a limit on the scope of such control.

That limit was to be negotiated with the civil administration. Civil officials controlled village forests in populated areas, but more importantly, also continued to exert influence over the creation of state reserves. The 1881 Act provided for the appointment of a civil official

---

[68] Brandis, *Suggestions.*

[69] *Ibid.*, p. 8

[70] *Ibid.*, p. 11.

[71] Ribbentrop, *Forestry in British India,* pp. 111-12; *Proceedings of the Council of the Governor General of India* (henceforth *Proceedings*) 20 (1881), p. 4.

as Forest Settlement Officer – the person responsible for leading the inquiry into a proposed reserve. A forest official could assist in the inquiry but 'it was intended that he should always act in subordination to the Forest Settlement officer'.[72] Cooperation between civil and forest officials was thus embedded in the 1881 Act.

Yet such cooperation was not thereby guaranteed. Bureaucratic conflict persisted after 1881 as a result of differing programmatic interests. The failure of the 1881 Act to specify the ultimate reserved area increased the likelihood of conflict. With large forested areas as yet unexplored, forest officials were reluctant to be precise on this matter. The almost inevitable result, however, was that as the Forest Department grew, and became more knowledgeable about the forests, it continually revised that total upwards. Thus, in 1874 Brandis had suggested a rough limit of 2,000 square miles, yet by 1883 a revised 1881 figure of 3,474 square miles had already been surpassed, and the ultimate area was disputed by the Chief Commissioner and the government of India.[73] The Burma Forest Act of 1881 did not eliminate conflict within the state over forest policy. Rather, it shifted the terms of the debate.

The debates of the 1870s were partly about seeking ways to coordinate forest and civil administration in a context of bureaucratic growth and differentiation. In the process, the role of the Forest Department as a resource manager was firmly situated in a broader institutional context shaped by bureaucratic politics. Yet these debates were not merely about the allocation of bureaucratic power within the state. They also reflected a broader need to establish the parameters of state forest control in relation to various groups in civil society – a prerequisite for effective scientific forest management. However, and as the remainder of this chapter shows, this process was vigorously contested by European timber traders, shifting cultivators and peasants and indigenous timber traders.

Resistance

The best indication of the political impact of scientific forestry in Burma was the increasing scope and intensity of the resistance of groups in civil society to the activities of the Forest Department

[72] A. Rivers Thompson, Secretary, Government of India, in *Proceedings*, 20 (1881), p. 3. Thompson was Chief Commissioner of Burma in 1875-8.

[73] A. Mackenzie, Secretary, Government of India, to Chief Commissioner, 7 December 1883, and Resolution, both in *RFA*, 1882-3; D. Brandis, 'Demarcation of State Forests in British Burma', and A.O. Hume to Chief Commissioner, 28 July 1874, both in Government of India, *Copy of Enclosures*.

entrusted with its introduction. Such resistance was quite complex, reflecting the vicissitudes of Department control, but also the often contradictory interests of the actors in question. At times, those interests even resulted in strategies in which cooperation with, rather than resistance to, the Forest Department were adopted. Further, the interests of different groups in society were not necessarily compatible – European timber merchants and shifting cultivators over the use of teak forests, for example.

Yet if one of our recurring themes is that there was no permanent or unbridgeable gulf between the Forest Department and groups in civil society, it was nevertheless the case that the assertion of state forest control in the decades after 1856 prompted widespread resistance characterized notably (but not exclusively) by the techniques of everyday resistance and avoidance protest discussed in Chapter 1. Resistance is most appropriately understood in the context of specific patterns of state forest control. Thus, attempts to control teak extraction earned the open opposition of European timber traders, whereas efforts to curtail shifting cultivation prompted a covert but no less powerful response. Forest Department efforts to regulate non-teak forest use, meanwhile, resulted in conflict with Burmese peasants hitherto at the margins of colonial forest politics. Relations between the Forest Department and these groups are outlined briefly here as the basis for a more detailed discussion in subsequent chapters.

European Timber Traders.   European timber traders were the earliest, and most vocal opponents of the Forest Department. Such opposition later turned to cooperation as a maturing industry sought to turn scientific forestry to its advantage. However, in 1856 the industry was fervently opposed to a system of forest management that seemed to be premised on their exclusion from the business.

The initial tone of relations between the Forest Department and the European timber traders was dictated by Dalhousie's 1855 Minute which had shown, it will be remembered, unremitting hostility to the idea of private enterprise working Pegu's teak forests. Consequently, upon taking charge of those forests in January 1856, Brandis initiated a system in which Burmese contractors extracted timber on the Forest Department's behalf. By taking 'forest work out of the hands of the mercantile community', he sought to develop a class of indigenous foresters – 'a kind of aristocracy' – instilled with the virtues of scientific forestry.[74] Denied direct access to Pegu's forests, European timber traders could only purchase teak at government auction in Rangoon.

---

[74] D. Brandis, 'Report for 1856', p. 34; D. Brandis to A.P. Phayre, 9 November 1859,

Yet Brandis's audacious plan failed in practice for two reasons. First, instead of encountering a class of upstanding Burmese contractors as hoped, Brandis was besieged, initially at least, by 'a host of rogues' who absconded with advances or perpetuated wasteful cutting practices. Unable to persuade Karen contractors to leave the Salween forests in sufficient numbers to establish Pegu forestry on a regular basis, the Superintendent was forced to rely on his own employees to get the contract system started. The pitfalls of this arrangement soon became evident. In Tharrawaddy district, for example, subordinates in league with independent contractors defrauded the government by substituting inferior timber for first-class logs, selling the latter to private parties. In the Sittang forests, timber was dragged north into monarchical Burma and then reintroduced to Pegu by river as foreign timber.[75]

In the late 1850s, the contract system began to coalesce as a more reliable set of indigenous foresters took to forest work. Tempted by a system of advances introduced to encourage local participation, foresters who were typically related to local notables began to acquire elephants and extract teak on an increasing scale.[76] However, the initial difficulties experienced with the contract system proved its undoing – extraction was simply not growing fast enough for the liking of senior colonial officials under pressure to enhance state revenue.

However, it was the strong and unremitting pressure of the European timber traders that sealed the fate of Brandis's plan for a system based exclusively on indigenous contractors. The European timber trading community in mid-nineteenth century Burma was relatively unstructured and small-scale in comparison with its counterpart in the early twentieth century.[77] It was also an industry in constant flux. Thus, firms which were prominent at the time such as Gladstone Wyllie, Bulloch Brothers and the Burmah Company had ceased operations in the country by the late 1870s.[78] In contrast, other firms

---

Selections from the Records of the Government of India (Foreign Department) 31 (1861), p. 149.

[75] Brandis, 'Report for 1856', pp. 26-7.

[76] D. Brandis, 'Report on the Pegu Teak Forests for 1857-58', *Selections from the Records of the Government of India (Foreign Department)* 31 (1861), p. 3; D. Brandis, 'Memorandum on the Revision of Forest Establishment', *IFP* (January 1870), p. 92.

[77] The timber trade was also 'highly speculative', J.S. Furnivall, 'Safety First: A Study in the Economic History of Burma', *Journal of the Burma Research Society* 40 (June 1957), p. 29.

[78] Ernest Andrews, *The Bombay Burmah Trading Corporation Limited in Burmah, Siam and Java*, vol. I: *Teak: The Cutting and Marketing*, n.p., 1930-1, p. 8; Conservator Leeds to Secretary, Chief Commissioner, 11 December 1865, *IFP* (February 1866), p. 31; B.R.

founded at this time later became the mainstays of the business.[79] Steel Brothers, for example, was founded in 1870 by William Strang Steel who purchased teak from the Salween and Prome forests. Romanian entrepreneur John Goldenburg founded a business in association with J.W. Darwood in 1860 that worked forests along the Anglo-Burmese border, and which later became Macgregor and Company. Foucar and Company was founded in 1878 by the French Huguenot Ferdinand Foucar, and was based in Moulmein, as was T.D. Findlay and Son which acquired a teak shipping firm about 1850.

The key European trader was the Scottish-born William Wallace who became involved in the Moulmein teak trade in the 1850s.[80] Thereafter, he worked the Ataran and Pegu forests, and with Phayre's assistance won a lucrative contract with King Mindon of Burma to work the Pyinmana forests just north of the border in 1862. In conjunction with other family members and Indian financiers, Wallace founded the Bombay Burmah Trading Corporation Limited (BBTCL) in the following year.

Wallace led the campaign by European timber traders to end the contract system. He blamed the poor financial performance during the 1850s on the Forest Department's incompetence and overregulation, which unnecessarily diminished the quantity and quality of timber supplies. In a vintage exposition of economic liberalism, Wallace claimed that the poor financial record was due to the Forest Department's 'unnatural' entrepreneurial role which was not in keeping with the economic principles that had brought Britain international fame and power.[81] Wallace also alleged that the Department, by interfering in what was properly a business concern, failed at its primary duty of forest conservation:

> Conservancy has been hitherto merely a name . . . the forests have neither been conserved nor improved – whilst the Department has presented the lametable [sic] spectacle of a Government trading institution, eminently unsuccessful and disastrously obstructive to the prosperity of the Provinces.[82]

Wallace promoted instead a permit system under which private enterprise would girdle, fell and extract the trees of its choice subject to minimal

---

Pearn, *A History of Rangoon*, Rangoon, 1939, p. 211.

[79] F.T. Morehead, *The Forests of Burma*, London, 1944, pp. 44-7; Alister McCrae, *Scots in Burma: Golden Times in a Golden Land*, Edinburgh, 1990.

[80] A.C. Pointon, *The Bombay Burmah Trading Corporation Ltd, 1863-1963*, Southampton, 1964, pp. 3-6.

[81] W. Wallace to Conservator Leeds, 19 July 1864 in *RFA*, 1863-4, p. 53.

[82] *Ibid.*, p. 56.

rules. The assurance that offenders would be severely punished if caught would keep permit holders within the law. By giving up the contract system in this manner, the Forest Department would have more time to attend to the forest conservancy work for which it was founded.

Such arguments found favour with officials in India and Burma who were opposed to excluding European timber traders from Pegu's forests. Wallace's shrewd argument even gained the support of certain forest officials, including Henry Leeds, Brandis's successor as Conservator of Forests in Burma. This support reflected frustration with the growing amount of time devoted to business at the expense of forest conservancy work. In Leeds's view, the permit system offered 'every advantage to Government' because it not only relieved the Forest Department 'of all money advances and their concomitant evils which by it devolve upon the permit-holder', but also meant that forest officials would have more time to devote to 'the cause of conservancy'.[83]

The campaign to re-open the forests to private enterprise forced Brandis on to the defensive. In February 1861, the government of India ordered Phayre to open the Pegu teak forests to European timber traders. With the support of the Chief Commissioner and the Secretary of State for India, however, Brandis retained in the most valuable forests key elements of the original system. While the government offered twelve-year leases, including permission to girdle trees, in a large area of less important forests, it offered leases only for three or six years in more valuable forests, and forest officials retained responsibility for tree selection and girdling. In the prime Tharrawaddy teak forests, the Forest Department continued to control all aspects of extraction through the contract system.[84] Following the return of teak extraction by European timber traders, teak production climbed from 20,462 tons in 1858-9 to 31,549 tons in 1866-7 (Table 3.2).

Subsequent efforts by Wallace to have the permit system extended were rejected by the government of India.[85] Indeed, by 1867 senior

[83] Leeds in *RFA*, 1863-4, p. 12. Leeds also recommended that girdling and even reforestation work be done by private firms, see *Ibid.*, pp. 72-81; H. Leeds, 'Memorandum', *IFP* (September 1870), appendix.

[84] Brandis, *Indian Forestry*, pp. 33-5; 'Correspondence Regarding the Opening of the Pegu Forests to Private Enterprise', in *Selections from the Records of the Government of India (Public Works Department)* 35 (1862).

[85] Government of India to Secretary of State for India, 26 July 1864, *IFP* (July 1864), p. 204. This decision was confirmed by London, see Secretary of State for India to Governor General of India, 25 January 1865, *SDI* (1965), p. 43.

officials in India were beginning to question the merits of the permit system itself.[86] However, it was the discovery of illegal extraction in the Sittang valley in 1871 that led to the demise of this system. An official inquiry revealed that leaseholders had illegally girdled or felled 9,707 teak trees.[87] In some cases, they had done so in connivance with local forest officials.[88] At the behest of Chief Commissioner Ashley Eden, the government of India ordered the end of the permit system in August 1874, and on expiry of the last lease in 1877 almost all of British Burma was once more under the contract system.[89] Total extraction simultaneously declined from a peak 57,086 tons in 1870-1 to only 17,585 tons in 1879-80, before once more resuming an upward climb in the 1880s (Table 3.2). Private enterprise was not readmitted to Pegu's teak forests until 1889, and then only under close government supervision.

Table 3.2. TONS OF TEAK EXTRACTED, 1858-1884

	Forest Department	License holder	Total
1858-9	20,462	–	20,462
1862-3	16,369	19,530	35,899
1866-7	9,793	21,756	31,549
1870-1	22,765	34,321	57,086
1874-5	16,393	21,517	37,910
1879-80	16,240	1,345	17,585
1883-4	34,404	3,200	37,604

Source: *Progress Report of Forest Administration in British Burma*, various years. The data is for selected years; quantities are in tons.

The events of the 1870s led to the end of the permit system, but as Chapter 4 highlights developments after 1886 in relation to the BBTCL Upper Burma leases restored the 1860s pattern at a

---

[86] C.H. Dickens, Secretary, Government of India (PWD), to Chief Commissioner, 8 May 1867, *IFP* (May 1867), pp. 204-5.

[87] The principal leaseholder involved was the Burmah Company. However, the BBTCL was also implicated, and its permit in the region was cancelled in 1872. See H. Carter, *Working Plan of the Kabaung Reserve*, Rangoon, 1895, p. 4; *Annual Report of the Bombay Burmah Trading Corporation Limited*, 1872-3, p. 5.

[88] Including the European forester W.C. Graham who was subsequently dismissed, *RFA*, 1872-3, pp. 9-18; see also Baden-Powell, *Forest System*, pp. 67-9; W.S. Oliphant, Secretary, Chief Commissioner, to Secretary, Government of India (PWD), 19 June 1872, *IFP* (September 1872), pp. 631-42.

[89] Government of India (DRAC) to Secretary of State for India, 4 August 1874, *IFL* no. 14 of 1874; Secretary of State for India to Governor General of India, 19 November 1874, *SDI* (1874), p. 91; Resolution, Chief Commissioner, *RFA*, 1877-8, p. 3.

Burma-wide level. Private extraction occurred in certain areas subject to greater supervision, and Forest Department extraction persisted in other forests. This arrangement was a central feature of forest administration during the remainder of colonial rule.

Shifting Cultivators. The Forest Department's quest to introduce scientific forestry to Burma also brought it into conflict with shifting cultivators who made hill clearings in the teak forest. In some respects a greater obstacle to scientific forestry than European timber traders, these cultivators resorted to covert resistance strategies that were none the less effective for all their surreptitiousness.

To understand why shifting cultivators opposed the Forest Department is to appreciate the social and ecological conditions of *taungya*. Such cultivation is a type of dry agriculture combining various techniques – partial forest clearance, shallow cultivation, multiple cropping, field rotation – to produce food and cash crops.[90] With an extensive network of hills, Burma was home to groups practising diverse forms of shifting cultivation. In the formulation of colonial policy, the tendency was to simplify complexity by classifying all such practices as '*taungya*'.[91]

Forest officials were not especially concerned about the social and ecological nuances of shifting cultivation. Their main concern was to protect the Pegu Yoma teak forests for long-term commercial exploitation from a small and predominantly Karen population which cleared annual fields there.[92] For this population, the teak forests were useful primarily when felled and burned because the resultant ashes were an important source of fertiliser in their agriculture. Hence, the widespread colonial view that Karen occupations were 'altogether unconnected with an article which is the source of wealth and industry everywhere, but in the place where it is produced' was simply not true.[93] Fundamentally different perceptions of the utility and value of teak were at work here: while the British (and many lowland

---

[90] J.E. Spencer, *Shifting Cultivation in Southeastern Asia*, Berkeley, 1966; Karl J. Pelzer, 'Swidden Cultivation in Southeast Asia: Historical, Ecological, and Economic Perspectives', in Peter Kunstadter, E.C. Chapman and Sanga Sabhasri (eds), *Farmers in the Forest: Economic Development and Marginal Agriculture in Northern Thailand*, Honolulu, 1978, pp. 271-86.

[91] Tao Hai, 'Some Notes on the Taungya Problem in the Shan States', *Indian Forester* 39 (August 1913), p. 364.

[92] There were about 5,000 Karen in the Tharrawaddy and Prome hills in 1876, see Brandis, *Suggestions*, pp. 10-11.

[93] J. McClelland, 'Report on the Southern Forests of Pegu', *Selections from the Records of the Government of India (Foreign Department)* 9 (1855), p. 13.

Burmese as well) saw teak as a valuable source of timber, hill Karen viewed teak (and other forest species) as the sources of nutrients for agriculture. Such perceptual differences were at the heart of conflict between Karen shifting cultivators and forest officials during the colonial era.

Just as colonial officials misunderstood the utility of teak forest to the Karen so too they misjudged the strength of the attachment of these shifting cultivators to their isolated home and itinerant lifestyle. Forest officials were surprised when Karen refused to trade that lifestyle for a more settled and financially remunerative life on the plains.[94] They should not have been surprised. Cultivators feared increased vulnerability to the predations of powerful political and economic groups which such a move implied. The British were newcomers to Pegu and an unknown quantity. There was also no guarantees that the British would stay or that Burmese rule might not be later reimposed. Relative financial deprivation was thus a small price to pay for greater security in the hills. These Karen also sought to protect a spiritually sanctioned animist way of life founded on *nat* (or spirit) worship. Cultivators submitted to a carefully codified personal and communal regime designed to propitiate divine *nats* who they believed controlled most aspects of their lives. So strong was the fear of *nats*, that fields were cleared and houses built only under auspicious circumstances; special ceremonies marked by the beating of great bronze drums were also held in their honour.[95] In a world populated by mostly malevolent spirits, the tenacity with which Karen resisted change must be seen in part as a quest for spiritual security and redemption.

This quest seemed incompatible with the official goal of long-term commercial teak exploitation. Accordingly, a basic conflict of interest was joined to a pseudo-anthropological belief in the 'backwardness' of shifting cultivators and their system of agriculture to criticize Karen use of the teak forests. Chapter 2 noted early criticism of shifting cultivation in colonial Tenasserim. Such criticism grew after 1856 as forest officials began to realise the extent of *taungya* – and hence the full scope of the threat to imperial interests. To be sure, it was periodically acknowledged that hill clearings did not inevitably lead to the elimination of teak. However, it was a tenet of colonial

---

[94] *RFA*, 1863-4, p. 9.

[95] H.I. Marshall, *The Karen People of Burma: A Study in Anthropology and Ethnology*, Columbus, OH, 1922, pp. 63-4, 76-8, 115-26; H.I. Marshall, 'Karen Bronze Drums', *Journal of the Burma Research Society* 19 (April 1929), pp. 1-14; Donald Mackenzie Smeaton, *The Loyal Karens of Burma*, London, 1887, p. 88; Nisbet, *Burma under British Rule*, vol. I, pp. 323-4.

foresters that shifting cultivators jeopardized forest conservancy.[96] The fact that commercial maturation of teak took anywhere up to 150 years, while a *taungya* rotation lasted for only 10 to 20 years, was taken as proof that unrestricted shifting cultivation threatened Pegu's forests as unfettered private enterprise had done earlier in Tenasserim. Such cultivation was also alleged to lead to soil erosion, flooding and localized drought.[97] For many colonial foresters, therefore, *taungya* was a great evil to be stamped out.

The Forest Department used various means to restrict shifting cultivation in teak tracts. As financial inducements proved ineffective, forest officials began to interfere systematically in hill Karen society. In precolonial times, cultivators paid annual imposts to specially appointed Burman *myo-wun* (governors). The British continued these imposts in the form of capitation and *taungya* taxes, but collected them with greater efficiency.[98] The Karen also now faced prosecution for breach of forest rules. Since teak was scattered throughout areas that they cleared, forest officials assumed that wherever there were *taungya* there would be evidence of teak destruction. Further, when caught, Karen had no legal recourse since as already noted shifting cultivation was not recognized as conferring a right to land in colonial law. Indeed, as Brandis noted, 'if anything of the kind were recognised, there would hardly be a square mile of forest in these Yoma hills, which could not be claimed by some Karen family or other.'[99] This statement highlighted the scale of the perceived threat of shifting cultivation to imperial forest interests, and explains why the hill Karen were no longer as safe from the exactions of the state under the British as they were under monarchical rule.

Karen resistance to state forest control encompassed both avoidance behaviour and everyday resistance. Cultivators in close proximity to the Burmese or Siamese frontiers could opt to flee, and in the 1860s Karen reportedly moved from Tenasserim into Siam for this reason. In certain cases, cultivators cleared fields and girdled teak along the border, only to slip into Siamese territory at a forest official's approach.[100]

---

[96] For example, Brandis, 'Report for 1856', pp. 31-4; Baden-Powell, *Forest System*, p. 11; Nisbet, *Burma under British Rule*, vol. II, p. 60; H.W.A. Watson, 'Taungya Cutting', *Indian Forester* 34 (May 1908), p. 265.

[97] *RFA*, 1870-1, p. 5; *RFA*, 1874-5, p. 17; Nisbet, *Burma under British Rule*, vol. II, pp. 60, 63-4.

[98]. These taxes were 6 rupees per individual per year, see Conservator Seaton to Chief Commissioner, 27 September 1869, *RFA*, 1869-70; see also Cady, *History of Modern Burma*, pp. 31, 42-3.

[99] Brandis, *Suggestions*, p. 11.

[100] *RFA*, 1879-80, pp. 45-6; *RFA* (Tenasserim), 1881-2, p. 4; *RFA*, 1865-6, p. 6; Resolution,

Groups that were unable or unwilling to flee resisted in other ways – destroying evidence of teak in their fields, for example.[101] Another tactic was to circumvent the intent, but not the letter, of the law – in Tharrawaddy district in 1859, for example, cultivators defeated the purpose of the fifty trees rule by clearing adjoining fields in which none were found to contain fifty or more trees.[102]

Karen non-cooperation often foiled official investigations of suspected infractions of the forest law. In Prome, for example, out of seventy-six cases involving teak destruction in 1869-70, sixty-seven cases lacked sufficient evidence to prosecute. Only six prosecutions obtained convictions.[103] Non-cooperation also extended to other aspects of forest administration. Forest topographical survey parties, for example, encountered passive resistance from Karen 'adverse to rendering any assistance'.[104] Perhaps the most successful form of resistance was to plead ignorance of the forest rules. This tactic was initially successful because it played on the Forest Department's reluctance to alienate forest dwellers unnecessarily.

Both Karen resistance and official restrictions on cultivators had their limits. The Karen could attenuate the worst effects of state forest control, but they could not escape it altogether. In contrast, forest officials lacked the personnel to enforce the law systematically, but in any event were reluctant to create enemies of potential allies in newly conquered and still largely hostile country.

It is in this context that a reforestation technique known as *taungya* forestry was implemented in the latter half of the nineteenth century.[105] First attempted with Karen in Prome District in 1856, this scheme was based on the idea that, if cultivators planted teak with their rice and cotton crops, the Forest Department would be left with young teak plantations once these cultivators had moved to new fields. The attraction of *taungya* forestry to forest officials was obvious – a practice that was considered an ecological vice would now be turned into a silvicultural virtue. Reforestation work could be done inexpensively, and would transform the Karen 'from an antagonistic nuisance to forest conservancy into the most loyal servants of the

RFA 1868-9, p. 1.

[101] *RFA*, 1866-7, p. 24.

[102] Brandis, 'Report for 1860-61', pp. 26-7.

[103] *RFA*, 1869-70, p. 7.

[104] RFA (Pegu), 1884-5, p. 7.

[105] For a more detailed discussion, see Raymond L. Bryant, 'Shifting the Cultivator: The Politics of Teak Regeneration in Colonial Burma', *Modern Asian Studies* 28 (May 1994), pp. 225-50.

Department.'[106] Yet Karen leaders realized that this scheme would undermine their way of life in the long-term, and it was only introduced after 1869 after a concerted campaign by the Forest Department which combined elements of persuasion and intimidation. The planted area expanded rapidly from about 100 acres in 1869 to more than 70,000 acres in 1906, but such growth only confirmed Karen fears that they would be eventually 'planted out' of a traditional way of life.[107] As with efforts to introduce *taungya* forestry elsewhere in the colonial world, the Burmese experience highlighted the short-term possibilities but long-term difficulties associated with any attempt to reconcile two essentially incompatible types of forest use.[108] Cooperation there certainly was under this system, but it was a cooperation which occurred against a backdrop of coercive forest management in aid of scientific forestry and commercial timber extraction.

Peasants. The state assertion of forest control that engendered an early reaction from European timber traders and shifting cultivators reflected these groups' close association with the teak forests. Groups that used the forests for other purposes initially noticed *decreased* government regulation upon the advent of British rule in Pegu, as forest officials focused exclusively on teak management.

Chapter 2 noted that the precolonial state taxed various non-teak forest products in addition to teak. Teak itself was probably a lesser source of revenue to the Burmese state (prior to the 1860s at least) than it was to the British, yet the taxation of other forest products was of greater importance to the former than it ever was to the latter.[109]

For this reason, colonial forest policy in the mid-nineteenth century was of little concern to Burmese peasants and timber traders. With the exception of teak, there were no restrictions on the subsistence or commercial use of forest products. Rejecting a proposal made by Conservator Leeds in 1866 to regulate non-teak timber extraction,

---

[106] Ribbentrop, *Forestry in British India*, p. 193.

[107] RFA, 1863-4, p. 9; RFA (Lower Burma), 1892-3, p. lxi. Data from Bryant, 'Shifting the Cultivator', table 1, p. 238.

[108] Nancy Lee Peluso, *Rich Forests, Poor People: Resource Control and Resistance in Java*, Berkeley, 1992, pp. 63-4; R.G. Lowe, 'Development of Taungya in Nigeria', in Henry L. Gholz (ed.), *Agroforestry: Realities, Possibilities and Potentials*, Dordrecht, 1987, pp. 137-54.

[109] Before 1880, colonial forest revenue derived almost entirely from teak sales, but in the 1920s teak still accounted for 70 per cent of total receipts. See D. Brandis, 'The Burma Teak Forests', *Garden and Forest* 9 (1895), p. 12; Great Britain, Indian Statutory Commission, *Memorandum submitted by the Government of Burma to the Indian Statutory Commission*, London, 1930, vol. XI, p. 55.

Chief Commissioner Phayre warned that such a move would only 'produce general alarm and discontent.'[110] Phayre's response in part reflected a misconception, popular among colonial officials at the time, that peasants traditionally enjoyed free access to forest products. In a context of widespread political unrest, the government was reluctant to introduce unpopular measures that might complicate the beginning of colonial rule in Pegu.

By the 1870s, however, British rule in Burma began to stabilize. Further, as noted earlier, an expanded and increasingly professional forest service was better placed by then to expand and enforce state forest control. Forest policy simultaneously began to be applied beyond the teak industry, encompassing the regulation of non-teak forest use in the indigenous forest sector. Resistance by Burmese peasants often acting in collusion with indigenous timber traders was the all but inevitable result.

The Forest Department soon realized the immensity of the task involved in regulation of non-teak forest use. To begin with, regulation needed to account for the great diversity that characterized such forest use in mid-nineteenth century British Burma.[111] If teak or *kyun (Tectona grandis)* was used traditionally for construction and other purposes, by the 1860s its relative scarcity and high price resulted in growing commercial prominence for other multi-purpose timbers like *padauk (Pterocarpus macrocarpus), in (Dipterocarpus tuberculatus), thingan (Hopea odorata), thitkado (Cedrela toon), pyinma (Lagerstroemia flos-reginae), kanyin (Dipterocarpus adatus/turbinatus)* and *pyinkado (Xylia dolabriformis).*[112] Bamboo was in even greater demand for conversion into mats, umbrellas, fences, lacquer ware, fishing traps, and in the case of poor villagers even houses.[113] Forests were also used for firewood, charcoal, rope, resins, dyes, fruit, and intoxicants.

Use of forest products was often conditioned by religious and cultural practice. As with animist Karen, many Burmese Buddhists built houses only under auspicious astrological conditions. Even the selection of timber for the construction of houses was carefully considered:

---

[110] Resolution, RFA, 1865-6, p. 2; see also C.H. Dickens, Secretary, Government of India (PWD), to Chief Commissioner, 25 August 1868, *IFP* (September 1868), p. 255; Secretary of State for India to Governor General of India, 15 November 1867, *SDI* (1867), p. 127.

[111] Nisbet, *Burma under British Rule*, vol. II, pp. 205-304; Shway Yoe (J. George Scott), *The Burman: His Life and Notions*, Edinburgh, 1989, (1882).

[112] *RFA*, 1865-6, p. 26.

[113] S. Kurz, 'Bamboo and Its Use', *Indian Forester* 1 (January 1876), pp. 219-69.

Posts are masculine, feminine, and neuter. Male posts are of equal size at both ends; females are larger at the base; those which swell out in the middle are a-thet ma-shi – without life; taing bilu, ogre's posts are largest at the top. As a general rule it may be taken for granted that if a house is built with neuter posts, its inmates will always be miserable and unlucky; if the posts are ogres, death and disaster will attend; male posts are easy-going and harmless; females, on the contrary, are fortunate and leading to honour [moreover] the presence or absence of knots, and if the former, their position, determines the luck of the householder.[114]

Such considerations affected the nature of timber extraction. The quest for 'auspicious' timber may even partly explain the apparently wasteful practices of Burmese woodcutters so often decried by colonial officials.[115]

Indigenous forest use was also influenced by market conditions. Even before the economic changes of the late nineteenth century, the domestic forest sector was becoming commercialized. Traders were already widely employed in the 1860s collecting forest products for peasants living on the plains.[116] These traders extracted timber and bamboo from accessible low-lying forests, but also worked the Pegu Yoma forests.[117] Transported by river and cart road to the plains villages, forest products were often then sold to artisans for the manufacture of everything from boats and carts to umbrellas and lacquerware.

British rule encouraged the further commercialization of indigenous forest use. As forests were cleared for agriculture, and the population in Lower Burma expanded, the domestic forest sector was affected in various ways. Forest clearance reduced or even eliminated local supplies, which then had to be obtained from further afield, increasing the dependence of peasants on traders. Migrants also increased local demand for agricultural implements, carts and boats. Conservator Leeds noted in 1866 that the value of boats had trebled within two years 'owing chiefly to the increased cultivation of rice' even though the number built had jumped from 200 to 400 boats in the mid-1860s in Toungoo alone.[118]

If the colonial state facilitated such development, it also restricted popular forest access. In addition to the bureaucratic conflict note

[114] Shway Yoe, *The Burman*, pp. 76-7.

[115] Baden-Powell, *Forest System*, pp. 13-14.

[116] *RFA*, 1865-6, pp. 26-7; *RFA*, 1866-7, pp. 17-18; *RFA*, 1868-9, p. 2.

[117] *RFA*, 1868-9, p. 2. Forest produce such as wood-oil (used in torches) was collected from as far afield as Mergui, see J. Butler, *Gazetteer of the Mergui District*, Rangoon, 1884, pp. 32-3.

[118] *RFA*, 1865-6, pp. 26-7.

earlier, restricted popular forest access was the occasion for conflict
between the Forest Department and Burmese peasants and timber
traders. Forest Department restrictions affected peasant access in two
ways. With the creation of the first reserved forest in May 1870,
the Forest Department began an enclosure campaign that reduced
popular access to teak and other areas. The Department usually provided
free access to meet local subsistence needs, but reserving forests
was nonetheless a divisive process. Enjoined to reduce 'general claims
to something definite and tangible', Forest Settlement Officers encountered much opposition.[119] Peasants who were permitted to obtain
forest products from reserves objected to the detailed restrictions placed
upon such access, while Burmese timber traders and others whose
claims were rejected protested their exclusion from these forests. The
reserved area increased gradually at first, however reserves still covered
1,410 square miles in 1878-9.

The Forest Department also limited popular access to selected
species even outside reserves. In 1873, it persuaded Chief Commissioner
Ashley Eden to proclaim *thitkado* and *thitka (Pentace burmanica)*
reserved trees, and three years later added another twelve species
to the list.[120] These trees could only be cut with government approval
and the appropriate permit. The government tried to differentiate between
local subsistence needs and commercial timber extraction. Local people
could acquire free permits, while commercial users were required
to purchase trade permits.

Peasants and traders alike opposed the new restrictions on access
to species and land. Everyday peasant resistance to species reservation
encompassed notably the illicit felling of reserved trees.[121] This practice
was at times nothing more than an attempt by peasants to obtain
forest products free for their own use without having to bother registering
with the Forest Department. Indeed, there may have been a calculation
here that such registration was merely a colonial ploy to gather information about peasant use of reserved species as a precursor to
subsequent taxation.

Yet peasant resistance to species reservation also reflected a opportunistic quest for economic gain borne of the new legal situation.
Thus, along with illegal extraction, there emerged simultaneously a
booming black market in free permits in which peasants colluded

---

[119] Baden-Powell, *Manual of Jurisprudence*, p. 190.

[120] Brandis, *Suggestions*, pp. 25-6; Ribbentrop, 'Special Report' in *RFA*, 1876-7.

[121] Discussion here is based largely on Ribbentrop, 'Special Report', which contains
extensive testimony by both forest and civil officials about Burmese reactions to species
reservation.

with indigenous timber traders to circumvent the law requiring the latter to acquire commercial permits. In some cases peasants extracted the wood themselves, but typically timber traders did the work. In each case, timber traders paid peasants to claim the timber on their behalf under the free-permit scheme. As Conservator Ribbentrop complained, 'the practical result of giving people, living in the vicinity of the forests, their wood free, is to allow the timber merchants to extract a certain proportion of their season's wood free of tax'.[122]

In contrast, peasants resorted to avoidance behaviour when they opted to avoid access restrictions on selected species altogether by switching to the use of unreserved species. This tactic of seeking to outflank official restrictions through shifted species use depended on such factors as local forest conditions and the relative substitutability of species. Yet this practice was reportedly widespread; indeed, in certain districts trade in reserved species virtually ceased. As one official remarked, peasants generally preferred 'to utilize trees of other kinds rather than go to the myooke [township officer] to obtain a free permit'.[123]

Peasants also resisted vigorously the creation of reserved forests. Here, law-breaking was associated with the conduct of such activities as timber extraction and cattle grazing that were illegal by virtue of the fact that they occurred within a prohibited area. Resistance in this case was spatially defined, a rejection, as it were, by peasants of colonial efforts to define 'inside/outside' via the mechanism of a network of reserved forests. In extreme cases, such resistance also included the intentional destruction of official property – teak plantations, forest offices and bungalows. The subject of peasant resistance to forest reservation is considered fully in subsequent chapters.

The Forest Department's decision to reserve selected non-teak species was guided by diverse considerations. Forest officials were often as critical of the practices of Burmese peasants and timber traders as they were about those of shifting cultivators. Such criticism reflected in part a concern that these groups were eliminating species of considerable export potential.[124] Certain forest officials also believed that taxing non-teak forest trade would 'add considerably to the revenue of the Department without any increase of expenditure.'[125] As Ribbentrop

---

[122] *Ibid.*, p. 28.

[123] *RFA* (Pegu), 1880-1, p. 19; see also *RFA* (Tenasserim), 1876-7, p. 11; *RFA*, 1879-80, p. 5; Nisbet, *Burma under British Rule*, vol. II, p. 57.

[124] Baden-Powell, *Forest System*, pp. 13-14; Brandis, *Suggestions*, p. 20; Ribbentrop, 'Special Report', pp. 25, 38; Nisbet, *Burma under British Rule*, vol. II, p. 56.

[125] Conservator Leeds in *RFA*, 1865-6, p. 26.

added, such a move would 'only give the state a legitimate revenue, which at present enriches individuals who have no particular claim whatever to it.'[126] These arguments persuaded government sufficiently of the need to impose some controls on indigenous non-teak forest use. Yet, as subsequent chapters show, such controls were the focus of sustained popular resistance, and the source of much political trouble for the Forest Department.

This chapter shows that the introduction of scientific forestry after 1856 resulted in major changes in the nature of Burmese forest politics. European timber traders, shifting cultivators and Burmese peasants (acting at times in collusion with indigenous timber traders) opposed the Forest Department's efforts to impose a system based on detailed regulation of their forest activities. Yet such resistance was not coordinated, a reflection of the diverse, and even conflicting interests of non-state forest users.

The fragmented nature of non-state resistance to the new system enabled the Forest Department to assert its authority in the forests more quickly and effectively then would otherwise have been the case. In only a matter of years in the mid-nineteenth century, it became a resource manager with which to be reckoned. Yet the Forest Department's ability to manage the forests was still relatively limited in 1881, and it would not be until the early twentieth century that forest officials would have the requisite financial and human resources to attempt a comprehensive rationalization of forest activities.

Part of the problem faced by the Forest Department as it introduced scientific forestry to Burma was the opposition that it encountered at times within the colonial state itself. The new system was linked to the bureaucratic growth and differentiation that transformed the state in Burma in the nineteenth century. Yet that transformation was also marked by bureaucratic rivalry and conflict associated with the establishment of state services on a functionally defined basis. As discussion of the relationship between forest and civil officials illustrated, such conflict was an important, if underrated influence on forest management in the country. Indeed, it is often overlooked that state control in colonial times could be as fragmented as the resistance in civil society that it often engendered.

The period 1856-81 thus witnessed the development of patterns of control and strategies of resistance that were to shape Burmese forest politics into the twentieth century. Yet the politics was relatively fluid, the battlelines rarely cast in stone, as subsequent chapters seek to demonstrate.

---

[126] *RFA*, 1874-5, p. 25.

Part III

RATIONALIZING FOREST USE

4

THE ERA OF EXPANSION, 1882-1901

During the last two decades of the nineteenth century, the Forest Department strengthened its hold over Burma's forests. Yet rationalization of forest use was conditioned by the bureaucratic politics and the popular resistance examined in the preceding chapter. This chapter addresses the implications of this situation for the development of forest control and conflict in the late nineteenth century.

The chapter is concerned with what may be termed the era of expansion (1882-1901). During this era, Upper Burma and the Shan States were annexed and all of Burma was under British rule for the first time. The modern Burmese nation-state replete with fixed external borders was born – a process earlier described as external territorialization. Such change had important implications for Burmese forest politics as Forest Department control expanded into new territories. The period was also marked by a rapid increase in the area of reserved forests. This internal territorialization aimed to clarify, if not completely separate state and non-state access rights to commercial forests in the newly unified country. Within and without reserves, forest officials further sought to regulate selectively non-teak forest use. The regulation of cutch (a water extract of the *sha* tree) and bamboo is discussed to illustrate that scientific forestry was not about either teak management or regulation within reserves exclusively.

These interrelated processes were linked to a broader quest to rationalize forest use. This topic is pursued further in Chapter 5 where Forest Department efforts to consolidate state forest control in the early twentieth century are examined. To fully appreciate forest rationalization, however, it is necessary first to explore the ways in which the Forest Department extended its activities in the late nineteenth century.

External Territorialization

Following the third Anglo-Burmese war (1885-6) the British controlled all of Burma's forests. But, as in 1852 in Pegu, colonial officials inherited a series of political, economic and ecological problems that conditioned policy formulation. Specifically, the Forest Department faced problems concerning precolonial timber leases, political unrest and overharvesting.

The Department first sought to gain a working knowledge of the newly acquired forests. Under the direction of Harry Hill, Upper Burma's first Conservator, foresters set out to 'explore, survey and roughly value the forests' beginning with the valuable Pyinmana teak tracts of the north Pegu Yoma in 1886.[1] By the early 1890s, all but the most remote forests had been investigated, and a preliminary survey confirmed widespread overharvesting. In the Pyinmana forests, for example, rough calculations indicated that for every thirty-three mature trees, twenty-seven had already been removed or killed; one-sixth of the girdled trees were also undersized (i.e. below 6 feet in girth).[2]

Although forest officials witnessed extensive overharvesting, this did not mean that irreparable damage had occurred to Upper Burma's forests. Contemporary popular accounts of pervasive deforestation may have served to belittle precolonial forestry, but they were otherwise highly misleading.[3] Yet this deforestation myth persists even today. Charles Keeton, for example, claims that

> the 1883-1885 'drought' and the other calamities attributed to [King] Thebaw's 'misrule' were, in the main, caused by 'modern' Deforestation. King Mindon had first leased extensive portions of his forests to the BBTC in 1862. Within twenty years many cutch, teak, and other timber areas in the provinces south of Mandalay and elsewhere were largely denuded of trees and other ground cover.[4]

What is important here is not the link between alleged deforestation

---

[1] *Progress Report of Forest Administration for Upper Burma* (henceforth *RFA*) for 1888-89, p. 6.

[2] *RFA* (Upper Burma), 1887-8, p. 8; *RFA* (Upper Burma), 1889-90, p. 6; Government of India, Home, Revenue and Agriculture Department, to Secretary of State for India, 6 November 1879, *India Forest Letters* no. 157 of 1878-9.

[3] For example, Grattan Geary, *Burma After the Conquest*, London, 1886, p. 312.

[4] Charles Lee Keeton III, *King Thebaw and the Ecological Rape of Burma: the Political and Commercial Struggle between British India and French Indo-China in Burma, 1878-1886*, Delhi, 1974, p. 143; see also Mark Poffenberger, 'The Evolution of Forest Management Systems in Southeast Asia', in Mark Poffenberger (ed.), *Keepers of the Forest: Land Management Alternatives in Southeast Asia*, West Hartford, CT, 1990, p. 17.

and drought in Upper Burma,[5] so much as the assumption that over-harvesting and deforestation were synonymous. That assumption is false for several reasons. First, it has been noted that teak in Burma rarely constitutes naturally more than 12 per cent of total forest cover. Thus, even if every teak tree in a given area was removed, much forest cover would remain. Further, teak extraction involved the use of elephants which hauled felled trees to streams so that logs could then be floated to market. This procedure resulted in minimal damage to surrounding forest. Second, leaseholders took only marketable trees, not the entire teak crop as frequently assumed. 'If 'undersized' trees were taken, the smallest timber was nevertheless typically left behind. Finally, loggers missed completely forests where logs could not be floated out due to natural obstruction. It was partly because these inaccessible forests were not logged that the Forest Department was able to expand production in the twentieth century, despite closure of accessible but overworked areas.[6] Overharvesting was probably greater in the cutch (*sha*) forests, but even here Upper Burma was not as denuded of these forests as Lower Burma was in 1885.[7] Extensive overharvesting of selected species under Burmese rule thus did not denote pervasive deforestation. Rather, deforestation occurred mainly in British-held Lower Burma in the latter half of the nineteenth century where the conversion of delta forests into paddy fields reduced forest cover much more extensively than timber extraction (whether under Burmese or British direction) ever did.[8]

Yet evidence of overharvesting in Upper Burma reiterated to forest officials the lesson learned already in Tenasserim and Pegu that private extraction in the absence of state regulation led to overharvesting. Nevertheless the Forest Department's ability to regulate private enterprise in 1886 was constrained by the question of precolonial forest leases held by the Bombay Burmah Trading Corporation Limited (BBTCL) and other firms in Upper Burma, and the conditions under which the colonial state would honour their terms.

For several reasons, the British government did not cancel these

---

[5] This link is still debated today, but was considered extensively in the early twentieth century in Burma, see below.

[6] A similar situation prevailed in Pegu after 1856, see Dietrich Brandis, 'The Burma Teak Forests', *Garden and Forest* 9 (1895), pp. 12-13.

[7] R.S. Wilkie, *Yamethin District Gazetteer*, Rangoon, 1934, p. 83; F.C. Owens, *Pakokku District Gazetteer*, Rangoon, 1913, p. 59.

[8] Michael Adas, 'Colonization, Commercial Agriculture, and the Destruction of the Deltaic Rainforests of British Burma in the Late Nineteenth Century', in Richard P. Tucker and J.F. Richards (eds), *Global Deforestation and the Nineteenth- Century World Economy*, Durham, NC, 1983, pp. 95-11.

leases. First, since its founding in 1863 the BBTCL had become a very powerful company with considerable influence in government.[9] Such influence was used to good effect on this issue. Second, as the largest lessee in Upper Burma it already possessed the staff and elephants that the Forest Department would require years to match. The BBTCL was thus best placed to maintain teak production, and hence government forest revenue, at least in the short-term.[10] Finally, it was in the colonial state's own interest to uphold precolonial law. Chapter 2 noted how the British claimed ownership of Pegu's teak forests in 1853 on the basis of such law. In 1886, this inherited prerogative was extended to Upper Burma and the Shan States. In the latter case, British proprietary rights, as expressed in *sanads* (treaties) granted to the *Sawbwas* (hereditary local rulers), were explicitly based on the putative control of Shan forests by Burmese monarchs.[11]

However as the colonial state sought to revise precolonial leases to render them compatible with scientific forestry practices, it met resistance from the BBTCL and other lessees as well as the Shan *Sawbwas* who simultaneously fought to protect their privileged forest access.[12] Negotiations between government and business began in January 1886 when the BBTCL conveyed to Chief Commissioner Charles Bernard its financial claims against the Burmese monarchy. Bernard felt that the Corporation's leases should be confirmed subject to cutting restrictions. However, he also argued that:

> It will be better for the country, the people, and the forests that at the end of the existing leases (1890 or 1891) the Forest department should

---

[9] Anon., 'Forest Administration under Lord Dufferin', *Indian Forester* 15 (January 1889), p. 7; A.C. Pointon, *The Bombay Burmah Trading Corporation Ltd., 1863- 1963*, Southampton, 1964; Ernest Andrews, *The Bombay Burmah Trading Corporation Limited in Burmah, Siam and Java*, n.p., 1930-1, vols I-III; *Annual Report of the Bombay Burmah Trading Corporation Limited for 1876-77* (henceforth *ARBBTCL*), p. 5.

[10] C. Bernard, 'Claims of the Bombay-Burma Corporation against the Government of Upper Burma', 29 January 1886, *Burma Forest Proceedings* (henceforth *BFP*) (February 1886), pp. 5-6.

[11] B. Ribbentrop, *Forestry in British India*, Calcutta, 1900, pp. 103-4; Resolution, *RFA* (Upper Burma), 1889-90, p. 2; C.U. Aitchison (ed.), *A Collection of Treatises, Engagement and Sanads relating to India and Neighbouring Countries*, Calcutta, 1909, vol. II, pp. 63-5. See also Benedict Anderson, *Imagined Communities: Reflections on the Origin and Spread of Nationalism*, rev. edn, London, 1991, pp. 174-5, who notes that Europeans generally were in the business of 'reconstructing the property-history of their new possessions. . . [and] the antiquity of specific, tightly bounded territorial units.'

[12] Lord Dufferin, 'Minute by His Excellency the Viceroy and Governor General of India, 17 February 1886, as to the Future Administrations of Upper Burma', *Further Correspondence Relating to Burmah*, London, 1886, vol. III, p. 31; *ARBBTCL*, 1887-8, p. 4; J. Nisbet, 'Suggestions for the Administration and Working of the Forests in the Southern Shan States', *BFP* (December 1898), pp. 98-102.

be free to arrange for the working of the forests after the most approved methods. Doubtless they would . . . employ largely the agency of the Bombay-Burmah Corporation; but they would regulate girdlings, fellings, and reproduction in the best way for securing permanent and steady yield from all the different teak forests in the country.[13]

Bernard thus sought to. balance the Forest Department's demands for sufficient authority to manage the forests scientifically and claims to 'rightful' usage made by the BBTCL.[14] Not satisfied with this plan, the Corporation lobbied the British government and in October 1886 the Secretary of State for India ruled that both existing contracts and rights to lease renewal would be recognized. Two further years of negotiation led to an agreement between the British government and the BBTCL that also formed the basis of agreements with the other lessees.[15] Under this agreement, the BBTCL retained the right to work Upper Burma's teak forests until the turn of the century. It was to extract not less than 100,000 tons per annum on payment of a royalty of ten rupees per ton on full-size timber and six rupees per ton on undersized timber, but the government could reduce or even eliminate the allowable cut in areas already overworked.[16]

This agreement confirmed the BBTCL as the preeminent extraction agency in Upper Burma. This situation led to further privatization of teak extraction as government sought to counterbalance BBTCL predominance in Upper Burma by allocating teak forests to other firms in Lower Burma. Yet the agreement also confirmed government ownership of the forests and its right to manage them. The Forest Department regulated BBTCL activities under the Upper Burma Forest Regulation (1887) and was in complete control of teak selection and girdling. The Department was thereby empowered to bring teak extraction in Upper Burma into line with practices already in place in Lower Burma.[17]

[13] Bernard, 'Claims', pp. 5-6.

[14] More than seventy European and indigenous timber merchants in Rangoon and Moulmein urged the government in January 1886 to cancel the BBTCL leases, fearful that a Corporation monopoly and overharvesting would otherwise ensue, *ibid.,* app. Q, pp. 22-3.

[15] U.K. Parliament, 'Return of Contract between the Secretary of State for India and the Bombay-Burma Trading Corporation referring to the Teak Forests of Upper Burma, and Correspondence relating thereto', *Sessional Papers* (Commons), *Accounts and Papers* – 12, vol. L VIII, 24 August 1889; *RFA* (Upper Burma), 1888-9, appendix; *RFA* (Upper Burma), 1889-90, appendix; H.C. Hill, 'Brief Report on Forest Administration in Upper Burma for the Year 1887- 88', *BFP* (August 1888), Upper Burma Circle, pp. 22-4.

[16] U.K. Parliament, 'Contract', pp. 14-15. The BBTCL continued to lobby government for a better deal thereafter, *ARBBTCL*, 1887-8, p. 4; *ARBBTCL*, 1893-4, p. 5.

[17] This mandate soon brought it into conflict with the BBTCL over the question of departmental girdling operations, S.F. Hopwood, *Working Plan for North and South Gangaw Working Circles*, Rangoon. 1916, p. 5; *ARBBTCL*, 1894-5, p. 4.

The British dealt with the Shan *Sawbwas* differently befitting their special political and economic status.[18] As developed in the late 1880s and early 1890s, government policy in the Shan States represented a delicate attempt to assert British control over the teak forests, but not so as to alienate the *Sawbwas* whose allegiance was actively solicited. As a result, a central feature of that policy was the retention of *Sawbwas* as lessees in their individual states. This policy affirmed conditionally the autonomy that many local rulers enjoyed in precolonial times. As one forest official noted, under Burmese rule:

> Such Sawbwas, whose wealth or whose extent of forest made them conspicuous, were from time to time called upon to pay a duty on teak extracted from their forests, but as a general rule the Sawbwas were accustomed to work their forests just when and how they pleased, and it is therefore not unnatural that they should have come to look upon them as their personal property, to be exploited to their own direct profit.[19]

However, such autonomy was gradually limited. In 1890, the colonial state introduced an annual tax of 200 rupees per timber elephant as was done in precolonial times. This fixed rate was soon abandoned for one geared to the profitability of individual forests, and a surcharge was levied in cases where *Sawbwas* operated sawmills.[20] The system was modified again in 1893 as an annual fixed assessment per state was introduced; richer states such as Kengtung and Mongpan paid 10,000 rupees, while poorer states paid as little as 200 rupees.[21] By the end of the decade, evidence of illegal extraction and overharvesting provided a pretext for further British intervention, hastening the demise of teak extraction by the *Sawbwas*. In the early twentieth century, their place was gradually taken by European firms, a change that was part of a general campaign to limit the autonomy of these rulers.[22]

The caution with which colonial officials treated the claims of

---

[18] D.T. Griffiths, *Working Plan for Southern Shan States Forest Division, 1940-41 to 1949-50*, Rangoon, 1949, vol. II, p. 3; Robert H. Taylor, *The State in Burma*, London, 1987, pp. 93-4.

[19] H. Jackson, 'Preliminary Report on Some of the Forests in the Shan States in the Basin of the Salween', BFP (September 1891), p. 33.

[20] Resolution, *RFA* (Upper Burma), 1891-2, pp. 6-7, *Sawbwas* also had to obey rules pertaining to teak girdling J. George Scott and J.P. Hardiman, *Gazetteer of Upper Burma and the Shan States*, Rangoon, 1900, vol. II, part I, p. 313.

[21] Resolution, *RFA* (Upper Burma), 1892-3, p. 6; *RFA* (Eastern), 1893-4, p. 17.

[22] Nisbet, 'Suggestions', pp. 97-104; F. Beadon-Bryant, Chief Conservator, to Revenue Secretary, 24 June 1905, *BFP* (October 1907), pp. 1-4; *RFA*, 1905-6, p. 68; Taylor, *State in Burma*, pp. 94-8.

the Shan *Sawbwas* and timber lessees must be situated in a broader context of political unrest following Upper Burma's annexation in 1886. The elimination of monarchical rule triggered the outbreak of rebellion in many areas as precolonial political and religious leaders led resistance to the British. The propensity of insurgents to take refuge in the forests when pursued by British-Indian forces prolonged the anti-insurgency campaign. The well-wooded Pegu Yoma and outer hills – 'an earthly paradise for outlaws' – were home to Burmese insurgents until 1890 if not later.[23] Forest administration was introduced gradually under these circumstance, and forest officials required an armed escort to go about their duties.[24] Moreover, the military practice of concentrating outlying villagers in stockaded villages deprived the Forest Department of a local labour supply to be used in fire-protection duties; difficulties experienced in hiring Burmese foresters, or persuading those hired to enter remote forests, only exacerbated this problem. Not surprisingly, Conservator Hill reported that it was 'either not possible or, where possible, unadvisable to proceed against offenders more than exceptionally', and with the exception of teak offences, violations of the law were overlooked in the 1880s.[25]

By the early 1890s, however, the Upper Burma forest administration was established on the model of that in Lower Burma. The territory was formed initially into one forest circle, but growing political stability led to its division into two in 1892, each circle thereafter managed by a Conservator.[26] Modelled on the Burma Forest Act (1881), the Upper Burma Forest Regulation (1887) was gradually enforced, and its provisions extended selectively to the Shan State.[27] Additional

---

[23] D. Wilson, 'General Report on the Ngamingyaung, Yinmale, Kinmundaung, and Kyaukmigyaung Reserves', *BFP* (January 1896), p. 214; Charles Crosthwaite, *The Pacification of Burma*, London, 1912, pp. 32, 61; *RFA* (Upper Burma), 1889-90, p. 18; *RFA* (Upper Burma), 1890-1, pp. 12-13; *RFA* (Upper Burma), 1891-2, p. 19.

[24] *RFA* (Upper Burma), 1887-8, p. 1; *RFA* (Upper Burma), 1888-9, pp. 12, 19; *RFA* (Upper Burma), 1889-90, p. 18. As did employees of the BBTCL, *ARBBTCL*, 1888-9, p. 5.

[25] Hill, 'Brief Report', pp. 18, 20; *RFA* (Upper Burma), 1887-8, Resolution, p. 3, p. 9; *RFA* (Upper Burma), 1888-9, Resolution p. 3, p. 9.

[26] Between 1892 and 1900, Upper Burma was divided into a Western Circle (the region to the west of Mandalay) and an Eastern Circle (the area to the south and north-east of Mandalay). In 1900, in the first of a series of administrative re-designations, these circles in a slightly modified form became the Northern and Southern Circles respectively.

[27] H.C. Hill, *Memorandum on the Forest Laws in Force in Upper Burma*, Rangoon, 1889; Secretary, Upper Burma, to Secretary, Revenue and Agriculture Department (RAD), Government of India, 3 February 1887, *Upper Burma Proceedings* (February 1887), p. 5; Chief Secretary, Burma, to Secretary, RAD, Government of India, 22 September 1888,

foresters were also posted to Upper Burma: from sixteen officers
in 1887-8, the superior service there totalled twenty-six men in July
1893.[28] These changes both reflected and reinforced the growing asser-
tiveness of the Forest Department in the newly acquired territory.
Burmese forest policy was thus standardized with the exception of
the Shan States (and other frontier areas).

Internal Territorialization

The standardization of forest policy was particularly evident with
regard to the creation of reserved forests. During the late nineteenth
century, forest officials focused on selecting and protecting these
forests as internal territorialization became the principal means of
asserting Forest Department control. This process provoked both popular
opposition and bureaucratic conflict.

The Burma Forest Act (1881) established a complex procedure
for the creation of reserved forests. A forest official prepared a proposal
for the Deputy Commissioner's comment, before it was passed on
via the Commissioner and Conservator to the Chief Commissioner.
Civil officials could thus object to proposals but the Conservator
also had the opportunity of 'explaining away their objections or adducing
additional arguments for reservation.'[29] If the Chief Commissioner
approved the proposal, a civil official was then appointed Forest
Settlement Officer to determine how reservation, if carried out, would
'affect the people in the neighbourhood, and the rights and privileges,
if any, to which they are entitled'; this officer could redraw boundaries,
buy out rights or specify rights within the reserve in the course
of the enquiry.[30] The proceedings of the enquiry were forwarded
to the Deputy Commissioner, and a three-month period ensued during
which local villagers could appeal the Settlement Officer's decision.
Appeals were reviewed by the Deputy Commissioner who could modify
or confirm the original decision, forwarding the proceedings up the
chain of command as before. Once a reserve was notified, all rights
not explicitly claimed were extinguished.

BFP (September 1888), Upper Burma Circle, p. 4; *BFP* (April 1889), Upper Burma
Circle, p. 1.

[28] Resolution, *RFA* (Upper Burma), 1887-8, p. 1; Hill, 'Brief Report', p. 18; Revenue
Secretary, Burma, to Secretary, RAD, Government of India, 6 July 1893, *BFP* (July
1893), p. 8.

[29] J. Nisbet, *Burma under British Rule and Before*, Westminister, 1901, vol. II, p. 67.

[30] 'Instructions for Forest Settlement Officers, Upper Burma', *BFP* (April 1891), p. 10;
Burma Forest Act 1881, Rangoon, 1884, nos 6-15.

Internal territorialization proceeded on the basis of this highly bureaucratic and legalistic system. Notwithstanding a shortage of civil officials to serve as forest settlement officers, extensive reservation took place in Lower Burma, and after 1890 in Upper Burma as well (Table 4.1). Indeed, most of the best teak forests of the Pegu Yoma were reserved by the turn of the century.[31]

Table 4.1. GROWTH IN RESERVED FORESTS, 1880-1905

	Lower Burma	*Upper Burma*	*Total*
1880-1	2,288	–	2,288
1883-4	3,759	–	3,759
1886-7	4,788	–	4,788
1889-90	5,574	–	5,574
1892-3	5,790	2,269	8,059
1895-6	7,379	5,438	12,817
1898-9	7,680	7,989	15,669
1901-2	9,471	9,135	18,606
1904-5	10,340	10,071	20,411

Source: Progress Report of Forest Administration in British Burma (various years). Selected years; area in square miles.

Two things are striking about changes to the reserved area during this period. The first concerns the steady increase in the reserved area in Lower Burma which occurred despite the political turmoil of the 1880s. As discussed below, forest administration was disrupted temporarily in Pegu during the third Anglo-Burmese war (1885-6). Yet work continued more or less as usual in neighbouring Tenasserim. This, in itself, is testimony to the power and resiliency of the bureaucratic structures and rational-legal techniques introduced by the British in Burma after 1856. In contrast, what is noteworthy about the pace of reservation in Upper Burma in the 1890s is its rapidity. Thus, whereas reserves in Upper Burma constituted 28 per cent of the total reserved area in 1892-3, six years later they represented 51 per cent. This record reflected the importance of Upper Burma's teak forests and growing stability in forest administration in the region.

However, rapid growth in the reserved area was a source of ongoing bureaucratic tension in the late nineteenth century. Conflict between civil and forest officials was reduced as a result of the Burma Forest Act (1881), but the silence of that Act on the ultimate extent of reservation remained a bone of contention. The internal territorialization that was at the heart of the Forest Department's programme of scientific

[31] H.W. A. Watson, *A Note on the Pegu Yoma Forests*, Rangoon, 1923, p. 4.

forestry was thus often still viewed in exclusionary terms by the civil administration.

As during the 1870s, civil officials opposed Forest Department proposals to reserve large areas adjoining populated areas. For example, a proposed reserve covering 637 square miles in Henzada District was rejected by the Deputy Commissioner for this reason in 1884. J. Butler noted that in the past, reservation had led to the 'total exclusion' of people from the forests, and that, even with new legislation the quest for 'a good balance sheet' might influence a forest official more than 'supplying the wants of a people whose prosperity or reverse do not immediately come under his observation.'[32] Forest officials hotly denied this claim, but Commissioner of Irrawaddy Division, G.J.S. Hodgkinson, supported Butler, deeming the proposed reserve 'unnecessary' and the arguments adduced in its favour 'unsubstantiated'; in the end, the Chief Commissioner sided with the civil officials.[33]

Civil officials supported other proposals but often only after recommending substantial areas be set aside to meet the objections of peasants or shifting cultivators. In the case of Aingdon-kun reserve (Shwegyin District), Forest Settlement Officer J.L. Long recommended in 1894 that the livelihood of 181 Karen shifting cultivators and their families be safeguarded by allocating to them 65 square miles (22 per cent) of a total proposed area of 294 square miles.[34] In 1903, the Namkwin reserve in Myitkyina District was sanctioned over 15 square miles, down from a proposed size of 60 square miles.[35] In some instances, exclusions encompassed so much of the proposed area that forest officials ultimately abandoned the proposal.[36]

Forest and civil officials thus became involved in ongoing negotiations as to the nature and extent of reservation and Forest Department control. These negotiations resulted in recurring bureaucratic tension and conflict reflecting differing programmatic interests. However much conflict may have bedevilled forest-civil relations, it is nevertheless important to situate such differences in the broader context of a

[32] J. Butler to Deputy Conservator, Western Division, 30 August 1884, BFP (December 1884), p. 29.

[33] BFP (December 1884), pp. 29-30. See RFA (Pegu), 1883-4, p. 3, and RFA (Tenasserim), 1888-9, p. 1, for similar episodes.

[34] BFP (November 1894), pp. 133-7; see also BFP (December 1884), p. 13; BFP (July 1896), pp. 229-32.

[35] W.A. Hertz, Myitkyina District Gazetteer, Rangoon, 1912, p. 96.

[36] For example, the proposed Kyaukchaw reserve (Myingyan District), W.F.L. Tottenham, Conservator, Southern Circle, to Revenue Secretary, 15 November 1911, BFP (January 1912), p. 17; and the Methe reserve (Shwebo District), BFP (July 1896), pp. 123-81.

common European (typically British) heritage, as well as a shared interest in the maintenance of imperial rule. Despite their differences, these officials were united in their capacity as representatives of the British government in a land acquired by force. Their common identity was formally acknowledged through hiring and promotion policies that, until the 1920s at least, reserved the top jobs for Europeans. That identity was also informally reinforced through various social fora, and notably the 'Club':

> All the social activities of the Europeans are centred in the Club, where outdoor games such as golf, tennis and polo, and indoor ones such as billiards, snooker and bridge can be played. Newspapers and magazines are also to be found, while a library is usually attached.[37]

In many respects, the Club was the 'spiritual citadel, the real seat of the British power'.[38] Here, deputy commissioners and forest officials had the opportunity to try and resolve policy and personal differences.

For reasons of social and imperial solidarity, then, the Burmese could not count on civil officials to defend their interests against forest officials. Thus, peasants and shifting cultivators routinely objected to forest settlements that often provided them with insufficient forest access for grazing, agriculture, woodcutting and the collection of forest products. Yet supported generally by civil officials, the Forest Department often overcame such opposition in the rapid creation of reserves. Unable to prevent their creation, cultivators used diverse covert methods to subvert rules imposed in these forests.

As part of the process of internal territorialization, forest officials imposed a complicated set of rules that sought to regulate all human activities within reserves. Together with silvicultural operations, these rules were at the heart of scientific forestry management in Burma. In essence, such management was about the systematic elimination of all natural and human hazards to the development of teak, and to lesser extent, other commercial imperial timbers such as *padauk* and *thitka*.

From the start, a primary concern was the exclusion of fire from reserved areas. The urgency with which forest officials sought to avert forest fires reflected, in turn, a belief that was widespread

---

[37] G.H. Ogilvie, 'A Forestry Officer's Life in Burma', *Sylva* (Edinburgh) 14 (1934), p. 20.

[38] George Orwell, *Burmese Days*, Harmondsworth, Middlesex, 1987 (1934), p. 17. It was also one of the few places where colonial officials were 'offstage': 'among their own...and no longer strutting before the audience of colonial subjects. Activities, gestures, remarks, and dress that were unseemly to the public role of sahib were safe in this retreat', James C. Scott, *Domination and the Arts of Resistance: Hidden Transcripts*, New Haven, 1990, pp. 12-13.

in the nineteenth century that fire was a major threat to teak. Indeed, this belief was part of a much broader European attitude towards fires which viewed this phenomenon as an inherently destructive force, and one which forest conservancy was required almost by definition to check.[39] In the Burmese context, colonial foresters recognized that forest fires occurred naturally. However, they also blamed lax indigenous practices for conflagrations in Burma's forests. As noted, the British condemned shifting cultivators for *taungya* fires that allegedly eliminated teak forest. However, they also criticized peasants for firing jungle in search of game or to promote good grazing for their cattle, and for damaging trees in collecting wood-oil, varnish and honey.[40] Thus, internal territorialization was about the creation of reserved forests within which intensive (mainly) teak management was practiced, but the exclusion of fire was considered by foresters to be essential to that process. Fire exclusion involved inevitably the restriction of 'unscientific' indigenous fire use in reserves.

However, such restriction was exceedingly difficult given the small number of forest officials available as well as the 'porous' nature of reserve boundaries. Further, the ability to control the fire-related activities of peasants and shifting cultivators became more difficult as the area designated for 'fire protection' increased. From only 150 square miles (6.6 per cent of the reserved area) in 1880-1, that area had expanded by 1898-9 to 3,157 square miles (20.1 per cent of the reserved area). At its peak in the early twentieth century, the fire protection programme embraced more than 40 per cent of the total area of Burma's reserved forests.[41]

The area protected from fire was invariably less than the official target. Fire protection was subject to the vagaries of climate in so far as drier than average seasons were typically associated with a greater failure rate. It was also affected by human factors since the fate of fire protection often depended on local support in fighting fires and adopting preventative measures. However, Forest Department efforts to restrict fire use in reserves was widely opposed by peasants and shifting cultivators, and encompassed the illegal use of fire, village complicity, labour strikes or slowdowns, and incendiarism.

Resistance commonly took the form of continuing fire-related prac-

---

[39] William Beinart and Peter Coates, *Environment and History: The Taming of Nature in the USA and South Africa*, London, 1995, p. 47.

[40] B.H. Baden-Powell, *The Forest System of British Burma*, Calcutta, 1873, pp. 12, 14; Nisbet, *Burma under British Rule*, vol. II, pp. 63-4.

[41] Raymond L. Bryant, 'Forest Problems in Colonial Burma: Historical Variations on Contemporary Themes', *Global Ecology and Biogeography Letters* 3 (July-November 1993), pp. 124-8.

tices that were now illegal. Thus, peasants fired reserves in search of game or to encourage better grazing for their cattle, while shifting cultivators failed to fire their clearings in the prescribed manner (a fire-trace around the designated area).[42] These forest users habitually denied any responsibility when caught, attributing the fires to natural causes. This explanation was more likely to succeed than pleading ignorance of the law in avoiding punishment given the highly publicized nature of the Forest Department's anti-fire campaign.

Resistance was facilitated by the fact that suspects could count on village complicity. Rewards were offered for information leading to the arrest of offenders, but strong social pressures within the village offset this measure.[43] Indeed, one frustrated colonial forester observed in 1891 that a 100-rupee reward for informers was useless because 'in no case was such information given in spite of the numerous incendiary or mysterious fires which occurred.'[44] An entire reserve was burnt in one instance but no arrest could be made as information was unattainable.[45]

Resistance also took the form of labour slowdowns and strikes. Under the forest rules, peasants were required to assist forest officials in fighting fires when requested to do so. However, these officials complained of peasant 'indolence' and 'negligence' in this regard. The case of Kyaungthaik village in Minbu Division is perhaps typical. Called upon at noon to assist with a fire, the villagers did not arrive until evening and 'only remained a short time, going away before the fire was put out.'[46] In other cases, villagers even refused to turn out when required to do so.[47]

Peasants and shifting cultivators thus used various methods to make plain their opposition to fire-related restrictions. All of these practices were associated with an unwillingness to cooperate with forest officials or to alter established practices. In contrast to these fairly innocuous methods, arson was a more serious and calculated form of resistance. Since it was often difficult to determine whether a fire was deliberate,

---

[42] *RFA* (Pegu), 1880-1, pp. 2, 9; *RFA* (Pegu), 1884-5, p. 18; *RFA* (Eastern), 1893-4, p. 11; J.P. Hardiman, *Lower Chindwin District Gazetteer*, Rangoon, 1912, p. 114.

[43] Forest Department circular no. 3 (1891), 13 August 1891, *BFP* (August 1891), p. 10.

[44] G.Q. Corbett to Conservator, Pegu, 21 September 1891, *BFP* (November 1891), p. 66; E.P. Popert, Conservator, Pegu, to Secretary, Chief Commissioner, 4 February 1886, *BFP* (March 1886), p. 4.

[45] *RFA*, 1894-5, p. lxii.

[46] *RFA*, 1898-9, p. ciii.

[47] *RFA* (Western), 1894-5, p. 11.

accidental or natural, arson was an anonymous, and at times highly effective, means of attacking forest valued by the Forest Department.

Many such attacks were isolated affairs by individuals with a particular grievance against the Forest Department. For example, a Karen cultivator in Sinzway reserve (Salween Division) 'believed to be ill-disposed to the forester' repeatedly fired the forest.[48] Other attacks suggested collective opposition to fire rules. In one Upper Burma village, these rules were explained to peasants, but two days later a fire was started by one villager near the colonial official's camp.[49] As with other forest rules, civil officials tended to caution against punishment that might alienate the Burmese. Thus, peasants living near the Minhla reserve (Tharrawaddy Division) were not punished in 1891 despite a series of arson attacks and the determination of the local forest official to impose a collective fine.[50]

During the third Anglo-Burmese war (1885-6), the Burmese used arson as a means of resistance extensively, and teak reserves, plantations and forest bungalows were thereby destroyed. Such resistance was part of a broader anti-British struggle. Thus, key reserves in Prome and Tharrawaddy Divisions were overrun by insurgents and used as bases from which to launch attacks on British and Indian troops.[51] In the course of the fighting, teak reserves and plantations that had been protected from fire since the 1870s were destroyed. These arson attacks occurred mainly in Pegu, while in virtually trouble-free Tenasserim the anti-fire campaign proceeded without interruption.[52]

Opposition to fire regulation was not universal. As part of the *taungya* forestry programme noted in Chapter 3, for example, hill Karen were employed to fight fires on the Forest Department's behalf. This situation was paradoxical in that the Department thereby employed as fire wardens the very people that it regularly blamed for causing many forest fires in the first place; and, it reflected labour shortages in the reserves as well as a tacit recognition by foresters that Karen were not necessarily as unskilled at fire management as officially portrayed.[53] Karen fire-fighting could be both effective and inexpensive. Three key reserves in the Salween Division were protected so successfully by local Karen, for example, that the Forest Department awarded

---

[48] *RFA* (Tenasserim), 1877-8, p. 8.

[49] *RFA* (Eastern), 1893-4, p. 10.

[50] G.Q. Corbett to Conservator, Pegu, 21 September 1891; F.D. Maxwell to Commissioner, Pegu, 22 September 1891, both in *BFP* (November 1891).

[51] *RFA* (Pegu), 1885-6, pp. 5-6; *RFA* (Pegu), 1886-7, p. 5.

[52] *RFA* (Pegu), 1885-6, pp. 5-6; *RFA* (Tenasserim), 1885-6, p. 5.

[53] *RFA*, 1874-75, p. 11.

each family a bonus of eight annas (one rupee for headmen's families).[54] Karen cultivators also contained fires in a number of reserves set alight by insurgents in 1885-6, for which action they became the target of insurgent attacks themselves.[55] Such loyalty assisted the Forest Department in restoring forest management rapidly in Pegu after the war.

Nevertheless, resistance was the predominant indigenous response to the anti-fire campaign. Yet the ability of such resistance to subvert that campaign was relatively limited and contrasts with the greater effect on forest management of the theft to forest products discussed in chapters 5 and 6. The explanation for this difference resides in the greater overall economic impact on the indigenous population of restrictions on access to forest products as opposed to fire restrictions. While fire use in aid of grazing and hunting was often important, the acquisition of forest products was typically a more pervasive and critical part of peasant livelihoods, and hence, the subject of a more extensive and ultimately 'successful' campaign of resistance to the colonial state.

Indeed, it was growing official disenchantment with the anti-fire campaign, and not a reaction to popular resistance, that led to its *de facto* termination in the early twentieth century. Chapter 2 noted how scientific debates about the ecological effects of deforestation influenced forest policy in Pegu in the 1850s. A similar process occurred at the turn of the century over the role of fire in teak propagation. Thus, the forester Herbert Slade turned conventional wisdom on its head when in 1896 he argued that annual ground fires 'should be considered as the friends and not the natural enemies of the teak' and that fire was 'one of the forest officer's most useful agents'.[56] Slade's article generated much debate, but by the second decade of the twentieth century, most forest officials were of the view that large-scale fire protection only wasted funds and threatened the teak forests; after the First World War the programme was restricted to young plantations only.[57]

Growth in scientific knowledge led to altered perceptions among

[54] *RFA* (Tenasserim), 1877-8, p. 8.

[55] Resolution, *RFA*, 1885-6, p. 3. *RFA* (Pegu), 1886-7, pp. 7-8; *RFA* (Pegu), 1885-6, p. 6; John F. Cady, *A History of Modern Burma*, Ithaca, 1958, pp. 137-8.

[56] Herbert Slade, 'Too Much Fire-Protection in Burma', *Indian Forester* 22 (May 1896), p. 176.

[57] H. Carter, 'Fire Protection in the Teak Forests of Burma', *Indian Forester* 30 (August 1904), pp. 363-6; R.S. Troup, 'Fire Protection in the Teak Forests of Burma', *Indian Forester* 31 (March 1905), pp. 138-46. Fire protection was attacked as early as 1875, M.J. Slym, *Memorandum on Jungle Fires*, Maulmain, 1876.

forest officials about the relationship between fire and teak such that the need to control indigenous fire use became less important. With the winding down of the anti-fire campaign, the use of fire as a means of popular resistance also declined. Yet resistance persisted in other guises. As patterns of control changed, so too did strategies of resistance.

Non-Teak Forest Use

Much forest conflict in colonial Burma centred on the question of access to reserved forests. Yet forest politics was not only a by-product of internal territorialization. The Forest Department also sought to control selectively non-teak forest activities that were not exclusively or even predominantly located within reserves. As Chapter 3 illustrated, forest officials encountered difficulties when they first attempted such regulation in Lower Burma in the 1870s. Here, discussion of cutch and bamboo management highlights how those difficulties persisted in the late nineteenth century.

Cutch was a forest product in great domestic and foreign demand in the latter half of the nineteenth century. A water extract of *sha*(*Acacia catechu*) wood, cutch was used primarily for tanning and dyeing purposes, but was also used in medicine and as an intoxicant (i.e. for chewing with the betel leaf).[58] Cutch was already the focus of an important cottage industry in Burma at mid-century, but under colonial rule the trade expanded rapidly and by the late 1860s officials were reporting widespread deforestation in accessible *sha* forests.[59]

Regulation of the cutch trade began in the early 1870s. In 1876 *sha* was declared a reserved tree and a five-rupee tax per cauldron was imposed.[60] Notwithstanding these actions, between 1876 and 1879

[58] F.T. Morehead, *The Forests of Burma*, London, 1944, p. 63; Alex Rodger, *A Handbook of the Forest Products of Burma*, Rangoon, 1951 (1921), pp. 66-7; F.J. Branthwaite, 'Cutch and Its Adulterants', *Indian Forester* 18 *(May 1892)*, pp. 184-5; Shway Yoe (J. Goerge Scott), *The Burman: His Life and Notions*, Edinburgh, 1989 (1882), p. 71; H. Slade, 'Manufacture of Cutch in Burma', *Indian Forester* 12 (June 1886), pp. 257-61; Nisbet, *Burma under British Rule*, vol. I, pp. 374-5; see also Bryant, 'Forest Problems in Colonial Burma', pp. 132-4.

[59] J. McClelland, 'Report on the Sitang and other Teak Forests of Pegu', *Selections from the Records of the Government of India (Foreign Department)* 9 (1855), pp. 141-2; Owens, *Pakokku District Gazetteer*, p. 54; D. Brandis, 'Memorandum on the Working Plan of the Forests for 1865, 1866 and 1867', *India Forest Proceedings* (henceforth *IFP*), (March 1865), p. 96. In 1871-2 alone, cutch exports from Burma were valued at £2 million, A.O. Hume, Secretary, Government of India, to Chief Commissioner, 14 September 1872, *IFP* (September 1872), p. 591.

[60] Baden-Powell, *Forest System*, app. A; *RFA*, 1874-5, p. 6. This became the standard

at least 750,000 trees were cut down in the Irrawaddy valley, and by decade's end, large cutch-yielding trees had all but disappeared from the Tharrawaddy, Prome, and Thayetmyo Districts outside of reserves.[61] Following passage of the Burma Forest Act (1881), additional measures such as the appointment of a *myo-ok* to supervise cutch manufacture, and legal provision for the creation of village cutch reserves, were introduced.[62] However, these measures failed to slow cutch deforestation in the 1880s.

Part of the problem related to the complex bureaucratic politics associated with the management of this distinctive trade. The cutch trade was located in relatively populated areas, and on lands that were used for agrarian purposes by shifting cultivators and peasants. Seasonal variations further complicated these land-use patterns – cutch boiling was a regular livelihood of the poor in Prome and Thayetmyo Districts, but when the rains failed their numbers were greatly increased by others desperate to eke out a subsistence.[63] For these reasons, cutch regulation was as much a civil matter as a forest concern. Yet the cooperation between civil and forest officials that was essential to the process was tempered by programmatic differences, notably maintenance of social order on the one hand and preservation of *sha* forest on the other.

Yet persistent cutch deforestation also reflected the strong resistance of cutch traders and workers to any restrictions placed on their trade. Following the annexation of Upper Burma in 1886, conflict spread as peasants and even shifting cultivators became implicated in the issue. Conflict between the latter and the colonial state was a by-product of the tougher rules introduced after 1889. In particular, strict enforcement of rules concerning felling of *sha* confronted shifting cultivators with a new challenge to their way of life. As hard-pressed cultivators openly defied the law, the number of prosecutions soared: out of a total of 1,838 forest offences in 1893-4, no less than 1,451 were in Thayetmyo and Prome Divisions, and many of which were related to illegal felling of *sha* in *taungya*.[64] One *thu-gyi* defiantly commented

method of taxation. Earthen pots or iron pans were used to boil the chipped heartwood of the *sha* tree.

[61] D. Brandis, 'Suggestions regarding Forest Administration in British Burma 1881', *IFP* (February 1881), p. 249.

[62] *RFA*, (Pegu), 1882-3, p. 25; *Burma Forest Act 1881*, nos 31-34; *RFA*, 1884-5, app. O; *BFP* (November 1888), pp. 1-10.

[63] Government of Burma, *Thayetmyo District Gazetteer*, Rangoon, 1911, pp. 45-6; A.H.M. Barrington, *Working Plan for Allanmyo Forest Division, 1927-28 to 1936-37*, Rangoon, 1928, p. 28.

[64] Resolution, *RFA*, 1893-94, p. 2.

that 'the people do not wish to preserve any cutch trees at all.'[65] Not surprisingly, officials reported that village cutch forests had failed as cultivators took 'no interest' in them.[66] Faced with such pervasive opposition, a conference of civil and forest officials held in Prome in March 1896 agreed that the Forest Department would reserve the best remaining cutch tracts, village reserves could be cancelled, and remaining areas would be abandoned to shifting cultivators.[67]

Yet the main conflict was between cutch traders and workers and the colonial state. As the price of cutch climbed, and supplies dwindled, cutch traders and workers ignored the rules and theft of trees was common. Of 135 breaches of the forest law in Pegu in 1886-7, 71 involved cutch, and when such offences later declined, scarcity rather than obedience to the law was the cause.[68] Scarcity was also reflected in the adulteration of cutch, as the bark of inferior species such as *than* (*Terminalia oliveri*) was used; when the government attempted to eliminate this practice by reserving *than*, the cutch industry simply shifted to new species.[69]

The government's difficulties over the cutch issue were compounded by a novel challenge to cutch regulation by peasants (acting often in conjunction with cutch traders) in Upper Burma in the 1890s. Following the depletion of *sha* supplies on private lands, peasants claimed adjoining tracts as *bobabaing* (ancestral) lands under precolonial law, and proceeded to employ workers to boil cutch.[70] Caught offguard by this unexpected challenge, colonial officials debated the legal merits of these claims. While forest officials denounced *bobabaing* claims as a cover for illicit cutch-boiling, some civil officials were sympathetic to the Burmese case in view of what they perceived to be heavy-handed treatment of suspects by forest officials.[71] Cutch traders, many of whom were from Lower Burma where forests were now largely depleted,

---

[65] Statement of Maung Shwe Ni, Chinle village, 23 November 1893, cited in C.H. Hampden and J.L. Long, 'Special Cutch Enquiry, Shwele Township, Prome District', *BFP* (August 1894), p. 11.

[66] Minutes of Proceedings of Cutch Conference, Prome, 24 March 1896, *BFP* (July 1896), p. 13.

[67] Resolution, 15 July 1896, *BFP* (July 1896), p. 16.

[68] G.Q. Corbett, *Working Plan for Taungnyo Forests*, Simla, 1891, p. 9; H. Carter, *Working Plan for Shwele Forests*, Calcutta, 1893, p. 7; *RFA* (Pegu), 1886-7, pp. 4-5; *RFA* (Pegu), 1889-90, p. 4.

[69] *RFA* (Pegu), 1888-9, p. 17; *RFA* (Pegu), 1889-90, p. 18.

[70] *RFA* (Eastern), 1892-3, p. 7.

[71] *RFA* (Western), 1893-4, p. 9; *RFA* (Eastern), 1893-4, p. 9; *RFA*, 1893-4, p. lxx.

took advantage of these divisions within the colonial state to expand their activities in Upper Burma.[72]

A ruling by Chief Commissioner Frederick Fryer in 1894 that claims would be adjudicated individually in the course of land settlements failed to halt deforestation of the country's *sha* forests. Indeed, civil officials subsequently encouraged such destruction during times of drought when they issued free licenses to cultivators.[73] Changing market conditions, not government regulation, ultimately saved *sha* from total elimination. As prices increased, cheaper substitutes such as mangrove extracts and aniline dyes gradually displaced cutch.[74]

The fate of cutch management was a humbling reminder to colonial officials of the limits of state forest control. The attempt to regulate the bamboo trade further illustrates the difficulties encountered by forest officials in the regulation of non-teak forest use. As Chapter 3 noted, bamboo served a wide variety of domestic and commercial purposes, and for peasants and shifting cultivators alike it was a 'chief necessity of life'.[75] Yet bamboo figured only peripherally in colonial forestry accounts.

The 'light' colonial regulation of bamboo use contrasts with the economic importance of the bamboo trade in the domestic forest economy. That trade was taxed in precolonial times, and the commercial value of bamboo was such that bamboo plantations were even created to supply a prosperous trade along the Irrawaddy river.[76] Under British rule the trade continued to expand. As with other types of forest products, bamboo became relatively scarce on the plains of Lower Burma in the latter half of the nineteenth century as forests were converted into paddy fields with the result that bamboo use became progressively commercialized in populated areas.[77] Traders sought out

---

[72] *RFA*, 1892-3, p. lxxi.

[73] Wilkie, *Yamethin District Gazetteer*, pp. 84-5; Pe Kin, 'Thayetmyo Forest Division', *Guardian* (Rangoon) 16 (February 1969), p. 48; P. Burnside and C.H. Thompson, *Working Plan for Thayetmyo Forest Division, 1931-32 to 1940-41*, Rangoon, 1933, vol. I, p. 17.

[74] Rodger, *Handbook of Forest Products*, pp. 66-7.

[75] A.J. Butterwick, 'The Bamboo Forests of the Pegu Forest Division and the Method of Extraction', *Indian Forester* 39 (April 1913), pp. 176-7; see also S. Kurz, 'Bamboo and its Use', *Indian Forester* 1 (January 1876), pp. 219-69.

[76] Frank N. Trager and William J. Koenig, *Burmese Sit-tans 1764-1826: Records of Rural Life and Administration*, Tucson, 1979, pp. 160, 169-70, 326, 354, 363. However, bamboo was not taxed in other districts, *ibid.*, pp. 167, 186, On precolonial bamboo plantations, see Anon., 'Memo [sic] on the Conservative Treatment of Forest of Bambusa Brandisii', *Indian Forester* 2 (January 1877), pp. 311-12.

[77] *RFA*, 1868-9, p. 2; B. Ribbentrop, 'Special Report on the Working of the Revenue Notifications nos. 33 and 34 of 8 March 1876', in *RFA*, 1876-7, p. 16; J.W. Oliver, *Working Plan of the Thonze Reserve*, Rangoon, 1885, p. 10.

the more valuable *Kyathaung* and *Tinwa* bamboo in the Pegu Yoma
which were cut and then rafted by river for sale in the country's
burgeoning towns and cities. It was estimated that annual bamboo
consumption in Rangoon alone in the mid-1870s amounted to 5,300,000
bamboos in a trade worth 150,000 rupees; by the turn of the century,
forest officials reported that nearly 12 million bamboos were being
traded in the country's second biggest city Mandalay.[78] Just as teak
was the mainstay of the colonial forest industry in Burma, so too
bamboo was a cornerstone of the indigenous forest economy.

The importance of the bamboo trade did not escape the attention
of colonial officials, and calls for its regulation began to be made
in the 1870s.[79] Beginning in the 1870s rules were drawn up under
both the Land and Revenue Act (1876) and the Burma Forest Act
(1881) that regulated bamboo use. However, these rules were applied
only sporadically and unevenly in the country, and revenue derived
from taxing commercial exploitation was negligible. Although government persisted in taxing traders in the early twentieth century, revenue
from the bamboo trade never realized even remotely that obtained
from commercial timber and cutch.[80]

The Forest Department never accorded a high priority to bamboo
management during the colonial era – hence its classification as a
'minor' forest product. To begin with, the sheer scale of the trade
dwarfed the ability of forest officials to regulate it effectively. Not
only was it a high-volume trade, but sources of supply were diverse
and scattered over the country, rendering supervision difficult. In
a context in which forest officials were primarily concerned with
regulating the teak trade, moreover, the management of such a large
and amorphous trade was not especially desirable. Further, although
bamboo supplies became scarce in populated areas, there was still
plenty of bamboo in more remote areas so that bamboo was never
in short supply nationally as was the case with cutch. Thus, unlike
the latter, conservation was never a burning issue with regard to
bamboo.

In addition, the centrality of bamboo in the domestic forest economy,
and in particular the reliance of poor people on bamboo, resulted
in civil officials taking an active interest in bamboo management.
During the 1880s, there was a 'confusion of authorities' as both
civil and forest officials regulated the bamboo trade. Under new
rules issued in October 1892, forest officials acquired new powers

---

[78] *RFA*, 1874-5, p. 25; *RFA*, 1903-4, p. 60.

[79] Baden-Powell, *Forest System*, p. 15; *RFA*, 1874-5, p. 25.

[80] Butterwick, 'Bamboo Forests', p. 178.

to manage bamboo (and other minor forest products) but this led some 'over-zealous forest officials . . . to levy taxes very extensively.'[81] Civil officials noted the hardship and resentment caused by such taxes, and argued that 'they hardly pay for the cost of collection and cause a great deal of friction and discontent.'[82] Accordingly, the Chief Commissioner curtailed taxation of bamboo and other minor forest products in June 1895. However, as Chapter 5 shows, the Forest Department continued to regulate non-teak forest use selectively, and such regulation was the basis of ongoing disputes between forest and civil officials in the early twentieth century.

Finally, the Forest Department's limited interest in bamboo management may have also reflected its inability to generate interest among European capitalists in the large-scale commercial exploitation of bamboo. Unlike cutch, bamboo was not the subject of an export trade; forest officials sought to alter this situation by encouraging the development of a pulp and paper industry based on the use of bamboo as a raw material. The government granted generous concessions to the manufacturer Thomas Routledge in 1882, and to Rangoon-based A. Scott and Company in 1884, but neither concession was ever acted upon. An inquiry by industry expert R. Sindall in 1906 nevertheless encouraged government in the belief that such an industry was feasible economically, but a renewed offer of concessions was not taken up by the private sector.[83]

For all of these reasons, bamboo was never as much a focus of attention for the Forest Department as was cutch in the late nineteenth century. Conversely, rules scarcely affected the development of the large bamboo trade, and revenue from this trade was well below that obtainable if rules were enforced systematically. Yet, the history of bamboo management highlights in its own way the limits of state efforts to rationalize forest use in Burma.

Discussion of the vicissitudes of cutch and bamboo management shows that state forest control was not always successful. Yet the ability of the Forest Department to regulate diverse forest activities was greater at the turn of the century than it was in 1882. A vast new forest estate was acquired in Upper Burma and the Shan States through a process of external territorialization. An increasing proportion

---

[81] Resolution, Chief Commissioner, 10 June 1895, *BFP* (June 1895), p. 55; see also Secretary, Chief Commissioner, to Secretary, Government of India (RAD), 9 November 1891, *BFP* (November 1891), p. 43.

[82] *RFA*, 1896-7, p. liv; *RFA*, 1893-4, p. lxxiii.

[83] R.W. Sindall, *Report on the Manufacture of Paper and Paper Pulp in Burma*, Rangoon, 1906; *RFA*, 1880-1, p. 12; F.T. Morehead, *The Forests of Burma*, London, 1944, pp. 62-3.

of Burma's commercial forests was thereafter enclosed in reserves. Such internal territorialization continued in the early twentieth century, and in 1911 reserves covered 26,077 square miles or 15 per cent of a total administered land area of 170,000 square miles.[84] This transition from unreserved to reserved status is central to subsequent developments in Burmese forest politics. Forest officials continued to regulate selectively practices outside of reserves, but during the early twentieth century their attention turned increasingly to the consolidation of control inside reserves.

[84] Shein, *Burma's Transport and Foreign Trade, 1885-1914*, Rangoon, 1964, p. 12.

5

THE ERA OF CONSOLIDATION, 1902-1922

While the Burma Forest Act of 1881 facilitated expanding state forest control, passage of the Burma Forest Act of 1902 was designed to consolidate such control. No great debates marked the latter's enactment as was the case with the earlier act. Yet, if the 1902 Act indicated business as usual in Burma's forests, this should not obscure its symbolical and practical importance. Forest management under this act became an ever more rigorous attempt to promote long-term commercial timber production in reserves according to scientific principles. The next chapter shows how the Forest Department's ability to fulfil that task was affected by Burmese nationalism after 1923. Here the objective is to explore ongoing rationalization of forest use in the early twentieth century.

The era of consolidation (1902-22) was relatively uneventful when compared with what came before or after. The reserved area expanded less dramatically than in the late nineteenth century, while the politics associated with Burmese nationalism had yet to have an impact on forest management. Nevertheless, three important changes took place at this time that were to shape subsequent forest politics in the country. First, teak extraction increasingly devolved upon the Bombay Burmah Trading Corporation Limited (BBTCL) and other European firms subject to supervision by the Forest Department. Second, forest officials produced elaborate working plans for long-term commercial timber production as they simultaneously paid increasing attention to broader ecological issues. Finally, the closing of the agricultural frontier in Lower Burma enhanced the pressure on residual forests, exacerbating conflict over access.

Timber Extraction by European Firms

The most dramatic change of the period concerned the European timber firms. From the turn of the century, five companies came to dominant the teak trade at the expense of Burmese timber traders and the Forest Department. Following the lead of the BBTCL, Steel

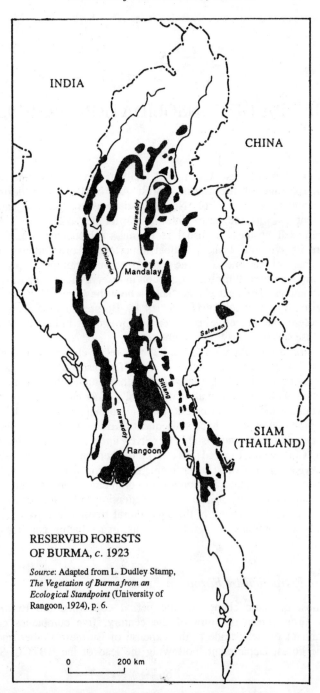

INDIA

CHINA

Irrawaddy

Chindwin

Mandalay

Salween

Sittang

Irrawaddy

SIAM
(THAILAND)

Rangoon

RESERVED FORESTS
OF BURMA, *c.* 1923

Source: Adapted from L. Dudley Stamp,
*The Vegetation of Burma from an
Ecological Standpoint* (University of
Rangoon, 1924), p. 6.

0   200 km

Brothers, Macgregor and Company, Foucar and Company, and T.D. Findlay and Sons acquired long-term leases encompassing Burma's key teak forests. Chapter 6 examines Burmese criticism of this arrangement, but here the goal is to describe the reasons for this change and the implications for the Forest Department.

The image that tends to be given in the literature about these firms is that their rise was both inevitable and 'natural'.[1] Nothing however, could be further from the truth. Rather, the rise of the European timber firms was the occasion for intense political debate within the colonial state, and reflected the growing political power and influence of these firms in government.

Many forest officials in the late nineteenth century viewed with alarm the prospect of a general return to teak extraction by private enterprise. Indeed, it was almost an article of faith in the Forest Department by then that such extraction was incompatible with scientific forestry. Forest officials could point to a lamentable record of over-harvesting by private firms in both Lower and Upper Burma prior to 1885. The 'green teak' scandal of 1898, in which BBTCL employees were caught illegally felling green teak in the Pyinmana forests, was seen as further evidence of the 'duplicity' of private enterprise.[2]

Instead, forest officials promoted the government contract system first introduced by Brandis in 1856. After the demise of the permit system in the mid-1870s, the government contract system was the basis for teak extraction in Lower Burma.[3] Although this system depended on small-scale Burmese contractors who required cash advances from the Forest Department to buy elephants and hire labourers, Burma's Conservators were satisfied with the arrangement, believing that it induced local inhabitants 'to take an interest in forest matters', and fostered an allegiance to the Forest Department.[4] Conservator

---

[1] A.C. Pointon, *The Bombay Trading Corporation Ltd., 1863-1963*, Southampton, 1964; H.E.W. Braund, *Calling to Mind: Being Some Account of the Hundred Years (1870 to 1970) of Steel Brothers and Company Ltd.*, Oxford, 1975; J.H. Williams, *Elephant Bill* London, 1950; A.A. Lawson, *Life in the Burmese Jungle*, Sussex, 1983; Hugh Nisbet, *Experiences of a Jungle-Wallah*, St Albans, 1936.

[2] The Corporation's lease in that area was cancelled and a 120,000 rupee fine was imposed, J. Nisbet Conservator, Eastern, to Revenue Secretary, 23 February 1898, *Burma Forest Proceedings* (henceforth *BFP*), (April 1899), pp. 87-90.

[3] Except in the Toungoo forests where, as noted, Macgregor and Company had been awarded a lease in 1889 as part of an attempt to counterbalance the preponderance of the BBTCL in Upper Burma. See J. Nisbet, 'The Development and Trade of Burma', *Imperial and Asiatic Quarterly Review* 25 (1908), p. 90; *Progress Report of Forest Administration in Burma (henceforth RFA)*, Pegu, 1889-90, p. 11.

[4] E.P. Popert, Conservator, Pegu, to Assistant Secretary, 6 January 1888, *BFP* (March 1888), p. 14; P.J. Carter, 'Note on the Extraction of Timber by Government Agency in

John Nisbet even predicted in 1896 that the system would be extended to Upper Burma as outstanding leases there expired.[5]

In the event, that prediction was mere wishful thinking. If it appeared in 1898 that the BBTCL might have to shift its 'centre of gravity to Siam' as a result of the green teak scandal, skilful lobbying by R.H. Macauley and C.B. Lacey (two of the BBTCL's senior managers) of senior members of the government of India succeeded in defusing the crisis, and the BBTCL was permitted to continue extracting teak in Upper Burma.[6] Indeed, the government of India went further in 1899 when it explicitly confirmed private extraction under the lease (or purchase contract) system, and offered leases to the smaller European firms as part of an ongoing campaign to prevent a BBTCL monopoly.[7] This decision did not sit well with many members of the Forest Department. Indeed, Burma's Revenue Secretary felt obliged to remind Upper Burma's Conservators in March 1899 that 'the general question of departmental extraction *versus* extraction by private firms has been settled and further remarks on it are not required.'[8]

Yet worse news was still to come for proponents of the government contract system. With the exception of the Toungoo forests, the 1899 decision did not apply in Lower Burma. However, Lower Burma's forests were opened to private enterprise in 1907 as part of a major reorganization of teak extraction. The Forest Department retained control over extraction in forests drained by the Myitmaka river, but all other forests – some worked by government for more than thirty years – were made over to European firms on fifteen-year leases (with a fifteen-year renewal).[9] European firms were responsible thereafter for a growing percentage of the total amount of teak extracted (Table 5.1).

Burma', *Indian Forester* 21 (May 1895), pp. 183-95.

[5] *RFA* (Eastern), 1896-7, p. 30.

[6] Ernest Andrews quoted in Pointon, *Bombay Burmah*, p. 41; *Annual Report of the Bombay Burmah Trading Corporation Limited* (henceforth *ARBBTCL*), 1897-8, p. 5.

[7] T.W. Holderness, Secretary, Government of India, Department of Revenue and Agriculture (DRA), to Revenue Secretary, Burma, 21 February 1899, *BFP* (June 1900), pp. 12-13; J. Wilson, Secretary, Government of India (DRA), to Revenue Secretary, Burma, 5 October 1906, *BFP* (October 1907), p. 49. Leases were for seven to ten years and all were accepted, Resolution, *RFA*, 1899-1900, p. 1; *RFA* (Northern), 1899-1900, p. 5.

[8] Revenue Secretary to Conservators, Eastern and Western Circles, 6 March 1899, *BFP* (June 1900), p. 14.

[9] 'Policy of government to be pursued in the Allotment of Forests in Burma to Timber Firms', 14 September 1907, *BFP* (October 1907), pp. 62-8.

Table 5.1. TEAK OUT-TURN BY AGENCY, 1900-1924

	Govt.	BBTCL	Other European	Non-European	Total
1900-4	69,077	65,081	24,621	46,847	205,626
1904-9	69,721	80,918	60,608	26,228	237,475
1909-14	47,636	110,575	106,457	19,052	283,720
1914-19	75,286	119,441	133,589	16,852	345,168
1919-24	108,490	172,847	208,950	23,119	513,406

Source: H.R. Blanford, 'Distribution of Teak Forests'. Note prepared for the Government of Burma, [1936], MSS Eur. D. 689. Average annual outturn in tons.

Although teak production rose steadily during this period, output increased most rapidly during and after the First World War. This increase was accompanied by a re-allocation of production among extraction agencies. The principle losers were the non-European or Burmese timber traders whose outturn fell from 23 per cent of total production in 1904-9, to under 5 per cent in 1919-24. Their outturn also fell in real terms: from an annual average of 46,847 tons in 1900-4, to only 16,852 tons per annum during 1914-19. This drop partly reflected wartime economic conditions – Burmese traders were often unable to borrow capital needed to meet license pre – payments due to a general credit squeeze. However, a very modest postwar increase in outturn indicated a broader trend.[10] Excluded from key teak tracts, Burmese firms were allocated residual forests under short-term contracts. As chapter 6 shows, different treatment of Burmese and European firms by the colonial state was the focus of sustained conflict after 1923.

Department extraction also became less prominent in the early twentieth century than it was in the late nineteenth century. Although it increased by volume during 1900-24 (the dip of 1909-14 notwithstanding), Department extraction as a percentage of total extraction fell from one-third at the beginning of the period to one-fifth at the end. By 1927-8 such extraction was only 11 per cent of the total, and outturn at 50,344 tons was less than half of the 1919-24 level. This shrinkage in output affected the Burmese contractors who had long worked for the Forest Department. Many became employees of the European firms: 'the native Government contractors lost their elephants and gradually became their servants.'[11]

[10] Burma Forest Department, *Review of Forest Administration in Burma during the five years 1909-10 to 1913-14*, Rangoon, 1916, p. 17; *RFA*, 1915-16, p. 20; H.C. Walker, 'The Issue of Timber Licenses in Burma', *Indian Forester* 43 (February 1917), pp. 70-5.

[11] Kyaw, 'An Old Forester Looks Back', *Burmese Forester* 6 (June 1956), p. 24; *RFA*,

Under the new system, the relative importance of the BBTCL in relation to the other European firms was reduced. Thus although the BBTCL's outturn virtually trebled between 1900 and 1924, extraction by other European lessees increased nearly three times as fast. The BBTCL share of total extraction by European firms fell during the same period from 73 per cent to less than 45 per cent. The colonial state was thus able to prevent a BBTCL monopoly through the judicious allocation of leases.

The new extraction policy was motivated by various concerns. As a result of previous overharvesting, quality teak was becoming scarce in Burma, and there were fears that high prices and diminished supplies would favour Siamese teak or the substitution of other woods on the international market.[12] These conditions favoured extraction by European firms since only they were in a position to conduct the capital-intensive extraction that was now required to open up remote teak tracts. By the early twentieth century, the depletion of accessible forests had altered the economics of teak extraction – large European firms which could muster hundreds, if not thousands of elephants and workers were favoured over small Burmese contractors unable to accumulate significant amounts of capital.

Teak extraction by the European firms also simplified forest management for government. Under the contract system, forest officials supervised a myriad of Burmese contractors, many of whom lived a hand-to-mouth existence on government advances. Chapter 3 noted that administration associated with this system led some officials to support private extraction in the 1860s. As forest management became more complex in the early twentieth century, forest officials once again saw advantages in private extraction.[13] With only five European firms on long leases rather than hundreds of Burmese contractors on annual licenses to supervise, the Forest Department could devote more time to forest conservancy without losing overall control of teak extraction. The revenue lost under the new system due to a lower rate of return on extracted teak would be partially offset by reduced management costs.[14] Revenue would also become more

1900-1, p. 28.

[12] Scarcity was reflected in a decline in the percentage of squaring logs in favour of less valuable planks and undersized (*yathit*) logs, Ernest Andrews, *The Bombay Burmah Trading Corporation Limited in Burmah, Siam and Java*, vol. I: *Teak: The Cutting and Marketing*, n.p., 1930-1, p. 44; T.A. Hauxwell, 'The Teak Timber Trade of Burma' *Indian Forester* 31 (November 1905), p 618; Shein, *Burma's Transport and Foreign Trade, 1885-1914*, Rangoon, 1964, pp. 161-2.

[13] Hauxell, 'Teak Timber Trade', pp. 629, 631-2; *RFA*, 1905-6, p. 8.

[14] W. J. Keith, *Burma Legislative Council Proceedings*, 5 April 1915, p. 396.

stable as annual extraction became less dependent on the vicissitudes of contractor finances.

Lobbying by the European firms also influenced government decision-making on teak extraction. The BBTCL was particularly important in this regard, and the prospect that it might shift production to Siam worried some officials. Not only would such a move benefit Burma's chief competitor, but it would also disrupt timber extraction in Upper Burma since the Forest Department had neither the staff nor the elephants to take over from the European firms.[15]

However, the European firms did not need to threaten a capital strike. After the turn of the century, senior officials in Burma, India and England were in agreement that extraction by these firms needed increasing at the expense of Department extraction. Echoing remarks made by the BBTCL's founder William Wallace forty years earlier, Indian Revenue and Agriculture Secretary J. Wilson summarized the new official mood in 1906:

> It is of great importance that the energies of the limited Forest Staff should be devoted mainly to the improvement of the forests under their charge, and that they should be relieved of operations which can be as efficiently conducted by private enterprise.[16]

Senior forest officials concurred with this view, and some even urged government to 'gradually abandon' Department extraction for the purchase contract system.[17] This about-turn reflected a growing recognition among forest officials that extraction work was hindering their ability to perform other tasks. It also was linked to a change of personnel. While no Conservator serving in 1906 had been in that post prior to 1900, senior conservators like E.P. Popert and John Nisbet whose views on private enterprise had been shaped by the overharvesting of the past, had left Burma.

The new official mood was cemented by a network of social affiliations between colonial officials and employees of the European firms that was already in evidence in the nineteenth century, but

---

[15] The BBTCL became involved in the Siamese teak industry in the late nineteenth century, *ARBBTCL*, 1883-84, p. 5; *ARBBTCL*, 1893-94, p. 4; Banasopit Mekvichai, 'The Teak Industry in North Thailand; The Role of a Natural-Resource-Based Export Economy in Regional Development', unpubl. Ph.D. thesis, Cornell University, 1988, pp. 110, 204; Ian Brown, *The Elite and the Economy in Siam, c. 1890-1920*, Singapore, 1988, pp. 111-12.

[16] J. Wilson to Revenue Secretary, Burma, 5 October 1906, *BFP* (October 1907), p. 49.

[17] As reported by Chief Conservator F. Beadon Bryant in 1906, and cited in Blanford, 'Distribution of Teak Forests', p. 3.

which only received its fullest expression in the twentieth century. That network operated at various levels: company directors met with Whitehall officials in London, local managers maintained links with senior administrators in Rangoon and Delhi, and assistants socialized with civil and forest officers in the district headquarter's Club. These affiliations served, among other things, to ensure that corporate interests were represented at key decision-making points in the imperial hierarchy. As the following statement by a Burmese forester makes plain, they were typically very effective in this regard too:

> The Forest Officers almost all of them, being Europeans, were very friendly with the managers and assistants of those European firms. Consequently, hardly any native forest officer could dare to write a report against the firms even when they infringed certain clauses of the lease; also it was difficult to give straight-forward and bold explanations to the [Divisional Forest Officer] if he received reports from the European lessees against his native officers.[18]

Burmese firms in contrast enjoyed little influence with government. These firms were run by small capitalists who may have been influential in their local communities, but who possessed negligible influence with senior officials in Rangoon, Delhi and London in charge of allocating the teak leases. This lack of influence was to prove fatal for many Burmese companies as European firms acquired the most profitable teak leases. The Burmese teak-trading community was effectively 'decapitated' in the early twentieth century.[19]

The new policy on teak extraction thus favoured the European firms. Yet the Forest Department did not give up completely its own extraction operations, and in the Myitmaka Extraction Forest Division, Timber Assistants supervised Burmese contractors as before.[20] Such extraction was a means to guarantee the British Admiralty a regular supply of quality timber. It also served to sustain small independent timber mills in Rangoon which, in turn, enabled the Department to avoid dependency on mills owned by the European firms.[21] Further, it enabled government to obtain accurate information as to

[18] Kyaw, 'An Old Forester Looks back', p. 24.

[19] Aung Tun Thet, *Burmese Entrepreneurship: Creative Response in the Colonial Economy*, Stuttgart, 1989, pp. 64, 80-3.

[20] *RFA* 1920-1, p. 49; Htao Hai, 'Commercial vs. Quasi-Commercial Departmental Teak Extraction in Burma', *Indian Forester* 43 (March 1917), pp. 111-16; H.W. A. Watson, *Note on Departmental Extraction of Teak in Prome, Zigon and Tharrawaddy Divisions, Pegu Circle, Lower Burma*, Rangoon, 1917.

[21] *RFA*, 1909-10, p. 14; *RFA* 1912-13, p. 26; Maria Serena I. Diokno, 'British Firms and the Economy of Burma, with Special Reference to the Rice and Teak Industries, 1917-1937', unpubl. Ph.D. thesis, University of London, 1983, chap. 6.

extraction costs and teak prices which was used in lease negotiations. Finally, Department extraction gave the government some leverage over the local teak market, and was the principal means by which it could prevent price fixing among the lessees.[22]

Forest officials were able to devote more time to forest conservancy in the measure that Department extraction was restricted. They used working plans and other measures to regulate forest access and use in ever greater detail.

Ecology and the Politics of Scientific Forestry

The main priority of the Forest Department after 1902 remained the long-term commercial development of Burma's teak forests. Working plans were compiled and reforestation work undertaken to this end. Forest officials also sought to rationalize forest use more generally. Scientific forestry was thus associated with forest protection on ecological grounds as well as the promotion of non-teak timber production. By the early 1920s, Burma's forests were managed much more intensively than had been the case in the late nineteenth century. This process had important implications for all forest users but perhaps none more so than shifting cultivators.

Working plans epitomized the more intensive style of forest management of the early twentieth century. The working plan was originally nothing more than a rough survey to facilitate immediate teak extraction. However, a more elaborate system was required as forest management became more complex, and in 1885 Deputy Conservator J.W. Oliver prepared the first modern working plan in Thonze reserve (Tharrawaddy Division). This plan sub-divided the reserve into blocks and compartments which were to be harvested on a rotational basis. As with other plans of the era, it was solely concerned with teak: 'ordinary jungle woods' were to be sold 'without restraint at nominal rates, as their removal would make room for teak.'[23] Indeed, to increase the proportion of teak in the forest, the cutting of climbers and the removal of other species ('improvement' fellings) were prescribed. Oliver's plan signalled the formal adoption of a 'teak selection' system in Burma.

The area under working plans expanded slowly at first as priority

---

[22] *RFA*, 1909-10, p. 14; Resolution, *RFA*, 1910-11. p. 2.

[23] J.W. Oliver, *Working Plan of the Thonze Reserve, Tharrawaddy Division, Pegu Circle, British Burma*, Rangoon, 1885, p. 18; see also H.R. Blanford, 'Forest Management and Preparation of Working Plans in Burma', *Empire Forestry* 4, 1 (1925), pp. 57-8.

was given to reservation. The need for working plans became more urgent as the government allocated teak leases to the European firms, and beginning in 1902, the government of Burma ordered the accelerated creation of working plans according to the principle that the effort expended on a plan was linked to the commercial value of its forests.[24] The start of the First World War in 1914 halted field work, but not before most of the valuable Pegu Yoma and Chindwin reserves had been covered.[25] The creation of working plans resumed in 1920 and a special branch within the Forest Department was formed to direct this work. Plans covered an increasing proportion of reserves in the 1920s (Table 5.2).

Table 5.2. WORKING PLANS AS A PERCENTAGE OF
RESERVED AREA, 1899-1930

	A. Working Plans	B. Reserved Area	A/B (%)
1899-1900	1,817	17,153	10.59
1904-5	3,388	20,411	16.60
1909-10	7,241	25,691	28.18
1914-15	8,857	28,239	31.36
1919-20	10,855	29,874	36.34
1924-5[a]	12,083	28,227	42.81
1929-30[a]	19,967	29,487	67.71

[a] Figures for the Federated Shan States excluded.

Source: *Report of Forest Administration in Burma* (various years); H.R. Blanford, 'Forest Management and Preparation of Working Plans in Burma', *Empire Forestry* 4, 1 (1925), p. 58. Selected years; amounts in square miles.

The data lump together plans of varying scope and detail, but the expansion in the area under working plans during this period was nonetheless remarkable. While the reserved area nearly doubled in size, the area covered by plans increased more than tenfold.

Yet these plans provided systematic guidelines for non-teak extraction only beginning in the 1920s. This omission reflected what Conservator F.B. Manson in 1903 suggested was 'the exaggerated importance' of teak on the export market and 'the comparative neglect, not to

[24] Resolution, RFA, 1902-3, p. 2; Blanford, 'Working Plans', pp. 58-9. An example of a minor plan prepared using the fast-track method is S.F. Hopwood, *Working Plan for the Thingadon-Yama and Patolon Working-Circles in the Lower Chindwin Forest Division, Northern Circle, Upper Burma*, Rangoon, 1915.

[25] Blanford, 'Working Plans', p. 59; H.W.A. Watson, *A Note on the Pegu Yoma Forests*, Rangoon, 1923, p. 22. Plans were later revised according to a standard procedure, Burma Forest Department, *Working Plans Manual Burma*, 3rd edn, Rangoon, 1948 (1938).

say contempt, of all other kinds.'[26] To be sure, strategically valuable woods such as *pyinkado (Xylia dolabriformis)* and *padauk (Pterocarpus macrocarpus)* were exported to India for conversion into railway sleepers and gun carriage wheels from the mid-nineteenth century. Forest Department attempts to expand this trade failed miserably.[27]

A similar fate befell government efforts to promote the export of other 'junglewoods' such as *in (Dipterocarpus tuberculatus)* wood. Used extensively in Burma for house building, the government encouraged exports of *in* by offering concessions to the European firms in 1898 (and again in 1906). Concessions included 5,000 tons of free timber in the first year, 10,000 tons at half royalty during the next five years, and a fixed royalty thereafter. The government also promoted this wood through the dissemination of information and samples. Despite these efforts, the export trade did not develop due to high freight charges and the conservatism of British timber buyers.[28]

If junglewood exports increased in the early twentieth century – from 9,923 tons per annum (1901-5) to 32,959 tons per annum (1911-15) – this trend merely reflected an attempt by traders to find substitutes for expensive teak. Moreover, teak continued to dominate Burma's timber exports; between 1911 and 1915, exports of all kinds of timber were 203,927 tons per annum but teak exports constituted 170,968 tons (84 per cent of the total).[29] During the First World War, the urgent need for timber led to the exploitation of woods hitherto never exported. Concurrently, a visiting Canadian forester, H.R. MacMillan, urged Burma's forest officials to develop the non-teak export trade, the revenue from which he believed should eventually rival that from teak.[30] Macmillan's visit prompted a Forest Department initiative designed to 'show the way' for private enterprise, and after the end of the war forest officials began to incorporate systematically

[26] F.B. Manson to Revenue Secretary, 8 June 1903, *BFP* (August 1903), p. 10; see also B.H. Baden-Powell, *Memorandum on the Supply of Teak and Other Timbers in the Burma Markets*, n.p., 1873, p. 5.

[27] R.S. Troup, *Burma Padauk*, Calcutta 1909, p. 39; *RFA*, 1874-5. pp. 23-4; *RFA*, 1879-80, p. 48. Between 1876 and 1900, the Department shipped 3,785,013 tons of *padauk* to Madras and Bombay, F.B. Manson, Conservator, Tenasserim, to Revenue Secretary, 21 September 1901, *BFP* (January 1902), p. 123.

[28] R.S. Troup, *Burmese In Wood*, Calcutta, 1909; Alexander L. Howard, 'Commercial Prospects of Burma Woods', *Asiatic Review* 19 (July 1923), pp. 396-9.

[29] Shein, *Burma's Transport and Foreign Trade*, pp. 161-2.

[30] H.R. MacMillan, 'Notes on the Prospect of Working the Hardwood Forests of Burma', *Indian Forester* 42 (October 1916), pp. 481-99; Htao Hai, 'Burma Jungle Woods and the Europe Market', *Indian Forester* 45 (June 1918), pp. 243-52.

provision of non-teak timber extraction in working plans.[31]

This interest in non-teak timber was part of a broader attempt to rationalize forest use. From 1909, for example, the Forest Department debated whether to abandon the teak selection system in favour of the uniform system – the latter combining clear felling and natural regeneration on a sequential basis.[32] The uniform system raised the prospect for the first time of comprehensive commercial forest exploitation. H.R. Blanford drew up an experimental working plan for the Mohnyin Reserve (Katha Division) in 1911, and devised a similar plan for the Tharrawaddy Division during the First World War.[33]

The elaboration of working plans and the quest to develop a non-teak timber export trade had important implications for forest users, notably shifting cultivators. Chapter 3 highlighted the ambiguous relationship between forest officials and shifting cultivators in the nineteenth century, which was both conflictual and co-operative. This relationship became more complicated in the early twentieth century as it was affected by changing scientific knowledge, extraction techniques, political and economic conditions and ecological concerns.

The fate of the *taungya* forestry system provides one indication of how changing imperial attitudes or political and economic conditions could affect shifting cultivators.[34] Chapter 3 suggested that a primary function of this system was to convert an ecological 'menace' into a silvicultural virtue. However, problems began to be encountered in maturing plantations that gradually brought into question the silvicultural merits of the scheme. Miscalculations as to the length of time required for the tending of young trees by shifting cultivators to ensure optimal teak growth resulted in poor plantation development. Further, as the area planted under this system expanded from 42,059 acres in 1896 to 98,740 acres in 1924, the ability of the Forest

[31] G.S. Hart, *Note on a tour of Inspection in the Forests of Burma*, Simla 1918, pp. 7-8; F.A. Leete, *Memorandum on Departmental Extraction v. Cooperation with Traders for the Development of Trade in Burma Hardwoods*, Rangoon, 1923; A.P. Davis, *Working Plan for Indaung Working Circle*, Rangoon, 1918; C.H. Philipp, *Working Plan for Yinke Working Circle*, Rangoon, 1921.

[32] *Proceedings of the First Burma Forest Conference held at Maymyo between the 13th and 20th June 1910*, Rangoon, 1910; H.C. Walker, 'The Uniform System in Burma', *Indian Forester* 41 (April 1915), pp. 105-11; H.R. Blanford, 'THe Uniform System in Burma', *Indian Forester* 41 (October 1915), pp. 366-71.

[33] H.R. Blanford, *The Mohnyin Working Plan, Katha Division*, Rangoon, 1911; H.R. Blanford and D. Ellis, *Working Plan for the Yoma Reserves in the Tharrawaddy Division*, Rangoon, 1918-19, vols I-III.

[34] For a fuller discussion of this scheme, see Raymond L. Bryant, 'Shifting the Cultivator: The Politics of Teak Regeneration in Colonial Burma', *Modern Asian Studies* 28 (May 1994), pp. 225-50.

Department to supervise plantation work declined. Left often to their own devices, cultivators frequently chose sites inappropriate to the aims of the scheme.[35] Serious doubts were also raised about the efficacy of a system premised on teak monoculture. Assistant Conservator H.N. Thomson, for example, warned that teak grown in 'pure patches' in *taungya* plantations 'is peculiarly liable to damage from insects, fungi and other pests, which danger is greatly reduced when it is mixed with other species'.[36] Scientific evidence that teak damage caused by the predations of an insect known as the bee-hole borer (*Xyleutes ceramica*) was much higher in plantations than in mixed forests strengthened the case against these plantations.[37]

The fortunes of *taungya* forestry were linked simultaneously to the question of extraction techniques. Thus, after a hiatus between 1906 and 1918 large-scale planting resumed after the First World War. At this time, such planting became an integral part of plans to transform Burma's forests into evenly aged timber stands under the uniform system.[38] Suddenly, as Chief Conservator Frederick Leete observed, shifting cultivators were now 'respectable'.

> The change of attitude with regard to the *taungya* cutter is remarkable. For many years Forest Officers looked upon him as an unmitigated curse. It is now recognized, however, that he can play a useful part, and that, in the *taungya* cutter Burma possesses an extremely valuable asset in the regeneration of forests.[39]

Yet this new respectability was short-lived. European firms proved reluctant to enter the non-teak timber trade and the government of Burma denied permission to the Forest Department in the early 1920s to undertake extraction operations itself. Since the uniform system was attractive partly because it was a means to facilitate the non-teak timber trade, the popularity of this technique quickly faded, and with

---

[35] Data taken from *ibid.*; table 1, p. 238. See also *RFA*, 1904-5, p. 11; J.D. Clifford, 'The Formation of Teak Taungya Plantations in Burma', *Indian Forester* 43 (March 1917), p. 121; *RFA*, 1905-6, p. 6; H.C. Walker, 'Reproduction of Teak in Bamboo Forests in Lower Burma', *Indian Forester* 30 (February 1904), p. 51.

[36] *RFA* (Tenasserim), 1895-6, p. 8.

[37] However, such evidence was contested by some foresters. See C.W. Scott, *Measurements of the Damage to Teak Timber by the Beehole Borer Moth*, Rangoon, 1932; H.G. Champion, *The Problem of the Pure Teak Plantation* Calcutta, 1932; Kyaw Sein, 'The Bee-Hole Borer of Teak', *Burmese Forester* 13 (December 1963), pp. 32-9.

[38] H.R. Blanford, 'Regeneration with the Assistance of Taungya in Burma', *Indian Forest Records* 11, 3 (1925), p. 83.

[39] *RFA* 1918-19, p. 4.

it, the favoured status of shifting cultivators.[40]

Broader political and economic considerations also affected the prospects of shifting cultivators under the *taungya* forestry system. That system was introduced in the mid-nineteenth century as part of an attempt to increase state control by winning Karen allegiance in the politically unstable, but economically important Pegu Yoma at a time of British weakness. By the early twentieth century, however, improved transport and communications links combined with a much more elaborate colonial administrative system had served to enhance imperial control; the need for Karen political support through schemes such as *taungya* forestry was accordingly much reduced.

The growing power of the colonial state was reflected in the ever more rigorous efforts of forests officials to control shifting cultivation in reserves in the early twentieth century. The Forest Department began to regulate *taungya* in Karen areas more strictly than hitherto was the case, and through a census of Karen living in the Pegu Yoma it developed an accurate picture of the extent of shifting cultivation in the region.[41] Under the Burma Village Amendment Act (1921), the Department also established forest villages for cultivators that it employed to do planting and other work. Forest officials in these villages possessed extensive powers to specify the rights and duties of cultivators.[42] In Pyinmana Division, for example, villagers were restricted to no more than six acres of land each as 'a greater grant merely means that the villager becomes too affluent or that most of his time is spent in cultivation.'[43] The prevailing mood of forest officials was thus one of paternalistic cooperation with shifting cultivators but on terms increasingly favourable to the colonial state. In the

---

[40] Both the BBTCL and Steel Brothers abandoned non-teak timber extraction after sustaining a financial loss, *ARBBTCL*, 1895-6, p. 4; *ARBBTCL*, 1900-1, p. 4; R. J. Sayres, *Working Plan for Pyinmana Forest Division, 1936-37 to 1946-47*, Rangoon, 1937, vol. II, p. 100; Braund, *Calling to Mind*, pp. 53-4.

[41] Karen areas were small plots of land set aside for the Karen's own use at the time of forest settlements. See also H.W.A. Watson, *Working Plan for Pyu-chaung and Pyu-kun Reserves*, Rangoon, 1902, p. 3; H.W.A. Watson, 'Taungya Cuting', *Indian Forester* 34 (May 1908), pp. 264-9. *Taungya* cutters in this area numbered 1,054 in 1922, down from 1,757 at the time of settlement, H.W.A. Watson, *Pegu Yoma Reserves*, app. IV.

[42] Government of Burma, *Village Manual*, Rangoon, 1940, pp. 119-25; A.P. Davis, 'Forest Villages in Burma', *Indian Forester* 49 (December 1923), pp. 641-5. Cultivators often resisted this more regimented work arrangement. See *RFA*, 1917-18, p. 31; *RFA*, 1921-2, p. 53; G.S. Shirley, 'Growing of Timber so far as Forest Villages and Taungyas are concerned (Burma)', *Third British Empire Forestry Conference Papers* (1928), pp. 612-15; A.F.R. Brown, *Working Plan for Yamethin Forest Division*, Rangoon, 1932, vol. I, pp. 30-1.

[43] F.G. Burgess and C.R. Robbins, *Working Plan for the Pyinmana Forest Division for the period 1927-28 to 1936-37*, Rangoon, 1929, vol. I, p. 121.

words of one forester, 'the taungya cutter is like a forest fire, he is a bad master, but, under control, he is the best servant the forest can have.'[44]

Other changes also affected the status of *taungya* forestry. Upon the annexation of Upper Burma in 1886, the British obtained a vast new forest estate. However, as the Forest Department extended its operations into this area limited funds and staff prevented regular planting in Upper Burma.[45] Instead, a system of natural regeneration based on improvement fellings was adopted. Under these conditions, it was almost inevitable that interest in intensive silviculture would decline (the brief interest in the uniform system notwithstanding). As Conservator John Nisbet noted, the introduction of *taungya* forestry was predicated in part on British control of the more limited teak forests of Lower Burma.[46]

Finally, the fate of *taungya*k forestry was conditioned by broader changes in the colonial economy and related state finances. Indeed, it was the onset of the Great Depression in the early 1930s that sealed the fate of this system. In a context of general and massive government retrenchment (see Chapter 6), the government of Burma in 1935 declared that *taungya* forestry was 'too speculative' an endeavour to be justifiable on economic or any other grounds, and ordered its gradual termination.[47] The demise of this system heightened the financial insecurity of cultivators who depended on emoluments from the Forest Department. For many hill Karen, *taungya* forestry had become a way of life. Yet, just as the colonial state undermined their relatively autonomous lifestyle in the 1860s, it now disrupted their new-found dependency in the late colonial period. Not for the last time, Karen who trusted the British, in the end felt betrayed.[48]

---

[44] J.W.A. Grieve, 'Note on Forest Policy in Burma', *Indian Forester* 42 (September 1916), pp. 446-7.

[45] Trials using Kachin cultivators in Bhamo Division were apparently stymied by 'the slackness and opium-smoking tendencies of the forest villagers'. See E.S. Hartnoll and F.T. Morehead, *Working Plan for the Kaukkwe Portion of the Bhama Forest Division, 1935-36 to 1947-48*, Rangoon, 1936, pp. 20, 25.

[46] J. Nisbet, 'Notes on Improvement Fellings for the Benefit of Teak in Fire-protected Reserved Forests, Burma', *Indian Forester* 25 (May 1899), pp. 202-14.

[47] *RFA*, 1939-40, p. 20; see also, *RFA*, 1934-5, p. 19; *RFA*, 1935-6, p. 20; C.W.D. Kermode, 'Natural and Artificial Regeneration of Teak in Burma', *Indian Forester* 72 (January 1946), pp. 15-21.

[48] Foresters recognized that constant policy changes were 'grossly unfair', H.W.A. Watson, 'Forestry in Lower Burma', *Indian Forester* 44 (May 1918), p. 215. Following the Second World War, the Karen felt betrayed when they were not granted independence by the British, Martin Smith, *Burma: Insurgency and the Politics of Ethnicity*, London, 1991, pp. 50-2, 72-87 *passim*, 110-12, 137-54 *passim*.

Changing imperial attitudes about ecological conservation in the late nineteenth and early twentieth century reinforced the likelihood of conflict between the colonial state and shifting cultivators. Chapters 2 and 3 noted that early imperial criticism of shifting cultivators related primarily to a concern about the protection of teak. By the turn of the century, in contrast, such criticism reflected a growing belief that shifting cultivation was also contributing to hill erosion, siltation and flooding.

There were several reasons for this change of attitude. First, as the main teak tracts were demarcated, the Forest Department reserved forest lands that were valuable for other reasons. Forests containing *sha* and other commercial species were thus sporadically demarcated.[49] However, forests were also reserved predominantly, if not exclusively for ecological reasons. The creation of ecological (as opposed to teak or *sha*) reserves was an integral part of the elaboration of state forest control in late nineteenth and early twentieth century colonial Burma.

Second, forest officials were influenced by the government of India's 1894 statement on forest policy. If Dalhousie's Minute of 1855 established the state's intention to manage commercially valuable forests (such as teak forests), the 1894 statement laid down general principles for managing British India's forests.[50] It recognized four types of forest; (1) protection forests to be maintained on climatic or physical grounds; (2) commercial forests to be managed for timber production; (3) local supply forests designed to satisfy subsistence needs; and (4) pasture lands. This statement was intended primarily to address criticism that the forest service in India was paying insufficient attention to the needs of the subcontinent's agricultural population.[51] As such, it was only partially applicable to Burma where different conditions (such as a more favourable population-to-land ratio) prevailed.[52]

The 1894 statement nevertheless prompted greater official ecological awareness. Forest officials sought to protect watersheds through reservation and new restrictions on shifting cultivators in the belief that this would safeguard plains villagers from flooding and decreased water supplies. They focused their attention at first on forests in

[49] F.C. Owens, *Pakokku District Gazetteer*, Rangoon, 1913, p. 59.

[50] Resolution, Government of India (DRA), circular no. 22F, 19 October 1894, *BFP* (December 1894), pp. 65-71.

[51] Specifically, the government was responding to a report on Indian agriculture by Dr Voelcker published in 1893, see Madhav Gadgil and Ramachandra Guha, *This Fissured Land: An Ecological History of India*, Delhi, 1992, p. 135.

[52] Revenue Secretary to Inspector General, 20 December 1894, *BFP* (December 1894), pp. 73-4.

central Burma, but later targeted more remote areas in northern Burma and the Shan States.[53] Between 1897 and 1909, over 2,000 square miles were reserved, and in the latter year, 3,700 square miles were being considered for reservation, for reasons 'at least partially climatic'.[54]

The impetus for ecological reservation came from a belief that deforestation was linked to agricultural decline and climate change. However, when the government of India inquired into this matter in 1909, it found that there was no evidence that rainfall, ground-water levels or flooding had altered appreciably in recent decades despite a substantial reduction in forest cover. Further, there was no sign that 'serious injury to cultivation or other interests' was occurring either.[55] Despite such inconclusive evidence, the governments of Burma and India confirmed watershed protection as a key objective of forest policy.[56] In a sense, this policy was more about regulating shifting cultivators then it was about watershed protection. As Chief Conservator J.H. Lace noted in 1909, 'reservation of large areas has done much to prevent the denudation of important catchment areas' but restriction of shifting cultivation remained the 'most urgent' task facing government.[57] Forest officials lumped together diverse hill peoples and practices and blamed them for erosion, flooding and landslips. Although these processes occurred naturally, this was rarely acknowledged in colonial reports.[58]

In addition to ecological reservation, the Forest Department also restricted shifting cultivation in ecologically fragile unreserved hills under the 1902 Act and Rules. Rule 19 thus prohibited cultivation in designated public forests, while other rules applied selectively to teak and (in Arakan) *pyinkado* forests.[59] These rules were a flexible

---

[53] A.M. Reuther, Conservator, Pegu, to Revenue Secretary, 21 May 1899, *BFP* (July 1899), p. 313; Review, Chief Conservator, *RFA*, 1905-6, p. 1; Alex Rodger, *Forest Reservation in Burma in the Interests of an Endangered Water-Supply*, Calcutta, 1909; Ralph Neild and J.A. Stewart, *Kyaukse District Gazetteer*, Rangoon, 1925, pp. 85-6; G.W. Dawson, *Bhamo District Gazetteer*, Rangoon, 1912, p. 46; *RFA*, 1909-10, p. 67.

[54] G.F. Arnold, Revenue Secretary, to Secretary, Government of India (DRA), 15 July 1909, *BFP* (December 1909), pp. 90, 96-9.

[55] *Ibid.*, p. 89.

[56] *Ibid.*, pp. 90-1; E.D. MacLagan, Secretary, Government of India, to Department of Revenue and Agriculture, circular no. 8F, 28 April 1911, *BFP* (June 1911), pp. 19-21.

[57] J.H. Lace to Revenue Secretary, 16 March 1909, *BFP* (December 1909), pp. 59-60.

[58] F.B. Manson, 'The Erosion of the Hills to the East of the Sittang River, Burma', *Indian Forester* 31 (April 1905), pp. 223-7; D.F.B. Manning, 'Some Aspects of the Problem of *Taungyas* in Burma', *Indian Forester* 67 (October 1941), pp 502-5; T.S. Thompson, *Soil Erosion and its Control in the Shan States, Burma*, n.p., 1944.

[59] Burma Forest Act (1902), sec, 33 (2a/b), Rules nos 17-19. The penalty for breach of

means to restrict *taungya* without having to resort to costly and time-consuming reservation. They also could be applied quickly over an extensive area. Rule 19 was used in 1909, for example, to cover 100 square miles in Arakan and 222 square miles in the Ruby Mines District.[60]

The ability of the Forest Department to enforce the new policy on ecological conservation as part of a wider quest to rationalize forest use was strengthened by Departmental expansion in the late nineteenth and early twentieth century. Thus, the forest service grew threefold between 1893 and 1923, and whereas in 1907 there were 91 officials on active service, by 1923 that total was 160 officials.

The Forest Department also became more complex as new posts were added. The most important addition was that of Chief Conservator in 1905. Prior to this date, the country's Conservators corresponded with the Inspector General on technical questions, but otherwise reported to the Lieutenant Governor through the Revenue Secretary. Since the latter was rarely familiar with forestry matters, the tendency when faced with new proposals was to act only when a majority of Conservators favoured the change.[61] In contrast, authority was concentrated after 1905 in the office of the Chief Conservator who was simultaneously head of the Forest Department and principal forestry adviser to the government of Burma.[62] Technical positions were also created. The post of Research Officer was established in 1913 followed by that of Silviculturist, Botanist and Forest Engineer after the First World War.[63] The posts of Zoologist, Forest Economist and Game Warden were added in the 1920s.

As manifested in its increased size and complexity, the Forest Department was more powerful in the early twentieth century than it had been in the nineteenth century. It could regulate timber extraction and shifting cultivation as never before. But as forest officials sought to strengthen their hold over Burma's forests in the early twentieth century, they met growing opposition from Burmese peasants. Broad societal and ecological changes limited the ability of the Department

---

these rules was 6 months, imprisonment, a 500-rupee fine, or both (Rule 98). See Government of Burma, *The Burma Forest Manual*, Rangoon, 1922.

[60] Review, Chief Conservator, *RFA*, 1909-10, p.1.

[61] Nisbet, *Burma under British Rule*, vol. I, p. 248.

[62] Great Britain, *Minutes of Evidence taken before the Royal Commission upon Decentralization in India*, London, 1908, vol. III. p. 131.

[63] H.R. Blanford, 'Highlights of One Hundred Years of Forestry in Burma', *Burmese Forester* 6 (June 1956), pp. 16-17; A.H.M. Barrington, 'Forest Development in Burma, *Empire Forestry* 4, 2 (1925), p. 256.

to protect forests in populated areas when the need for such protection was most pressing.

Forest Crime as Everyday Resistance

That inability was especially evident in the case of the plains and delta reserves.[64] In a sense, Forest Department efforts to safeguard these forests went against the grain of colonial policy since the British had long encouraged Burmese cultivators to convert forest to field. Indeed, the colonial state provided financial and legal incentives (i.e. tax holidays, legal title to land) for them to do so. It also funded transport and infrastructure projects 'to facilitate the movement of labour and export products and to make cultivation of empty lands possible.'[65] The British also recognized that selected plains forests had to be spared the axe in order to provide villagers with a ready supply of timber and fuel. This task was always difficult in a context of rapid agricultural expansion, but it became ever more so as residual forests were whittled away.

In this regard, the sheer scale of agricultural expansion under British rule needs to be emphasized. Between 1852 and 1906, the rice-growing area in Lower Burma expanded from between 700,000 and 800,000 acres to nearly 6,000,000 acres, while the delta's population climbed from about 1 million in 1852 to over 4 million in 1901.[66] Land clearance before 1880 was concentrated in Prome, Henzada and Tharrawaddy Districts, and around the expanding towns of Rangoon, Bassein and Pegu. Subsequently, it spread throughout the lower delta region, and in total at least 3 million hectares of *kanazo (Heritiera fomes)* forest alone were eliminated in this manner.[67]

Adas suggests that this ecological transformation was viewed with equanimity by peasant and official alike.

> Colonial administrators, Indian migrants, and Burmese peasants all became so caught up in the rewarding process of clearing, cropping,

---

[64] No distinction is made here between plains and delta reserves. For a brief description, see J.B. Carrapiett, 'Plains Forests', *Burmese Forester* 2 (March 1952), pp. 15-18; Pe Kin, 'From the Hills to the Delta', *Guardian* (Rangoon) 15 (October 1968), pp. 39-44, and 15 (November 1968), pp. 12-16.

[65] Michael Adas, *The Burma Delta: Economic Development and Social Change on an Asian Rice Frontier, 1852-1941*, Madison, 1974, p. 35.

[66] *Ibid.*, p. 58.

[67] Michael Adas, 'Colonization, Commercial Agriculture, and the Destruction of the Deltaic Rainforests of British Burma in the Late Nineteenth Century', in Richard P. Tucker and J.F. Richards (eds), *Global Deforestation and the Nineteenth-Century World Economy*, Durham, NC, 1983, p. 106.

marketing, milling, and exporting rice that no one gave a though to the destruction of the great rainforests that was a central consequence of the delta's development to participants at all levels the forest was seen only as an obstacle. To British officials it was a striking symbol of precolonial back-wardness, ignorance, and neglect. Its transformation into rice paddies was repeatedly cited buy colonial administrators as clear proof of the superiority of European over indigenous rule.[68]

Benefits derived from agriculture undoubtedly obscured the ecological effects of deforestation. Yet some British officials were concerned about the social implications of this change, and beginning in the late 1890s, government created plains reserves intended for the agricultural population's benefit.[69] Forest and civil officials disputed the size and management of these reserves, while Burmese peasants and timber traders subverted their purpose through illegal extraction. There was no consensus of opinion about deltaic deforestation. Indeed, it was because the issue was in dispute that forest politics in late colonial Burma was so closely associated with the status of plains reserves. The next chapter examines this question in greater detail. Here is described the erratic creation of plains reserves, and the everyday resistance that frustrated their management.

The distinction between 'plains' and 'hill' reserves only became meaningful with the great land clearances of the late nineteenth and early twentieth century. In the 1870s and 1880s, forest officials created reserves in the Irrawaddy and Sittang valleys to protect teak and *sha*, as well as as to provide fuel for rail and river transport.[70] At first indistinguishable from the surrounding forest, these reserves were gradually transformed into isolated patches of forest as peasants converted unreserved forests into paddy fields. Located 10 miles east of Zigon, the case of the Myodwin teak plantation is illustrative. As described by Brandis in 1860, the village where this plantation was located was 'surrounded' by forest, but by 1915 the Myodwin plantation was 'entirely surrounded by paddy fields and temporary cultivation'.[71]

---

[68] *Ibid.*, 104-5.

[69] Resolution, *RFA*, 1896-7, p. 2; *RFA* (Pegu), 1899-1900, p. 3; *RFA*, 1902-3, p. 23; Pe Kin, 'From the Hills to the Delta', p. 41; J.S. Furnivall and W.S. Morrison, *Syriam District Gazetteer*, Rangoon, 1914, p. 92.

[70] Resolution, *RFA*, 1870-1, p. 2; *RFA*, 1874-5, pp. 9-10; S.G. Grantham, *Tharrawaddy Districts Gazetteer*, Rangoon, 1920, p. 63. Imported coal became the main fuel for the railway as fuel reserves were depleted. See Shein, *Burma's Transport and Foreign Trade*, p. 77.

[71] D. Brandis, 'Report on the Pegu Teak Forests for 1859-60', *Selections from the Records of the Government of India (Foreign Department)* 31 (1861), pp. 76-8; A, Rodger, 'The Myodwin Teak Plantations, Zigon Division, Lower Burma', *Indian Forester 41 (October*

Such land clearance raised the question of peasant forest needs. However, this question illustrated, once more, differences between civil and forest officials over forest management. Thus, civil officials criticized regularly the Forest Department's policy of requiring cultivators to pay for minor forest produce and for grazing rights in reserves. Noting the negligible income derived from the latter, the Commissioner of Sagaing Division remarked in 1898 that it was this kind of 'petty economy' that made forest officials 'so thoroughly unpopular with the people'.[72] In contrast, forest officials seeking to impose user fees or close reserves emphasized tree damage caused by cattle in reserves.[73]

Bureaucratic conflict also developed over village fuel and fodder reserves. Entrusted with their creation in Lower Burma in 1886, civil officials failed to implement the policy, and in 1895 the Chief Commissioner was forced to intervene and order once more their creation.[74] At the same time, civil officials were quick to recommend the 'disforestation' (forest clearance for permanent agriculture) of plains or delta reserves. In the case of the Kamase and Yitkangyi reserves in 1901, for example, the Commissioner of Pegu Division recommended their disforestation even though, as Conservator Hauxwell observed, they represented virtually the last opportunity in Pegu District to maintain a local fuel supply.[75] In other instances, civil officials in Hanthawaddy District questioned the long-term closure of several fuel reserves, even though they acknowledged their depleted condition.[76] Moreover, in the reserves that they did establish, civil officials often granted user rights that undermined their long-term management. In 1902-3, rights admitted by Settlement Officers in the Toungoo, Pegu and Thaton Districts were subsequently restricted for this reason.[77] Not surprisingly, Chief Conservator C.G. Rogers noted in 1915 that fuel reserves created after 1896 had 'largely failed' to guarantee

---

1915), p. 372; see also Pe Kin, 'History of Forest Management in British Burma', Guardian (Rangoon) 15 (December 1968), p. 14; A.J. Page, *Pegu District Gazetteer*, Rangoon, 1917, p. 80.

[72] *RFA* 1897-8, p. cxix.

[73] *RFA* 1903-4, p. 9; *RFA* (Tenasserim), 1897-8, p. 10; F. Beadon Bryant, Conservator, Southern, to Revenue Secretary, 25 December 1904, *BFP* (January 1906), p. 47; Grantham, *Tharrawaddy District Gazetteer*, p. 63.

[74] Resolution, 8 October 1895, *BFP* (January 1896), pp. 121-2; Resolution, 13 October 1894, *BFP* (October 1894), pp. 270-3.

[75] T.A. Hauxwell, Conservator, Pegu to Revenue Secretary, 12 August 1901, *BFP* (November 1901), pp. 4-5; see also Tan Chein Hoe, *Working Plan for Delta Forest Division, 1947-48 to 1956-57*, Rangoon, 1951, vol. II, p. 2.

[76] *BFP* (January 1910), pp. 252-3.

[77] *RFA*, 1902-3, p. 23.

local supplies or prevent the destruction of remaining unreserved forests.[78]

More than such bureaucratic conflict, the colonial state's inability to deal effectively with the question of village forest needs reflected widespread popular resistance to access restrictions. As Scott notes, the power of everyday resistance derives primarily from its pervasiveness and anonymity.

> Just as millions of anthozoan polyps create, willy-nilly, a coral reef, so do thousands upon thousands of individual acts of insubordination and evasion create a political or economic barrier reef of their own. . . .It is only rarely that the perpetrators of these petty acts seek to call attention to themselves. Their safety lies in their anonymity.[79]

At various stages, this book has documented the ability of Burmese peasants, timber traders and shifting cultivators to disrupt state forest control through everyday forms of resistance. Chapter 3 noted how regulation of shifting cultivation and non-teak forest use was resisted through illegal timber felling or burning. Such resistance grew thereafter, and as Chapter 4 illustrated, impeded colonial efforts to protect reserves and regulate the cutch and bamboo trades. The ability of these groups to sabotage forest policy was nowhere more evident, however, than with regard to the depletion of the plains reserves.

One indication of the intensifying conflict over these reserves is to be found in the growing number of breaches of the forest law. Although the data contained in Table 5.3 summarize all forest crime, a substantial proportion of the offences pertained to the plains reserves. In 1918, for example, 90 per cent of reported forest offences in Tharrawaddy Division concerned these areas.[80] Peasants apprehended for illegal possession of timber or illicit cattle grazing formed the bulk of detainees and were fined under the 'compounding' clause (sec. 62) of the 1902 Act. This clause was a flexible means to punish petty offenders on the spot without recourse to the courts. However, serious cases of large-scale theft and fraud were habitually taken to court.

---

[78] C.G. Rogers, 'Note on Proposal to Form Reserves in Unreserved Forests (Public Forest Land) for the Supply of Forest Produce to the Agricultural Population of Burma', *BFP* (June 1917), pp. 363-5.

[79] James C. Scott, *Weapons of the Weak: Everyday Forms of Peasant Resistance*, New Haven, 1985, p. 36.

[80] Hart, *Tour of Inspection in the Forests of Burma*, p. 8.

Table 5.3. BREACHES OF THE FOREST LAW, 1889-1930

	Cases tried	Cases compounded	Total
1889-90	440	946	1,386
1894-5	639	2,983	3,622
1899-1900	663	1,527	2,190
1904-5	867	2,403	3,270
1909-10	878	2,429	3,307
1914-15	843	3,786	4,629
1919-20	701	4,993	5,694
1924-5	1,153	6,672	7,825
1929-30	1,687	9,014	10,701

Source: Report of Forest Administration in Burma (various years). Selected years.

The evolution of forest crime between 1889 and 1930 is revealing on several counts. First, although the total number of cases more than doubled in the early 1890s, thereafter they declined, and until 1912 fluctuated between 2,500-3,500 offences annually. The initial increase is accounted for by the cutch crisis which peaked during this period. Conversely, the easing of cutch restrictions explains the declining number of offences in the late 1890s. Although cutch crime in the 1890s is only loosely related to the issue of the plains reserves, it nevertheless foreshadowed developments after 1912 when the latter were the focus of popular resistance. At first glance,the period 1896-1912 represented a relative lull in forest crime. However, this result reflected not so much the quiescence of peasants and shifting cultivators as the way in which legal violations were treated. During this period, the power to compound offenses was removed from subordinates below the rank of Deputy Ranger as part of an anti-corruption drive. In the process, the government effectively reduced the number of reported offences. Forest crime was not in abeyance during this period, it was simply less likely to be reported

Second, the period after 1912 reveals a steady increase in the number of reported offences, with the 1929-30 figure more than treble that of 1909-10. As discussed below,this increase reflected broad social and ecological changes arising from the closing of the agricultural frontier in Lower Burma around the time of the First World War.

Finally, Table 5.3 is revealing because it shows an interesting trend in the way that the Forest Department handled offences. Notwithstanding the restrictions placed on its use by the subordinate service, the compounding clause became the predominant means by which foresters attempted to deter crime. Whereas in 1889-90 compounding cases made up 68 per cent of the total, in 1929-30 that figure had risen to 84 per cent. This shift to on-the-spot punishment partly reflected the increasing incidence of petty offences as desperate peasants took greater risks to obtain needed forest products.

Greater use of the compounding clause also reflected the vicissitudes of the judicial system. Forest officials complained of delayed proceedings and the tendency of magistrates to dismiss cases or only nominally punish offenders.[81] However, the high acquittal rate was also linked to inadequate case preparation by foresters.[82] The result, as Table 5.4 illustrates for the Pegu Circle between 1899 and 1902, was a system in which conviction was uncertain and the deterrent effect of the law accordingly weakened.

Table 5.4. RESULTS OF COURT CASES, PEGU CIRCLE, 1899-1902

Division	1899-1900			1900-1901			1901-1902		
	C	A	%	C	A	%	C	A	%
Thayetmyo	74	–	–	46	6	12	28	3	10
Prome	55	19	26	20	20	50	10	7	41
Tharrawaddy	34	4	10	7	2	22	28	10	30
Rangoon	11	9	45	24	1	4	24	6	20
Pegu	23	4	15	5	1	16	10	3	23
Bassein	22	4	15	50	47	48	53	16	23
Henzada	24	5	17	17	3	15	8	3	27
Agency	9	–	–	38	3	7	10	2	16
Total	252	45	15	207	83	29	171	50	23

Note: C = Convictions; A = Acquittals; % = % of failure.

Source: *Report on Forest Administration in Burma* (various years).

The rate of conviction showed considerable annual and regional variation. In aggregate, the conviction rate fell from 85 per cent in 1899-1900, to 71 per cent the following year, before rising to 77 per cent in 1901-2. Such variability was even more pronounced at the divisional level. Thus, in Bassein Division the conviction rate dropped from 85 per cent in 1899-1900, to only 52 per cent the year after, before climbing to 77 per cent in 1901-2. Finally, the

---

[81] *RFA* (Pegu), 1894-5, p. 5; *RFA*, 1901-2, p. 5; *RFA* 1904-5, p. 6; *RFA* 1906-7, p. 15; *RFA*, 1911-12, p. 17. Civil officials often viewed the situation differently. In 1898-9, for example, Deputy Commissioner D. Ross opined that 'it is well for the people that there is an unbiased Magistrate between them and the Forest Officer', see *RFA*, 1898-9, p. xcv.

[82] RFA, 1900-1, p. 4; *RFA*, 1901-2, p.5.

variation was often quite large between divisions. In 1899-1900, the conviction rate was 100 per cent in the Thayetmyo and Agency (or depot) Divisions, but only 55 per cent in the Rangoon Division. It is not surprising when faced with such volatility that foresters preferred to commute offenses to a simple fine.

It is doubtful whether any law, however well enforced, could have prevented depletion of the plains reserves. The difficulties associated with law enforcement in populated areas were enormous. Reported offenses were only a fraction of the real number of cases; the number of undetected cases ran 'into the thousands' because foresters did not record a case unless the identity of the offender was at least suspected.[83] Offenders typically stole forest products from reserves at night, and were usually 'screened by the surrounding villagers'.[84] Illegal activity was more blatant in cases where subordinates shielded villagers. In one Pegu reserve in 1907-8, a surprise visit by a civil official led to the discovery of twenty-six cattle camps with six hundred cattle as well as illegal fisheries all tolerated by the local Ranger.[85] Peasants living in the delta used boats to penetrate reserves taking advantage of the numerous streams to escape detection; foresters even discovered a 'fair-sized' village of fuel cutters inside one reserve. Forest officials blamed Burmese timber traders for much of this illegal activity as the latter exceeded the terms of their trade permits or paid villagers for local free timber.[86]

The financial loss to government of such resistance was considerable. The illicit removal of bamboo from the Prome and Thayetmyo Divisions in one year alone deprived the treasury of 10,000 rupees; in 1919-20 it was estimated that 25,000 tons of *kanazo* (used for firewood) valued at 250,000 rupees was illegally extracted from the delta reserves. Indeed, theft from the latter was so rife that at least 75 per cent of timber, and 50 per cent of fuel, was harvested in this manner.[87] Forest officials were thus largely unable to control or tax this trade.

---

[83] *RFA*, 1908-9, p. 5; *RFA*, 1916-17, p. 6.

[84] *RFA*, 1906-7, p. 5. Timber theft was most prevalent during the dry season (November to June) when carting was easiest. See R.S. Troup, *Working Plan for Satpok, Sitkwin and Thindawyo Working Circles*, Rangoon, 1905, p. 39; H.C. Smith, *Working Plan for South Toungoo Forest Division, 1923-24 to 1932-33*, Maymyo, 1923, p. 17.

[85] *RFA*, 1907-8, pp. 8-9; *RFA* (Pegu), 1897-8, p. 7.

[86] *RFA*, 1918-19, p. 22; Pe Kin, 'From the Hills to the Delta', p. 40; Carter, Conservator, Southern, to Revenue Secretary, 16 August 1905, *BFP* (December 1906), pp. 344-5; *RFA*, 1911-12, p. 17; *RFA*, 1914-15, p. 19.

[87] *RFA*, 1910-11, p. 6; *RFA*, 1919-20, p. 23; *RFA*, 1918-19, p. 22; A.W. Moodie, *Working Plan for Delta Forest Division for the period 1924-25 to 1933-34*, Maymyo, 1924, vol. I, p. 33.

The growing scarcity of forest products that became noticeable around the time of the First World War intensified the struggle over the plains reserves. However, the willingness of a growing number of peasants to flaunt the forest law must also be situated in the broader context of increasing agricultural landlessness and deprivation in Lower Burma. In contrast to conditions in the nineteenth century, unoccupied land was scarce in the twentieth century. This closing of the agricultural frontier had important political and economic implications:

> The Delta rice frontier closed gradually and unevenly. No government proclamations marked its end; in fact few government officials noted its demise and only a handful understood its importance. As the frontier closed, however, the potential and protection that it had provided for the cultivating classes also came to an end. With the open land buffer gone, problems inherent in the nature of economic development in Lower Burma grew more intense and an era of apparent prosperity and content gave way to decades of conflict and unrest.[88]

Thus, between 1906-7 and the onset of the Great Depression in 1930, the area let to tenants climbed from 30 per cent to nearly 46 per cent of the total occupied land in the Delta.[89] As a growing proportion of cultivators became tenants or were otherwise marginalized, restrictions on forest access had a more devastating effect. Moreover, the failure of the Forest Department to develop fuel and timber plantations (as in the teak sector),[90] meant that its sole contribution to the issue of peasant forest needs was a coercive one. Access to reserves was limited (if not cut off altogether) to permit natural regeneration in overworked areas, and those who transgressed the rules were punished. As a result, foresters were in the paradoxical position of 'protecting the reserves against the very people in whose interests they are being protected'.[91]

The most serious consequence of this policy was that it enhanced the opportunities for corruption among subordinates. Such corruption was fairly common and partly explains why the Forest Department was so unpopular.[92] The low pay, difficult work conditions and limited

---

[88] Adas, *The Burma Delta*, pp. 128-9

[89] *Ibid.*, p. 150.

[90] For an exception, see J.M.D. Mackenzie, 'Fuel and Bamboo Plantations in the Sittang Delta of the Pegu District, Lower Burma', *Indian Forester* 43 (January 1917), pp. 2-9.

[91] *RFA*, 1918-19, p. 22; see also C.W. Scott, *Working Plan for Insein Forest Division, 1927-28 to 1936-37*, Rangoon, 1928, p. 14.

[92] *Report of the Bribery and Corruption Enquiry Committee 1940*, Rangoon, 1941, pp. 28-9.

prospects that encouraged indolence and corruption among Burmese forest officials in the nineteenth century had scarcely changed in the early twentieth century. Thus, a Forest Guard in 1905 still earned less in many districts than an unskilled labourer.[93] Burmese foresters expressed their dissatisfaction by moving to more remunerative and less hazardous employment in other departments or in the private sector. What colonial officials termed 'wastage' was high among subordinates. In 1919-20, of a permanent subordinate staff of 2,637, the number of men who left the service was 732 17 retired, 57 died, 375 resigned and 283 were dismissed.[94]

Yet the data highlight that many subordinates were fired. Some officials were guilty of defrauding the government of revenue or failing in their duties, but others extorted money from the public. In this regard, the power to compound offences was a potent weapon. As one civil official observed in 1896,

> What is complained of so much is the enormous power which is placed in the hands of subordinates of levying blackmail. It is a case of either subsidizing the forest gaungs [i.e. guards] or being run in.[95]

It was to stop the compounding clause from becoming 'an engine of oppression' that reforms were introduced at the turn of the century restricting this power to the rank of Deputy Ranger or higher.[96] Indeed, subordinates below that rank were expressly forbidden to receive any money on the government's behalf.[97] Nevertheless, corruption continued to be rife in the subordinate service. As Burma's Conservators observed in 1905, 'the venality of these underpaid subordinates is proverbial' and was a 'veritable blot on Forest Administration in Burma.'[98]

Senior colonial officials met between 1917 and 1919 to seek a way in which to diffuse the growing confrontation between peasants

---

[93] *RFA*, 1904-5, p. 18.

[94] Review, Chief Conservator, *RFA*, 1919-20, p. 11. The turnover in other years was about 300-350 men, F.A. Leete, Chief Conservator, to Revenue Secretary, 1 March 1920, *BFP* (December 1920), pp. 1-2; Review, Chief Conservator, *RFA*, 1920-1, p. 13; *RFA*, 1922-3, p. 3.

[95] G.M.S. Carter (Deputy Commissioner, Thayetmyo) quoted in *RFA*, 1895-6, p. lxviii.

[96] D. Ibbetson, Secretary, Government of India (DRA), to Revenue Secretary, 29 June 1897, in *RFA*, 1895-6, p. 2; Burma Forest Act (1902), sec. 62 (1), and Forest Department circular no. 19 of 1919, both in Government of Burma, *Burma Forest Manual*, pp. 28, 228-30.

[97] Burma Forest Department, *Manual of Standing Orders for Forest Subordinates*, Rangoon, 1919.

[98] Conservators to Revenue Secretary, 12 February 1905, *BFP* (October 1906), pp. 13-14.

and forest officials over peasant forest needs. After much debate, Lieutenant-Governor Sir Reginald Craddock proposed a scheme in November 1919 in which village reserves would be created under the Forest Department's control. Forest products from these reserves would not be free, but foresters would devote greater attention than before to their management.[99] Craddock suggested that it was 'just as much the duty of the Forest Department to conserve forests' for the agricultural population as it was 'to conserve them for commercial purposes or for climatic reasons.'[100] The Lieutenant Governor was in a sense simply reiterating the government of India's 1894 statement on forest policy which had emphasized the agricultural population's needs. Yet Craddock's scheme also fit well with the post-war quest to rationalize forest use in Burma. However, that quest was soon overshadowed by political developments which culminated in the introduction of partial self-rule or dyarchy in January 1923. The issue of the plains reserves and peasant forest needs was thereafter integral to the political process in the late colonial era.

The preceding two chapters have described the Forest Department's efforts to rationalize forest use between 1882 and 1922. This forty-year period comprised an era of expansion (1882-1901) in which state forest control was asserted over a widening territory and range of activities, and an era of consolidation(1902-22) during which the gains of the late nineteenth century were consolidated. This process affected forest politics in different ways. An expanding Forest Department was forced at nearly every turn to negotiate shared powers with a distrustful civil administration. The relationship between the Forest Department and the European firms changed from one rooted predominantly in conflict to one based on mutual understanding and advantage – a change which enabled forest officials to attend to other matters. Yet, social and ecological changes were undermining the ability of those officials to manage forests in populated areas. As illustrated notably in conflict over cutch use and the plains reserves, the actions of peasants, traders and shifting cultivators demonstrated that there were definite limits to the Forest Department's ability to rationalize forest use. Those limits became even more apparent as a result of post-1923 forest politics.

---

[99] Reginald Craddock, 'Minute on Forest Produce in Burma', *BFP* (November 1919), pp. 246-50.
[100] *Ibid.*, p. 246.

Part IV
FIGHTING OVER THE FORESTS

6

FORESTS AND NATIONALISM, 1923-1947

The Forest Department was at its most powerful in the years immediately following the First World War. It had created an extensive network of reserved forests in which intensive management was being practiced. Growing cooperation between the Forest Department and the European firms was the basis of a prospering timber industry, and both teak production and forest revenue were at an all-time high. Efforts were underway to develop an export-oriented non-teak timber trade and forest officials were even beginning to address more systematically than hitherto was the case the question of peasant forest needs. In short, the Forest Department had effectively achieved its goal of a system of rationalized forest use in Burma.

Yet 1923 marked the high point of Forest Department power. Thereafter, that power was gradually but inexorably undermined as conflict over Burma's forests intensified, and the system of rationalized forest use so painstakingly developed in the late nineteenth and early twentieth century began to collapse. Previous chapters have shown how the introduction of scientific forestry after 1856 prompted opposition from civil officials, European and Burmese timber traders, shifting cultivators, and peasants. Such opposition was never static but changed over time in keeping with the evolution of state forest control as well as the interests of particular forest users. Indeed, opposition turned into cooperation in certain cases: Karen shifting cultivators assisted the Forest Department under the *taungya* forestry scheme (albeit subject to ongoing tensions) and the European timber firms extracted teak in the twentieth century under the watchful but increasingly sympathetic eye of colonial forest officials. By the early 1920s, internal territorialization was all but completed with the result

127

that a perennial source of forest-civil official tension had largely disappeared.

In contrast, the period extending from the advent of partial self-rule (or dyarchy) in 1923 to the attainment of independence in 1948 was characterized by at times quite intense conflict between the Forest Department and Burmese peasants and timber traders. Peasant opposition to the plains reserves intensified, while timber traders pressed the British to re-allocate the teak leases in their favour. Japanese rule between 1942 and 1945 did not fundamentally alter this conflict. Although the interests of Burmese peasants and timber traders were not the same, it was nevertheless the case that the nationalist struggle against the British provided a context within which inter-class cooperation flourished. Chapter 7 examines how fighting over the forests persisted following independence in 1948 but in an altered political context in which the anti-British struggle was replaced by conflict between diverse political and ethnic groups over who was to control the country's people and natural resources. Here, the goal is to explain Burmese forest management in the late colonial era, and to link that explanation to the growing politicization of forest access and use that ultimately subverted imperial scientific forestry in Burma.

Forests, Nationalism and Politics

Writing in December 1947 on the eve of Burmese independence, the eminent colonial forester and historian E.P. Stebbing congratulated the colonial forest service for having done 'a magnificent work for Burma' and for having left 'a great heritage to the Burmans'.[1]

However, the evidence presented in this chapter calls into question this rose-tinted vision of imperial forestry, and suggests an alternative historical reading centred on the primacy of politics and conflict in Burmese forest management. Later sections explore the evolution of such conflict in the context of a discussion of peasant forest access and Burmanization of the forestry sector. This section explores the broader political context within which conflict over these two issues took place.

The origins of dyarchy may be traced back to the years 1919-22. Acting upon the advice of the Viceroy of India, Lord Chelmsford, and the Secretary of State for India, Edwin Montagu, the British

---

[1] E.P. Stebbing, 'The Teak Forests of Burma', *Nature* 160 (December 1947), p. 820; see also, F.T. Morehead, *The Forests of Burma*, London, 1944; H.R. Blanford, 'Highlights of One Hundred Years of Forestry in Burma', *Burmese Forester* 6 (June 1956), pp. 12-23.

Parliament passed the Government of India Act in 1919 as part of a plan to establish the dyarchy system of tutelary democracy on the Indian sub-continent. The omission of Burma (thought to be politically less advanced than India) from the 1919 reforms was the occasion for the 'first sustained campaign' of the Burmese nationalist movement against the British.[2] Surprised by this political agitation, the British Parliament voted in 1921 to extend dyarchy to Burma. A Burma Reforms Committee (the Whyte Committee) was then appointed to sort out the details.[3]

A central concern of that Committee was to decide whether forests would become a transferred subject. However, the status of Burma's forests was the occasion for much dispute. As the Whyte Committee noted, on this question 'there was a more definite cleavage of opinion among our witnesses than on any other subject.'[4] The European community was opposed generally to the transfer of forests. The government of Burma's submission to the inquiry expressed that opposition in suggesting that Burma's forests were too valuable to be left to inexperienced Burmese management.[5] Teak extraction by the European firms might be disrupted by Burmese ministers intent on promoting indigenous enterprise. Forest conservancy could also be jeopardized by a Burmese Minister who would be accountable to 'an electorate which is as yet completely untrained, and incapable of appreciating the importance of a policy of scientific and far-sighted development.'[6] Chief Conservator Frederick Leete expressed similar sentiments in a separate brief to the Whyte Committee. Although government had always been 'prodigal in its liberality' in granting popular access to reserves, forest management nevertheless remained unpopular in Burma reflecting the lack of a 'healthy public opinion' on forest matters. It was premature therefore to transfer forests to indigenous control.[7]

Burmese testifying before the Whyte Committee contested this

---

[2] Robert H. Taylor. *The State in Burma*, London, 1987, pp. 119-23; Albert D. Moscotti, *British Policy and the Nationalist Movement in Burma, 1917-1937*, Honolulu, 1974, pp. 24-30, 71-6; Reginald Craddock, *The Dilemma in India*, London, 1929, p. 116.

[3] Burma Reforms Committee, *Report and Appendices* (henceforth *BRCR*), and *Record of Evidence* (henceforth *BRCE*), Rangoon, 1922, vols I-III.

[4] *BRCR*, p. 17.

[5] F. Lewisohn, 'Note of the Local Government's views on the subject of the Franchise and of Transferred Subjects, etc.', *BRCR*, app. IV, p. 41; see also J.A. Swan, Steel Brothers, *BRCE*, vol. I, p. 126; H,A, Thornton, Commissioner, Mandalay, and D.F. Chalmers, Deputy Commissioner, Thaton, *BRCE*, vol. II, pp. 144-5, 207.

[6] Lewisohn, 'Local Government's views', p. 41.

[7] *BRCE*, vol. III, pp. 81, 93.

claim and highlighted the pitfalls of the status quo. Although Burmese witnesses were mainly pro-British officials and lawyers, their complaints about forest management foreshadowed many of those made subsequently by radical politicians.[8] They noted, for example, that Burmese were being eliminated from the teak trade in favour of the European firms, and that they were also confined to small leases when extracting other hardwoods.[9] Concurrently, the emphasis on commercial timber extraction interfered with the satisfaction of peasant forest needs. The Pyinmana lawyer Maung Kan Baw observed that since reserves (*kyo-waing*) had been created, the forests were 'given by compartments . . . a man who obtains a lease . . . won't allow the villagers to come and take firewood.'[10] As another witness pointed out, village access was being 'gradually circumscribed' to the 'great economic loss' of the peasantry, and sheer necessity was forcing peasants to steal from reserves.[11] The existing system was non-democratic, illegitimate and ineffective, but under an elected Burmese Minister, the Tharrawaddy barrister Maung Kyaw believed, forest management would be 'more in accordance with the wishes of the people'.[12] Such change might result in an easing of access restrictions, but peasants would not abuse their new liberty as they were against unfair restrictions and taxation, and not conservation. Indeed, the message of conservation would have a better chance of success coming from a Burmese Minister who would 'bring home to his countrymen the importance of the subject'.[13] The transfer of forests would not only reduce conflict over reserves, therefore, but it would also facilitate their conservation.

The Whyte Committee agreed with this argument much to the dismay of Burma's European community. By allowing the Burmese to manage a large revenue-earning department, the government would promote the legitimacy of its reforms simultaneously facilitating the

---

[8] Most radical nationalists boycotted the Whyte Committee at the insistence of the General Council of Buddhist Associations (GCBA), a prominent nationalist organization of the 1920s. See Maung Maung, *Burma's Constitution*, 2nd edn, The Hague, 1961, p. 17; Moscotti, *British Policy*, pp. 32, 78.

[9] Maung Kan Baw, Advocate, Pyinmana, *BRCE*, vol. II, pp. 57, 62; Saw Pah Dwai, Karen National Association, Thaton *ibid.*, pp. 240, 242-3.

[10] *Ibid.*, p. 61.

[11] Taw Sein Ko, Bahuthuta Association, Mandalay, *ibid.*, p. 68; see also Maung Po Hla, Deputy Commissioner, Pyapon, *BRCE*, vol. III, p. 24.

[12] *BRCE*, vol. I, p. 274.

[13] Maung Shwe Tha, Deputy Commissioner, Sagaing, *BRCE*, vol. II, p. 127; see also *BRCE*, vol. I, p. 278; Maung Shwe Tha, Deputy Commissioner, Sagaing, *BRCE*, vol. II, p. 132; Maung Po Yun, Advocate, Kyaukse, *ibid.*, p. 181.

emergence of a trained Burmese administrative elite. Moreover, the Committee believed that conservation measures 'in the interests of the villagers would be much more likely to gain general acceptance' if proposed by an elected Burmese Minister than if put forward by the British.[14] The Whyte Committee assumed that the appointment of such an individual would undercut popular opposition to forest management. It also took for granted that the interests of an elected Burmese Minister and peasants would coincide.

The introduction of dyarchy on 1 January 1923 granted Burma greater administrative autonomy within the British Indian empire. Forests became a transferred subject as per the Whyte Committee's recommendations.[15] Formal control of the Forest Department now passed to the Minister of Agriculture, Excise and Forests who was appointed by the British Governor from among the elected members of the Burma Legislative Council.

The Governor favoured pro-British conservative politicians in appointments to that post. Thus, in January 1923 the conservative barrister Joseph A. Maung Gyi was chosen by Governor Harcourt Butler as the first Forests Minister.[16] A fellow conservative (and member of Burma's small but influential Chinese population) Lee Ah Yain held the Forests portfolio from December 1925 until his death in 1932. However, the Governor also appointed opponents of the government as Forest Minister. During 1924-5, for example, the post was held by Yamethin U Pu, a vocal critic of the government and a member of the Twenty-One Party (named after the twenty-one GCBA members who left that association in 1922 to participate in the first dyarchy elections). U Kyaw Din, a supporter of the anti-dyarchist leader Dr Ba Maw, was appointed in December 1932, but was replaced as Forests Minister in April 1934 by the veteran nationalist and leader of the Twenty-One Party U Ba Pe.

The Governor was required to act on the advice of the Forests Minister unless there was 'sufficient reason to dissent'.[17] The Minister

[14] *BRCE*, p. 18.

[15] Some Conservative MPs in London opposed this move. However, Secretary of State Lord Winterton suggested that in making such a transfer Britain was meeting 'the acid test of her sincerity' toward reform in Burma. The Burma Reform Bill was approved without difficulty. See John F. Cady, *A History of Modern Burma*, Ithaca, 1958, pp. 239-40; Moscotti, *British Policy*, p. 80.

[16] On J.A. Maung Gyi, see Maung Maung, *Burma and General Ne Win*, London, 1969, p. 16; Nyo Mya, 'Profile: Sir Joseph Augustus Maung Gyi', *Guardian* (Rangoon) 2, 6 (April 1955), pp. 10-11; Frank N. Trager, *Burma: From Kingdom to Independence: A Historical and Political Analysis*, London, 1966, p. 51.

[17] F.S.V. Donnison, *Public Administration in Burma: A Study of Development during*

was advised, in turn, by a Forest Secretary acting in conjunction with the Chief Conservator. Beginning with H.O. Reynolds in 1923, this position was filled by a senior British official, but in the 1930s Burmese officials such as U Kyaw Min and U Tin Tut were appointed Forest Secretary.

The new system placed strict limits on the ability of a Burmese Forests Minister to effect policy change. Thus, control over the allocation of teak leases remained under the firm control of the Secretary of State in London and the Governor in Rangoon. Senior British officials also retained control over all aspects of personnel management in the Forest Department.[18] Similarly, the Minister had no say over forest management in the Shan States and other 'excluded' border areas. Indeed, the creation of the Federated Shan States had been partly designed to shelter the *Sawbwas* from 'the effects of a more democratic government and of Burmese nationalism'.[19] After 1923, British forest officials seconded from the Burma cadre controlled these forests under the direction of the local Commissioner.[20] Control over much of the Chin Hills, likewise, was transferred from the Forest Department to British Political Officers in 1927.[21]

Many nationalists denounced these limitations on Burmese ministerial authority. Tharrawaddy U Pu expressed a popular sentiment when he suggested in February 1930 that the system 'was 'not good at all for this country . . . the Ministers are merely puppets in the hands of their glorified Secretaries.'[22] The government of Burma's submission to the Indian Statutory Commission (Simon Commission) in 1930 indirectly supported these claims. It suggested that relations between the legislature and the colonial executive over the Forest Department since 1923 had been 'more in the direction of education of the legislature than of effective interference by it' in forest management.[23] Since dyarchy left unchanged the basic operation of transferred

---

the British Connexion, London 1953, pp. 54-5.

[18] Great Britain, Indian Statutory Commission, *Memorandum submitted by the Government of Burma to the Indian Statutory Commission*, London, 1930, vol. XI, p. 31.

[19] Taylor, *The State in Burma*, pp. 96-7; Reginald Craddock, *Speeches by Sir Reginald Craddock, Lieutenant-Governor of Burma, 1917-1922*, Rangoon, 1924, pp. 233-4.

[20] H.W.A. Watson, *A Note on Forest Administration and Policy in the Federated Shan States*, Rangoon, 1929, pp. 1-3. Forest officials working in the Shan States received a 40 per cent 'Compensatory Local Allowance' in excess of the going rate in Burma. See Commissioner, Federated Shan States, to H. Butler, Governor of Burma, 5 May 1927, Clague Papers, MSS Eur E. 252/3.

[21] *Report of Forest Administration in Burma* (henceforth *RFA*), 1927-8, p. 3.

[22] *Burma Legislative Council Proceedings* (henceforth *BLCP*), 28 February 1930, p. 541. As noted, this did not stop some nationalists from accepting ministerial posts.

departments, the government of Burma felt itself able to support additional reform. For this very reason, however, dyarchy was 'almost a term of abuse' to most Burmese.[24]

Yet it would be inappropriate to dismiss the dyarchy reforms. Burmese appointed as Forests Minister were able to use their positions to lobby British officials for policy reform. Further, nationalists kept up a steady barrage of criticism of forest policy in the Legislative Council from the opposition benches. Whereas before 1923 British forest officials acted without having to take into account the local political implications of their actions, under dyarchy that was no longer possible. As Burmese political leaders challenged imperial forest policy, British forest officials were obliged to defend that policy as being in the interests of Burma. In the process, the behaviour of the colonizer towards the colonized began to change.[25]

On 1 April 1937, moreover, the Burmese acquired significant new powers over forestry (and other) matters when the Government of Burma Act (1935) became operative. Under this legislation, Burma was constitutionally separated from India, and was granted a system of parliamentary government modelled on that of Westminster. For those willing to cooperate with the British, as did politicians such as Dr Ba Maw, Shwegyin U Pu and U Saw, these reforms were a golden opportunity to acquire real political power.[26] Concurrently, and as elaborated below, forest management became increasingly intertwined with the party political process in Burma.

These reforms were cut short in January 1942 by Japan's invasion of Burma. During the Japanese occupation (1942-5), forest management was disrupted by the fighting and by the timber requisitions of the Japanese army. Yet Japanese rule provided new opportunities for nationalists since it removed from Burma the British officials and timber traders who had controlled the key elements of the colonial

[23] Great Britain, *Memorandum by the Government of Burma*, p. 64. Sir John Simon was appointed by the British government in 1927 to review the operation of dyarchy and to recommend further reform.

[24] Governor Butler quoted in Maung Maung, *Burma's Constitution*, p. 20.

[25] An incident related by the Burmese forester, U Pe Kin, although in itself of a trivial nature, gives some idea of the often subtle, but nevertheless important changes that dyarchy imposed on British behaviour. In the late 1920s, R. Unwin (a future Chief Conservator) lectured at Rangoon University. On one occasion, he used derogatory language in referring to students in the class, an event which was reported to Forests Minister Lee Ah Yain. The latter took the matter up with the University authorities, and Unwin had to apologize to the students. See Pe Kin, 'Life in the Forest Service', *Guardian* (Rangoon) 15 (March 1968), p. 17. This event would have been inconceivable in pre-dyarchy days.

[26] Robert H. Taylor, 'Politics in Late Colonial Burma: The Case of U Saw', *Modern Asian Studies* 10 (April 1976), p. 161.

forest economy. For Burmese forest officials, peasants and timber traders who were left behind, the Japanese period was one of considerable hardship. Yet, the British absence afforded them an opportunity to pursue their individual forest interests, albeit subject to Japanese authority.

In order to win Burmese allegiance, the Japanese established a *Baho* (or Central) Administration in April 1942 composed of Burmese allies under the nominal leadership of Tun Ok. Prior to 1942, the Japanese had developed contacts with young nationalists opposed to British rule, notably among *Do Bama Asiayon* ('Our Burma Association') members. [27]Founded in July 1933, this political group gained influence with many Burmese upon its affiliation with the All Burma Student's Union (ABSU) in 1938. The quest for ways in which to overthrow British rule led in 1940 to contact being made with the Japanese and in July 1941 thirty *Thakins* received military training from the Japanese on Hainan Island. These 'Thirty Comrades' were the basis of the Burma Independence Army which accompanied the Japanese into Burma in 1942, and many of whom then joined the *Baho* government. However that government proved relative powerless and its orders (such as the prohibition against the cutting of teak and other species) were ignored.[28] Peace Preservation Committees that operated at the local level similarly enjoyed little success as they sought to protect reserves.[29] The Japanese appointed a new government under Dr Ba Maw in August 1942 who appealed to prewar politicians and officials to join it. A Forest Bureau modelled on the pre-war Department was formed as part of the Ministry of Forests and Mines and foresters were instructed to re-organize the subordinate staff. One year later, Burma was formally granted independence by the Japanese. Yet such independence lacked authenticity. Thus, the Forest Bureau remained subordinate to the Japanese military and the Nippon Burma Timber Union (see below). As U Hla Pe, a wartime Forests Minister recalled, the Forest Bureau required the approval of the Union before it could extract any timber.[30]

However limited, the Burmese experience with self-rule under the Japanese strengthened the nationalist movement which, following the

[27] A detailed discussion is provided by Taylor, *The State in Burma*, pp. 202-16.

[28] J. Russell Andrus, *Burmese Economic Life*, Stanford, 1956 (1948), p. 111.

[29] Burma Ministry of Finance, *Financial and Economic Annual of Burma, July 1943*, Rangoon, 1943, p. 31.

[30] Hla Pe, *Narrative of the Japanese Occupation of Burma*, recorded by Khin, Ithaca, 1961, p. 65. Of Karen origin, Hla Pe's appointment as Forests Minister represented a Burman attempt to win the confidence of that minority group: Hugh Tinker, *The Union of Burma: A Study of the First Years of Independence*, London, 1957, p. 11.

resumption of British rule in 1945, mounted a major campaign for independence. Members of the increasingly powerful *Do Bama Asiayon* joined with other groups to form the Anti-Fascist People's Freedom League (AFPFL), and under the leadership of U Aung San (a prewar leader of the ABSU and one of the Thirty Comrades), this organization threatened a nation-wide revolt if the British did not quit Burma. Such pressure forced Governor Sir Hubert Rance to appoint an AFPFL – dominated Executive Council in September 1946, and led ultimately to the Aung San-Attlee Agreement of 27 January 1947 which promised full independence for Burma within one year.

In a context of intensifying nationalist agitation, it is not surprising that British forest officials failed to restore scientific forest management in Burma's forests after the war. Subject to criticism by the nationalists, these officials also had to confront pervasive unrest in rural areas. Conflict between rival Burmese political factions combined with a surfeit of military equipment at war's end to produce 'triumphant lawlessness' in Burma's forests. As independence neared, fighting over the forests intensified and the system of rationalized forest use introduced by the British in the late nineteenth and early twentieth century finally disintegrated. Yet the origins of such disintegration lie in the period after 1923 when forests became an integral part of the political process in Burma. As the remainder of this chapter shows, two issues in particular – peasant access to the plains reserves and Burmanization of the forestry sector – dominated Burmese forest politics in the late colonial era.

Peasant Access to the Plains Reserves

The struggle over the plains reserves did not suddenly emerge in the 1920s. Conflict grew during the late nineteenth and early twentieth century, and as Chapter 5 noted, was exacerbated by the closing of the agricultural frontier around the time of the First World War. Dwindling unreserved forests and growing landlessness combined to guarantee that access to residual stands would be a central nationalist demand during the 1920s and 1930s. In certain instances, peasants sought access to obtain timber and non-timber forest products or to graze cattle. In other cases, they demanded individual title to land which, although forested, was suitable for permanent agriculture. However contradictory, these objectives formed the basis of a political campaign that directly challenged the Forest Department's system of rationalized forest use.[31]

[31] As a British forester protested in 1925: 'Some balance must be stuck between the

As the anti-colonial struggle intensified, the status of the plains reserves took on a new meaning. Before they had been widely resented and actively subverted. Now these reserves symbolized imperial domination. From the early 1920s, peasants challenged diverse aspects of British rule – including forest management – through village-level nationalist organizations known as *wunthanu athin*. Combining everyday forms of resistance with overt collective action, these organizations derived their strength from specific peasant grievances as well as general anti-British sentiments.[32]

The affiliation of *wunthanu athin* with national organizations such as the GCBA and the General Council of Sangha Sammeggi (GCSS), the latter an organization founded by monks in 1920, enhanced the position of these local organizations *vis-à-vis* British officialdom in two ways. First, peasant grievances were now expressed nationally, and could no longer be treated by the colonial state as being of a purely local, and hence 'minor' significance. The GCBA and GCSS served as fora in which peasants learned that their individual or village grievances were not unique; the actions of local forest officials were situated in the broader context of an imperial forestry policy inimical to indigenous interests. Second, the GCBA in particular served as a link between the increasingly politicized peasantry and the urban middle class. If, at times, these two groups had differing interests and objectives, through the medium of the GCBA they nevertheless found common ground in the 1920s. At GCBA meetings, peasant demands were incorporated in conference resolutions. The 1925 conference, for example, resolved that 'the poor should be allowed to use *thit-pok* [i.e. *thitkado*], firewood and bamboo free'; four years later, the Forest Department was urged to recognize 'the just rights of the poor people concerning the forest products'.[33]

Peasant grievances were also aired in the Legislative Council by nationalist leaders eager for the political support of the peasantry.

---

individual demand for land and the communal need for cheap fuel, bamboo and houseposts', see A.H.M. Barrington, *Working Plan for North Toungoo Forest Division, 1920-21 to 1928-29*, Rangoon, 1925, pp. 19-20. However, the Forest Department's neglect of peasant forest needs only reinforced the tendency of the Burmese to assert individual over communal claims, see below.

[32] Taylor, *State in Burma*, pp. 192-3. Opposition was also expressed through localized rebellions, see Michael Adas, 'Bandits, Monks, and Pretender Kings: Patterns of Peasant Resistance and Protest in Colonial Burma, 1826-1941', in Robert P. Weller and Scott E. Guggenheim (eds), *Power and Protest in the Countryside: Studies of Rural Unrest in Asia, Europe, and Latin America*, Durham, NC, 1982, pp. 93-4.

[33] Maung Maung, 'Nationalist Movements in Burma, 1920-1940: Changing Patterns of Leadership from Sangha to Laity', unpubl. M. A. thesis, Australian National University, 1976, pp. 593, 601.

In March 1923, for example, the prominent journalist and politician, U Ba Pe, charged that 'the general complaint all over the country' was that forest rules prevented the poor from 'enjoying the fruits of the country'.[34] The Thayetmyo-based politician U San Lu drew attention in 1930 to the plight of peasants in his district whose livelihoods were in jeopardy due to proposals to extend a local reserve.[35] Legislative amendments designed to relax forest access restrictions were also put forward. Thus, in September 1926, U San Lu proposed that the 1902 Forest Act be amended so as to extend the radius of free domestic consumption of forest products from 10 to 20 miles; however, the resolution was defeated by 43 votes to 26.[36] These initiatives did not result in reform. They were nonetheless significant in so far as they were a means by which nationalists could confront the colonial state with the social implications of its forest policy.

Those implications were not addressed by the Burma Forest Committee appointed in 1924 to consider the organization of the Forest Department and timber extraction, and composed mainly of pro-British officials, politicians and businessmen. In the Committee's view, commercialization of forest products in populated areas was 'an inevitable result of progress and prosperity' and it found 'little that requires remedy' in the Forest Department's relations with the peasantry.[37] Three nationalists on the Committee (U Ba Pe, U E Maung and U Thin Maung) disagreed. They argued that the Forest Department oppressed peasants by making them pay for forest products that were hitherto 'free'. Further, official allowances for domestic consumption of these products were inadequate, forcing the poor on to the market. As a transferred subject, they concluded, the time was right to administer the forests 'more in the interests of the sons of the soil'.[38] Once again, such dissent registered a protest by middle class nationalists on behalf of the peasantry. It did not alter the status quo but nonetheless strengthened inter-class cooperation on forestry issues.

These efforts by nationalist politicians to effect change by legal means occurred against a backdrop of rising peasant militancy over the plains reserves. Increased illegal extraction from these reserves

[34] *BLCP*, 21 March 1923, p. 292.

[35] *BLCP*, 20 February 1930, pp. 220-2. Local peasants extracted fuelwood for local mills as well as for the Irrawaddy Flotilla Company, see P. Burnside and C.H. Thompson, *Working Plan for Thayetmyo Forest Division, 1931-32 to 1940-41*, Rangoon, 1933, vol. I, p. 17.

[36] *BLCP*, 1 September 1926, pp. 86-90.

[37] *Report of the Burma Forest Committee 1925*, Rangoon, 1926, pp. 24, 27.

[38] Note of Dissent by U Ba Pe, U E Maung and U Thin Maung, *ibid.*, pp. 37-8.

boosted dramatically the number of forest offences: from 6,310 cases in 1922-3 to 10,922 offences six years later. Offences became more serious. Teak-related incidents increased as peasants and traders challenged the very essence of colonial policy. There was, in the words of the Chief Conservator, a 'lessening respect for teak as a royal tree'.[39] Burmese subordinates were also attacked. Thus one official in Thayetmyo Division was murdered in 1925, and such violence was not unusual.[40] The political significance of these events was not lost on British officialdom. As Chief Conservator H.W.A. Watson observed in 1928:

> The actual numbers and results of forest offences are becoming serious ...[a] general gradual increase would under existing conditions be the normal result of expansion of cultivation and population eating into the unclassed forest available for domestic supply; but the sharp increase of the past six years appears to be largely an expression of general lawlessness closely connected with political agitation.[41]

One indication of such politicization was the increasing employment of expert defence lawyers, a trend which forced the Forest Department to turn to the Criminal Investigation Department for help. A public prosecutor was also hired in the Tharrawaddy District, and additional officers were deputed to investigate cases.[42]

The *wunthanu* movement facilitated such peasant resistance, but it also prompted repressive new legislation, coercive tax collection and military reprisals. This cycle of repression and resistance culminated in the Hsaya San rebellion of 1930.[43] A district leader of the GCBA, Hsaya San was commissioned by that organization in the late 1920s to investigate popular complaints against the state, including its denial of public access to plains reserves. In 1929 he proposed a confrontational strategy in which free timber and bamboo for family use must be guaranteed or a campaign of non-violent resistance would begin. When the GCBA leadership rejected this strategy, Hsaya San began secretly to promote civil disobedience and armed insurrection.[44]

The insurrection broke out on 22 December 1930 in Tharrawaddy District but spread to adjoining areas. As Hsaya San's headquarters

---

[39] *RFA*, 1925-26, p. 21.

[40] *RFA*, 1924-25, p. 3; *RFA*, 1925-26, p. 21. Such violence was part of a broader campaign against Burmese and Indian accomplices of the British, see Taylor, *The State in Burma*, p. 194; Adas, 'Bandits, Monks, and Pretender Kings', pp. 94-7.

[41] *RFA*, 1927-8, pp. 21-2.

[42] *RFA*, 1928-9, p. 30.

[43] Taylor, *State in Burma*, pp. 192-9.

[44] Maung Maung, 'Nationalist Movements', pp. 180-1.

was located in the Pegu Yoma east of the town of Tharrawaddy, work in those forests came to a halt. As in 1885-6, both Forest Department employees and property were attacked by insurgents. Thus six employees were killed and a further three were wounded while 'extensive burning of Forest Department buildings' occurred.[45] Following the importation of troops from India, the insurrection was soon quelled. By 1932 it was essentially 'a thing of the past' and forest work was resumed. Yet Karen working in South Pegu Division remained armed, and foresters in Myitmaka Division required armed escorts, as late as 1934.,[46] For their help in suppressing the insurgency, meanwhile, Burmese and British forest officials were honoured by the government.[47]

Yet peasant resistance to the colonial state did not end with the defeat of Hsaya San. It simply resumed its earlier covert and 'everyday' character. Thus, following the restoration of 'order', forest offences soared from 9,298 in 1931-2 to a record 13,192 in 1935-6. By the mid-1930s, 50 per cent of offences in Lower Burma occurred in plains reserves leading Conservator A.W. Moodie to lament that 'the growing stock in many reserves is gradually diminishing'.[48]

Ironically, this rising tide of forest 'crime' during the interwar period took place against a backdrop of sporadic official attempts to placate the peasantry. In November 1919, for example, the creation of new plains reserves was effectively frozen by a rule requiring that future reservation must not be undertaken without the consent of neighbouring villagers.[49] Bowing to political pressure, the government in 1938 raised the radius of free peasant domestic consumption of forest products in unreserved forests from ten to twenty miles.[50] The

---

[45] *RFA* 1930-1, p. 50; *RFA*, 1931-2. p. 46.

[46] *RFA* 1934-5, p. 65; *RFA* 1933-4, p. 44; Blanford, 'Highlights', p. 19. As in 1885-6, the hill Karen sided with the British during the insurgency, E.C.V. Foucar, *I Lived in Burma*, London, 1956, p. 74; *RFA*, 1930-1, p. 47.

[47] On the role of forest officials in fighting the insurgency, see *RFA*, 1930-1, p. 49; Maung Maung, 'Nationalist Movements', pp. 187-8; C.G.E. Dawkins to Enid Dawkins, Dawkins Papers, MSS Eur. D. 931/15; F.G. Burgess, 'Touring under Difficulties in Burma', *Indian Forester* 57 (June 1931), pp. 257-64; J.S. Vorley, 'The Forest Department and the Burma Rebellion', *Indian Forester* 62 (January 1936), pp. 9-11; Blanford, 'Highlights', p. 19.

[48] *RFA*, 1932-3, p. 23; see also Kyaw Zan, 'Choice of Species in the Thitcho Plains Reserve of the Zigon Forest Division', *Burmese Forester* 2 (March 1952), p. 21; *RFA*,1935-6, p. 30.

[49] Resolution, Government of Burma, 15 November 1919, *Burma Forest Proceedings* (henceforth *BFP*), November 1919, pp. 232-7; Royal Commission on Agriculture in India, *Evidence Taken in Burma*, London, 1928, vol. XII, p. 116.

[50] *RFA*, 1938-9, pp. 43, 73; *Burma Legislature House of Representatives Proceedings* (henceforth *BLHORP*), 23 August 1938, p. 123.

question of peasant forest needs began to be treated in a series of revised working plans prepared during the 1920s and 1930s, and in 1940 forest officials even began a propaganda campaign to explain to the population why forest conservation was necessary.[51]

These initiatives failed to diffuse peasant opposition to restrictions on access to plains reserves. Indeed, peasants often acting in league with nationalist politicians pressed their advantage in the face of perceived colonial weakness. Thus, the halt to further plains reservation in 1919 simply encouraged the Burmese to press even harder for the elimination of existing plains reserves whose status became increasingly ambiguous with each passing year.[52] Petitions by peasants and politicians to 'disforest' reserves in favour of permanent cultivation increased in number to such an extent in the 1920s that forest officials in some areas were devoting much of their time to this issue. The case of the Kanyutkwin reserve (South Toungoo Division) is typical of the disforestation 'campaign'. Petitions to disforest this reserve prior to 1923 were rejected by the government because of its importance as a source of timber. However, it was soon disforested under dyarchy.[53]

During the 1930s, the Forest Department's ability to protect the remaining plains reserves was further weakened. During the Great Depression, teak prices and exports fell dramatically.[54] In turn, forest revenue plummeted from 21,737,618 rupees in 1926-7, to only 7,999,782 rupees in 1933-4.[55] The government of Burma responded by cutting

---

[51] *RFA* 1939-40, p. 69. For examples of revised working plans, see M.V. Edwards, *Working Plan for South Toungoo Forest Division, 1933-34 to 1947-48*, Rangoon, 1938, vol. II, p. 5; R.J. Sayres, *Working Plan for Pyinmana Forest Division, 1936-37 to 1946-47*, Rangoon, 1937, vol. II, p. 100; A.F.R. Brown, *Working Plan for Yamethin Forest Division, 1930-31 to 1939-40*, Rangoon, 1932, vol.I, P. 63.

[52] In 1935, Forest Department circular no. 35 decreed that 'many' plains reserves were to be disforested and made over to peasants as Village Common Lands. Yet as late as 1940 applications to disforest reserves were being held up pending a final resolution of the plains reserves question. See RFA, 1935-6, pp. 10, 12; D.J. Atkinson and F. Allsop, *Working Plan for Insein Forest Division, 1937-38 to 1946-47*, Rangoon, 1940, vol. II, p. 121.

[53] H.C. Smith, *Working Plan for South Toungoo Forest Division, 1923-24 to 1932-33*, Maymyo, 1923, p. 47; *BLHORP*, 4 September 1939, pp. 470, 472; see also *Report of the Burma Forest Committee 1925*, pp. 24-5.

[54] During 1930-4, annual teak exports averaged 163,000 tons compared with 234,000 tons in 1925-1929, S.F. Hopwood, 'The Influence of the Growing Use of Substitutes for Timber upon Forest Policy with Special Reference to Burma', *Indian Forester* 61 (September 1935), p. 562. The teak price fell from 97.9 rupees per ton in 1928-9 to 40.3 rupees per ton in the early 1930s, Harry Champion and F.C. Osmaston (ed.), *E.P. Stebbing's The Forests of India*, London, 1962, vol. IV, p. 464.

[55] Net revenue also declined since expenditure fell more slowly than revenue. During 1921 and 1931, the forest surplus fluctuated between 17 and 23 per cent of total government

forest administration.[56] Such was the magnitude of these cuts that the total number of staff in 1936-7 (3,001 men) was little more than it had been just before the First World War (2,940 men), while the strength of the subordinate staff was less in the mid-1930s than it was 1913-14.[57] With fewer staff to patrol the forests, protection of the plains reserves became more difficult. As Conservator C.E. Milner noted in 1934, peasants refused to extract designated trees, 'preferring to steal' what they needed, safe in the knowledge that there was little that the Forest Department could do to stop them on a reduced staff.[58]

Political changes in the late 1930s only intensified these difficulties. Following suppression of the Hsaya San insurrection, the link between peasants and urban middle-class nationalists was briefly disrupted. As noted, the former resumed everyday resistance strategies; in contrast, the latter became embroiled in constitutional politics.[59] Yet the advent of parliamentary government in April 1937 enhanced the ability of the Burmese political elite to intervene in forestry matters and peasant lives.

This politicization of forest administration is discussed below. What needs to be noted here, however, is that applications to disforest plains reserves were no longer judged according to technical criteria.[60] Rather, these applications were used in the context of a general shortage of agricultural land to advance Burmese elite interests.[61]

---

revenue, but in 1932-3 it was 12 per cent, *Report of the Burma Retrenchment Committee 1934*, Rangoon, 1934, p. 28.

[56] It was guided by several committees – *Report of the Burma Retrenchment Committee 1934; Second Interim Report of the Fiscal Committee 1938*, Rangoon, 1938; *Report of the Committee on Expenditure on the Public Services, 1939-40*, Part I, Rangoon, 1940 – but was still reviewing the latter two reports in 1942, see *BLHORP*, 18 February 1941, p. 57; F.T. Morehead, 'Organisation of the Forest Service in Burma with particular reference to the Report of the Fiscal Committee of 1938,' *Burma Office File* (henceforth BOF) M/3/1531; H.C. Smith, 'Reconstruction in Burma, the Forest Department; Preliminary Review of Past Administration (1942),' BOF M/3/1531.

[57] Champion and Osmaston, *Forests of India*, vol. IV, p. 441.

[58] *RFA*, 1933-4, p. 22; Thein Lwin, 'Why We Had Failed', *Burmese Forester* 6 (June 1956), pp. 34-5.

[59] Cady, *History of Modern Burma*, pp. 322-55; Taylor, *State in Burma*, pp. 195-6.

[60] Which is not to say that before 1937 applications were necessarily always judged according to these criteria see J.S. Vorley, *Working Plan for North Pegu Forest Division, 1936-37 to 1945-46*, Rangoon, 1937, p. 16 Before 1937, however, the application process was only partly politicized.

[61] Land alienation accelerated after 1930 as landowners could not repay debts. Thus, while the area held by non-farmers climbed from 31 per cent in 1929-30 to nearly 50 per cent in 1934-5, the area let to tenants increased form 46 per cent to 59 per cent.

For this reason, after 1937 the fate of applications to disforest plains reserves depended on the views of the Parliamentary Secretary, and never on the technical advisers, 'unless the two happened to agree', indeed, politicians 'vied with each other for the "honour and glory" of being responsible for the disforestation of reserved forests'.[62]Members of the newly created House of Representatives petitioned the government to disforest reserves in their districts; but if the official objective was to provide land to the rural poor, in practice local notables affiliated with national politicians were often the ultimate beneficiaries of disforestation.[63] Plains reserves were disforested in, among other places, Meiktila, Myingyan and Magwe Districts as a result of political interference.[64]

Degradation of residual plains reserves intensified after 1942 in the context of a virtual breakdown of forest management in the country. The Japanese army used without restraint these forests as a convenient source of timber supplies ignoring the pleas of Burmese forest officials that they abide by the forest law.[65] The Forest Bureau also failed to halt the theft of forest products from reserves by a peasantry pressed harder than usual by the deprivations of life under harsh wartime conditions. The resumption of British rule in 1945 did not alter this situation. Thus, efforts to restore order in the plains reserves were nullified by 'increasing disrespect for forest laws' in a context of chronic political unrest and economic hardship.[66] Indeed Communist leader Than Tun, among others, actively encouraged peasants to raid reserves in defiance of the law.[67] However, degradation of the plains reserves in the final years of colonial rule was more a continuation of the everyday forms of resistance that characterized

---

See Michael Adas, *The Burma Delta: Economic Development and Social Change on an Asian Rice Frontier, 1852-1941*, Madison, 1974, pp. 188-9. In this context, the pressure to clear residual plains forests increased, see *BLHORP*, 4 September 1939, pp. 469-73.

[62] Smith, 'Reconstruction in Burma'; see also J.W.R. Sutherland, *Working Plan for Minbu Forest Division, 1937-38 to 1951-52*, Rangoon, 1938, vol. I, p. 17; Tan Chein Hoe, *Working Plan for Delta Forest Division, 1947-48 to 1956-57*, Rangoon, 1951, vol. II, p. 14; A. Long, 'Village or Community Forests', *Burmese Forester* 2 (March 1952), pp. 28-9; J.B. Carrapiett, 'Plains Forests', *Burmese Forester* 2 (March 1952), p. 15.

[63] *BLHORP*, 23 March 1939, pp. 1362-3; *BLHORP*, 6 April 1939, pp. 1871-2.

[64] Thein Lwin, 'Why We Had Failed', p. 34.

[65] Hla Pe, *Narrative*, p. 65.

[66] Forest Department Report (March 1947), BOF M/4/883.

[67] Forest Department Report (January 1947), BOF M/4/883; Martin Smith, *Burma: Insurgency and the Politics of Ethnicity*, London, 1991, p. 70. Than Tun was himself the son of a timber merchant.

prewar Burmese forest politics than a response by peasants to the contemporary political situation.

There is a paradox in the politics surrounding the plains reserves issue. Never of much economic significance to the colonial state, the reserves were created in the late nineteenth and early twentieth century almost as an afterthought by a Forest Department preoccupied with the management of the lucrative teak forests. Yet, the closing of the agricultural frontier in Lower Burma, combined with the growth of nationalism, guaranteed these reserves a high political profile after 1923. That Europeans were favoured in the allocation of forest leases and jobs only reinforced the general image of an exploitative and anti-Burmese central state.

Burmanization of the Forest Sector

The plains reserve issue was primarily a concern that related to the peasantry. In contrast, the Burmanization question was of central importance to the urban middle class. This group generally prospered under colonial rule, but by the 1920s its position was under attack from Indian, Chinese and European interests. However, the dyarchy reforms provided a political-legal context within which the urban middle class could lobby for change. The promotion of Burman control of the forest sector was thus part of a broader effort to protect elite interests in the transition to self-rule.

There were two aspects to that process. First, the Burmese elite sought to remove obstacles that prevented Burmese from attaining senior posts in the Forest Department and the European firms. Second, it fought for a reallocation of the teak leases in order to advance Burmese economic interests. The former was designed to ensure the representation of Burmese elite interests within existing state and non-state decision-making structures. In contrast, the latter was an attempt to transform gradually those structures through a reconstitution of teak lease-holdings.

Burmese advancement within the Forest Department and the European firms remained slow under dyarchy. The subject of Burmese advancement in the European firms was first taken up systematically only in 1938 when the Ba Maw government proposed that 25 per cent of the superior service of the European lessees should be Burmese within five years. The extent to which each firm complied with this scheme would be taken into account in the future disposal of leases.[68] The

---

[68] Government press release, 'Burma's Forest Reserves, Extraction Policy, Big Lessees and Burmanisation', *Rangoon Gazette* 27 May 1938, BOF M/3/501; Bruce, 'Burma

Ba Maw government was defeated in 1939, but the issue was raised again by Premier U Saw in a meeting with the European firms on 17 September 1941. He urged them to meet a 50 per cent target in return for which they would be awarded a concession on timber royalties then under negotiation (see below). An agreement was reached in principle, but the Japanese invasion interrupted the conclusion of a final deal.[69] The pre-eminent role of the European firms came under growing attack following the war, and calls for nationalization ('complete Burmanization') began to be heard ever more frequently.

Gradual progress was made in Burmanizing the Forest Department. As a public institution responsible for managing the country's forest resource in the 'national' interest, the Forest Department was always more vulnerable to Burmese pressure than were the privately – owned European firms. Even here, though, nationalists faced an uphill battle in the 1920s and 1930s as existing bureaucratic practices and imperial resistance combined to delay the Burmanization campaign.

As noted, the appointment of a Burmese Forests Minister in 1923 did not alter British control over appointments to the Forest Department. However, this Minister was in a unique position to lobby fellow ministers and the Governor on this issue. Further, over the years nationalists repeatedly attacked the government over the absence of Burmese in the superior service. In 1923, for example, Yamethin U Pu moved that forest expenditure be cut in protest at the lack of Burmese in this service. This resolution was narrowly defeated after a heated debate.[70] Similar resolutions were made in 1924 and 1926, and at the height of the Great Depression in 1932, U Ba Thi (Mandalay) cleverly pointed out that government could simultaneously save funds and promote Burmanization by replacing highly paid Europeans with their lower paid Burmese counterparts.[71] These efforts maintained the Burmanization issue on the political agenda and contributed to incremental change in this area.

Burmese comprised about one-quarter of the senior service in 1942; in contrast prior to 1923 no Burmese had served in this select group.[72]

Recollections', MSS. Eur. E. 362/3

[69] Note of the Meeting between Premier U Saw and Lessees, 17 September 1941, BOF M/3/501; Bruce, 'Burma Recollections'.

[70] *BLCP*, 21 March 1923, pp. 279-96.

[71] *BLCP*, 25 February 1932, pp. 460-3; see also Note by M.M. Ohn Ghine and U Shwe Tha, *Report of the Burma Retrenchment Committee 1934*, p. 227; *BLCP*, 20 March 1924, pp. 555-7; *BLCP*, 18 March 1926, pp. 426-9;

[72] With the exception of Assistant Conservator Poh Oh in the 1870s as noted in Chapter 3. On Burmese advancement after 1923, see Great Britain, *Memorandum by the Government of Burma*, p. 58; *Report of the Forest Reconstruction Committee* (1944), app. VI, BOF,

After 1937, the Burmese political elite sought to accelerate this process of change. The most significant step in this regard came in November 1941 when the government of Premier U Saw appointed a committee to enquire into recruitment policy; several meetings were held but the war interrupted completion of a report. Nevertheless, the Recruitment Committee's deliberations indicated that European recruitment to the Forest Department was not acceptable to an increasingly assertive Burmese leadership.[73] In taking this stance, the Burmese were able to point to the growing number of trained local men: by 1938, forty-two individuals had been awarded a Bachelor of Science in Forestry from Rangoon University, all but one of whom had entered the Forest Department thereby creating a pool of recruits awaiting promotion to the senior service.[74]

If politicians sought to accelerate the Burmanization campaign, they also intervened actively in Forest Department activities. Such intervention partly reflected frustration at the slow pace of reform, but was also indicative of the growing politicization of forest administration, particularly after 1937.

This process was most evident during U Saw's term as Forests Minister. Appointed in February 1939, Saw skilfully used the numerous patronage opportunities of the Department to promote his quest for the premiership. [75] As the Forests Ministry was 'used as a political instrument', the Chief Conservator became marginalized, and political appointees ignored the recommendations of forest officials. The appointment of Palit Maung Maung – a former Forest Department employee dismissed for corruption – as Saw's personal assistant was particularly significant in this regard as this individual was a senior official in Saw's own *Myochit* Party.[76]

Even routine administrative matters were now subject to political interference. Thus, Saw's assistants overruled officials in a move which 'undermined the authority of the executive' and interrupted the carriage of justice.[77] The senior Burmese forest official, U Thein

---

M/3/1531; Smith, 'Reconstruction in Burma'.

[73] Smith, 'Reconstruction in Burma'. Premier U Saw was committed to Burmanization throughout government, *BLHORP*, 26 September 1940, p. 1348; *BLHORP*, 18 February 1941, p. 57.

[74] *Burma Legislature Senate Proceedings*, 23 February 1938, pp 6-7.

[75] Saw retained the Forests portfolio even after he became Premier in September 1940, Taylor, 'The Case of U Saw', p. 179; John LeRoy Christian, *Burma and the Japanese Invader*, Bombay, 1945, p. 250.

[76] Smith, 'Reconstruction in Burma', Thein Lwin, 'Why We Had Failed', pp. 37-8; *BLHORP*, 19 March 1941, pp. 1010-11.

[77] Smith, 'Reconstruction in Burma', *BLHORP*, 31 August 1939, pp. 320-1.

Lwin, related how on one occasion he compounded a forest offence that was committed by a politician. Subsequently, he was ordered to withdraw the case by the Minister; that order was communicated through the accused person.[78] Similarly, the traditional practice of allocating free timber for the construction of *pongyi kyaung* (monasteries) was also used for political purposes – to ensure Saw of the support of key religious leaders.[79] Perhaps most seriously, direct political control was exerted over the subordinate service such that the belief became widespread that 'appointments were bought and sold.'[80] In the years immediately prior to 1942, a kind of *de facto* parallel administration thus emerged. Based in the Burmese-controlled Secretariat located in Rangoon, it linked forest management to party politics as never before, and in the process, undermined the authority of colonial officials.

The Japanese occupation provided the context for a rapid Burmanization of the Forest Department. British forest officials evacuated to India along with other colonial officials in early 1942. Based in India, they planned the postwar resumption of colonial rule based on the political and economic *status quo ante bellum*. Thus, since the Burmese were still 'unprepared' for senior posts, Europeans would still run the Forest Department.[81] However, even as Chief Conservator H.C. Smith was writing this assessment in 1942 from exile in Simla, Burmese forest officials were beginning to reorganize the Forest Department in the British absence under Japanese direction. As noted, a Forest Bureau modelled on the prewar Department was established in 1942 under a Director of Forests reporting to the Forests Minister. The prewar bureaucratic structure was retained as far as possible; it was even proposed to open a Forest School at Thindawyo (Tharrawaddy District) for the training of subordinates at the same time as university-level instruction would be provided in Rangoon for officials destined for the senior service.

Under Director U Thein Lwin, Burmese forest officials sought to restore order in the forests. In doing so, they used the same techniques, and justified their actions with recourse to the same principles, as did their British predecessors. Such continuity was set out in the first annual report:

[78] Thein Lwin, 'Why We Had Failed', p. 37; see also *BLHORP*, 6 April 1939, p. 1868.

[79] Taylor, 'Case of U Saw', p. 173; Smith, 'Reconstruction in Burma'; *BLHORP*, 18 February 1941, p. 61.

[80] Smith, 'Reconstruction in Burma'; Taylor, 'Case of U Saw', p. 173; Thein Lwin, 'Why We Had Failed', p. 37.

[81] Smith, 'Reconstruction in Burma'; see also Taylor, *The State in Burma*, p. 230.

The Forest policy has been and still is to administer and manage the State Forests on sound scientific principles, in order to produce the highest, sustained annual yield of timber for export and home consumption, while trying to improve the condition and stocking of the valuable tree species.[82]

The pursuit of this policy proved impossible in wartime Burma. Dislocation caused by the war itself hindered the reassertion of forest control by the Forest Department. Thus, movement of officials around the country and the central coordination of their activities was disrupted by Allied bombing of Burma's transport and communications infrastructure. Further, forest rules were ignored by the Japanese army which permitted unlimited extraction in aid of their war effort. When Burmese forest officials tried to halt the destruction of teak plantations by fuelwood contractors, for example, they were over-ruled by the military; indeed, anyone 'on friendly terms with the local Japanese officer could go into the forests at leisure and cut whatever tree he liked'.[83] U Thein Lwin even cited international law on one occasion when he pleaded with a Japanese officer to stop such practices.[84]

Burmese forest officials nevertheless sought wherever possible to reintroduce prewar practices. Thus, they resumed charging peasants for the extraction of forest products from reserves; the tapping of trees for wood-oil, for example, required once more a license.[85] subordinates also reported breaches of the forest rules in a (largely futile) attempt to contain illegal extraction from the plains reserves. The perpetuation of long-term commercial teak exploitation, meanwhile, remained a central concern of the wartime all-Burmese forest service. Thus, forest officials girdled teak trees in the forest in the prescribed manner, and as noted sought to prevent contractors from felling teak plantations.[86] They also sought permission to extract teak, but were forced in general to cede this activity to the Japanese (see below).[87] These wartime efforts were important because they enabled the Burmese to gain experience managing the country's forests in the absence

---

[82] Burma Ministry of Finance, *Financial and Economic Annual*, p. 31.

[83] Hla Pe, *Narrative*, p. 65.

[84] Thein Lwin, 'Why We Had Failed', p. 38.

[85] M.V. Edwards, 'Use of Minor Forest Products in Burma during the Japanese Occupation', *Indian Forester* 73 (December 1947), p. 534. Anon., 'Ministry of Forests and Public Works', *Guardian* (Rangoon) 8 (March 1961), p. 25.

[86] Burma Ministry of Finance, *Financial and Economic Annual*, p. 32; A.N. Barker, 'The Forest Position in Burma – January 1946', *Empire Forestry Review* 25, 1 (1946), p. 38; Toke Gale, *Burmese Timber Elephant*, Rangoon, 1974, p. 86.

[87] Anon., 'Forests and Public Works', p. 25.

of the British – albeit subject to the disruptions of war and Japanese rule. In a process that foreshadowed post-independence forestry practices, Burmese forest officials sought to restore order in the forests in keeping with colonial scientific forestry management. The British may have gone but their practices were to continue.

The return of British forest officials to Burma in 1945 marked a formal return to the prewar Forest Department. Once more, British resumed charge of the senior service and the Burmese returned to more junior positions. However, the British were no more successful at restoring order in the forests between 1945 and 1948 than were their Burmese counterparts during the war. The pervasive rural unrest noted earlier prevented the resumption of regular forest work in most parts of the country. As in prewar times, subordinates bore the brunt of attacks directed against the Forest Department, and several men were murdered. Not surprisingly, the Forest Department experienced difficulties in recruiting Burmese youth. Indeed, and reflecting the growing power and influence of the nationalist movement *vis-à-vis* the British, subordinates started 'Forest Subordinate Unions', especially in the areas worst affected by the unrest, to protest their work conditions.[88]

As independence drew ever nearer, however, politically motivated violence intensified, overwhelming the little forest work that had been undertaken. In the Pyinmana and Yamethin Divisions, for example, it was reported that 'teak plantations are being clear felled and contractors and lessee's logs in hundreds are being removed illicitly ... subordinates are powerless.'[89] The armed escorts that accompanied forest officials everywhere were 'merely a succulent bait for the large bands of well armed rebels roaming the country.'[90] Forest management was thus virtually impossible throughout the country. Teak extraction was disrupted, and 40,000 tons of teak worth 6,000,000 rupees were stolen in 1946 alone.[91] A substantial loss of revenue, such theft also frustrated efforts to restore production to prewar levels. At independence, the British thus handed over to their Burmese counterparts a Forest Department whose effective remit extended little beyond the city limits of the national capital, Rangoon.

During the late colonial era, therefore, the Burmese political elite

---

[88] Forest Department Report (October 1946); Forest Department Report (January 1947), both in BOF M/4/883.

[89] 'Confidential Note on Illicit Extraction of Timber and General Lawlessness', Conservator, Sittang Circle, to Agricultural and Rural Economy Secretary, 8 May 1946, BOF M/4/626; Timber Project Report (July 1947), BOF M/4/6.

[90] 'Confidential Note'.

[91] Forest Department Report (January 1947), BOF M/4/883; Timber Project Report (April 1946), BOF M/4/6.

sought to promote its interests through the Burmanization of the Forest Department and the European firms. However, it also demanded that Burmese be allotted a greater share of the teak leases as part of a gradual re – allocation of the lease holdings. Yet firm British control over this strategic timber resource obviated rapid change.

Ironically, the emergence of a Burmese middle class in the early twentieth century was based partly on success in the timber trade. Indeed, several politicians of the interwar period owed their position to success in that trade.[92] Shwegyin U Pu, who was Premier in 1939-40, was born into a family of timber merchants in Shwegyin, and profit earned from the business enabled him to be educated in England. The grandfather and father of another leading politician, U Chit Hlaing, prospered in the timber business; the family financial legacy was later used in the nationalist struggle.[93] U Thin Maung, a Hanthawaddy-based politician and critic of the Forest Department, had been in the business since before 1923.

Yet the allocation in 1907 of the key teak forests to the European firms under a system of long-term renewable leases effectively eliminated the possibility that Burmese firms would ever be able to compete on equal terms with their European counterparts. In 1925, and again in 1937, a government committee reviewed the timber allocation question, but each time recommended against major change. To be sure, a few Burmese obtained teak leases for extended periods, but most remained confined to short-term contracts and the least valuable forests.[94] Chapter 5 noted the twentieth-century pre-eminence of the European firms in terms of teak extraction. Such pre-eminence was also reflected in their share of the teak leases. These firms held twenty-eight leases covering an area of 56,926 square miles in 1925. In contrast Burmese firms held 15 leases comprising only 1,614 square miles.[95]

Under the system of renewals, moreover, the only way that the Burmese could acquire forests from the European firms was if the latter violated the terms of their leases or could not agree with the government over royalties. There were lease violations by the European firms over the years, but the government did not revoke their leases.[96]

[92] Taylor, *State in Burma*, pp. 169, 171.

[93] Upon his return from England in 1903, Chit Hlaing urged his father to leave the timber trade because 'the forest laws were so framed that no [Burmese] could escape being penalised'. In 1910 Chit Hlaing's father quit forestry for agriculture. See *BLHORP*, 14 March 1940, p. 1056

[94] For details on the leading interwar Burmese lessees, see On Gyaw, *Burma Teak Lease*, Rangoon, 1947, pp. 2-3; Morehead, *Forests of Burma*, p. 43.

[95] *BLCP*, 10 March 1925, p. 29.

[96] F.A. Leete, 'Inspection Note on Teak Fellings and Extraction in the Nawin Forests,

Consequently, the allocation of teak leases remained essentially un-changed throughout the interwar period.

British forest officials believed that this state of affairs reflected the superior organizational and financial skills of the European firms. While Burmese timber traders lacked the capital and experience to undertake large-scale teak extraction, especially in remote areas, the European firms had the financial and human resources to do the job. In 1924, for example, their invested capital in Burma was 100,000,000 rupees and they employed a total of 55,000 men.[97] It was the highly capitalized and international European firm, then, and not the small-scale and under-financed Burmese trader, that was best placed to develop the teak trade in Burma.

Nationalists rejected this argument and pointed to a forest policy that systematically favoured European over Burmese firms. Whereas the former were granted fifteen-year renewals, the latter were largely confined to short-term contracts (1-5 years) without such a clause. The Europeans thus had security of tenure, while the Burmese did not.

Favouritism was also reflected in the royalty system. To begin with, the rate paid by the European firms was generally lower than that paid by Burmese traders.[98] The Europeans also paid for timber after, and not before, extraction. In contrast, the Burmese were required to pay royalties in advance despite the fact that pre-payment only 'played into the hands' of the money-lenders on whom they were dependent.[99] Under the terms of their contracts, moreover, the Europeans could reject all but the best teak as 'refuse' timber. As the latter was disposed of by the Forest Department and the proceeds then

---

Prome Division under the 15 Year Lease dating from 1908-09 held by Messrs. Steel Bros. and Co. Ltd.', *BFP* (November 1916), pp. 95-128; E.S Hartnoll and F.T. Morehead, *Working Plan for the Kaukkwe Portion of the Bhamo Forest Division, 1935-36 to 1947-48*, Rangoon, 1936, p. 21.

[97] H.R. Blanford, 'Distribution of Teak Forests', Note prepared for the Government of Burma, [1936], MSS Eur. D. 689; Morehead, *Forests of Burma*, p. 43.

[98] Maria Serena I. Diokno, 'British Firms and the Economy of Burma, with Special Reference to the Rice and Teak Industries, 1917-1937', unpubl. Ph.D. thesis, University of London, 1983, p. 187; *BLHORP*, 26 February 1937, p. 132. In Thaton Division, for example, T.D. Findlay and Sons paid 23 rupees per ton on full-sized timber as compared with 45 rupees per ton by U Bah Oh and Sons and 40 rupees per ton by Saw Tha Dwe and Saw Po Nyein, see W.S. Shepherd, *Working Plan for Thaton Forest Division, 1935-36 to 1944-45*, Rangoon, 1937, p. 6. Rates varied depending on timber accessibility and quality, but these factors do not account for the discrepancy in the European and Burmese rates.

[99] H.C. Walker, 'The Issue of Timber Licenses in Burma', *Indian Forester* 43 (February 1917), pp. 70-1.

split with the firm in question, this arrangement partially sheltered the European firms from market downturns in so far as the average royalty rate was reduced.[100] The Burmese, meanwhile, paid royalty on all contracted timber whether extracted or not; indeed, often such timber had already been rejected by the Europeans as sub-standard.[101]

But it was during the Great Depression that favouritism shown by the colonial state towards the European firms became most evident. As teak prices plummeted, the European firms pressed for, and obtained, a substantial royalty rebate.[102] On 1 July 1933, the government reduced the rate by 30 per cent 'in order to assist the lessees in maintaining the market for teak by lowering the price and placing it on a competitive basis.'[103] At a time when substantial cuts in forest administration were being implemented, this decision cost the government 1,450,000 rupees in 1933-4 alone. The full royalty rate was only restored in 1937-8. The government's 'broad-minded policy' was praised by the BBTCL, and as a result of which that company's profits were 'rather better' than expected.[104]

In contrast, the colonial state was slow in extending to Burmese traders the same advantage. Yet, it was precisely because they were less capitalized than their European counterparts that the Burmese were most in need of such a reduction.[105] In 1936, the government even raised the duty on Siamese teak imported into Burma via the Salween river from 7 per cent to 25 per cent. This move was in response to lobbying by the European firms, and was bitterly opposed by Burmese traders in Moulmein whose interests were adversely affected, but who were not consulted on the matter.[106] A representation by

---

[100] The average rate fell from 25.6 rupees per ton in 1931-2 to 18.9 rupees per ton in 1932-3, Champion and Osmaston, *Forests of India*, vol. IV, pp. 465-6; A.C. Pointon, *The Bombay Burmah Trading Corporation Ltd., 1863-1963*, Southampton, 1964, pp. 80-1.

[101] *BLCP*, 25 February 1932, pp. 451-2; *BLHORP*, 8 March 1938, p. 759; *BLHORP*, 15 February 1940, p. 51.

[102] The government assisted these firms through royalty concessions even before the 1930s, see Smith, *South Toungoo Forest Division*, p. 17; W.C. Rooke, *Working Plan for Minbu Forest Division, 1927-28 to 1936-37*, Rangoon, 1928, p. 9; A.J.S. Butterwick, *Working Plan for South Pegu Forest Division, 1937-38 to 1946-47*, Rangoon, 1938, vol. II, p. 4.

[103] Hopwood, 'Growing Use of Substitutes', p. 567.

[104] *Annual Report of the Bombay Burmah Trading Corporation Limited* (henceforth *ARBBTCL*), 1934-5, pp. 3-4; *ARBBTCL*, 1935-6, p. 3.

[105] Timber trader and politician U Ba charged that a belated 20 per cent reduction on non-teak royalties was 'so low that it was not possible for the small traders to go on working', see *BLHORP* 3 March 1937, pp. 285-6; see also *BLCP*, 9 February 1933, p. 37; *BLCP*, 2 March 1935, pp. 392, 394-5; Aung Tun Thet, *Burmese Entrepreneurship: Creative Response in the Colonial Economy*, Stuttgart, 1989, pp. 63-4.

the Moulmein Timber Traders' Association calling for the repeal of this duty was rejected by government.[107]

It is hardly surprising, therefore, that Burmese who had once been 'very much engaged' in the timber business, by the 1930s were increasingly peripheral. As U Thin Maung noted, this trend had much to do with the fact that 'the larger firms are quite able to make their points of view heard [by government], but the local traders are not and their opinions are often ignored.'[108]

Following the 1937 political reforms, the Burmese political elite stepped up the pressure on British officials to reverse this trend. The goal of that elite between 1937 and 1942 was not, however, a sudden or dramatic re-allocation of the teak leases. Rather a gradual shift was sought. There were various reasons for such pragmatism. First, and notwithstanding the substantial political powers transferred to the Burmese in 1937, Burma remained a colony subject to British control.[109] Given the centrality of European interests in the teak industry, senior British officials would not have allowed politicians to effect major change in the lease holdings – at least in the short term. From the start of the lease negotiations in the mid-1930s, British policy was thus to maintain 'as far as possible the outturn of the five European teak firms.[110] This policy was confirmed by the Forest Enquiry Committee whose report was submitted to the Governor as the first Burmese government under the new constitution took office.[111] For the benefit of that government, the Committee warned that disrupting the status quo 'would lead to disorganization of the teak trade and would in all probability seriously affect Government revenue.' However, it also recommended that in order to facilitate 'more and wider opportunities for indigenous enterprise', the new European leases should not include rights of renewal or first refusal as in the past.[112] This

---

[106] *BLCP*, 12 August 1936, pp. 87-91; *BLCP*, 13 August 1936, pp. 123-4. The *BBTCL* closed its operations in the Salween forests in 1932-3, see *ARBBTCL*, 1932-3, p. 3.

[107] *BLCP*, 17 August 1936, pp. 274-5; *BLHORP*, 8 March 1937, pp. 425-30.

[108] *BLCP*, 4 March 1935, p. 404; see also *BLCP*, 2 March 1935, pp. 394-5.

[109] Ba Maw, *Breakthrough in Burma: Memoirs of a Revolution, 1939-1946*, New Haven, 1968, pp. 18-19; Trager, *Burma: From Kingdom to Independence*, pp. 52-3.

[110] Blanford, 'Distribution of Teak Forests'.

[111] *Report of the Forest Enquiry Committee 1937*, Rangoon, 1937. In soliciting the views of Burmese timber traders, the Committee noted that many traders 'ventilated grievances, such as methods of collection of royalty,which are not the concern of this Committee' (p. 1). Yet, as noted, it was precisely this issue which was of preeminent concern to these traders during the interwar period.

[112] *Ibid.*, p. 13.

move would keep open the option of future lease re-allocations in favour of Burmese firms.

Second, Burmese politics in the years 1937-42 was highly volatile, and government was accordingly unstable. Thus, the Ba Maw government (1937-9) held power only at the sufferance of the European and ethnic minority members in the House of Representatives – groups hardly favourable towards radical change.[113] Third, the pragmatism of the Burmese political elite also reflected a generally conservative outlook borne of personal business interests, as well as those of their wealthy financial backers. It was for this reason that nationalization was never an option prior to the war.[114]

Yet the fact that the Burmese political elite now controlled forest administration was the most compelling reason of all for a moderate strategy on the lease question. A sudden change would have seriously disrupted government revenue as there were no Burmese firms even remotely in a position to replace the European lessees in the foreseeable future. A disruption in revenue would have limited patronage opportunities in a highly competitive political environment. If the political elite was 'intensely keen' to gain access to 'the privileges and protections that the mantle of state authority would provide them with in both their intra-elite conflicts and their contest with British officialdom', then it would have been illogical (and impolitic) on their part to limit in any way that authority through precipitous action.[115]

For these reasons, no prewar Burmese government challenged the continued short-term predominance of the European firms. As set out by successive Burmese governments, the new policy aimed for continuity in a context of long-term change: the major teak forests would continue to be worked by the European firms for fifteen years while smaller accessible forests would be allocated to Burmese firms. At that stage, the Burmanization issue would play a central part in the re-allocation of leases.[116] However, this arrangement was never finalized before the war owing to disagreement over royalty rates.[117]

Nationalists had little opportunity to pursue Burmanization further

---

[113] Cady, *History of Modern Burma*, pp. 386, 389.

[114] Taylor, 'Case of U Saw', pp. 166-8; *BLHORP*, 24 March 1937, pp. 738-9; *BLHORP*, 13 March 1939, pp. 937-8.

[115] Taylor, *State in Burma*, p. 187.

[116] Government of Burma, 'Burma's Forest Reserves, Extraction Policy, Big Lessees and Burmanisation'; Bruce, 'Burma Recollections'.

[117] The European firms encountered more trouble from British forest officials than they did from Burmese politicians over royalty rates, see Bruce, 'Burma Recollections', Pointon, *Bombay Burmah*, p. 86.

during the war. Under the Japanese, the timber trade was given over to supporting the war effort. Four Japanese firms comprising the Nippon Burma Timber Union (NBTU) virtually monopolized the trade after May 1942, and extracted timber from accessible forests, often in violation of the forest rules.[118] Burmese timber traders sought, wherever possible, to continue timber extraction. This was invariably on a small scale. Thus, U Ba Oh extracted 15,000 tons of timber form the Pyinmana forests for conversion into railway sleepers.[119] Further, all timber had to be sold to the NBTU under the terms and conditions set by that organization. Under these conditions, Burmese timber traders were unable to take advantage of the absence of the European firms to expand their operations. Indeed, as a result of Allied bombing and sabotage operations of the transportation network, as well as chronic labour shortages, timber outturn was well below both wartime targets and prewar levels.[120]

In India, meanwhile, the British planned for a resumption of Burma's teak trade on the prewar model – that is, based on the continued preeminence of the European firms. Thus, in 1944 an Expert Advisory Committee based its advise to Burma's Governor on the rehabilitation of the timber industry on the assumed preeminence of these firms in the postwar trade.[121] Significantly, however, this assumption was criticized by Burmese Committee member U Htoon Aung Gyaw who argued that since much of the invested capital (e.g. timber elephants) of the European firms would have likely disappeared as a result of the fighting, it was time to consider Burmanization or even nationalization of the forest industry. He further noted a 'definite school of thought' among the Burmese that extraction should not be by European firms unless new technology required their continued presence.[122]

Yet the British ignored this warning as they sought to restore British rule in Burma after 1945.[123] Thus, the government implemented

---

[118] Anon, 'The Nippon Burma Timber Union', *Guardian* (Rangoon) 7 (December 1960), pp. 19-20; Barker, 'Forest Position', p. 37.

[119] Barker, 'Forest Position', p. 37; On Gyaw, *Burma Teak Lease*, p. 4.

[120] In 1943, for example, the goal was 241,200 tons but actual production was only 71, 388 tons, see Won Zoon Yoon, 'Japan's Occupations of Burma, 1941-1945', unpubl. Ph.D. thesis, New York University, 1971, p. 214; Barker, 'Forest Position', pp. 37-8.

[121] Expert Advisory Committee, 'Report on the Rehabilitation of the Timber Industry in Burma 1944', BOF M/3/1234; see also Note by Sir Hugh Watson (12 December 1942), and Note by H.R. Blanford (6 February 1943), both in BOF M/3/501.

[122] Htoon Aung Gyaw, 'Comment on His Excellency the Governor's Consultative Committee' (2 August 1944), in Expert Advisory Committee, 'Rehabilitation of the Timber Industry'. Htoon Aung Gyaw was a Finance Minister in U Saw's government.

[123] Attention at first focused on supplying military needs, but civil rule was restored in

the Waight Plan (after Financial Adviser Leonard Waight), a plan negotiated during the war between the government of Burma, the Burma Office in London, and the European firms. Under the Plan, a Timber Project Board comprising the European firms and the government was set up for 'managing and controlling the extraction, conversion, and marketing of forest produce in Burma.'[124] The Board would revive timber production while new leases were settled, and the Forest Department would restore scientific forest management in the country's forests. However, the shortage of Project staff was such that the Department focused almost exclusively on timber extraction duties in 1946-7.

This arrangement between the European firms and the government was attacked vociferously by an increasingly assertive and radical nationalist movement. Thus, Deputy Chairman of the Governor's Executive Council and AFPFL leader Aung San condemned in 1947 the Project Boards for 'killing what indigenous enterprises there are instead of promoting them or benefiting the people to the extent they should', and added that 'nationalisation of all important industries' – including the forest industry – would be a central goal of a future AFPFL government.[125] Burmese timber traders simultaneously protested the restoration of the prewar status quo in the guise of the Timber Project Board. To make their 'legitimate claims' heard, they formed the All Burma Timber Trades Federation in Rangoon in 1947 to lobby government for a change of policy. Such initiatives were reported widely in the Burmese media as part of a broader anti-British campaign in the lead-up to independence.[126] As the formal date for the end of British rule in Burma neared, it was increasingly apparent that the predominance of the European firms in the country's teak industry was also nearing its end.

This chapter has shown how the Forest Department's system of rationalized forest use was undermined between 1923 and 1948. If the introduction of dyarchy in 1923 did not spell immediate change, it nevertheless enabled an increasingly assertive nationalist movement

January 1946, see Burma Forest Department, 'Empire Forests and the War: Burma' in *Fifth British Empire Forestry Conference; Statements* vol. I (1947), app. II, pp. 23-6; D.J. Atkinson, 'Situation in 1945 [and 1946]', TMs [1946-47], Oxford Forestry Institute, Oxford; Barker, 'Forest Position', pp. 38-9.

[124] Timber Project Order 1945', reprinted in Burma Forest Department, 'Empire Forests and the War', p. 19; Memorandum on the Timber Project (1945), BOF M/4/3; also the extensive correspondence in BOF M/3/501.

[125] Aung San, 'This Burma', *Burma Digest* 2 (15 March 1947), p. 4.

[126] On Gyaw, *Burma Teak Lease*, pp. 4-5; Tan Chein Hoe, 'One Hundred Years of Forestry in Burma', *Burmese Forester* 6 (June 1956), p. 47.

to focus attention on hitherto neglected issues. Above all, partial self-rule in conjunction with peasant resistance in the countryside meant that British forest officials could no longer ignore the local political implications of their action as had been the case in the pre-dyarchy period.

On the one hand, an increasingly desperate peasantry stepped up its challenge to the colonial state. In the process, peasant grievances were politicized and linked to broader nationalist issues by middle-class politicians seeking peasant support through attacks on the Forest Department and its plains reserves policy. On the other hand, and as the Burmanization issue illustrates, the advent of partial self-rule was seized upon by the urban middle class as an opportunity to assert its claim to the top forestry jobs and a share of the valuable teak leases.

In many respects quite different, the peasant access and Burmanization issues were nonetheless linked insofar as they illustrated a common grievance: Burma's forests were not being managed in the 'best' interests of the Burmese by the Forest Department. That grievance was the basis of inter-class cooperation over forestry matters that weakened gradually the Forest Department's resource management capabilities. Yet as forestry in Burma became less a matter of bureaucratic politics and 'scientific' management, and more a question of nationalist grievances and party politics, it was not clear what those 'best' interests were, and who was to define them. However much forest politics was transformed between 1923 and 1948, conflict still remained at the heart of that process. Following independence, the fight over the forests continued, but as the next chapter shows, under new political conditions.

7

RESTORING ORDER IN THE
FORESTS, 1948-1994

Since Burma achieved independence on 4 January 1948, the Forest Department has operated in a radically altered political and economic context. During most of the postcolonial era, the country has been racked by civil war as diverse political and ethnic groups have challenged the authority of the Rangoon-based Burmese state. Until recently, moreover, a loosely defined socialism has been the ethos guiding the economic development policies of that state. These political and economic conditions have inevitably affected the policies and practices of the Forest Department in the postcolonial era. Thus, civil unrest has meant that the restoration of order in the forests has been a perennial concern of that Department, while the quest for socialism prompted the creation of a State Timber Board that has proven to be a powerful rival in the field of forest management. However, this chapter shows that continuity has also been a hallmark of Burmese forest management since 1948. Thus, while the timber industry was nationalized in a two-stage process beginning in 1948 and ending in the mid-1960s, this departure from the prewar situation did not alter the state's emphasis on commercial as opposed to subsistence forest use. Similarly, the forestry techniques and land management practices geared to commercial timber extraction developed by the British have been perpetuated since independence.

This chapter thus highlights both continuity and change in postcolonial Burmese forest policies and practices when compared with the colonial experience. In doing so, the goal is to explore two broad themes – reterritorialization and socialism – that have strongly shaped forestry in Burma since independence. Chapter 4 highlighted how forest management in the late nineteenth century was largely given over to the quest for territorialization. Since 1948, the Forest Department acting in conjunction with the Burmese army has been caught up in a similar process. Concurrently, the Department also needed to absorb the implications for its role as a resource manager of a shift towards a system of socialist forestry, and in particular, the rise of a powerful

State Timber Board in charge of timber extraction. However, since the *coup d'état* of 18 September 1988 which brought the State Law and Order Restoration Council (SLORC) to power, forest management in Burma has undergone various changes which, in aggregate, may signal a new direction for Burmese forestry in the 1990s – a question explored in the last section of this chapter.

Re-territorialization

If the early 1920s marked the high point of Forest Department power, then the period 1942-52 witnessed a low point in that agency's fortunes. Chapter 6 described the virtual disintegration of forest management in the lead up to independence in 1948. Thereafter the political troubles that had disrupted forestry intensified as one group after another took up arms against the new Burmese state. As much of the country fell under the control of one insurgent group or the other in 1949, the authority of the U Nu government extended little beyond the limits of Rangoon. Indeed, it was not until 1953 that the key low-lying areas of south and central Burma were largely cleared of insurgents, and a semblance of regular governance was introduced in those areas.[1]

For these reasons, in the years immediately following independence, the Forest Department was a department that was literally without forests to manage. The country's key commercial forests were held by insurgents, and Burmese forest officials could only plan for the day when their scientific management would be possible. Yet even when the military situation began to improve after 1952, the Forest Department's ability to manage the forests remained limited. Indeed, the Burmese army's success may have exacerbated the problems facing forest officials in some respects since insurgents retreated into the relative security of the hill forests that those officials sought to manage. As during the third Anglo-Burmese war (1885-6) and Hsaya San insurrection (1930-2), most of the Pegu Yoma fell under the control of the insurgents, but unlike in British times, this region was to remain largely off limits to the Forest Department for more than twenty-five years.

Rather than a regular system of forest management, 'forestry on the run' became the norm in areas subject to insurgent attack. As a result, practices that were integral to scientific forestry under colonial rule – *taungya* forestry, improvement fellings, the collection of field

---

[1] On Burma's civil war see Hugh Tinker, *The Union of Burma: A Study of the First Years of Independence*, London, 1957, pp. 34-61; Martin Smith, *Burma: Insurgency and the Politics of Ethnicity*, London, 1991.

data, and the protection of reserved forests – were impossible. Even basic tasks such as teak girdling and timber extraction were only possible under armed escort. At first, the Forest Department (responsible for teak girdling) and the State Timber Board (in charge of teak extraction) worked separately in the forest, but beginning in 1955 the two agencies coordinated their operations so as to obtain economies of scale in security operations; in turn, this enabled each agency to meet its allotted production target.[2] Thus, whereas 34,300 teak trees were girdled, and 38,700 trees were felled, in 1953-4, 270,400 trees were killed, and 114,300 trees were extracted, in 1956-7.[3] The recovery in timber extraction lagged behind that of girdling due both to the three-year time lag between teak girdling and extraction as well as to the shortage of timber elephants available for such work; during the mid-1950s the State Timber Board possessed fewer than 2,000 elephants compared with more than 6,000 available to the timber industry in 1941.[4]

Both girdling and extraction operations remained subject to constant insurgent attack. Indeed, one forest official remarked:

> The bigger the party the more attractive it became to the insurgents, as was a fatter sambur [deer] to a hungry tiger. No doubt the insurgents were hungry for food, provisions, stores, tents, elephants, money, and above all for firearms and ammunition of which they were in short supply and with all of which the girdling parties were fully equipped. No wonder they were stalking all the time.[5]

Each year, armed forest guards as well as Forest Department and State Timber Board employees were killed in battles with insurgents, underscoring the deadly nature of forestry in the immediate postwar period.[6] Security in central Burma improved gradually in the late

---

[2] *The Nation* (Rangoon), 10 November 1955. The relationship between the Forest Department and the State Timber Board is discussed more fully below.

[3] Louis J. Walinsky, *Economic Development in Burma, 1951-1960*, New York, 1962, p. 321.

[4] *Ibid.*, p. 321. This situation was essentially unchanged in the early 1960s, see *The Nation* (Rangoon), 11 February 1961.

[5] Aung Tin, 'Girdling in Abnormal Times: Zigon Forest Division, 1955-56', *Burmese Forester* 6 (June 1956), p. 106. The insurgency also severely limited the area open to extraction operations. In 1955, that area was only about 20 per cent of the total leased area, but by 1958 that figure had risen to 60 per cent. See Tun Kyaw, 'A Short Note on the Working of the State Timber Board', *Burmese Forester* 6 (June 1956), p. 71; 'The State Timber Board', *Burma* 8 (January 1958), p. 115.

[6] For example, see Aung Tin, 'Girdling in Abnormal Times', p. 105; 'The State Timber Board', *Burma* 6 (January 1956), p. 158; 'Scientific Management of Burma's Forest', *Burma* 7 (January 1957), p. 186.

1950s and early 1960s, but it was not until the mid-1970s that this part of the country was largely pacified.[7]

There were additional difficulties in transporting logs from the timber depots to the mills. Thus, teak was stored 'for years' in Toungoo because rafting operations were too dangerous along the Sittang river. In 1955, the government responded with 'Operation Teak': a large-scale operation in which the Burmese army secured the riverbanks between Toungoo and Rangoon as well as providing river escorts for the rafts themselves.[8] Yet the scale of this security operation only confirmed the major obstacles confronting the government as it sought to restore prewar levels of teak production.

As a result, postwar growth in teak exports was sluggish. From only 36,000 tons in 1953-4, such exports climbed to 87,000 tons in 1956-7, and reached 119,000 tons by 1961-2.[9] Yet, even the latter figure was well below the prewar average of 227,000 tons that was the government's symbolically important production target.[10] Forestry in the years immediately following independence was thus intimately associated with the vicissitudes of the civil war, and in key areas such as the Pegu Yoma was for all intents and purposes a military operation.[11]

---

[7] Director of Information, *Is Trust Vindicated? A Chronicle of the Various Accomplishments of the Government headed by General Ne Win during the Period of Tenure from November, 1958 to February 6, 1960*, Rangoon, 1960, pp. 126, 129-30; 'The State Timber Board', *Burma* 10 (January 1961), p. 319; 'Forest Department', *Burma* 11 (January 1962), pp. 233-4; Director of Information, *Burma: National Economy*, Rangoon, 1963, p. 28; Shwe Bo, 'Burma's Teak', *Forward* 1 (15) (7 March 1963), p. 18; and see below.

[8] *The Nation* (Rangoon), 10 November 1955; see also Tinker, *Union of Burma*, p. 248; 'The State Timber Board', *Burma* 8 (January 1958), p. 115. For a description of rafting operations, see Maung Tun Thu, 'Hardy Raftmen of Our River', *Forward* 2 (18), (22 April 1964), pp. 16-20.

[9] Walinsky, *Economic Development in Burma*, p. 321; Nafis Ahmad, *Economic Resources of the Union of Burma*, Natick, Massachusetts, 1971, p. 82. Burma provided about 25 per cent of total world teak exports in 1957 compared with a figure of 85 per cent before the Second World War, see M.N. Gallant, *Report to the Government of Burma on the Teakwood Trade*, Rome, 1957, p. 2.

[10] Tun Kyaw, 'Short Note', p. 71. The insurgency also affected the quality of teak exports. Thus, the State Timber Board was forced to export mainly low grade timber since much of the Pegu Yoma where high grade teak was to be found was off limits, see Gallant, *Report on the Teakwood Trade*, p. 43.

[11] Critics of nationalization blamed the relatively poor recovery in teak production on an inefficient State Timber Board, as well as the government's belated recognition in 1954 of the need to step up girdling operations, see Walinsky, *Economic Development in Burma*, pp. 319-23; see also Knappen Tippetts Abbott McCarthy, *Economic and Engineering Development of Burma*, London, 1953, vol. II, p. 815; T.L. Havill, 'Social Forces affecting Technical Assistance Programs in Forestry, a Case Study: Burma', unpubl. Ph.D. thesis, Syracuse University, 1966, p. 162. Although these factors played a part,

A key preoccupation of the Burmese state immediately after independence was thus to gain access to the country's main teak forests
in the face of insurgent attacks. While such attacks also occurred
in the low-lying plains reserves, here the problem was more a question
of dealing with a legacy of several decades of deforestation. Chapter
6 showed how these reserves became the focus of mounting nationalist
agitation and peasant resistance in the late colonial era, and how,
in the process, they were gradually but inexorably whittled away.
As a result of the Japanese occupation, and subsequent civil unrest
in the country, residual reserves were thereafter largely depleted as
an expanding population felled timber with relative impunity in the
political turmoil.[12] Accessible unreserved forests in the populous parts
of central and southern Burma suffered a similar fate as the twin
quest for land and forest products (especially fuelwood) placed growing
pressure on Burma's forests.[13]

It is in the context of a growing fuelwood shortage in state-
controlled areas that the government launched a major tree planting
programme in 1954. The programme centred on a plan to afforest
200,000 acres in the country's Dry Zone over an eight-year period
with the objective of promoting both soil conservation and local
fuelwood supplies. This plan was under the immediate control of
the newly created Agricultural and Rural Development Corporation,
but the Forest Department played a prominent role in its design
and implementation.[14] Concurrently, the government encouraged the
public to plant trees, and beginning on 27 June 1954 with the 'World
Festival of Trees Day', a campaign was mounted to provide seeds

---

the key factor is nonetheless the ability of insurgents to disrupt forest operations, see
Ahmad, *Economic Resources*, p. 82.

[12] It was estimated in 1952 that 70,000 acres of plantations and 2,000 square miles of
reserved forests were destroyed at a cost of some £36 million, see Aung Tin, 'Forest
Policy with reference to Forest Propaganda for the Union of Burma', unpubl. manuscript,
Commonwealth Forestry Institute, Oxford, 1962, p. 14. However, in the case of the
Shwekyundaw reserve in Prome Forest Division, the forest was protected by a local
belief that the trees was guarded by *nats* (spirits), and that disaster would befall all who
felled this forest. See Thein Maung, 'Girdling the Enchanted Teak in the Shwekyundaw
Reserve of the Prome Forest Division', *Burmese Forester* 11 (June 1961), pp. 44-5.

[13] Thein, *The Fuelwood Situation in Burma*, Rome, 1959. One retired civil servant recalled
how forests were 'quite extensive' around his hometown of Taungdwingyi in central
Burma at the end of the Second World War. However, in a process repeated in many
parts of the country, the forest were thereafter quickly degraded, and by the 1990s had
'long since disappeared'. Interview with U Tin Myint, 30 July 1994, Rangoon.

[14] Nu, 'World Festival of Trees Day', *Burma* 5 (October 1954), p. 64; Tan Chein Hoe,
'Forestry in Independent Burma', *Indian Forester* 80 (December 1954), p. 788. By the
end of 1957, a total of 11,304 acres (including demonstration plots) had been planted.
See Thein, *Fuelwood Situation in Burma*, pp. 105.

and saplings to the population. The tree planting programme received the firm backing of Premier U Nu who warned in a 1954 public broadcast that much of Burma would eventually 'become a desert' if the people did not start planting trees.[15] A deeply religious man, the Premier even appealed to the Buddhist faith of his compatriots when he warned that a failure to plant would 'invite the curse of the *Rokkasoe*' (guardian spirit of the trees).[16]

The prominence attached to the afforestation programme reflected the political exigencies of the times. Since regular forest management was impossible in much of the country due to the insurgency, the afforestation programme was a means by which the Burmese state could nevertheless assert generally its claim to being Burma's resource manager. If regular forest management was not possible in the 'insurgent-infested' hills, it could nonetheless be put into practice in the plains where central authority was typically greater after 1952. Further, the plan to afforest lands so as to provide the public with needed fuelwood supplies was a means to win over a peasantry simultaneously subject to communist propaganda.[17] Although the military battle for the central lowlands was largely won by the Burmese army in the mid-1950s, the allegiance of the peasantry remained in doubt, and measures such as the afforestation programme were designed to win the hearts and minds of this vital social group. Finally, the plan needs to be situated in the context of the competitive party politics of the 1950s. Thus, since factionalism was the norm within the ruling Anti-Fascist People's Freedom League (AFPFL), politicians used their control over state agencies and programmes as a source of patronage to reward supporters and punish opponents.[18] The afforestation programme launched in the political heartland of the country was not exempt from such patronage politics.

The afforestation programme also indicated that the Forest Department was devoting greater attention than before to local supply issues. Yet there was nonetheless a large measure of continuity with the colonial past – notwithstanding the change in personnel upon independence. One of the first moves of the U Nu government in 1948 had been to Burmanize the Forest Department, thereby meeting a long-standing nationalist demand. Four British officials were temporarily retained as advisors, but Burmese foresters replaced their British counterparts (42 men in total) and U Hman became the first Burmese Chief

---

[15] Nu, 'World Festival of Trees Day', p. 63.

[16] Nu, 'Do Grow Trees', *Burmese Forester* 7 (December 1957), p. 102.

[17] Robert H. Taylor, *The State in Burma*, London, 1987, pp. 242-73.

[18] *Ibid.*, p. 246.

Conservator of the postcolonial era. This change in personnel was accompanied by a general affirmation of scientific forestry principles and the system of rationalized forest use put in place by the British. Thus, the Government's initial two-year plan declared that 'the policy of Government in regard to the exploitation of the Forests shall be directed towards optimum economic development consistent with proper and scientific conservation.'[19] The launch of the ambitious *Pyidawtha* national economic development plan in 1954 reiterated this commitment to scientific forestry, and senior Burmese forest officials regularly emphasized the centrality of the colonial system of scientific forestry to the ethos of the postcolonial Forest Department.[20]

As during colonial times, that ethos included a strong antipathy towards shifting cultivation. Indeed, insofar as the afforestation policy was in part motivated by the fear of deforestation-induced drought in the country, then attention almost inevitably was directed towards stopping this 'destructive' form of agriculture. Chapter 5 noted the efforts of colonial forest officials in the early twentieth century to regulate shifting cultivators in order to protect key watersheds from degradation. During the 1950s, Burmese forest officials attempted a similar campaign to halt 'this spreading evil'.[21] In the Dry Zone, efforts to prevent *taungya* cultivation were linked to the afforestation campaign, and included a high-profile attempt to rehabilitate Mount Popa.[22]

Forest officials also operated in the peripheral regions of the country populated mainly by ethnic minority groups. Since shifting cultivation was practiced extensively in the Chin, Kachin and Shan hills, these areas were a major target for policy action. Thus, a Chin Hills Development Committee (comprising representatives from various departments) was established to encourage terrace farming and other 'less destructive' forms of agriculture; a Chin Hills Forest Division was thereafter also created in March 1956 to facilitate greater Forest Department supervision in the region. In the Shan States, a Soil Conservation

---

[19] *Two-Year Plan of Economic Development for Burma*, Rangoon, 1948, p. 18.

[20] Economic and Social Board, *Pyidawtha: The New Burma*, London, 1954, pp. 49-51; Thein Han, 'Forestry in the Union of Burma', *Burmese Forester* 1 (March 1951), pp. 5-7; Tan Chein Hoe, 'One Hundred Years of Forestry in Burma', *Burmese Forester* 6 (June 1956), pp. 45-53.

[21] Tin Htut, 'A Note on "Shifting Cultivation"', *Burmese Forester* (December 1955), p. 108.

[22] *The Nation* (Rangoon), 6 February 1955; 'Scientific Management of Burma's Forests', *Burma* 7 (January 1957), p. 204; Thein, *Fuelwood Situation in Burma*, pp. 105-6. However, these efforts were largely ineffectual as shifting cultivators continued to clear fields outside of designated areas, see Aung Tin, 'Forest Policy', p. 14.

Department under the charge of the region's senior forest official was responsible for the conduct of a similar campaign, notably on the Myelat plateau.[23] The ability of the Forest Department to restrict shifting cultivation in these areas was quite limited. This reflected partly the distinctive political status of Burma's hill areas during the 1950s.[24] More important, civil unrest was rife in these areas in the 1950s as a result of Burmese army and insurgent (notably Kuomintang) activities and the general quest of the Burmese state to impose central rule there.[25] The full implementation of initiatives to regulate shifting cultivation was thus not possible.

Indeed, the fate of this campaign to restrict shifting cultivation highlights once again the manner in which forestry initiatives were constrained by the waxing and waning of the Burmese state's territorial fortunes. During the early 1960s, the campaign was all but abandoned as diverse ethnic groups joined the Karen in their struggle against the Burmese central state, and much of the country's hill areas fell under insurgent control. The failure of constitutional talks over the place of the ethnic minority peoples in the Union of Burma, and the associated seizure of power in March 1962 by General Ne Win and a self-styled 'Revolutionary Council' of military commanders, set the stage for an intensification in the civil war that lasted into the 1980s. In the process, Burma's forests were witness to some of the most severe fighting since the Second World War. However, those forests were often not only the *site* of conflict between government and insurgent forces, but also the *subject* of conflict as rival armies fought for control over commercially valuable forests. In a general context of spiralling military expenditures, timber revenue was a coveted prize for all of Burma's combatants.

The ebb and flow of the conflict was such that the scope and nature of Burmese forest management tended to fluctuate in keeping with the fortunes of war. Yet two general trends characterize the period 1962-88. First, the period was marked by a gradual extension and consolidation of the Burmese state's control over the key central

[23] Nu, 'World Festival of Trees Day', p. 64; 'Scientific Management of Burma's Forests,' *Burma* 7 (January 1957), pp. 184, 204.

[24] State governments in the border regions were not especially powerful during the 1950s, but they possessed selective jurisdiction over forest matters, and enjoyed the right to timber royalties from the Burmese state. See Thein, *Fuelwood Situation in Burma*, p. 115; *The Nation* (Rangoon), 11 July 1960; Taylor, *The State in Burma*, pp. 227, 268-70.

[25] Chinese Nationalist KMT troops controlled a significant proportion of the Shan States during the 1950s. For details, see Robert H. Taylor, *Foreign and Domestic Consequences of the KMT Intervention in Burma*, Ithaca, 1973; Smith, *Burma: Insurgency and the Politics of Ethnicity*, pp. 190-5.

areas of the country. A counter-insurgency campaign known as the *Pya Ley Pya* (Four Cuts) was developed by the Burmese army in order to deprive insurgents of the local food, funds, intelligence and recruits that were essential to their operations.[26] First applied systematically in the Irrawaddy Delta against Karen and Communist insurgents in the late 1960s, the Four Cuts campaign was subsequently focused on the strategically and economically important Pegu Yoma. Operation Aung Soe Moe began in late 1973 and ended in April 1975 when the Burmese army cleared these hills of the last insurgent forces.

The importance of the Burmese army's victory in the Pegu Yoma to Burmese forest management cannot be overestimated. For the first time in a generation the Burmese state controlled the country's most valuable commercial forests. Faithful to the colonial model, the Forest Department sought to re-introduce the system of rationalized forest use first elaborated in the region by the British in the late nineteenth century. A regular system of tree girdling was resumed, field data for working plans was collected, and a major plantation programme was undertaken.

The expansion of the latter was especially noticeable. Hampered at first by a shortage of labour (partly a result of the army's strategy of evacuating villagers from the forests to secure hamlets on the plains as part of the Four Cuts campaign), the Forest Department had to rely on local People's Councils and other government officials to help in the recruitment of a labour force. However, by 1977-8, 4,000 full-time workers and 20,000 part-time workers were engaged in the establishment of plantations.[27] The area annually planted (mainly with commercial and industrial species) thereafter grew rapidly: from 7,722 acres in 1976, to 16,634 acres in 1979, before climbing to a record 89,799 acres in 1985.[28] Such data need to be treated with caution given the unreliability of official Burmese data as well as the often high failure rate of plantations.[29] Yet the growth in the

---

[26] Smith, *Burma: Insurgency and the Politics of Ethnicity*, pp. 258-68.

[27] *Forest News for Asia and the Pacific* 2, 1 (February 1978), p. 8.

[28] Commercial species were mainly teak and pyinkado, while industrial species were largely of the eucalyptus family. Data from Forest Department, *Forestry Situation in Myanmar*, Yangon, 1989, appendix 1. Planning began on a small scale in the early 1960s but it was not until the East Pegu Yoma plantation project was launched in 1979 that planting was conducted on a large scale, see Mehm Ko Ko Kyi *et al.*, 'Forest Management in Myanmar', paper prepared for the ESCAP/UNDP regional seminar-cum-study tour, Yangon, 1990, pp. 7, 15; Myanma Athan Tin Maung, 'Little Known Workers of the Forests', *Forward* 8 (15 January 1970), pp. 5-7.

[29] The figures, for example, do not take into account wastage due to illegal felling, pests

planted area in and around the Pegu Yoma is real enough – and may be seen as particularly vivid indicator of the Burmese state's restoration of order in central Burma. That such a restoration of order was also associated with unsustainable timber extraction by the State Timber Board is a subject explored in the next section.

Second, the period 1962-88 also witnessed the elaboration of rival forestry operations in insurgent-held areas which, at their most sophisticated, represented a material and symbolic challenge to forest management by the Burmese state. The felling of timber and the taxation of forest products by insurgents was nothing new, and even predated independence in selected areas. Yet such taxation was usually small-scale, erratic and opportunistic reflecting the vicissitudes of war.[30] However, as the Burmese army pushed insurgent forces from the plains and into ever more remote border areas, the revenue base of insurgent armies was altered and became centred on relatively well-defined 'national' territories; in certain cases, this meant that insurgent forces came to depend more heavily on forest revenue than was the case in the past. Such revenue, in turn, was lost to the Burmese state – a loss estimated in 1978 to amount to more than 200,000 mature trees valued at US $100 million.[31]

An increasingly essential source of revenue, the regulation and taxation of the timber trade in the territories under insurgent control was often also imbued with symbolic meaning. Thus, insofar as the ethnic insurgencies in the border areas were predicated on demands for greater autonomy, if not outright independence, from the Burmese state, then insurgent forest management needs to be seen as a practical everyday means by which such autonomy or sovereignty was asserted. Such conflict was thus quite different from that which occurred between the colonial state and peasants, shifting cultivators and timber traders. As this book has shown, the latter was a battle over access to specific forests that did not necessarily call into question the state's role as a resource manager. Peasants, shifting cultivators and timber traders may have challenged the colonial state's policies, but their actions could hardly be construed as an attempt to redraw the political map

---

and disease, poor seed or site quality. See Conrad F. Smith, *Report on the Myanma Forestry Sector*, Yangon, 1991, p. 2; Forest Department, 'Myanmar Country Report', paper to be presented at the Project Advisory Committee, 26-8 July 1994, Hanoi (Vietnam), p. 5.

[30] *The Nation* (Rangoon), 2 April 1954.

[31] Forestal International Limited, *Forest Feasibility Study: Forest Resources*, Rangoon, 1978, vol. I, p. 16. This study formed part of a larger investigation by Sandwell Management Consultants of Canada into the status of the forestry sector conducted between 1976 and 1978.

of Burma itself. In contrast, the struggle between the Burmese state and insurgent forces was as much about which groups had the right to call themselves a 'resource manager' as it was about the details of resource access. In short, it was a struggle over territorial political control – a struggle that was at the very heart of what it means to be a state in modern times.[32]

The case of the Karen National Union's (KNU) struggle to establish the State of Kawthoolei illustrates better than any other example the link between insurgency, sovereignty, territoriality and forest management in Burma.[33] Although a Forestry Department was created in 1950, the forests were not critical to KNU finances during the early years of the insurgency.[34] The need for revenue to buy arms was limited since they were plentiful after the Second World War. Further, the KNU initially controlled much of the Burma delta including the outskirts of Rangoon. The Government of Kawthoolei thus had access to a wide variety of sources of revenue; considerable revenue was obtained, for example, from agriculture and mining. Finally, in terms of forestry itself, there was little work that was required to begin with as the KNU was able to seize logs left in the forest or at timber depots by the departing British in 1948.

This relatively favorable situation changed after the mid-1950s as an increasingly powerful Burmese army pushed Karen forces out of the delta – by the mid-1970s the latter were largely confined to a slice of thickly forested hills along the Thai-Burmese border.[35] As the territory controlled by the KNU contracted, so too did the range of opportunities available to Karen leaders for earning a livelihood. An illicit border trade in natural resources and consumer goods that expanded rapidly in the 1960s and 1970s in response to the catastrophic economic policies of Ne Win's Burmese Way to Socialism provided a growing income for the KNU.[36] Yet such revenue was variable and uncertain, dependent as it was on political and economic developments beyond the control of the Karen. In contrast, the forests of Kawthoolei provided a more secure source of potential revenue to

[32] Michael Mann, 'The Autonomous Power of the State: Its Origins, Mechanisms and Results' in John A. Hall (ed.), *States in History*, Oxford, 1986, pp. 109-36.

[33] For an introduction to the KNU insurgency, see Smith, *Burma: Insurgency and the Politics of Ethnicity*; Jonathan Falla, *True Love and Bartholomew: Rebels on the Burmese Border*, Cambridge, 1991.

[34] Tinker, *Union of Burma*, pp. 46-7, 266; Smith, *Burma: Insurgency and the Politics of Ethnicity*, pp. 137-54.

[35] Smith, *Burma: Insurgency and the Politics of Ethnicity*, pp. 258-67.

[36] *Ibid.*, pp. 98-9; David I. Steinberg, *Burma's Road Toward Development: Growth and Ideology under Military Rule*, Boulder, 1981, pp. 27-41.

the Karen.[37] Indeed, forest revenue (mainly derived from teak extraction) was one of the only important sources over which the KNU had some control (another one – tin mining – was significant in the 1970s but collapsed with the price of tin in the early 1980s).[38] Not surprisingly, therefore, the forest sector assumed growing political and economic importance to the KNU beginning in the 1960s.

The importance of the forests was reflected in the power of the Forestry Department. From only a handful of officials in the 1950s and early 1960s, it had become a key part of the Karen state in the 1980s. By the early 1990s, there were 463 forest officials at work in Kawthoolei's forestry districts (Papun, where most of the teak extraction occurred being the most important), and forest earnings, by then, constituted most of total state revenue.[39]

The politics of border logging is discussed more fully below. What is important to emphasize here is the sheer scale and organization of such insurgent forest management. Indeed, the very existence of the Kawthoolei Forestry Department was a challenge – both in practice and in principal – to the authority of the Burma Forest Department to manage the country's forest resources. Yet, paradoxically, in many ways an even greater challenge to that role was mounted from within the Burmese state itself as the postwar quest for socialist economic development led to the creation of a powerful state agency responsible for timber extraction.

Socialism

A recurring theme of this book has been the power of ideas to shape forest management in Burma. Thus, while the notion of *laissez-faire* was used in the early nineteenth century to justify unfettered teak extraction by private enterprise in colonial Tenasserim, the growing influence of scientific ideas was at the heart of the system of 'rational' forest use that was introduced by the Forest Department in the late nineteenth and early twentieth century. However, that system was challenged in the late colonial era as nationalist ideas came to dominate Burmese forest politics. Following independence, nationalism remained a potent force in the country's politics, yet was joined to a programme of economic development premised on socialism.

[37] Teak was exported to Thailand throughout the Karen struggle, see *The Nation* (Rangoon), 2 April 1954.

[38] Falla, *True Love*, pp. 356-7.

[39] Additional staff served at the Mannerplaw headquarters. Author's interviews, August 1994, Mannerplaw.

If there was a general consensus among Burma's new political elite about the need for national development to be based on a combination of nationalism and socialism – a 'Burmese way' to socialism as it were – there was much disagreement over the precise definition of such a development path. In general, it is possible to differentiate two phases in Burma's socialist experiment: the reformist 'welfare socialism' of the U Nu government (1948-58, 1960-2); and the revolutionary Burmese Way to Socialism programme of General Ne Win's military regime (1962-88). Yet the relative weakness of the postcolonial Burmese state – only partly remedied by the military after 1962 – provided a set of practical limits to the implementation of the new socialist policies. A common theme of governance throughout the period 1948-88 was thus the existence of a discrepancy between the rhetoric of ambitious development plans and the reality of a poor economic performance that ultimately led to Burma's relegation to 'least developed country' status by the United Nations in 1987.[40]

The forest sector inevitably became caught up in Burma's postcolonial socialist experiment. Most obviously, the quest to control the 'commanding heights' of the economy was reflected in the nationalization of a teak industry long dominated by European firms. This objective was signalled in Section 44 (2) of the Constitution of the Union of Burma, which said that the state would exploit the country's natural resources 'by itself or local bodies or by people's co-operative organizations', but was more fully spelled out by the government in 1948 in its first economic development plan.[41] Thus, the major leases were to be taken over by the state or by indigenous traders acting on the state's behalf over three years. The first third of the leases (located in central Burma) were accordingly nationalized on 1 June 1948, and a Forest Nationalization Committee met with representatives of the European firms to sort out compensation. However, conflict broke out between these firms and the government over the valuation of company assets, and it took a ruling by Burma's High Court to break the logjam.[42] A draft Joint Working Agreement was thereafter drawn up with regard to the disposal of the remaining two-third of the teak leases, but was never signed due to the outbreak of civil war. As insurgent forces overran the country, the European firms sought to cut their losses; in June 1949 they agreed to surrender their remaining forests in exchange for 54,750 tons of teak logs

---

[40] *Far Eastern Economic Review*, 22 October 1987.

[41] *Two-Year Plan of Economic Development*, pp. 18-19.

[42] Tan Chein Hoe, 'One Hundred Years', p. 48.

to be disposed of as they saw fit.[43] This transaction was completed by November 1952, and with the purchase of the Steel Brother's Dunneedaw sawmill soon thereafter, the departure of the European firms from Burma was complete.[44] From the viewpoint of the European firms, this process was a 'salvage operation'; but from the perspective of the Burmese state it marked the resumption of indigenous control over a key economic sector.[45]

Yet the nationalization of Burma's teak industry was motivated by much more than simply the desire to satisfy a long-standing nationalist grievance. It was above all a cornerstone of the state's attempt to establish a socialist forest industry in the country.[46] Three aspects to the nationalization campaign need to be noted here. First, this campaign brought into question the role of indigenous timber traders in Burma. Nationalization targeted not only European firms, but Burmese traders as well. Thus, in 1948, teak leases held by U Ba Oh and U Po Dan were acquired by the state and by 1953 only four teak leases held by Burmese traders were outstanding.[47] Indigenous timber traders may have hoped to control the country's teak trade after the European pull-out, but the Burmese state was committed to its management as a government concern.[48]

Indigenous timber traders nonetheless retained control of the non-teak timber trade during the 1950s and early 1960s. Indeed, and in contrast to the state teak trade, this privately owned trade recovered rapidly

[43] 50,000 tons were allotted to the Bombay Burmah Trading Corporation Ltd and Steel Brothers in Rangoon, while 4,750 tons were handed over to T.D. Findlay and Sons in Moulmein, see *ibid.*, p. 49; see also A.C. Pointon, *The Bombay Burmah Trading Corporation Ltd, 1863-1963*, Southampton, 1964, p. 103. The outbreak of the civil war was the final straw for the European firms, which had experienced great difficulty in going about their business even before; see, *Annual Report of the Bombay Burmah Trading Corporation Limited*, 1945-6 to 1947-8.

[44] Tan Chein Hoe, 'One Hundred Years', p. 49; 'The State Timber Board,' *Burma* 7 (January 1957), pp. 182-3.

[45] Arthur Bruce, 'Burma Recollections', MSS Eur. E. 362/3; *Two-Year Plan of Economic Development*, pp. 18-19; Frank H. Golay *et al.*, *Underdevelopment and Economic Nationalism in Southeast Asia*, Ithaca, 1969, p. 227.

[46] Further, and unlike the mineral and oil industries which were operated on a joint-venture basis with Western capital until the early 1960s, it was an industry which the Burmese state felt confident about running without Western assistance right from the start, see Golay, *Underdevelopment*, pp. 229, 237-8.

[47] Tan Chein Hoe, 'One Hundred Years', p. 48; 'The Forest Department', *Burma* 3 (April 1953), p. 71.

[48] On Gyaw, *Burma Teak Lease*, Rangoon, 1947, p. 4. However, private traders continued to extract teak on a small scale during the late 1950s and early 1960s, see Gallant, *Report on the Teakwood Trade*, p. 40; *The Nation* (Rangoon), 20 October 1960.

after the war and soon exceeded prewar production levels. Seeking to take advantage of their financial success as well as the political factionalism in government, these traders formed the Union of Burma Timber Trader's Association (UBTTA) in order to press the U Nu government for more favourable treatment. At the first annual meeting in December 1953, UBTTA resolutions condemned the State Timber Board for not operating according to 'commercial principles', called for a general reduction in taxation, and demanded 'the release of more forest reserves to private extractors'.[49] Speaking at the meeting, the Industries Minister, U Kyaw Nein, sought to reassure traders, going even so far as to claim that it was the Government's hope that indigenous traders would one day assume 'the privileges and profits formerly enjoyed by the foreign firms'.[50]

Yet the Minister's speech also highlighted the vulnerability of private traders in 1950s Burma. Noting that some traders had paid 'protection taxes' to anti-government forces, U Kyaw Nein warned the assembled traders against 'being bullied into procuring ammunition and medical supplies for the insurgents'.[51] Although the government at first turned a blind eye to collusion between private traders and insurgents, as the military situation improved in central Burma, the government cracked down on such activities. Errant traders were arrested, and a government embargo was placed on timber procurement from insurgent-held areas.[52] Yet the persistence of an illegal timber trade from which private traders were seen to be making a profit reinforced the argument of those in the state, and especially in the army, calling for complete nationalization of the forest industry.

Second, the nationalization of the teak industry did not result in the empowerment of the Forest Department. Indeed, it was the occasion for a weakening of the Department as timber extraction became the preserve of the newly created State Timber Board. Chapter 5 noted how timber extraction by the Forest Department was restricted to the Myitmaka Extraction Division to allow the European firms to expand their production in the early twentieth century. In 1948 residual department extraction was transferred to the State Timber Board, and for the first time in its one hundred year existence the Forest

[49] *The Nation* (Rangoon), 23 December 1953.

[50] *Ibid.* The U Nu government's position with respect to indigenous timber traders reflected a broader ambivalence on its part toward the private sector beginning in the mid-1950s. See Golay, *Underdevelopment*, pp. 203-65 *passim*; also Taylor, *The State in Burma*, pp. 280-2, 292.

[51] *The Nation* (Rangoon), 23 December 1953.

[52] *The New Times of Burma*, 23 September 1952; *The Nation* (Rangoon), 15 June 1954; *The Guardian* (Rangoon), 26 November 1959.

Department became an agency that was concerned with forest conservation work exclusively. Thus nationalization not only removed
private enterprise from the teak trade, but it was also the occasion
of a major reorganization of the way in which the Burmese state
managed the forests. Under the new arrangement an institutional separation of powers and responsibilities was affected that has conditioned
Burmese forest management to the present day.

Finally, the nationalization campaign resulted in the creation of
a powerful new State Timber Board. This agency replaced the colonial
Timber Project Board, assuming the latter's assets and liabilities.[53]
Yet whereas the Timber Project Board was nothing more than a
transitional structure designed to restore order while new teak leases
were sorted out, the State Timber Board was a mechanism by which
socialism was to be introduced into the forest industry. Created on
10 April 1948 under the State Timber Board Order, the agency was
formally legislated into existence by an act of the Union Parliament
in 1950. Although both the State Timber Board and the Forest Department
came under the control of the Ministry of Agriculture and Forests,
they were distinct entities.[54] To be sure, the two agencies were linked
formally (the Chief Conservator of Forests sat on the State Timber
Board) and informally (through the transfer of Forest Department
staff to the new agency).[55] Yet, just as the functional definition of
the colonial state in the mid-nineteenth century led to bureaucratic
conflict between forest and civil officials, so too the institutional
elaboration of Burmese forest management after 1948 resulted in
a growing rivalry between employees of the State Timber Board
and the Forest Department.

However, that rivalry was conducted on highly unequal terms.
The State Timber Board (or Timber Corporation after 1974) was
both much larger, and was responsible for a greater diversity of
functions, than was the Forest Department (Table 7.1).

If the State Timber Board has always been a larger organization
than the Forest Department, Table 7.1 nevertheless highlights that
the discrepancy in size between the two agencies increased dramatically
between 1952 and 1977. Thus, while the State Timber Board grew
nearly sevenfold during this period, the Forest Department grew scarcely

---

[53] 'The State Timber Board', *Burma* 2 (January 1952), p. 36.

[54] This relationship was not materially affected by the creation of separate Ministry of
Forestry in 1992.

[55] The two agencies have also drawn their professional recruits from the same B.Sc
course in Forestry. On forest education in Burma, see Kyaw Tint, 'Forestry Education
in Myanmar', *Myanmar Forestry* 1 (October 1993), pp. 23-5.

at all. The latter was just over one-third of the size of the former in 1952, but was a mere one-seventeenth of its size in 1977.

Table 7.1. STATE TIMBER BOARD AND FOREST DEPARTMENT
(SIZE AND FUNCTION), 1952 and 1977

	Size		*Function*
	1952	1977	
State Timber Board	under 6,000	under 41,500	Extraction Milling Marketing
Forest Department	2,237	2,403	Conservation Research

Note: Data on the Forest Department excludes support staff (e.g. clerical, drivers), while data on the State Timber Board excludes private contractors working on that agency's behalf.

Source: J.A. von Monroy, *Report to the Government of Burma on Integration of Forests and Industries*, Rome, 1952, pp. 8, 67; Forestal International Ltd., *Forest Feasibility Study: Forest Resources*, Rangoon, 1978, vol. I, pp. 24, 38.

Much of the State Timber Board's growth took place during the mid-1960s as the agency benefited from the sweeping nationalization campaign that was at the centre of the Ne Win regime's Burmese Way to Socialism. Private sector involvement in the timber trade was ended after 1 October 1963 as the State Timber Board took responsibility for extracting, milling and marketing all kinds of timber.[56] The end result of this process was an agency increasingly able to pursue its mandate to exploit the forests commercially.[57] In contrast, the position of the Forest Department weakened gradually after 1962 as Burma's military rulers prioritized exploitation over conservation. A consultant's report to the Burmese government in 1978 described a Forest Department in crisis: it was 'seriously understaffed', under-capitalized, and there was 'ample evidence of frustration and a deterioration of morale at all levels of staff'.[58] As one senior Burmese forest

[56] Maung Tun Thu, 'Burma's Teak and Other Hardwoods', *Forward* 3 (15 September 1964), p. 15. The Board also took charge of the country's 250 'People's Timber Shops', but experienced difficulties with their management, Ahmad, *Economic Resources*, p. 80; Interview with U Myint Than, General Manager (Planning), Myanma Timber Enterprise, 28 July 1994, Rangoon.

[57] Extraction was thereafter conducted by the State Timber Board through a Timber Extraction Worker's Union, an organization that encompassed all forest workers, see Theike Myint Oo, 'A Song in the Forests', *Forward* 2 (7 September 1963), pp. 17-19.

[58] Forestal International, *Forest Feasibility Study*, pp. 27, 29. This parlous state of affairs continued in the 1980s, see John Blower, 'Conservation Priorities in Burma', *Oryx* 19 (April 1985), p. 85; Smith, *Report on the Myanma Forestry Sector*, p. 9. However, even in the 1950s low morale in the Forest Department was a problem, see Tinker, *Union of Burma*, p. 248.

official later conceded, 'the Forest Department viewpoint was not heard during the socialist era.'[59]

Yet size alone tells only part of the story. The State Timber Board was also responsible for the key economic functions of the forest sector (extraction, milling, marketing), while the Forest Department was confined to the 'supportive' functions of forest conservation and research. Although the latter were critical for long-term commercial timber production, the tendency after 1948 has been for Burma's leaders to favour immediate economic returns over long-term considerations. The Burmese state's quest for forest revenue has thus privileged the short-term production-oriented thinking of the State Timber Board over the longer-term conservationist ideas of the Forest Department.[60]

The political influence of the State Timber Board has derived from the growing importance of teak in the export economy after 1962. Unable to restore Burma's rice export trade to its prewar level, the Burmese state under military rule was forced to rely heavily on teak in order to boost export earnings. Thus, while timber (mostly teak) exports in 1938-9 represented 7 per cent of the value of total exports, falling to 4 per cent in 1951-2, by 1970 that figure had risen to 25 per cent, and climbed further to 27.4 per cent in 1984-5; in the late 1980s, teak exports constituted as much as 42 per cent of the country's total official exports by value.[61] Although the importance of teak exports varied from year to year, it was nonetheless clear that the teak trade was increasingly central to the fortunes of the Burmese state after 1962.

The implications of this situation were twofold. First, it guaranteed that the State Timber Board would be granted a virtual *carte blanche* in its activities, notwithstanding the protests of the Forest Department that those activities were often not compatible with scientific forestry. Thus, although the two agencies were required to cooperate over girdling and extraction operations, such cooperation was generally lacking. Just as during the colonial era, the imperatives of silviculture

[59] Interview with U Ye Myint, Advisor, Ministry of Forestry, 27 July 1994, Rangoon.

[60] Short-term thinking was also reflected in the Burmese state's reluctance to fund the development of an integrated forest-based industry as recommended by outside consultants. See J.A. von Monroy, *Report to the Government of Burma on Integration of Forests and Industries*, Rome, 1952; Forestal International, *Forest Feasibility Study*, p. ii.

[61] Frank N. Trager, *Toward a Welfare State in Burma: Economic Reconstruction and Development, 1948-1954*, New York, 1954, p. 26; Steinberg, *Burma's Road Toward Development*, p. 117; Ministry of Planning and Finance, *Report to the Pyithu Hluttaw on the Financial, Economic and Social Conditions of the Socialist Republic of the Union of Burma for 1985-86*, Rangoon, 1985, p. 107; Smith, *Report on the Myanma Forestry Sector*, p. 5.

and commerce often diverged with the result that there was frequent disagreement over which trees – and areas – were to be girdled. While the Forest Department girdled trees in areas deemed to be inaccessible by the State Timber Board, the latter insisted on extra girdlings in accessible areas. Since the final decision was based on 'current political and financial expediency rather than on a sound, long-term, technical basis', the outcome invariably favoured the latter.[62]

The power imbalance between the two agencies was also reflected in the royalty rates which the State Timber Board was required to pay to the Forest Department on all timber extracted. Between 1948 and 1977 the rates were not changed despite significant changes in production costs and sales prices. The government revised the rates in April 1977 but even the new rates bore 'little relation' to contemporary prices.[63] Thereafter they remained fixed until 1992-3 when once again they were abruptly increased.[64] Here again the State Timber Board was the beneficiary of this system in as much as the timber was obtained at 'bargain' prices, but also because the low rates shielded the performance of that agency from any possibility of external evaluation and accountability.[65] Indeed, the State Timber Board was accountable only to the country's political leadership.

Yet the perennial demands of that leadership for forest revenue placed enormous pressure on the State Timber Board to increase timber (especially teak) production.[66] The inevitable result was further conflict between that agency and the Forest Department:

> There is evidence in Burma that the Forest Department is being put under pressure to ignore the basic principle of sustained yield and to permit overcutting of the forest resource, especially teak, in the more accessible areas. This is because the Timber Corporation cannot meet set timber quotas due to difficult access and insecurity in the remote areas, shortages of extraction power, high extraction losses, and many other problems.[67]

---

[62] Forestal International, *Forest Feasibility Study*, pp. 49, 108.

[63] *Ibid.*, p. 31.

[64] The teak royalty was raised from Kyat (K) 200 per ton to K400 per ton, while the rate for premium hardwoods went from K40 per ton to K360 per ton, see *ibid.*, p. 35; Smith, *Report on the Myanmar Forestry Sector*, p. 5; Interview, U Tin Aye, Director, Budget and Accounts Division, Forest Department, 9 August 1994, Rangoon.

[65] Forestal International, *Forest Feasibility Study*, p. 35.

[66] Increased pressure on the State Timber Board was notably linked to the government's decision in 1972 to prioritize natural resource production and exports, see Steinberg, *Burma's Road Toward Development*, pp. 43-61.

[67] Forestal International, *Forest Feasibility Study*, p. 20.

Thus, an increase in teak production – from 262,361 tons in 1961-2 to a postwar peak of 435,592 tons in the 1981-2 – was only possible through systematic overharvesting in accessible areas.[68] In effect, the State Timber Board was set production targets by government based on the entire national forest area, but was necessarily restricted to secure accessible areas due to the insurgency. With as much as one-third of Burma's national forests (including important northern and eastern teak forests) under the control of insurgents between the early 1960s and mid-1980s, the need for overcutting in the face of inflexible government demands was overwhelming. The reluctance or inability of the State Timber Board to extract timber from remote or otherwise difficult areas due to a shortage of timber elephants and extraction machinery only increased the pressure to log accessible teak forests. The relative 'antiquity' of the Burmese timber industry may have inadvertently spared some remote forests, but only at the expense of the forests immediately at hand; the potential sustainability of Burma's reliance on elephants for timber extraction should not be confused with the reality of State Timber Board activities in postcolonial Burma.

A central feature of Burmese forest politics in the postcolonial era has been the clash between the politically and economically driven reality of State Timber Board activities and the efforts of the Forest Department to re-introduce a system of rationalized forest use based on scientific principles in the country. Yet such bureaucratic conflict needs to be set in the broader context of a civil war that denied to both agencies the opportunity to pursue their respective interests at a nationwide level. Burma's socialist experiment changed the way in which the Burmese state went about managing the forests. However, the state's inability to restore central authority throughout the national territory, as well as the internal contradictions of the Burmese Way to Socialism itself, limited the overall impact of that experiment in Burma's forests.

The advent of State Law and Order Restoration Council (SLORC) rule on 18 September 1988 initially appeared set to alter very little in this equation. The move was widely seen at the time as merely a cosmetic change designed to facilitate the restoration of order in the wake of widespread anti-regime protests during the spring and

---

[68] Data from Ministry of Planning and Finance, *Report to the Pyithu Hluttaw for 1985-86*, p. 115. The charge of overharvesting appears in Forestal International, *Forest Feasibility Study*, p. iv; Smith, *Report on the Myanma Forest Sector*, p. 7; and see below. The official view was that extraction was sustainable, see, for example, Mehm Ko Ko Kyi *et al.*, 'Forest Management in Myanmar', pp. 18, 22.

summer of 1988.[69] Yet, Burma's political and economic situation in the mid-1990s is quite different from that which existed prior to 1988. The Burmese state has largely abandoned socialism in favour of a gradual opening to the global capitalist economy, while its armed forces have apparently prevailed over the country's insurgent forces. Burma's altered political economy has inevitably affected the country's forest sector, but the precise impact of the changes is as yet unclear.

SLORC Forestry: New Directions?

Burma's forest sector has undergone dramatic change since 1988. Burmese forestry has been thrust into the international limelight as a result of the SLORC's decision to sanction large-scale logging along the Thai-Burmese border. Less well known to the outside world, but of potentially greater long-term significance, are a series of policy changes that may signal a new direction in forestry management in the country.

If Burmese forestry has been the subject of unprecedented international coverage in recent years, most of that coverage has related to the Thai logging deals of the late 1980s and early 1990s. These deals were a series of agreements concluded between the Burmese state and Thai businesses (acting in conjunction with the Thai military) to log hardwood forests along the Thai-Burmese border. Within three months of the coup which brought the SLORC to power in September 1988, Thailand's senior general, Chaovalit Yongchaiyuth, visited the SLORC leader General Saw Maung in Rangoon. In early 1989 Burma announced twenty logging concessions to Thai firms, and further concessions were subsequently awarded to Thai firms closely affiliated with the Thai government. In all, as much as 18,000 square km. may have been alienated in this way to forty-seven companies.[70]

The logging deals reflected a convergence of interests on the part of the Thai and Burmese authorities around the issue of opening up to large-scale exploitation the hitherto remote and lightly worked border forests. On the Thai side, the logging deals were a response to Thailand's growing timber shortage. As a result of decades of overharvesting, forest cover in the late 1980s was down to about 15 per cent of Thailand's total land area, and residual forests were the subject of increasingly bitter conflict between villagers, environ

---

[69] Bertil Linter, *Outrage: Burma's Struggle for Democracy*, London, 1990.

[70] Kate Geary, *The Role of Thailand in Forest Destruction along the Thai-Burmese Border, 1988-1993*, Bangkok, 1994, p. 6.

mental groups, business, and the state.[71] Indeed, such conflict was instrumental in the Thai government's 1988 decision to ban all further logging in the country. Clearly, if the country's timber industry was to survive, new sources of supply needed to be found urgently.

On the Burmese side, the logging deals reflected various political and economic interests of the SLORC. In the short term, the deals satisfied the regime's urgent need for hard currency in the context of a worsening foreign exchange situation. The domestic political unrest that culminated in 1988's 'summer of discontent' had underscored the political vulnerability of the Burmese state. The response – a massive and bloody crackdown on all dissent and an accelerated build-up of military capabilities – was predictable. Yet if the need for funds to purchase military equipment was great, Burma's financial position in the late 1980s were dire. As the country was ostracized by much of the international community, foreign trade came to a virtually halt, foreign exchange reserves declined to as little as Us $12 million, and the government faced the prospect of being unable to service its nearly US $6 billion debt.[72] In this situation, the need to intensify exploitation of the country's natural resources becomes readily apparent. The significance of teak in this process was considerable; in 1989-90 timber exports (mostly teak) worth US $135,790,000 accounted for 42 per cent of all official export earnings.[73]

Yet the logging deals were also linked to the political interests of the Burmese state in bringing to a close the country's long-running civil war. As the SLORC stepped up its campaign to eliminate ethnic insurgent (especially Karen) forces along the Thai-Burmese border, the logging issue became intertwined as never before with the military conflict. The deals were thus designed in part to facilitate the Burmese army's anti-insurgency campaign insofar as the construction of a network of logging roads as well as clearcut logging practices simultaneously deprived Karen forces of strategic forest cover and facilitated Burmese troop mobility in contested areas.[74]

---

[71] Phil Hirsch, 'Deforestation and Development in Thailand', *Singapore Journal of Tropical Geography* 8 (1987), pp. 129-38; P. Leungaramsri and N. Rajeesh, *The Future of People and Forests in Thailand after the Logging Ban*, Bangkok, 1992.

[72] *Far Eastern Economic Review*, 22 July 1993.

[73] Smith, *Report on the Myanma Forestry Sector*, pp. 5-6. Other estimates place the SLORC's annual income from timber as high as US $200 million, see Martin Smith, *Paradise Lost? The Suppression of Environmental Rights and Freedom of Expression in Burma*, London, 1994, p. 13. For its part, the SLORC denied that the deals reflected a foreign exchange shortage, see *Working People's Daily*, 26 June 1990.

[74] Geary, *Role of Thailand*, p. 4; Rod Harbinson, 'Burma's Forests Fall Victim to War', *The Ecologist* 22 (March/April 1992), p. 73; Smith, *Paradise Lost*, pp. 13-14.

The logging deals were also an attempt by the SLORC to undermine a key source of revenue for the KNU. Many of the logging concessions granted to Thai firms by the SLORC were located in KNU-controlled territory.[75] However, as these firms were supported by the Thai military, there was little that the KNU could do to stop the advance of Thai loggers into Karen forests without alienating the Thai state – something that a KNU already weakened by military setbacks could scarcely afford to do. If the KNU had little choice but to accept the logging deals, it nonetheless fought to maintain the forest revenue that was the lifeblood of the Karen insurgency. The KNU ostensibly succeeded in this endeavour: between 1989 and 1993, Thai companies reportedly paid the KNU $40 to $80 per cubic metre of teak at the same time as they paid the SLORC $80 per cubic metre for the right to harvest the same timber.[76]

Yet the KNU was badly weakened by this 'teak war'. As the forestry rules of the Kawthoolei Forest Department were waived, widespread teak overharvesting was the norm.[77] Not only did Thai loggers fell more timber than was allowed under the terms of their contracts, they also took advantage of the political turmoil to extract extra timber free of charge outside of designated areas. In addition, illegal logging persisted even after the SLORC formally terminated all border logging in December 1993. The border forests were thus rapidly depleted prompting widespread environmental degradation as well as a crisis in the Government of Kawthoolei's finances.[78] The Burmese army's capture of the KNU capital, Mannerplaw, in early 1995 effectively spelled the end of Kawthoolei.

The SLORC suspended the Thai logging deals in December 1993 ostensibly due to the illegal and unsustainable practices of Thai loggers.[79]

[75] In border areas controlled by the Burmese state (i.e. parts of the southern Shan States), employees of the Myanma Timber Enterprise and the Forest Department supervised the trade in conjunction with local army units, see, for example, *Working People's Daily*, 15 March 1989, 6 April 1989, 10 April 1989.

[76] Indeed, to cut costs many Thai firms reportedly chose to deal exclusively with the insurgents, see Geary, *Role of Thailand*, p. 7. The imposition of tougher conditions on logging concessions was the SLORC's initial response to this situation, see *The Nation* (Bangkok), 13 October 1990.

[77] Karen forestry management generally followed the colonial model. Thus, forest officials girdled teak, supervised teak extraction, and managed reserved forests as per the British example. Interview with Saw Aung San, Forests Minister, 22 August 1994, Mannerplaw.

[78] On the environmental implications of the teak war, see *Asiaweek*, 25 May 1994; Falla, *True Love*, p. 354; Geary, *Role of Thailand*, pp. 10-11. As noted above, by the 1990s the KNU was dependent for most of its revenue on logging. Author's Interview, 22 August 1994, Mannerplaw.

[79] The reason given to the Thai government for the suspension of the logging deals was

However, a more likely explanation centres on the reduced dependence of the SLORC on this particular source of revenue.[80] By 1993, the SLORC's financial position had improved as Burma benefited from the 'constructive engagement' policies of its Asian neighbours. Further, as the Burmese army advanced, the ability of the Burmese state to supervise directly logging in the border areas also increased, and hence the need for 'surrogate' Thai loggers was greatly diminished.[81]

However, the forest politics associated with the Thai logging deals needs to be situated in the broader context of the SLORC's more general success in ending the country's various insurgencies. Following the collapse of the Communist Party of Burma's People's Army in 1989, the SLORC stepped up the pressure on its remaining opponents to agree to a cease-fire. In a strategy that combined the massive use of force (including Four-Cuts-style tactics) with the promise of concessions to cooperative groups, the SLORC was able to reap a rich harvest of cease-fires beginning with the Wa and Kokang in 1989, but culminating with the Kachin Independence Organization in February 1994.[82] Although conflict persisted in selected areas (notably in parts of the Shan States where Khun Sa's army operated), and there is no guarantee that the various cease-fires will not break down in the future, the ever increasing power of the Burmese army would appear to rule out a return to the generalized unrest of the past.

The defeat of the insurgencies is also a defeat for the resource management claims of the insurgent groups. In the process, Burmese forest management appears to be on the brink of entering a new phase in which policies can be planned and implemented by the central state on a nationwide basis.[83] As the question of external

---

that the move reflected the SLORC's commitment to 'environmental protection and sustainable development of forest resources'. The SLORC did not rule out future deals but set out more stringent conditions than in the past. See Thailand-Myanmar Joint Commission on Bilateral Cooperation, *Agreed Minutes of the First Meeting of the Thailand-Myanmar Joint Commission on Bilateral Cooperation*, Yangon, 16-18 September 1993.

[80] *Far Eastern Economic Review*, 22 July 1993. In contrast, the belief that international pressure forced the SLORC to change its policy lacks plausibility given both the SLORC's improving financial position at the time and its traditional defiance of external opinion, *The Nation* (Bangkok), 16 July 1992.

[81] One of the main reasons originally given by the regime for working with Thai loggers was that its employees could not extract the timber themselves due to the insurgency, see *Working People's Daily*, 26 June 1990. Nonetheless, Thai firms were still involved in Burma's logging trade thereafter, notably through individual barter deals and joint ventures, see, for example, *The Nation* (Bangkok), 16 July 1992.

[82] Martin Smith, *Ethnic Groups in Burma: Development, Democracy and Human Rights*, London, 1994, pp. 35-63.

[83] Diverse ethnic groups are involved extensively in border logging, but such activity

territorialization is apparently resolved, attention can now turn to the consolidation of political control through internal territorialization. For the first time since the colonial era, Burma's forest managers may have an opportunity to rationalize forest use in much of the country.

On the face of it, this situation represents a chance for the Forest Department to reclaim much of its former glory as Burma's preeminent resource manager. The need to restore the country's forests, seriously degraded as a result of decades of warfare, logging, and shifting cultivation, would appear to place a premium on the Forest Department's conservationist mandate. Further, the growing international emphasis on sustainable development in the wake of the 1992 Earth Summit held in Rio de Janeiro is being reflected in new SLORC policies that appear to take seriously the type of conservation thinking for which the Forest Department has long been known.[84]

Indeed, after years of stagnation the Forest Department has assumed a more prominent role than before in the management of the country's forests. A new Forest Law passed by the SLORC in November 1992 to replace the 1902 Forest Act is the basis of the Forest Department's renewed mandate.[85] Although the new law replicates much that is in the old colonial law, it goes beyond its predecessor insofar as it links forestry management explicitly to social and environmental considerations. Chapter 2 of the 1992 Forest Law, for example, requires forest officials to implement the law in keeping with a series of basic principles that include traditional concerns associated with commercial timber management, but which also emphasize for the first time environmental conservation, public participation, and international commitments. Other chapters, meanwhile, explore how biodiversity conservation, watershed protection, and encouragement for the private sector, are to be taken into account.[86]

A National Forest Policy prepared by the Forest Department in 1994 is designed to complement the new Forest Law. Although the need for a new forest policy has been a recurring theme of forest officials since 1948, the issue was not accorded a high priority by

---

is not linked to politicized resource sovereignty claims as before, see *Far Eastern Economic Review*, 22 December 1994; Smith, *Paradise Lost*, p. 15.

[84] Interview with U Ye Myint, Adviser, Ministry of Forestry, 27 July 1994, Rangoon.

[85] State Law and Order Restoration Council, *The Forest Law*, SLORC Law no. 8.92, Yangon, 3 November 1992.

[86] For example, Chapter III (4 c/d), Chapter IV (9 b), in SLORC, *Forest Law*; see also Ye Myint, 'The Forest Law that Serves State Interests', *Myanmar Forestry* 1 (October 1993), pp. 18-19. The Forest Rules have also been redrafted in keeping with the new Forest Law.

government, and the Forest Department had to make do with the 1894 policy statement of the British Indian government.[87] However, that statement was no longer adequate in light of the Forest Department's expanded mandate under the 1992 Forest Law. Thus, the National Forest Policy, as with that Law, emphasizes the need to integrate the goals of timber production, wildlife and environmental conservation, the role of the private sector in the timber industry, the maintenance of biological diversity, and social forestry.[88]

In order to meet the goals contained in the Forest Law and National Forest Policy, the Forest Department is planning an unparalleled expansion in the area designated as reserved forest. Although further expansion in the reserved area has been a long-standing goal of the Forest Department, the insurgency combined with a lack of staff prevented any real progress in this quarter. Thus, while the reserved area in 1952-3 was 34,800 square miles, by 1992-3 that figure was only marginally higher at 39,347 square miles.[89] In contrast, current plans would see the area enclosed as reserved forest increase from 14 per cent to 30 per cent of the total national forested area, and the land set aside as protected area – i.e. parks, upper watershed areas – from just over 1 per cent to 5 per cent of the total forested area. As much of central Burma is already enclosed in reserves, the growth in reserved area will occur mainly in more remote regions long subject to insurgent activity.[90] From the bamboo forests of Arakan in the west to the evergreen forests of Tenasserim in the south-east, the Forest Department is proposing to reserve all remaining forests in the country of commercial or conservationist interest.

A prominent goal of the reservation campaign is to protect all of the country's critical watersheds from degradation. In the process,

---

[87] A revised statement of forest policy was prepared by the Director General of the Forest Department in 1976 but not thereafter formally adopted, see Forestal International, *Forest Feasibility Study*, p. 20; see also Forest Department, *Myanmar Country Report*, p. 2.

[88] Forest Department, *Myanmar Forest Policy* (fourth draft), Yangon, July 1994. The policy is designed to link forestry to the new 'global outlook'. Interview with U Tun Hla, Director, Policy and Planning Ministry of Forestry, 11 August 1994, Rangoon.

[89] A. Long, 'The Forests in the Economy of Burma', *Burmese Forester* 3 (March 1953), pp. 20-21; Ministry of National Planning and Economic Development, *Review of the Financial, Economic and Social Conditions for 1993-94*, Yangon, 1994, p. 105. In contrast, it was proposed in the 1960s to increase the reserved area to 64,299 square miles, see A. Long, 'The Forests of Burma', *Burmese Forester* 14 (June and December 1964), p. 26.

[90] Interview with Lieutenant-General Chit Swe, Minister of Forestry, 15 August 1994, Rangoon; and with U Tun Hla, Director of Policy and Planning, Ministry of Forestry, 11 August 1994, Rangoon.

the Forest Department is necessarily confronting once more the 'problem' of shifting cultivators. At the height of the insurgency, forest officials had neither the time nor the opportunity to regulate *taungya* systematically. As a result, shifting cultivators were able to cut their clearings more or less as they saw fit. However, as the Burmese army restored order in central areas, the Forest Department resumed its campaign to reform shifting cultivation practices. Cultivators in and around the Pegu Yoma, for example, were persuaded to undertake commercial plantation work according to the *taungya* forestry scheme in the late 1970s.[91] In upland areas, meanwhile, watershed management schemes were devised (often in conjunction with international agencies) in order to 'stabilize shifting cultivators through incentives, demonstration and technical assistance.'[92] As forest management is extended gradually to border areas, this goal is being pursued by forest officials with regard to the estimated 2.6 million shifting cultivators living in these areas.[93] However, it is difficult to foresee how the pacification of the shifting cultivator in remote areas will be achieved without extensive conflict – especially given the Forest Department's ambitious reservation campaign. In effect, that campaign seeks to complete in peripheral areas the internal territorialization achieved by the British in central Burma in the late nineteenth and early twentieth century. If successful, it will spell the end of shifting cultivation as a way of life in Burma at the same time as it will facilitate the consolidation of central authority in border regions.

In central Burma, meanwhile, the Forest Department is also playing a prominent role in the SLORC's 'greening project'. The project covers forty-two townships in nine drought-prone districts of the Dry Zone, and is designed to tackle the fuelwood shortages that are linked to widespread deforestation and soil erosion in this densely populated part of the country.[94] Between 1994/5 and 1996/7, 51,300 acres of fuelwood plantations are to be created composed of species like *sha*

---

[91] *Forest News for Asia and the Pacific* 2 (February 1978), pp. 6-8.

[92] Kyaw Myint Than *et al.*, 'Watershed Management in Myanmar', unpubl. manuscript, Yangon, 1990, p. 5; see also Sein Maung Wint, 'Myanmar Strategy for Forest Resource Development', *Myanmar Forestry* 1 (October 1993), p. 16; K.S. Choi, 'Watershed Management in Myanmar', *Myanmar Forestry* 1 (October 1993), pp. 26-9; Government of the Union of Myanmar, *Government of the Union of Myanmar Pilot Watershed Management Project for Kinda Dam, Phugyi and Inle Lake*, Yangon, 1992; *Forest News for Asia and the Pacific* 1 (November 1977), p. 39.

[93] Sein Maung Wint, 'Myanmar Strategy', p. 16.

[94] Forest Department, *Greening Project for the Nine Critical Districts of the Arid Zone of Central Myanmar*, Yangon, 1994; see also Smith, *Report on the Myanma Forestry Sector*, p. 4.

(*Acacia catechu*) and *tama* (*Azadirachta indica*) used by peasants. The SLORC has allocated Kyat 102.6 million (about US $1 million) for the greening project, but this figure understates the true magnitude of the project. Thus, it does not include the contribution of government departments (and notably the Forest Department) or the army which are all extensively involved in the project. Further, it does not take into account the mandatory and unpaid participation of the peasantry in land clearance and planting operations.[95] Such participation guarantees the state a supply of free labour and also is designed to inculcate a conservationist ethos among the public.

The high priority attached to the greening project by the SLORC has given the Forest Department an unaccustomed public prominence. Although the project is in the charge of three senior military officers, and implicates a range of government departments (who cooperate through specially created national, regional and township committees), it is the Forest Department that is the lead agency involved – right down to the preparation of a documentary about the project broadcast on national television.[96] Further, plans to extend this afforestation campaign to other parts of the country will serve to keep the Forest Department in the public eye for the foreseeable future.[97]

The growing importance attached by the SLORC to the work of the Forest Department is reflected in staff numbers. Table 7.1 above, illustrates how staffing levels remained essentially unchanged between 1952 and 1977. When support staff are included, the Forest Department employed 4,556 people in 1977; in contrast, in 1992 that figure was 9,529, and had climbed to about 10,000 individuals in 1994 – with further growth anticipated in order to reach the Department's sanctioned strength of 14,751.[98]

Yet the power and influence of the Forest Department is not

---

[95] Forced labour is a ubiquitous phenomenon in Burma under the SLORC, but has been especially notorious in the border areas, see Smith, *Ethnic Groups in Burma*, pp. 84-93. The use of such labour by the army in logging operations is commonplace, and is documented, for example, in the reports of the Karen Human Rights Group.

[96] Forest Department, *Greening Project*, p. 11. Ministry of Forestry documentary entitled the 'Green and Lush Nine Districts' broadcast in 1994. The project has received extensive coverage in the state-controlled media, see *The New Light of Myanmar*, 14 August 1994.

[97] *The New Light of Myanmar*, 7 August 1994. An Arboriculture Committee of the Forest Department is also responsible for distributing millions of trees seeds annually to local communities and government departments for the planting of private and public woodlots.

[98] Union of Myanmar, *Brief Notes on the Ministry of Forestry and its Department and Enterprises*, Yangon, n.d.; Interview with U Ye Myint, Adviser, Ministry of Forestry, 8 August 1994, Rangoon. In contrast, the sanctioned strength of the Myanma Timber Enterprise in the early 1990s was 47,989.

to be overestimated. Both pay and morale remain low in the agency. As a result of salaries that are 'below the poverty line for most of the staff ... infidelity is on the increase as a matter of necessity.'[99] Indeed, 'income-generating activities' are rife as forest officials at all levels either tolerate illegal activities (for a fee) or participate in those activities themselves. Although a few forest officials have been imprisoned for illegal logging operations, the need to supplement official income just in order to make ends meet has resulted in a relatively relaxed attitude towards 'corruption' within Department ranks.[100] However, such practices tend to undermine the moral authority of an agency whose central purpose is to uphold the Forest Law. They also reduce the ability of the Forest Department to function generally since 'income generation' rather than forest conservation is uppermost in the minds of most forest officials, most of the time. Thus, the size of the Forest Department has increased, but the agency is still constrained in the pursuit of its mandate as a result of its impoverished conditions.

Moreover, the imbalance in the relationship between the Forest Department and the Myanma Timber Enterprise persists today notwithstanding the Forest Department's increased prominence.[101] That imbalance is reflected notably in the persistence of widespread over-cutting. As noted above, teak overharvesting was a feature of Burmese forest management in the socialist era as the national annual allowable cut was applied unadjusted to smaller accessible and 'secure' areas. This practice has been perpetuated under the SLORC. Indeed, following the 1988 coup, the Myanma Timber Enterprise also sold teak exports in advance in order to improve cash flow; in 1991, the discrepancy between advance sale and delivery was two years. A financially-risky practice, it also created 'undue pressure to over-harvest accessible teak'.[102]

Such pressure is reflected in ongoing tensions between the Forest Department and the Myanma Timber Enterprise over timber extraction.[103]

---

[99] Smith, *Report on the Myanma Forestry Sector*, p. 9.

[100] Personal observations, July-August 1994, Burma.

[101] The Timber Corporation became the Myanma Timber Enterprise in 1989 in a name change purportedly designed to reflect the shift from a socialist to a market-oriented approach, see Myint Kyu Pe, 'Some Facts of Myanma Timber Enterprise', *Myanmar Forestry* 1 (October 1993), p. 33.

[102] Smith, *Report on the Myanma Forestry Sector*, p. 8. This practice was apparently terminated in 1993. Interview with U Myint Than, General Manager (Planning), Myanma Timber Enterprise, 28 July 1994, Rangoon.

[103] The discussion in this paragraph is based on the author's interviews in Burma, August 1994.

Thus, the former has had to abandon the prescriptions contained in its working plans in order to meet the latter's demands for timber from accessible forests. Yet as teak supplies in many accessible areas dwindle, the pressure to meet annual production targets is leading the Myanma Timber Enterprise to rely increasingly on green or partly seasoned teak.[104] In some cases, it has even taken unmarked timber from the forest in a move that undermines one of the key functions of the Forest Department. Thus, revenue generation continues to take precedence over forest conservation in Burmese forest management. Not surprisingly, a national teak shortage is predicted for early in the next century.[105]

The Forest Department is also seemingly incapable of putting a halt to the popular encroachment on accessible reserved forests that has gone on largely unchecked since the Second World War. However, the Department has been constrained in this regard. As noted, it was not until the mid-1970s that the insurgency was effectively eliminated in central Burma; prior to that time, therefore, it was not practical to enforce the forest rules systematically. As a result, peasants were largely free to help themselves to needed forest products as they saw fit in many areas. Further, the general interest of both civilian and military regimes since 1948 in winning the support of the peasantry has militated against an excessively firm stance on the part of forest officials. Thus, in the mid-1950s, the U Nu government provided free grants of fuel, firewood, bamboos, and thatch, as well as freedom to graze cattle, to peasants during difficult times – at the same time as it was warning of a fuelwood crisis in populated areas.[106] After 1962, a central goal of the military regime was to win the support of the peasantry through mass organizations, producer cooperatives and People's Councils.[107] These mechanisms served as a means for the state to educate the public on the need for forest conservation as well as to organize labour for plantation work.[108] They also served as a means for the state to control the trade in non-timber forest products. In West Katha Forest Division, for example, firewood collection and tree tapping was permitted during the Burmese Way to Socialism

---

[104] To some extent, the reliance on green teak reflects a postwar shift in demand. Thus, Burma began to fell green teak in the late 1950s to meet the new demand for teak veneer.

[105] Smith, *Report on the Myanma Forestry Sector*, p. 9. In contrast, the Forest Department estimated in 1959 that there would be enough teak to last 'the next hundred years', see *The Guardian* (Rangoon), 23 October 1959.

[106] 'Scientific Management of Burma's Forests', *Burma* 7 (January 1957), p. 204.

[107] Taylor, *The State in Burma*, pp. 330-1, 353.

[108] *Forest News for Asia and the Pacific* 1 (November 1977), p. 39.

period, but peasants were required to sell their products to the Agricultural and Multi-Purpose Cooperative.[109] The state thus probably obtained a greater control over the non-timber forest trade in secure areas than was the case hitherto. Yet these measures nonetheless failed to halt the depletion of accessible forests by the peasantry. The Forest Department was simply not able to protect the forests from depredation due to a lack of staff and resources. This loss of control inevitably resulted in 'severe degradation in value, quality, and quantity of the forest'.[110] Although the size of the Forest Department has increased since the late 1980s, so too has the range of tasks assigned to the Forest Department: the Greening Project, reservation programme etc. As a result, the resources of the Department have been stretched such that encroachment on reserve forests continues in the 1990s.[111]

Perhaps most seriously of all, the authority of the Forest Department in the forests is being undermined by the practices of the Burmese army itself. Thus, members of the army have been active participants in the country's booming illegal logging trade. The SLORC has sought to prevent this trade from getting out of control through well-publicized prosecutions; in early 1994, for example, 127 officers (including an army colonel) were jailed for up to seven years for illegal logging in the upper Sagaing Division and in the Kachin State.[112] Yet this move is not so much an attempt to stamp out corruption in the military as it is a move to assert the SLORC's ultimate control over this important source of political patronage. Participation in the 'legal' private sector timber trade, for example, is used as a means to ensure the loyalty of the armed forces.[113] Further, the SLORC itself is reported to be actively involved in the timber trade as its members or their families export timber to neighbouring countries.[114] Just as revenue earned from timber contributed to the survival of the regime in the late 1980s and early 1990s, so too timber is now being used increasingly for the personal enrichment of Burma's political and economic elite. As Burma opens up to the international economy, therefore, it would appear that its leaders are following in the footsteps

[109] Maung Maung Moe, 'Intwe and Pwenyet from Burmese Forests', *Forward* 4 (15 March 1966), pp. 12-18.

[110] Smith, *Report on the Myanma Forestry Sector*, p. 9.

[111] Memo, Conrad F. Smith to FAO Resident Representative, 1 January 1991, Yangon, p. 10; Author's interviews and personal observations, August 1994, Burma.

[112] Smith, *Paradise Lost*, pp. 15-16.

[113] Memo, Conrad F. Smith to FAO Resident Representative, 1 January 1991, Yangon, pp. 6, 8.

[114] For example, see *The Nation* (Bangkok), 22 July 1994.

of their counterparts in Thailand, the Philippines, Malaysia and Indonesia who have profited immensely from 'crony capitalism'.[115]

Less clear, however, is the role that private business will play in the forest sector as the national economy is re-oriented along market principles. Soon after the 1988 coup, the SLORC announced that the private sector would be permitted to extract, process and export non-teak hardwoods and other species (the teak trade remaining the exclusive preserve of the Myanma Timber Enterprise).[116] This decision reversed the nationalization programme of the 1960s which had placed all extraction in the hands of the State Timber Board. As the Forest Department issued logging concessions to Burmese traders, private extraction, milling and export activities expanded rapidly.[117] From only 851 tons in 1989-90, for example, private sector timber exports had reached 83,190 tons in 1992-3.[118] But the growth in private extraction was accompanied by extensive illegal logging as firms ignored cutting restrictions laid down by the Forest Department. These 'cut and run' practices led the SLORC to ban all private extraction in January 1994.

However, most private firms subsequently continued to extract timber as contractors working for the Myanma Timber Enterprise.[119] Further, the SLORC remained committed to the principle of extraction by private firms, but subject to tougher rules governing their conduct in the forests. The ultimate goal, as Forestry Minister Lieutenant-General Chit Swe explained in August 1994, was to 'nurture a responsible private sector'.[120] Burma's leaders, ironically, thus face in the late

---

[115] Philip Hurst, *Rainforest Politics: Ecological Destruction in South-East Asia*, London, 1990.

[116] The SLORC targeted the private sector in Burma initially, but has invited foreign investment mainly in the form of joint ventures with the Myanma Timber Enterprise or local Burmese timber traders. The latter have included traders from the 1950s and early 1960s but also (in roughly equal measure) new entrants to the business. See Ministry of Forestry, Planning and Statistics Department, *An Outline of the Forest Situation and Investment Opportunities in Myanmar*, Yangon, 1993; interview with U Myint Than, General Manager (Planning), Myanma Timber Enterprise, 28 July 1994, Rangoon.

[117] Although the Forest Department was the licensing body, it was effectively powerless to halt applications, see Memo, Conrad F. Smith to FAO Resident Representative, Yangon, 1 January 1991, p. 13.

[118] *Myanmar Forestry* 1 (October 1993), p. 37.

[119] Interview with U Tin Aung Hla, Assistant General Manager (Extraction), Myanma Timber Enterprise, 10 August 1994, Rangoon.

[120] Interview with Lieutenant-General Chit Swe, Minister of Forestry, 15 August 1994, Rangoon. In contrast, the relationship between foreign firms and the Burmese state appears to be good, if still at a small scale. Joint ventures between the Myanma Timber Enterprise and Korean and Malaysian firms are under way in the plywood/veneer industry, and a

twentieth century a similar challenge to that encountered by their colonial counterparts a century earlier – that is, to find a way in which to ensure that private extraction occurs in keeping with the policies of the state. The specific context may be different, but the apparent need to reconcile state and business interests is the same.[121]

Nonetheless, Burmese forest management in the 1990s takes place in a distinctive political and economic context that sets it apart from both the colonial and the socialist eras. In this regard, the growing international concern about environmental degradation, and the associated worldwide interest in the wake of the 1992 Earth Summit in the promotion of sustainable development policies, has had a noticeable impact on the way in which the Burmese state approaches environmental questions. On the one hand, Western concern about tropical deforestation has prompted unparalleled international scrutiny – and criticism – of Burmese forest management.[122] On the other hand, the SLORC has sought to turn such concern to its advantage as it has extolled the virtues of Burma's longstanding tradition of 'sustainable' forestry to which it professes unswerving allegiance.[123]

Yet the SLORC's response has not only been confined to discursive battles over the sustainability or otherwise of contemporary Burmese forest management. Rather, the SLORC has also adopted an ambitious environmental agenda in line with its international commitment to promote sustainable development policies in the country. Thus, as already noted, one area of activity has centred on revitalizing the Forest Department with a expanded mandate to conserve the forests. The SLORC has also developed a series of other policies, committees, and projects, designed (in theory at least) to 'green Myanmar'.

Notable in this regard was the creation in February 1990 of the National Commission for Environmental Affairs (NCEA). The NCEA is chaired by the Minister of Foreign Affairs and comprises cabinet ministers and senior government officials. It is primarily concerned

---

counter-trade (logs for diesel and parts) is also taking place with foreign firms. *The New Light of Myanmar*, 7 August 1994; interview with U Saw Myo, General Manager, Myanmar Korea Timber International Limited plywood factory, 2 August 1994, Swa.

[121] On Burma's hesitant adoption of a pro-market approach, *see Far Eastern Economic Review*, 16 February 1995.

[122] For example, *Far Eastern Economic Review*, 22 February 1990; Harbinson, 'Burma's Forests Fall Victim to War', pp. 70-2; *Asiaweek* 25 May 1994.

[123] For example, see *The Working People's Daily*, 18 March 1989; 29 June 1990; Forest Department, *Forestry Situation in Myanmar*, Yangon, 1989, p. 15; Major General Chit Swe, Minister for Agriculture and Forests, 'Country Statement to the Twenty-fifth Session of the United Nations FAO Conference', Rome, 1989, p. 5.

with the development and coordination of national environmental policy, but also is the agency in charge of relations with other countries and international organizations on environmental matters.[124] In practice, the NCEA delegates its work to four specialized sub-committees which meet three or four times a year to discuss problems and proposed solutions relating to the conservation of natural resources, the control of pollution, research, information and educational matters, and international cooperation. The main task of the NCEA and its sub-committees since 1990 has been to formulate a National Environmental Policy. Although still in the planning stage in 1994, the general aim of the policy is to promote an integrated approach to environmental management in keeping with the national goal of sustainable development and the country's international treaty commitments, and based on state-of-the-art environmental knowledge as well as the support of an informed public.[125] Once established, the National Environmental Policy will provide a framework for the subsequent enactment of a series of environmental laws and regulations.

Eschewing Burma's isolationist past, the SLORC's environmental agenda has also encompassed the country's active participation in international agreements and organizations concerned with environmental matters.[126] A signatory to both the Framework Convention on Climate Change and the Convention on Biodiversity, as well as participant in the Global Environment Facility, Burma decided to join the International Tropical Timber Organization (an organization of timber exporting and importing countries based in Japan) in 1993, and has drawn up a national Tropical Forestry Action Plan.[127] It is also active in regional fora on wildlife conservation as part of its formal commitment to the protection of endangered wildlife.[128]

---

[124] National Commission for Environmental Affairs, *Environmental Policy and Legislation for Myanmar*, Yangon, 1993.

[125] *Ibid.*; National Commission for Environmental Affairs, *The Need for a National Environmental Policy in Myanmar*, Yangon, 1993. The NCEA has distributed leaflets in order to promote environmental consciousness among the public, for example, its 'One Earth, One Family' leaflet produced for World Environment Day 1994.

[126] However, the Ministry of Forestry has a long, if rather erratic tradition of cooperating with international agencies on industrial development, extraction, conservation and education matters. See Charles L. Coltman, 'Burma and the FAO', *Burma* 4 (January 1954), pp. 56-9; *The New Light of Myanmar*, 31 July 1994.

[127] Interview with U Tun Hla, Director, Policy and Planning, Ministry of Forestry, 11 August 1994.

[128] For example, the Global Forum on the Conservation of the Tiger held in New Delhi in March 1994. The Wild Life, Natural Forests and Nature Preservation Law (1994) replaces the 1936 Wildlife Act, and is to be enforced by the Wild Life and Sanctuaries Division of the Forest Department. See Thein Lwin, 'Wildlife Conservation in Myanmar';

These various initiatives highlight the SLORC's intention to participate actively in international fora on environmental issues – and hereby tap funds that might be available for environmental conservation.[129]

These initiatives reflect the prominence of green issues in SLORC thinking in the 1990s.[130] However, and as countries throughout the world are discovering, it is one thing to make a formal commitment to undertake sustainable development policies, but quite another to introduce such policies in the face of often pressing economic considerations. In Burma's case, the commitment to sustainable development would appear to be in direct conflict with the SLORC's simultaneous quest for rapid economic development as well as the personal enrichment of the SLORC itself. That quest is more often than not associated with unsustainable use of the country's forests.[131]

Both directly and indirectly, logging has been responsible for much deforestation in the country, but as Burma is integrated into the international economy new development projects are placing an added strain on the country's forests.[132] A case in point is the SLORC's plan to develop the country's natural gas resources. Thus, a pipeline linking recently discovered natural gas fields in the Andaman Sea · to the Thai border village of Pilok in Khanchanburi province (where

Myanmar Forestry 2 (January 1994), pp. 20-3; Thein Lwin, 'Status of Wetlands in Myanmar: Problems and Conservation', *Myanmar Forestry* 2 (April 1994), pp. 11-16; *The New Light of Myanmar*, 5 July 1994. These initiatives follow decades of relative neglect of wildlife conservation, see Burma Wildlife Survey, 'Burma's Wilderness: One of the World's Last Vast Tracts', *Burma Weekly Bulletin* 8 (31 December 1959), pp. 342-6, 357; Blower, 'Conservation Priorities', pp. 79-85; John Blower *et al.*, 'Burma (Myanmar)' in N. Mark Collins *et al.* (eds), *The Conservation Atlas of Tropical Forests: Asia and the Pacific*, London, 1991, pp. 103-10; Glen Hill, 'Wildlife Trade in Mergui Tavoy District, Kawthoolei, December 1991-April 1993', TRAFFIC Southeast Asia Field Report No. 2, Chiang Mai, 1993.

[129] One indication of this strategy is the growing use in official documents of current 'buzzwords' in the international environment and development community. For example, see Forest Department, *Greening Project*.

[130] The environment even figures in the proposed state constitution which says that 'the state shall protect the natural environment' (paragraph 31), in National Commission for Environmental Affairs, *Environmental Policy and Legislation*, p. 2.

[131] The official view is that deforestation is the result of shifting cultivation, fuelwood collection, agricultural expansion, population growth, underdevelopment and poverty. For example, see Forest Department, *Myanmar Country Report*, p. 1; National Commission for Environmental Affairs, *Need for a National Environmental Policy*, pp. 6-7; *The New Light of Myanmar*, 5 October 1994.

[132] Estimates of forest loss in Burma vary widely. For example, while the government claims a rate of only 220,000 hectares annually between 1975-89, other estimates suggest that 6,000 square km. per year were being cleared by the late 1980s. See Kyaw Tint and Tun Hla, *Forest Cover of Myanmar: The 1989 Appraisal*, Yangon, 1991, p. 14; Blower *et al.*, 'Burma (Myanmar)', p. 107.

it will be joined to a pipeline built by the Petroleum Authority of Thailand) has resulted in forest destruction along the pipeline's route across the south Tenasserim hills.[133] It is the SLORC's plan to tap Burma's enormous hydro-electric potential through the construction of a series of large dams on rivers along the Thai-Burmese border that represent perhaps the greatest threat yet to Burma's forests. One proposal alone would see the establishment of a 166-metre-high dam on the upper Salween river that would be dedicated to the production of electricity for export to Thailand, but which would entail the flooding of vast areas of low-lying forest as well as the removal of countless Karen communities in the affected area.[134]

If such mega-projects raise the prospect of widespread deforestation and population displacement, they also increase the likelihood of conflict within the Burmese state itself as departments promote their own institutional interests. Thus, conflict such as that which occurred recently between the Forestry and Mining Ministers over a proposed mining project in south Tenasserim is likely to become more frequent as difficult choices over the direction of national development will be required.[135] Such conflict will test the unity of the SLORC as never before. In a sense, the most important goal of an institution such as the National Commission on Environmental Affairs may be to serve as a forum for inter-departmental conflict resolution as environment and development issues prompt the need for ever more complicated bureaucratic negotiations and trade-offs.[136]

Conflict over Burma's forests may thus be entering a new phase. This chapter has shown that for much of the period since 1948 that conflict has been closely associated with the political and military struggle between the Burmese state and insurgent groups. During this time, the Forest Department and the State Timber Board practiced 'forestry on the run' – an opportunistic and short-term form of forest management rather than the regular system of scientific forestry practiced

---

[133] P. Wellner, 'A Pipeline Killing Field: Exploitation of Burma's Natural Gas', *The Ecologist* 24 (1994), pp. 189-93; Faith Doherty and Nyein Han, *Burma: Human Lives for Natural Resources Oil and Natural Gas*, Bangkok, 1994.

[134] Smith, *Paradise Lost*, pp. 21-3. Previous dam construction for both hydro-electric and irrigation purposes has been approved without prior consultation with the Forest Department, whose interest have been materially affected by the outcome, see Smith, *Report on the Myanma Forestry Sector*, p. 10.

[135] Interview with Lieutenant-General Chit Swe, Minister of Forestry, 15 August 1994, Rangoon; also with U Tun Hla, Director, Policy and Planning, Ministry of Forestry, 11 August 1994, Rangoon.

[136] A similar role can be envisioned for the country's national, regional, and district forest conservation committees set up by the SLORC in October 1993 to coordinate the activities of concerned ministries in order to promote forest conservation.

for much of the colonial era. However, by the mid-1990s the struggle of the Burmese state to restore order in the forests was nearly over, thereby raising the prospect that Burmese forest management for the first time in more than fifty years would soon be practiced throughout the national territory. Indeed, not since the early 1920s has the state been as well placed as today to introduce a rationalized system of forest use in the country.

Yet the likelihood that such a system will be introduced is arguably as remote as ever. As Burma becomes more integrated in the international economy, its leaders will be constantly subject to the temptation to deplete the country's forests as part of the broader quest to 'catch up' with its more economically advanced neighbours. If that temptation could not be resisted during the relatively isolationist years of the Burmese Way to Socialism, when the state Timber Board practiced unsustainable logging despite the protests of the Forest Department, then there would appear to be little room for hope that forestry in a more market-oriented Burma will be the salvation of the national forests. Indeed, the experience of other Asian countries shows that widespread deforestation is often intimately linked to economic development. As Burma appears set to embark on a development path similar to that of some of its neighbours, Chapter 8 briefly considers by way of conclusion how Burmese forest management and politics compares with that of other countries in the region.

Part V. CONCLUSION

8

BURMESE FOREST POLITICS IN COMPARATIVE PERSPECTIVE

This book has analyzed the politics of forest management in Burma between 1824 and 1994. It has emphasized the ambiguities of forest control and conflict. In the process, what has emerged is not a picture of 'progress' or 'romance' as some foresters would have it. Rather, Burmese forest management has been at each and every stage a political process in which resource access and use has been bitterly contested.

The patterns of state forest control and popular resistance at the centre of such resource contestation were elaborated during the period of colonial rule beginning with the creation of the Forest Department in 1856 and ending with the Japanese invasion in 1942. At the centre of this process was the Forest Department, which asserted control over forest access and use. This attempt was, of course, not new. In precolonial Burma, the monarchical state regulated access. What was new, however, was the method and scale of the attempt, as well as the greater coercive and administrative power of the colonial state. If early colonial forestry was virtually synonymous with teak overharvesting under *laissez-faire* conditions, than Brandis's appointment as Superintendent of Forests in 1856 signalled a new approach. As the European doctrine of scientific forestry was introduced, the Forest Department controlled a widening territory and range of activities.

Resistance to such control took various forms and changed over time. Burma's shifting cultivators, peasants and timber traders used strategies of everyday resistance and avoidance protest to circumvent forest rules. In the case of the latter two groups, such opposition was also expressed after the First World War through the nationalist movement. In contrast, early conflict between the Forest Department and the European firms gave way to cooperation based on perceived mutual advantage in the twentieth century. Differences over royalty rates notwithstanding, European predominance in the teak trade was an integral part of the government's system of rationalized forest use. The altered political circumstances of the late colonial era gradually undermined that system.

Following independence in 1948, the Burmese state sought to restore order in the forests as part of a general attempt to re-introduce a system of rationalized forest use in the country. In the process, however, it sought to modify that system in light of the political and economic goals of the postcolonial leadership – notably, the promotion of national security in the face of widespread insurgency as well as the nationalization of key sectors of the economy in keeping with socialist ideas. The advent of rule by the State Law and Order Restoration Council (SLORC) in 1988 may mark a new phase in this process of adapting the colonial model of forest management. Yet the underlying dynamic of attempted state control and popular resistance has endured, and continues to condition Burmese forest politics in the late twentieth century.

This book has suggested that Burmese forest politics needs to be understood in relation to three notions: (1) the forests as a contested resource, (2) the Forest Department as a resource manager, and (3) conflicting perceptions of forest use. These notions are used in this chapter to situate the Burmese experience in a comparative perspective. Specifically, the chapter first summarizes the Burmese experience, and the compares it with that of India, Indonesia and Thailand in light of these three notions. Although forest politics in these Asian countries have been shaped by often quite different political and economic circumstances, there are nonetheless comparable patterns of control and resistance that have developed in each country which lead themselves to a fruitful comparison with the Burmese situation. The chapter concludes by relating the general findings of the book to broader issues associated with the political ecology of forest use in the Third World.

Contesting the Forest Resource

Conflict was an integral part of British exploitation of Burma's forests. At first, conflict was limited by the colonial state's focus on teak and that state's relative political and economic weakness. In the mid-nineteenth century, the British imposed fewer restrictions on forest access than did their Burmese predecessors. Before the 1870s, Burmese peasants and timber traders enjoyed unprecedented freedom of access to non-teak forest products. Only shifting cultivators and European teak traders were seriously disrupted by the new forest policy.

The Forest Department began to control forest access systematically in the 1870s. Reserves were created and the non-teak sector was regulated. These measures exacerbated conflict, and forest administration became one of the more unpopular aspects of colonial rule. The confrontation between forest officials and peasants was particularly fierce in the early twentieth century as the conversion of low-lying forest to agriculture increased the pressure on the plains reserves. Moreover, the closing of the agricultural frontier and growing peasant deprivation coincided with the emergence of a nationalist movement such that forest access restrictions became a central component of the anti-British struggle.

Forest politics in colonial Burma was an escalating process of control and resistance. The forest bureaucracy grew, but so too did the number and the severity of forest offences. Even before administrative retrenchment and political intervention began to weaken the Forest Department in the 1930s, it could scarcely be said that Burma's forest users were becoming more law-abiding.

The nature of this conflict also changed as political, economic and ecological changes re-arranged the 'landscape of resistance'. In the twentieth century, the interests of the Forest Department and the European firms converged, even if differences (notably over royalty rates) remained. By affirming the predominance of these firms, the colonial state eliminated the possibility of Burmese control of the teak trade. Yet, such favouritism virtually guaranteed that the question of the teak leases would become a central concern of nationalists. Under the post-1923 dyarchy system, politicians sought to advance the economic interests of the Burmese middle class through a campaign to Burmanize the forestry sector.

In contrast, an increasingly hard-pressed peasantry seized the opportunity presented by the rising nationalist movement to become more militant after the First World War. As Guha observes in the Indian context, 'larger historical forces' such as mass nationalism 'served to legitimize protests oriented towards forest rights, enabling peasants to claim these rights more insistently and with greater militancy.'[1] Through the *wunthanu athin*, peasants sought to undermine British rule by denying its financial demands at the same time as they rejected the legitimacy of its laws. With the Hsaya San rebellion, such resistance turned into outright revolt. But, if peasants used these

---

[1] Ramachandra Guha, *The Unquiet Woods: Ecological Change and Peasant Resistance in the Himalaya*, Delhi, 1989, p. 134.

occasions to signal in no uncertain terms their opposition to colonialism, they also persisted with safer strategies of everyday resistance when faced with the superior coercive power of the state. As manifested in the inability of the Forest Department to protect the plains reserves from illicit deforestation, those covert strategies could be highly effective indeed.

Conflict between the Forest Department and shifting cultivators followed a different course. In the teak-bearing Pegu Yoma, forest officials sought to win over the hill Karen through introduction of the *taungya* forestry system. However, this system represented at best an uneasy compromise between two essentially incompatible land uses, and failed to resolve conflict in non-teak areas. As the cutch crisis of the 1890s illustrated, cultivators resisted regulation by illegally felling and burning reserved species. In remote areas, flight remained an option throughout the colonial era.

Although independence in 1948 marked the advent of indigenous rule in Burma, it did not lead to a reduction in conflict over forest access. Rather, such conflict became caught up in the broader civil unrest associated with armed insurrection as divergent political and ethnic groups fought for power in the wake of the British departure. The effect of this situation was twofold. On the one hand, it meant that for much of the postcolonial era the 'traditional' struggle between the Forest Department and the peasantry has been largely in abeyance – quite simply, the former has not been in a sufficiently powerful position to enforce systematically the access restrictions that were the source of so much conflict during the colonial era. Forest officials have been keen to re-impose the access rules that are an integral part of scientific forestry, but a lack of resources and secure forest access has hindered their ability to do so outside of selected central areas. The attempt to regulate shifting cultivators has been similarly handicapped even if a succession of programmes have illustrated the Forest Department's commitment to addressing the 'problem' of shifting cultivation. On the other hand, conflict over forest access has been embedded in the context of a wider armed struggle as various groups (notably the Karen National Union) have struggled for control over forest lands and revenue. In the 1990s the Burmese state looked set to restore order soon in most of the country's forests; as a result, the Forest Department may soon be in a position to re-impose systematically access restrictions in reserved forests – raising, in turn, the prospect that conflict with the peasantry 'on a colonial scale' may resume in the near future.

A prominent theme in Burmese forest politics since the mid-nineteenth century, then, has been conflict over forest access linked to the state's efforts to restrict and regulate forest-related activates. Yet this process of attempted state control and popular resistance is not unique to Burma. Indeed, the various stratagems of peasants and shifting cultivators designed to circumvent state control are remarkably similar to those used in other parts of Asia where the introduction of scientific forest management prompted local resistance. As in Burma, the creation of reserves and the multiplication of rules were bitterly contested by a peasantry loath to recognize the restriction of its forest access.

In northern India, for example, deforestation of sal and deodar forests in the nineteenth century was crucial to the growth of that country's cities and railways, but also led to the creation of the India Forest Department (1864) and the passage of the India Forest Act (1865). These steps marked the advent of a new management system that struck 'at the very root of traditional social and economic organization'.[2] Prior to the 1890s, attention focused on demarcating residual sal forest in the Himalayan foothills, but the discovery of improved methods of processing chir pine resin led to an escalating series of restrictions on peasants living in the upland Kumaun forests.[3] In 1894, eight species (including sal, deodar and chir) were reserved, and rules were framed that limited peasant access to fuel and timber supplies. With the creation of reserves after 1911, customary practices such as tree lopping, grazing and the annual burning of the forest floor (for pasture), were banned. In response, peasants ignored the new rules, and the number of forest offenses soared. Such resistance became increasingly militant, and culminated in 1921, when a strike against compulsory labour (*begar*) and an incendiary campaign paralysed local forest administration. Shortly, thereafter, the government abandoned many reserves in the area.[4]

Elsewhere in British India, a similar dynamic of control and resistance developed. The forests of southern India were originally valued for their teak, but later became an important source of timber and fuel for India's growing cities.[5] In Uttara Kannada district, for example, forests were reserved for this latter purpose.[6] But as peasants experienced

[2] *ibid.*, p. 185.

[3] *Ibid.*, pp. 43-5; Richard P. Tucker, 'The British Colonial System and the Forests of the Western Himalayas, 1851-1914' in Richard P. Tucker and J.F. Richards (eds), *Global Deforestation and the Nineteenth-Century World Economy*, Durham, NC, 1983, pp. 164-5.

[4] Guha, *Unquiet Woods*, chap. 5.

[5] Mahesh Rangarajan, 'Imperial Agendas and India's Forests: The Early History of Indian Forestry, 1800-1878', *Indian Economic and Social History Review* 31 (April-June 1994), pp. 154-5. Forests were also cleared as part of the development of coffee plantations, see C.A. Bayly, 'Indian Society and the Making of the British Empire' in *The New Cambridge History of India*, vol. 2, part I, Cambridge, 1988, p. 140.

growing hardship, they resorted to everyday forms of resistance: theft, illegal grazing, and so on. Peasants also openly contested access restrictions at public meetings specially convened to examine forest-related grievances. As in Burma, however, the inability of these various measures to more than marginally alleviate peasant oppression led to increased conflict. Thus, popular opposition turned into open defiance of the colonial state when in 1930 a forest *satyagraha* (revolt) broke out in this district.[7] A similar process of attempted control, everyday resistance and protest meetings were occurring simultaneously in other parts of India as well.[8]

As in Burma, India's shifting cultivators were the subject of strong official condemnation and regulatory campaigns. Not surprisingly, some of the most bitter forest conflict was associated with such campaigns as India's tribal minorities fought to protect a way of life often premised on the practice of *jhum* (shifting cultivation). They did so both covertly, and when pressed, openly through *fituris* (small risings).[9] Thus, the Koya and Konda peoples of the Gudem and Rampa hill tracts in what is today Andhra Pradesh resisted for many decades the efforts of colonial officials to eliminate their lifestyle – the Rampa rebellion of 1879-80 was of sufficient size and intensity to require several hundred police officers and ten army companies to suppress it.[10]

Following independence in 1947, Indian forest officials sought to control and develop the country's forests in much the same manner as did their colonial counterparts. Indeed, 'exclusionary processes accelerated as successive Indian governments strove to consolidate state authority over forest resources and increasingly bind their ex-

---

[6] Vandana Shiva, *Ecology and the Politics of Survival: Conflicts over Natural Resources in India*, London, 1991, pp. 94-5; Madhav Gadgil, 'India's Deforestation: Patterns and Processes', *Society and Natural Resources* 3 (1990), p. 136.

[7] Shiva, *Ecology and the Politics of Survival*, p. 97.

[8] Madhav Gadgil and Ramachandra Guha, *This Fissured Land: An Ecological History of India*, Delhi, 1992, pp. 158-71; Atluri Murali, 'Whose Trees? Forest Practices and Local Communities in Andhra, 1600-1922', in David Arnold and Ramachandra Guha (eds), *Nature, Culture, Imperialism: Essays on the Environmental History of South Asia*, Delhi, 1995, pp. 86-122; Richard H. Grove, 'Colonial Conservation, Ecological Hegemony and Popular Resistance: Towards a Global Synthesis', in John M. MacKenzie (ed.), *Imperialism and the Natural World*, Manchester, 1990, p. 33; Ajay S. Rawat (ed.), *History of Forestry in India*, New Delhi, 1991.

[9] Ramachandra Guha and Madhav Gadgil, 'State Forestry and Social Conflict in British India', *Past and Present*, 123 (May 1989), pp. 153-7; Indra Munshi Saldanha, 'The Political Ecology of Traditional Farming Practices in Thana District, Maharashtra (India)', *Journal of Peasant Studies* 17 (April 1990), pp. 433-43.

[10] Gadgil and Guha, *This Fissured Land*, pp. 154-5.

ploitation to state goals and interests.'[11] Unlike in Burma, the state in India has been able to assert its authority from the start over much of the national territory; it has not been faced, in other words, with the crisis of national unity that has for so long been characteristic of the Burmese situation. Yet as the Indian state has used its superior position in intensify commercial exploitation of residual forests, it has been confronted with growing popular opposition. The Chipko movement of Uttarakhand (northern India), which has won national and even international fame since the mid-1970s, is the best known example of Indian peasant protest and resistance in the face of commercially-driven forest management.[12] Yet, there are literally hundreds of groups and movements throughout the country today fighting state and business efforts to deny them access to needed forest supplies.[13] Thus, the British may have left India, but their legacy of contested forest control lives on to the present day.

In Indonesia, Dutch rule resulted in a comparable history of attempted control and conflict. Here, colonial attention centred on the island of Java where, as in Burma, teak was the chief object of forestry concern. Beginning in the seventeenth century, the Dutch sought teak supplies (notably for ship-building) from Java's forests, but it was not until 1849 that they established a regular and permanent forest service (with the help of German forest officials) to introduce scientific forestry in those forests.[14] Rules declaring all forest land and teak government property led to a confrontation with Javanese peasants who persisted with wood gathering and grazing practices that were now illegal. That confrontation was particularly severe in teak-forest villages where forest police considered even 'the smell of teakwood ... as evidence of punishable theft'.[15] As with the hill Karen in Burma, Java's teak-forest villagers were favourite targets of the Forest Department because they were considered a major threat to the teak monopoly. Not surprisingly, peasant resistance was especially militant in these areas. The millenarian Samin movement that caused the Dutch much trouble around the turn of the century was born, and remained centred,

---

[11] Richard Haeuber, 'Indian Forestry Policy in Two Eras: Continuity or Change?', *Environmental History Review* 17 (spring 1993), pp. 49-50.

[12] Guha, *Unquiet Woods*, pp. 152-84.

[13] Madhav Gadgil and Ramachandra Guha, 'Ecological Conflicts and the Environmental Movement in India', *Development and Change* 25 (January 1994), pp. 101-36.

[14] Peter Boomguard, 'Forest Management and Exploitation in Colonial Java, 1677-1897', *Forest and Conservation History* 36 (January 1992), pp. 10-12; Nancy Lee Peluso, 'The History of State Forest Management in Colonial Java', *Forest and Conservation History* 35 (April 1991), pp. 67-9.

[15] Peluso, 'History of State Forest Management', p. 72.

in Java's central teak forests. Like Burma's *wunthanu athin*, this movement rejected the laws and financial demands of the colonial state, and again, as in Burma, forest access restrictions were a leading source of peasant grievance.[16]

In the immediate aftermath of the Second World War, Indonesia was wracked by civil unrest linked first to the anti-Dutch struggle (independence was finally won in 1949), and subsequently to power struggles between various political factions that were not resolved until the installation of the military-led New Order government of President Soeharto in 1967. As in Burma, this initial period of political turmoil was associated with much forest degradation as both peasants and rival political groups typically ignored the forest rules of Indonesia's State Forestry Corporation. However, the basic tenets of scientific forestry introduced under the Dutch remained central to that agency, and during the New Order regime have formed the basis of an organized and highly repressive campaign of forest access restrictions and social forestry in Java.[17] Elsewhere in the Indonesian archipelago the Soeharto regime has encouraged large-scale logging and mining activities that have prompted widespread popular resistance, notably from indigenous groups, and which has resulted in an equally repressive state response.[18] As in Burma (but unlike in India), popular protest in Indonesia is not officially permitted; as a result, much protest has taken the form of everyday resistance to forest restrictions: illegal extraction, arson, and the like.

The discussion so far has highlighted the role of direct colonial rule in the development of Asian forest conflict. Even in the case of Thailand (or Siam as it was known before 1939) – a country never formally colonized by the European powers – a pattern of attempted state control and popular resistance similar to that which developed in nearby colonized nations also emerged. Thus, the introduction of scientific forest management in the country's north-western teak forests coincided with the assertion of royal control in this area in the late nineteenth and early twentieth century. As in the adjoining British-ruled Shan States, conflict at first centred on the struggle between the

---

[16] Nancy Lee Peluso, *Rich Forests, Poor People: Resource Control and Resistance in Java*, Berkeley, 1992, pp. 69-72.

[17] *Ibid.*, pp. 91-232.

[18] Philip Hurst, *Rainforest Politics: Ecological Destruction in South-East Asia*, London, 1990, pp. 1-45; Lesley Potter, 'Environmental and Social Aspects of Timber Exploitation in Kalimantan, 1967-1989', in J. Hardjono (ed.), *Indonesia: Resources, Ecology, and Environment*, Singapore, 1991, pp. 177- 211; Shannon L. Smith, *The Politics of Indonesian Rainforests*, Monash University, Centre of Southeast Asian Studies Working Paper 76. Clayton, 1992, pp. 16-22.

central authorities and the *Chao* (hereditary local rulers) for control of these forests.[19] Assisted by Herbert Slade and other British forest officials seconded from British Burma and India, the Siamese state prevailed, and a forest department modelled on the one in Burma was created in 1896.[20] Popular access to the teak forests was thereafter gradually limited. A 1914 decree allowed villagers free teak for domestic use, but the inconvenience and informal costs associated with acquiring a permit led many peasants to extract produce illegally.[21] Illegal extraction and forest clearance bedeviled Siamese forest officials in the the early twentieth century as similar offences occupied the time of their counterparts in Burma, Indonesia and India. Moreover, such resistance continued to grow because the more that the teak trade grew, 'the less people were allowed to use the resource, whether for private use or for commercial purposes.'[22]

Since the Second World War, successive Thai governments have promoted extensive logging of the national forests as part of the promotion of an indigenous forest industry.[23] Although state forest control in Thailand was limited to a certain extent as a result of the post-war communist insurgency (notably during the 1970s), the Thai situation has resembled more closely the Indian experience than that of Burma, where the lack of state forest control was a major limitation on forest management. Yet, as in India, maximum commercial exploitation of the Thai forests has resulted in rapid deforestation, increasing restrictions on popular forest access, and the growth of a vocal peasant movement that contests state and business control over residual forests.[24] Under Thai military rule, such protest was

[19] Banasopit Mekvichai, 'The Teak Industry in North Thailand: The Role of a Natural-Resource-Based Export Economy in Regional Development', unpubl. Ph. D. thesis, Cornell University, 1988, pp. 124-223. As noted below, Siam was an 'informal colony' of Britain.

[20] British forest officials experienced 'great trouble' in persuading local rulers to relinquish forest ownership to the Bangkok-based Siamese state, see W.F.L. Tottenham, 'The Formation of the Forest Department in Siam', *Indian Forester* 31 (August 1905), p. 447; see also D. Bourke-Borrowers, 'General Thoughts and Observations on Forestry in Siam', *Indian Forester* 54 (March 1928), pp. 152-4; Malcolm Falkus, 'Early British Business in Thailand', in R.P.T. Davenport-Hines and Geoffrey Jones (eds), *British Business in Asia since 1860*, Cambridge, 1989, p. 144.

[21] David Feeny, 'Agricultural Expansion and Forest Depletion in Thailand, 1900-1975', in John F. Richards and Richard P. Tucker (eds), *World Deforestation in the Twentieth Century*, Durham, NC, 1988, pp. 124, 126.

[22] Mekvichai, 'Teak Industry in North Thailand', p. 252.

[23] Larry Lohmann, 'Land, Power and Forest Colonization in Thailand,' *Global Ecology and Biogeography Letters* 3 (July-November 1993), pp. 182-3.

[24] Phil Hirsch, 'Deforestation and Development in Thailand', *Singapore Journal of Tropical Geography* 8 (1987), pp. 129-38; Phil Hirsch and Larry Lohmann, 'Contemporary

dangerous and often took the form of everyday resistance as practiced elsewhere in the region. However, since the mid-1980s a more democratic context has permitted public organization and protest on a scale un-thinkable today in SLORC-ruled Burma (or, for that matter, New Order Indonesia). As Chapter 7 noted, moreover, such popular resistance to forest access restrictions in a Thai context has had direct ramification in Burma. Thus, the 1988 logging ban which prompted growing Thai interest in Burma's border forests was partly the result of popular protests over the further degradation of Thailand's already much depleted national forests.[25] In this manner, the connection between Thailand and Burma over forest management and conflict first elaborated in the nineteenth century continues in the late twentieth century.

In the nineteenth and early twentieth centuries, British, Dutch and Siamese officials sought to limit and control popular forest access and use. Since the Second World War, this process has been intensified whenever the military situation has been conducive to central state forest control. That this process has provoked popular opposition to the policies and practices of the forest department is not surprising. In the process, the role of this agency as a resource manager in both colonial and postcolonial times has come to be contested as bitterly as the dwindling forest resource itself.

Resource Management and the Forest Department

To understand forest conflict is to appreciate the often pivotal role of the forest department in resource management. In Burma, the creation of the forest service in 1856 marked a new phase in state forest control. With this agency, a powerful means of political control was established.

The central purpose of the Forest Department was the long-term development of Burma's teak forests. The combination of a func-tionally-defined department and scientific principles was a felicitous means of promoting that goal. Emphasizing regulation, enumeration and calculation, scientific forestry was ideally suited to the rationalistic outlook of the colonial state. As German experts helped to organize the forest service in Burma, British recruits were sent to Germany and France for training. The result was a professional service that

---

Politics of Environment in Thailand', *Asian Survey* 29 (1989), pp. 439-51; P. Leungaramsri and N. Rajesh, *The Future of People and Forests in Thailand after the Logging Ban*, Bangkok, 1992.

[25] Leungaramsri and Rajesh, *Future of People and Forests*; Kate Geary, *The Role of Thailand in Forest Destruction along the Thai-Burma Border, 1988-1993*, Bangkok, 1994.

adapted European techniques to the Burmese setting. Teak forests were mapped, enumerated and demarcated as reserves. Subsequently, tree planting, fire-protection and other silvicultural operations were conducted under working plans the promoted the incidence of teak in these areas. By the early twentieth century, the growing complexity of forest management was reflected in the department's greater size and specialist appointments, as well as in its growing emphasis on non-teak timber production and the protection of ecologically-sensitive areas. Bureaucratic development and scientific management were thus linked in a process which enhanced state forest control.

Such control was not unambiguous. The advent of the Forest Department led to programmatic differences between forest and civil officials. A common paternalistic faith and interest in colonial rule meant that such conflict was kept within definite bounds, but differences over jurisdiction were nonetheless important. With the Burma Forest Act (1881), an attempt was made to eliminate such conflict by partially integrating the two services, but inter-departmental friction, as manifested notably in the cutch and plains reserves issues, remained a feature of colonial rule. Burma may have been run as a 'business concern',[26] but there was not always agreement over which business was to be accorded the most concern.

This image of a 'business concern' is apt for another reason. British forest officials were torn between their self-image as stewards of Burma's forests, and their duty to develop those forests in order to maximize revenue. As the administrative retrenchment of the 1930s indicates, senior officials were prepared to sacrifice the former in pursuit of the latter. Even before the Great Depression, however, forest revenue was an overriding concern of government. Scientific forestry may have been generally compatible with the development of a rational state, but in the quest to make financial ends meet, short-term expediency often proved the more powerful policy influence.

In contrast, long-term considerations led government to concentrate control of the teak trade in the hands of the European firms at the turn of the century. This move simplified forest management, and was part of a broader rationalization of forest activities. In the nineteenth century, European firms had been the bane of the Forest Department. In the early twentieth century, they were an essential bulwark of colonial rule.

Yet a key feature of the forest sector in postcolonial times has been a nationalized timber industry – beginning with the acquisition

---

[26] This imagery is from J.S. Furnivall as noted in Robert H. Taylor, *The State in Burma*, London, 1987, p. 8.

of the European teak leases in 1948 and culminating in the take-over of the entire timber trade after 1963. However, the gradual consolidation of Burma's timber trade (i.e. extraction, milling, marketing) in state hands has been associated with a weakening in the power of the Forest Department as responsibility for that trade was allocated to the newly created State Timber Board. While the latter was given the task of maximizing commercial forest exploitation, the former was assigned the function of conserving the forests. Bureaucratic conflict was almost inevitable under these circumstances, and tension between the Forest Department and the State Timber Board has been a recurring feature of Burmese forest management since 1948. The central importance of forest revenue to state finances – especially since the mid-1960s – has meant that the State Timber Board has been in a strong position to assert its interests despite the protests of forest officials that overharvesting was occurring in direct contravention of scientific forestry principles. Since 1988 the role of private enterprise has been emphasized by a SLORC regime seemingly bent on re-orienting the Burmese economy along market lines. That role has yet to be adequately defined, however, and the Myanma Timber Enterprise retains control over much of the timber trade, including the lucrative teak trade.

The link between scientific forestry, bureaucratic growth and private enterprise in Burma has been an important but complex one. Elsewhere in Asia, that link has also been crucial to the political economy of forest use. In Siam, British forest officials supervised the introduction of scientific forestry as the Siamese state asserted central control over a notoriously chaotic teak trade.[27] Siamese forest officials were sent to India and Burma for training just as their British counterparts had once gone to Germany and France. By the Second World War, valuable forests and species were being reserved by a trained staff that was also beginning to address conservation issues.[28] As in Burma, however, the quest to maximize revenue overshadowed this stewardship role.[29]

In rationalizing teak extraction, Siamese policy also entrenched

---

[27] Mekvichai, 'Teak Industry in North Thailand', pp. 196-207.

[28] Feeny, 'Forest Depletion in Thailand', pp. 124-5; Kamon Pragtong and David E. Thomas, 'Evolving Management Systems in Thailand', in Mark Poffenberger (ed.), *Keepers of the Forest: Land Management Alternatives in Southeast Asia*, West Hartford, CT, 1990, p. 169. However, the emphasis during this period nonetheless remained on exploitation and not conservation, see Colin De'Ath, 'A History of Timber Exports from Thailand with Emphasis on the 1870-1937 Period', *Natural History Bulletin of the Siam Society* 40 (summer 1992), p. 64.

[29] Bourke-Borrowes, 'Forestry in Siam', pp. 157-60.

the preeminence of British firms under a system of long-term leases.[30] This move was dictated by political and economic considerations – the Siamese were anxious not to provoke a British invasion as the Burmese had done in 1885. By affirming British economic power, the Siamese capitalized on Britain's desire 'to keep Thailand as an economic colony, if not a political one.'[31] This policy also reflected the fact that the Siamese were in no position at the turn of the century to extract their own timber. As in Burma, the working of remote forests (as a result of the exhaustion of accessible tracts) demanded 'an investment of fixed and working capital on a scale that only the major Western companies could provide.'[32] In the end, the result in early twentieth-century Burma and Siam was the same: the assertion of political and economic control over teak forests by a central state acting in conjunction with private (mainly British) firms.

Unlike Burma, however, Siam was never formally colonized. The significance of this situation only because fully apparent in the 1930s. In Burma, British rule – even under partial self-government – ensured that, in the end, the Burmese political elite was unable to rapidly alter the predominance of the European firms. In contrast, the absence of formal colonial control in Siam meant that indigenous political groups, such as the young military and civilian officials who ended that country's absolute monarchy in the 1932 revolution, had more of an opportunity to challenge European control of the teak trade. The movement to nationalize the teak industry after 1932, for example, signalled a shift in Siam's forest policy that was simply not possible in colonial Burma at that time.[33] Yet, the importance of Siamese autonomy during the colonial era must not be overrated. Despite the expansion of state logging operations, it was not until 1960 that British domination of the country's teak industry was brought to an end; that is, a decade after the Burmese, who had meanwhile gained their independence in 1948, nationalized their own teak industry.[34]

---

[30] Falkus, 'Early British Business in Thailand', pp. 133-46.

[31] Mekvichai, 'Teak Industry in North Thailand', p. 207. The quasi-colonial status was symbolized in the creation after 1883 of a British Consulate at Chiangmai to protect British interests in the area.

[32] Ian Brown, *The Elite and the Economy in Siam c. 1890-1920*, Singapore, 1988, pp. 118-9. Before 1925, these firms also selected and girdled their own trees as the government had insufficient men to do the job, see Bourke-Borrowes, 'Forestry in Siam', p. 155.

[33] Mekvichai, 'Teak Industry in North Thailand', p. 227.

[34] It should be noted that the Second World War was a major set-back to Siamese efforts to nationalize the teak industry. As a consequence of its alliance with Japan, Thailand was forced to restore British teak concessions by the Allies. It was not until 1953 that

Yet, if the expansion of the state-owned Forest Industry Organization after 1953 signalled a Thai interest in asserting central indigenous control over the timber trade, the role of the private sector in that trade has been far greater in 'postcolonial' Thailand than it has ever been in the Burmese trade. In a pattern repeated elsewhere in capitalist South-East Asia, the development of the Thai forest industry has been characterized by the inter-penetration of state (notably military) and business interests. In this regard, Thai forest politics has been dominated by 'crony capitalism' – a process whereby logging concessions are granted to friends and relatives of the politically powerful in return for political and economic support. Between 1969 and 1979 alone, 516 concessions covering almost fifty per cent of the country's total land area were granted in this manner; by the late 1980s most of Thailand's forests were depleted, but 300 concessions were still active at the time of the logging ban.[35] As noted, Thai state-business interests have been inter-linked in the border logging deal concluded with the SLORC between 1989 and 1993.[36] Although the role of the private sector in the timber trade has differed in Burma and Thailand during the postcolonial era, in both countries overharvesting has been the norm (albeit at a more rapid rate historically in Thailand than in Burma). Moreover, the Forest Departments in each country have been largely powerless to enforce the scientific forestry management that was a key reason for their establishment in the first place.

The Indonesian case provides an interesting contrast to that of both Burma and Thailand. Thus, the relationship between state forest control and private enterprise was more ambiguous in Dutch-ruled 'Netherlands India' (Indonesia) than it was in either colonial Burma or Siam. In the early to mid-nineteenth century, the Dutch colonial state worked the main Java teak forests directly, but with the introduction of the 1865 forest regulations that arrangement was phased out. Private enterprise then assumed a growing role until, in 1894, it controlled 95 per cent of the trade.[37] But, whereas in Burma the British moved to concentrate extraction in private (European) hands at about this

---

the Thais were able to resume nationalization through expansion of the state-owned Forest Industry Organization, see *ibid.*, pp. 228-9.

[35] Lohmann, 'Land, Power and Forest Colonization in Thailand', p. 182. Similar state-business links are associated with the rapidly expanding national afforestation campaign, see Apichai Puntasen *et al.*, 'Political Economy of Eucalyptus: Business, Bureaucracy and the Thai Government', *Journal of Contemporary Asia* 22 (1922), pp. 187-206.

[36] Geary, *Role of Thailand*, appendix A; and Chapter 7.

[37] Boomgaard, 'Forest Management and Exploitation', p. 12. J.S. Furnivall, *Netherlands India: A Study of the Plural Economy*, Cambridge, 1967 (1939), p. 201.

time, the Dutch in Java followed a reverse course: 'private enterprise, so important at the turn of the century, was slowly but surely crowded out.'[38] In part, this decision reflected the under-developed nature of Dutch capitalism in the forest sector.[39] There was no firm in Java of equivalent stature to the Bombay Burmah Trading Corporation Limited (BBTCL) in Burma and Siam.[40]

The decision also reflected the ability of Dutch forest officials to exert greater control over Java's compact teak forests than their counterparts elsewhere. As with the British, the Dutch imported German personnel and techniques to assist in the assertion of state forest control.[41] Reserves were established and rigorously protected by forest police. The creation of working plans paralleled developments in Burma, and reflected a similar quest to 'get full value from the scientific regulation of the forest districts.'[42] The Dutch may ultimately have forsworn private extraction, but their control of Java's teak forests was, if anything, more pronounced than in Burma. And, while some Dutch officials disapproved of the severe access restrictions imposed on peasants, their protests were 'no match for the increasingly efficient state forest protection machine'.[43]

The attainment of independence in 1949 did not alter the basic character or purpose of the forest service in Indonesia. Although civil unrest during the Sukarno era (1949-66) disrupted the postwar restoration of state forest control in Indonesia (as did civil unrest in Burma), most forest officials remained committed to a system of scientific forestry predicated on commercial exploitation and the restriction of popular access. Indeed, the State Forestry Corporation has been described as 'a business run by principles of capitalist production', and following the advent of the New Order in 1967,

[38] Boomgaard, 'Forest Management and Exploitation', p. 12. An 1897 Forest Regulation provided for the gradual exclusion of private enterprise. Thus, whereas in 1900 private firms managed all of Java's teak forests, by 1930 they controlled only 12 per cent of the total area, see Furnivall, *Netherlands India*, pp. 202, 325.

[39] Furnivall, *Netherlands India*, p. 201. This situation was in marked contrast to that in the agricultural sector, see Richard Robinson, *Indonesia: The Rise of Capital*, Sydney, 1986, pp. 6-10.

[40] The BBTCL's attempt to establish operations in Java's teak forests in the early twentieth century was ultimately frustrated by its inability 'to come to any satisfactory arrangement with the Dutch Government for a continuity of working rights', see *Annual Report of the Bombay Burmah Trading Corporation Limited* (henceforth *ARBBTCL*), 1911-12, p. 4; see also *ARBBTCL*, 1913-14, p. 4; *ARBBTCL*, 1906-7, pp. 4-5.

[41] Similarly, the Dutch required that officers destined for the superior service be trained in forestry at a university in Europe, see Furnivall, *Netherlands India*, p. 325.

[42] Peluso, 'History of State Forest Management', p. 71.

[43] *Ibid.*, p. 72.

that business was run on increasingly repressive lines.[44] The years since 1967 have witnesses a 'militarization' of that Corporation and an accompanying intensification of central forest control in the name of scientific forest management in Java.

Yet if strict control by the forest service has been the norm in the traditionally important Javan teak forests, an altogether different situation has characterized forest management elsewhere in Indonesia. State control and exploitation of forests in colonial times was largely confined to Java, and it was not until the New Order era that the Indonesian state began to encourage systematically commercial forestry in the Outer Islands. In 1967, the Basic Forestry Law was passed (confirming much in the original Dutch legislation) as well as a new foreign investment law designed to attract foreign firms to Indonesia; thereafter mainly Japanese and American firms acquired logging concessions, notably in heavily forested Kalimantan.[45] However, as in Thailand, Indonesia's leadership has been directly involved in the expansion of logging by the private sector in the Outer Islands. Indeed, Indonesian firms linked to President Soeharto's family and political associates have assumed growing control of the country's timber industry since the 1970s.[46] In a context of rapid deforestation and 'crony capitalism', the Indonesian forest service has not been able to apply the principles of scientific forestry in the Outer Islands as it has been able to do (by and large) in Java. Just as Burma's leaders have been actively involved in illegal logging in Burma, thereby subverting the Forest Department's efforts to manage the forests scientifically, so too the Indonesian and Thai leadership have prevented their respective forest bureaucracies from establishing a state system of long-term commercial forest use and management on a nationwide basis.

In the case of India, the quest to exploit the country's forests commercially on a large-scale basis has been a constant theme of the colonial and postcolonial state, and it has fallen to the Forest Department to take the lead on this matter. Yet the assertion of state forest control in mid-nineteenth-century India was the occasion of bitter inter-departmental wrangling. As in Burma, programmatic differences between the Forest and Civil (Revenue) Departments were the source of the problem. Although these differences cropped up

---

[44] Peluso, *Rich Forests, Poor People*, pp. 125, 132.

[45] Hurst, *Rainforest Politics*, pp. 11, 16, 20-1, 34-5; Smith, *Politics of Indonesian Rainforests*, pp. 18-19.

[46] Peter Dauvergne, 'The Politics of Deforestation in Indonesia', *Pacific Affairs* 66 (winter 1993/4), pp. 497-518.

in different places and at various times, they were nowhere more evident than in the unwillingness of the Madras government to accede to the India Forest Act (1878). If that government had a 'tradition' of upholding village rights, it also objected to the 'greatly enlarged powers' that the Forest Department would enjoy under the proposed legislation.[47] Moreover, civil officials feared that the new law, 'by sharply restricting customary usage, would adversely affect the agrarian economy.'[48] In early-twentieth-century Kumaun (northern India), Commissioner Percy Wyndham questioned the wisdom of a Forest Department that acted as if 'the world were made for growing trees and men were vermin to be shut in.'[49] As elsewhere in British India, it was feared that such an attitude would lead to civil unrest.

The role of the Forest Department in India was accentuated by the absence of large European firms in the extraction business. In the timber trade of northern India, for example, British merchants after 1860 were rare, and private extraction was 'almost entirely in Indian hands'.[50] However, the Department's role in that trade was also important, and extended to the operation of a resin processing plant.[51] As in Burma, forest management became more complex in early twentieth-century India. The introduction of working plans led to a more systematic forest exploitation: 'a variety of tree species that had previously been considered of no commercial value' were harvested and 'new uses for familiar species were developed.'[52]

Following independence in 1947, the Indian state embarked on an ambitious national development programme in which forest exploitation has figured prominently.[53] India's leaders and forest officials

---

[47] Ramachandra Guha, 'An Early Environmental Debate: The Making of the 1878 Forest Act', *Indian Economic and Social History Review* 27 (1990), pp. 69-70.

[48] *Ibid.*, p. 71.

[49] Quoted in Guha, *Unquiet Woods*, p. 108.

[50] This trade was controlled by Hindu and Sikh merchant sects, see Tucker, 'Forests of the Western Himalayas', pp. 162-3; see also Richard P. Tuker, 'The British Empire and India's Forest Resources: The Timberlands of Assam and Kumaon, 1914-1950' in John F. Richards and Richard P. Tucker (eds), *World Deforestation in the Twentieth Century*, Durham, NC, 1988, p. 107, where it is noted that Calcutta firms were given leases on favorable terms in the 1920s to develop Upper Assam's forests.

[51] It was also responsible for railway-sleeper production, see Tucker, 'India's Forest Resources', p. 100.

[52] *Ibid.*, p. 97; see also Gadgil and Guha, *This Fissured Land*, pp. 136-8.

[53] Forest management in India is complicated by the federal structure of the Indian government. State governments are formally in charge of forest matters, but the central state through control over key revenue sources as well as national policy formulation has sought to influence the direction of forestry in the states. See Akhileshwar Pathak, *Contested Domains: The State, Peasants and Forests in Contemporary India*, London,

have 'wholeheartedly adopted' the principles of the colonial system of scientific forestry; thus, as in Burma, the country's forest officials have sought to manage the forests in keeping with the colonial model.[54] However, and also as in Burma, the quest for rapid national economic development has been associated with widespread overharvesting of timber species in violation of that model. Indeed, forest-based in-dustrialization has progressed much farther in India than it has done in Burma with the result that deforestation has been even more rapid and extensive in the former than in the latter. The use of bamboo in India's growing paper industry is a case in point – from only 5,800 tons in 1924-5, the amount of bamboo used for this purpose had jumped to over five million tons in 1987 necessitating the import of bamboo from ever more remote areas of the country.[55] Such un-sustainable use of the forests has been associated as in Thailand and Indonesia (and more recently Burma) with crony capitalism – as Indian businesses have linked continued forest access to political support in state and national elections. Yet, as noted, increasing pressure on India's dwindling forests has prompted the development of a vocal peasant movement resistant to large-scale commercial exploitation of the forests.

Caught in the middle of this increasingly tense situation have been the country's forest officials. As in Thailand today (but not as yet in authoritarian Indonesia and Burma), Indian forest officials have been the target of mounting public criticism whether in the context of a national campaign against new forest legislation in the early 1980s or in a myriad of local and state settings where forest management has been disrupted by popular protest and covert resis-tance.[56] The Indian example, as with that of contemporary Thailand, highlights the extent to which the role of the forest department as a resource manager is the subject of popular contestation in a relatively open 'democratic' political system. It is likely that under less authoritarian conditions, similar contestation would occur in Indonesia and Burma.

Beginning in the colonial era, Asia's forest departments have ac-cumulated knowledge about the forests that has been used to rationalize forest activities along commercial lines. In each case, an expanding bureaucracy has sought to use 'scientific' principles to assert control over valuable forests often, but not always (as much of Burma's

---

1994, chap. 2.

[54] Haeuber, 'Indian Forestry Policy in Two Eras', p. 73.

[55] Gadgil and Guha, *This Fissured Land*, pp. 198-203.

[56] Shiva, *Ecology and the Politics of Survival*. Contemporary Indian forest politics is also characterized by intense bureaucratic conflict, see Pathak, *Contested Domains*.

postcolonial experience has illustrated), in conjunction with capitalist enterprise, and typically despite the opposition of officials in other state agencies or departments. But Asian forest politics in colonial and postcolonial times has not only been about the empowerment (or occasionally the disempowerment) of forest departments, and ensuing conflict with diverse forest users. It has also been a struggle of ideas that has embraced conflicting perceptions of what constitutes legitimate forest use.

Conflicting Perceptions, Contested Forests

One of the most important colonial legacies in Asia concerned the new ideas that transformed the politics, economics and ecology of the conquered territories. That transformation was particularly evident in Burma where the country's forests bore the imprint of powerful new ideas of social practice. For three decades after the first Anglo-Burmese war (1824-6), the British subjected the Tenasserim forests to unchecked exploitation according to *laissez-faire* principles. The ensuing degradation only confirmed what scientists had all along predicted: *laissez-faire* forestry and long-term timber production were incompatible. The acquisition of Pegu in 1852 coincided with an altered imperial context in which new forms of state forest control were possible.

To this end, the British employed German ideas and personnel to manage Burma's forests 'scientifically'. The new approach transformed Burmese forest politics as *laissez-faire* forestry never did. Whereas *laissez-faire* forestry emphasized freedom of access, scientific forestry was based on strictly limited access. While the former eschewed state intervention, the latter was premised on such action. As such, scientific management was bound to come as a shock to forest users accustomed to erratic or lax forest rules. That shock turned to resistance wherever its impact was felt in Lower Burma (after 1856) and Upper Burma (from 1886). But, if all forest users felt the bite of the new restrictions, some groups were more adversely affected than others. As the objective of scientific forestry was long-term commercial timber production, it was not surprising that the system ultimately found favour with the European firms (once Forest Department extraction was curtailed after the turn of the century). Indeed, with its emphasis on large-scale production over an extensive and difficult terrain, scientific management was ideally suited to the structure and resources of the BBTCL and other capitalist enterprises.

In contrast, scientific forestry limited indigenous access with few, if any compensating benefits. Burmese traders may have prospered, particularly in the nineteenth century, but the rationalization of the teak trade reduced generally their economic opportunities. To the peasantry, scientific management was an escalating series of restrictions that were all the more acutely felt as unreserved forests were depleted in the early twentieth century. For certain shifting cultivators, such management was, as manifested in the *taungya* forestry system, an opportunity to minimize state exactions and earn a small income. But, as the struggle to implement this system indicated, these cultivators were well aware that *taungya* forestry was ultimately based on the elimination of their way of life. Moreover, that system did not embrace all shifting cultivators. In the twentieth century, the campaign against these groups spread even to remote parts of Burma.

That scientific forestry proved inimical to indigenous interests was only to be expected. It privileged export-oriented production over the domestic forest economy. It also aimed to convert Burma's species-rich forests into uniform stands of high-value timber. Whereas the former were of considerable use value to the Burmese, the latter were not, and in any case, were primarily destined for external markets. Concurrently, forest officials showed little interest in peasant needs, as illustrated in their failure to seriously address the local-supply issue and their arbitrary classification of peasant produce as 'minor'.

Scientific forestry was also used to belittle indigenous practice. If long-term commercial timber production was scientific, then subsistence-oriented extraction was 'unscientific'. Of course, some practices were considered more unscientific than others. The degree of official disapprobation depended on the threat that a given practice posed to commercial production, as well as the general pseudo-anthropological reasoning that shaped European perceptions of indigenous peoples in the colonial era.[57] Thus, peasants living on the plains were 'wasteful', but the 'primitive' hill Karen who inhabited the teak-bearing Pegu Yoma were the very antithesis of responsible forest use.

However, the fundamental divide was between Europeans and Burmese. Whereas Europeans were scientific, modern, rational and ecologically-minded, the Burmese were unscientific, backward, irrational and anti-ecological. In practice, this perceptual dichotomy had important implications for forest management. Thus, Burmese traders failed to obtain sizable teak leases not because they were the victims of official discrimination, but rather because they were 'inefficient', 'unreliable' and 'wasteful'. Peasants were unable to manage their own village forests not because they were given insufficient powers and opportunity,

[57] Robert H. Taylor, 'Perceptions of Ethnicity in the Politics of Burma', *Southeast Asian Journal of Social Science* 10, 1 (1982), pp. 7-22; E.R. Leach, *Political Systems of Highland Burma: A Study of Kachin Social Structure*, London, 1986 (1954).

but rather because they were 'improvident'. Shifting cultivators were to be dissuaded from their lifestyle not because it conflicted with state forest control, but because such a lifestyle was ecologically 'destructive'. In short, because the 'natives' could not manage their own forests, Europeans had an obligation to do it for them.

Scientific forestry was thus a highly paternalistic but useful justification for British rule. In response, peasants could always hark back to a precolonial era in which customary usage was reputedly integral to a subsistence-oriented economy. Under the Burmese kings, it was believed, forest access was guaranteed and peasant needs provided for. That such a 'tradition' was largely invented did not detract either from its emotive appeal or its usefulness as a justification for everyday resistance. After the First World War, the rise of Burmese nationalism was an additional means of building an alternative perception of forest use. Thus, access restrictions were not only a violation of traditional rights; they were also fundamentally 'anti-Burmese' in character. It was this combination of perceptions that underlay the events of the 1920s and 1930s which ultimately undermined the colonial system of rationalized forest use.

Following independence in 1948, nationalism was conjoined with socialism as the basis of 'new' approach to the forest sector. At the centre of this approach was the nationalization of the timber trade beginning with the European teak leases in 1948 and ending in the mid-1960s with the take-over of the entire forest industry. However, formal adoption of a system of socialist forestry did not result in the rejection of the basic premises of the system of rationalized forest use introduced under the British. Thus, the postcolonial Burmese state has privileged commercial export-oriented extraction over subsistence-oriented local use just as did its colonial predecessor. Similarly, the Forest Department has remained firmly committed to scientific forestry as the principal upon which to base forest management. Accordingly, it has sought to eliminate shifting cultivation and restrict peasant forest access in reserved forests in a manner reminiscent of its colonial counterpart.

Yet the ability of the Forest Department to pursue scientific forestry has been limited both by the state's insatiable quest for forest revenue (manifested in State Timber Board overharvesting) and by the need to conduct 'forestry on the run' in a context of generalized postcolonial civil unrest. Thus forestry in independent Burma has been associated with a change in the ownership of the timber trade, but not with any fundamental reorganization of the purpose or objectives of the trade itself. Indeed, if the SLORC delivers on its promise to permit an expanded role for the private sector in the timber trade, then the main difference between colonial and postcolonial forestry – a nationalized forest industry – will have been eliminated. It is highly unlikely that privatization of the forest sector will encompass all of the timber trade (i.e. the teak trade) or that foreign interests will ever control the trade to the extent that they did during the colonial era.

Burmese forest politics has been conditioned by conflicting perceptions of forest use associated with issues of management control and appropriate use. However, this situation is hardly unique to Burma. Thus, the introduction of scientific management elsewhere in Asia represented a belated attempt by various states to rectify the damage caused to valuable forests by earlier *laissez-faire* policies. In the process, the new management system set forest departments on a collision course with indigenous peoples who resisted the subversion of preexisting patterns of forest access and use.

In India, as in Burma, scientific forestry was introduced as a response to widespread overharvesting during the *laissez-faire* era.[58] If in Burma the depletion of Tenasserim's teak forests under early British rule led to the imposition of state forest control in 1856, then in India it was 'the large-scale destruction of accessible forests in the early years of railway expansion [that] led to the hasty creation of a forest department' in 1864.[59]

As India's Forest Department moved to protect valuable forest, it converted areas that, in many cases, were already communally managed as common property resources into reserves.[60] By 1900, over 20 per cent of India's land area had been so acquired such that 'the working of state forestry could not fail to affect almost every village and hamlet in the subcontinent.'[61] Shifting cultivators were the worst affected, because, as with the hill Karen of Burma, their fields were located in those areas that contained the most valuable timber.[62] As in Burma, though, the peasantry was also adversely affected, because as access to common forests was reduced, forest

---

[58] Rudimentary state control was introduced in the Malabar teak forests of southern India in 1806 but the protests of timber merchants led to the elimination of such control in 1823, see B. Ribbentrop. *Forestry in British India*, Calcutta, 1900, pp. 64-6; Rangarajan, 'Imperial Agendas and India's Forests', pp. 155-6.

[59] Guha, *Unquiet Woods*, p. 37.

[60] On the difference between 'communally managed' and 'open access' common property resources in India (and how the British failed to distinguish between the two), see J.E.M. Arnold and W.C. Stewart, *Common Property Resource Management in India*, Tropical Forestry Papers no. 24, Oxford, 1991, pp. 2-5; Gadgil, 'India's Deforestation,' pp. 131-5.

[61] Guha and Gadgil, 'State Forestry', p. 147.

[62] *Ibid.*, p. 152.

officials made no provision for the long-term production of 'minor' forest products. As local forests deteriorated from a lack of management, peasants resented the fact that in nearby reserves 'plants that provided their forest resources disappeared under management practices that favored timber species'.[63] Forest officials denigrated peasant practices as 'destructive', and these officials were especially critical of the activities of shifting cultivators, who were seen as being 'the last remnant of an uncivilized past'.[64] Indian peasants and shifting cultivators responded, in turn, by asserting traditional claims. In Kumaun, for example, the firing of the forest floor noted earlier derived much of its appeal as a resistance strategy from the fact that it re-asserted an important traditional practice. The Indian nationalist movement reinforced such rural resistance when it launched a country-wide campaign against British rule after the First World War that linked nationalist objectives to defiance of the forest regulations.[65] As in Burma, the assertion of traditional claims combined with nationalist agitation to undermine scientific forestry practices.

Yet independence in India (as in Burma) was associated with the affirmation of the basis tenets of scientific forestry as introduced during the colonial era. However, in postcolonial India (unlike in Burma) private enterprise has played a more prominent role in the development of the forest industry.[66] In part, this difference reflects Burma's long-standing, and, at times, quite zealous attachment to socialism as compared with India's general adherence to a more market-oriented approach (albeit subject to state planning). Also, the fact that the colonial Indian timber trade was not controlled by European enterprise as in colonial Burma may help to explain the absence

---

[63] Peter S. Ashton, 'A Question of Sustainable Use' in Julie Sloan Denslow and Christine Padoch (eds), *People of the Tropical Rain Forest*, Berkeley, 1988, pp. 191-2. Local forests deteriorated because precolonial management had been eliminated and these forests were now treated as an open-access resource, see Gadgil, 'India's Deforestation', pp. 134-5.

[64] Jacques Pouchepadass, 'British Attitudes towards Shifting Cultivation in Colonial South India: A Case Study of South Canara District, 1800-1920' in David Arnold and Ramachandra Guha (eds), *Nature, Culture, Imperialism: Essays on the Environmental History of South Asia*, Delhi, 1995, p. 148. That forest officials typically viewed shifting cultivators in this manner does not mean, however, that all colonial officials shared this perspective. In this regard, see Sarah Jewitt, 'Europe's "Others"? Forestry Policy and Practices in Colonial and Postcolonial India', *Environment and Planning D: Society and Space* 13 (1995), pp. 67-90.

[65] Guha and Gadgil, 'State Forestry', p. 161.

[66] Which is not to say that state involvement in the forest industry has not occurred. See, for example, Gadgil and Guha, *This Fissured Land*, p. 201.

of a comprehensive nationalization programme in India after 1948.

What is clear, however, is that in both countries the postcolonial state has given priority to commercial exploitation over subsistence-oriented use. Indeed, the Indian state's greater control over its national territory combined with its longstanding commitment to large-scale national development projects has meant that it has been better placed, and perhaps more inclined, than its Burmese counterpart to enforce rigorously the restrictions on popular forest access that are at the heart of scientific forestry. In the process, the postcolonial Indian forest service has justified its actions with reference to a colonial-style discourse about the ecological irresponsibility of local people (and especially shifting cultivators) and the concomitant need for professional 'scientific' management by trained forest officials.[67]

Indonesian forest politics has been similarly influenced by conflicting perceptions of what constitutes appropriate and 'efficient' forest use. Once again, the influence of perceptions and practices from the colonial era has been felt in postcolonial times. Thus, the destruction of as much as 30 per cent of Java's teak forests between 1840 and 1870 prompted the introduction of scientific management in that territory.[68] During these years, the Dutch had imposed the so-called Cultivation System, an arrangement whereby Javanese peasants were required to dedicate a certain amount of land (20 per cent) and labour (66 days annually) to the production of specified commercial crops (notably sugar) grown on the state's behalf.[69] In the process, however, the demand for timber both as a building material (sugar factories, coffee warehouses, plantation housing), and as a fuel (used in the processing of sugarcane, coffee and tobacco), resulted in teak extraction 'without regard for logging regulations'.[70] If, in Burma and India, forest depletion was broadly associated with military-strategic concerns (shipbuilding railway construction), in mid-nineteenth-century Java, overharvesting reflected a Dutch concern to boost sugar and other agricultural exports. In Java, as in India and Burma, 'the power of other government sectors was sufficient to make the state itself the forests' major enemy.'[71]

State-sanctioned overharvesting led to fears of a timber famine that prompted the imposition of strict rules after 1870.[72] Yet, as

---

[67] Jewitt, 'Europe's "Others" ', pp. 82-3; Pathak, *Contested Domains*, pp. 27-8.

[68] Boomgaard, 'Forest Management and Exploitation', p. 12.

[69] Robinson, *Indonesia: The Rise of Capital*, p. 6; David Joel Steinberg *et al.*, *In Search of Southeast Asia: A Modern History*, rev. edn, Sydney, 1987, pp. 157-8.

[70] Peluso, 'History of State Forest Management', p. 68.

[71] *Ibid.*

[72] Furnivall, *Netherlands India*, pp. 201-2.

in the British colonies, the advent of scientific management in Java's teak forests affected indigenous forest users. Subsistence needs were subordinated to the dictates of commercial timber production as the colonial state usurped control over Java's 'unowned' forests. But, rules that required the purchase of wood and fuel only encouraged illicit trade and 'theft' as peasants sought to meet their needs at the same time as they asserted a 'culture of resistance'.[73]

Like their British counterparts, Dutch forest officials extolled the virtues of scientific forestry. Whereas the demarcation of reserves was beneficial because it protected watersheds, teak planting under a local *taungya* forestry scheme known as *tumpang sari* gave employment and temporary forest access to labourers. However, this scheme also gave rise, as in Burma, to 'a new kind of forest-dependent proletariat' in which the system's success was premised on the poverty of its labourers.[74] In Java, official rhetoric notwithstanding, scientific forestry was a doctrine in which basic village needs were given little attention in the quest to maximize timber production. But in a context of effective Dutch repression, no nationalist movement developed in the 1920s and 1930s that could effectively assist peasants (as in Indian and Burma) in their challenge to the *status quo*.[75]

During the years of civil unrest during the Sukarno era (1949-66), political divisions within the state prevented the Indonesian forest service from uniting around, and acting on, a common set of management principles. Yet, if anything, the political turmoil of the early post-colonial years reinforced the tendency of conservative senior forest officials to support the establishment of a system of forest management predicated on the same repressive and 'scientific' practices perpetrated by the Dutch. Thus, as in India and Burma, these officials never made the crucial shift from 'the trade/export orientation emphasized by [the colonial state] ... to distributing wood fairly, inexpensively, and directly to the people.'[76] Under the New Order government, this conservative viewpoint triumphed (many radical forest labourers and officials were killed during the bloodshed of the mid-1960s) with the result that the key tenets of scientific forestry have remained enshrined at the heart of forestry in Java. Simultaneously, the commercial thrust of New Order forestry has been accompanied by a managerialist discourse in which the professional knowledge and experience of

---

[73] Peluso, *Rich Forests, Poor People*, pp. 12-17.

[74] Peluso, 'History of State Forest Management', p. 71.

[75] Steinberg *et al.*, *In Search of Southeast Asia*, p. 309.

[76] Soepardi city in Peluso, *Rich Forests, Poor People*, p. 113.

forest officials is contrasted with the perceived ignorance or back-wardness of peasants and shifting cultivators on forestry matters. Thus, and notwithstanding the move in recent years to promote 'social forestry' (in which local participation in forestry management is sought), the 'moral economy of the forester' in Indonesia (but also elsewhere in Asia) remains wedded to a system of scientific forest management in which central state control and commercial exploitation is linked to oppressive restrictions on popular forest access and use.[77]

As adopted in turn-of-the-century north-west Siam, scientific forestry also had a commercial focus. The rapid depletion of the teak forests in the nineteenth century was less a function of government policy (as in Burma, India and Java), as it was a reflection of the absence of central authority in the region. Nevertheless, teak overharvesting served as a 'major excuse' for the Siamese state to extend its rule over 'what were previously vassal states.'[78] In 1899 the region's forests were formally claimed by the central state, and responsibility for their management was transferred to the Royal Forest Department. This move not only marginalized the local *Chao*, it also made the practice of shifting cultivation in highland forests illegal.[79] However, the Department was too weak to stop such practices, and in any event, focused on the teak trade until the 1930s.[80] Lacking the administrative and coercive powers of the British and the Dutch, the Siamese were unable to attain more than an imperfect control over the forest sector. As a result, the impact of scientific forestry on the subsistence economy was not as pronounced during the colonial era in Siam, as it was in Burma, India and Java. Nevertheless, there was, and still is, a 'considerable tension between the traditional Thai villager's view of forests and forest products as common property resources and official government policy.'[81]

Since the Second World War, the Thai state has moved systematically to incorporate peripheral regions of the country into the national economy as part of a concerted effort to boost economic growth

[77] *Ibid.*, p. 236; see also Charles Victor Barber, 'The State, the Environment, and Development: The Genesis and Transformation of Social Forestry Policy in New Order Indonesia', unpubl. Ph.D. thesis, University of California, Berkeley, 1989.

[78] Mekvichai, 'Teak Industry in North Thailand', pp. 207-8. Siamese action reflected, in turn, growing British disquiet over deforestation in this area, and the feeling of the latter that action of some sort was required, see De'Ath, 'History of Timber Exports from Thailand', p. 57.

[79] Peter Kunstadter, 'Hill People of Northern Thailand', in Julie Sloan Denslow and Christine Padoch (eds), *People of the Tropical Rain Forest*, Berkeley, 1988, p. 103.

[80] Feeny, 'Forest Depletion in Thailand', pp. 124-5.

[81] *Ibid.*, pp. 125-6.

in the country.[82] In the process, the Royal Forest Department has sought to extend central control through a national system of scientific forestry in which commercial timber extraction has taken precedence over subsistence forest use. As in Burma, India and Indonesia, this process has resulted in widespread over-harvesting as well as social conflict as local forest users, such as peasants and shifting cultivators, find themselves (and their forest practices) displaced as a result of state-sanctioned logging activity.[83] Yet, as in these other Asian countries, in Thailand it has been the norm for state officials to blame deforestation on shifting cultivators rather than on the loggers who are typically closely linked to senior Thai political and military leaders, and thus beyond official criticism.[84] In Thailand, as elsewhere in the region, scientific forestry in postcolonial times has thus been harnessed to the broader quest for national economic development in a process whereby local practices are disrupted and suborned to the 'greater national interest'. The widespread popular resistance to state-led 'development' that is characteristic of much Asian forest politics today illustrates that the application of scientific forest management in this new guise has not defused public opposition. Indeed, if anything, such opposition has intensified as groups oppose at the discursive and material level practices that subordinate local interests to 'national' concerns.[85]

It is the impact of scientific forestry (itself a response to earlier *laissez-faire* policies) on preexisting indigenous practices that is at the heart of Asia's colonial and postcolonial forest politics. There is of course a danger of romanticizing 'traditional' practices by accepting 'honeyed grandmothers' tales'.[86] Yet it is nonetheless apparent that the growing commercialization of Asia's forests since the early nineteenth century has transformed popular forest access and use. In many respects, this process has simply repeated what had occurred in early modern

---

[82] Philip Hirsch, *Development Dilemmas in Rural Thailand*, Singapore, 1990.

[83] Leungaramsri and Rajesh, *Future of People and Forests*; Phil Hirsch and Larry Lohmann, 'Contemporary Politics of Environment in Thailand', *Asian Survey* 29 (1989), pp. 439-51.

[84] For example, see Thiem Komkris, 'Forestry Aspects of Land Use in Areas of Swidden Cultivation' in Peter Kunstadter *et al.* (eds), *Farmers in the Forest: Economic Development and Marginal Agriculture in Northern Thailand*, Honolulu, 1978, pp. 61-70; see also Hurst, *Rainforest Politics*, p. 221.

[85] Lohmann, 'Land, Power and Forest Colonization in Thailand', pp. 188-90; on Asia generally, see James Rush, *The Last Tree: Reclaiming the Environment in Tropical Asia*, New York, 1991, especially chap. 5.

[86] Lenin quoted in Peter Linebaugh, 'Karl Marx, the Theft of Wood, and Working Class Composition: A Contribution to the Current Debate', *Crime and Social Justice* 6 (fall-winter 1976), p. 13.

Europe, where forests were enclosed, and peasants dispossessed of their rights.[87] In seventeenth-century England, for example, labourers who were 'notoriously better off in woodland areas' fought enclosure, but were forced to give way as their needs 'conflicted with the rational exploitation of woods for the production of timber.'[88] A similar pattern of events unfolded in Germany where by the end of the eighteenth century 'no State organization was more hated . . . than the forest police.'[89] In France, meanwhile, peasant hostility towards the restrictive policies of the central Forest Service grew and in the early nineteenth century resulted in incidents of arson as well as attacks on forest guards.[90] However, the advent of scientific forestry in Asia (and Africa) occurred in a different context in which resource extraction was tailored to the needs of the European powers with effects that are still in evidence today. Thus, to understand the political ecology of forest use in the Third World today it is essential to relate contemporary forest politics to policies and practices introduced during the colonial era.

The Political Ecology of Forest Use

As Chapter 1 highlighted, the political-ecology literature has begun to explore the interaction between political, economic and ecological forces on the one hand, and historical and contemporary developments on the other hand. Much more work needs to be done in order to clarify patterns and processes associated with forest use as well as other human impacts on the environment in the Third World. In light of this study, what are some of the general implications for analysis that may be derived from an understanding of forest politics in Burma?

One central finding concerns the central role of the state in forest politics. As the Burmese experience illustrates, the colonial state facilitated the growth of capitalist enterprise. Yet it also pursued its own distinctive, if variable interests. This was most evident in its efforts to balance revenue creation with long-term timber production.

---

[87] Guha, *Unquiet Woods*, pp. 186-9; E.P. Thompson, *Whigs and Hunters: The Origin of the Black Act*, London, 1975.

[88] Keith Thomas, *Man and the Natural World: Changing Attitudes in England, 1500-1800*, Harmondsworth, 1983, p. 200.

[89] Endres cited in Franz Heske, *German Forestry*, New Haven, 1938, p. 254; see also Linebaugh, 'Theft of Wood', pp. 9-14.

[90] John F. Freeman, 'Forest Conservancy in the Alps of Dauphiné, 1287-1870', *Forest and Conservation History* 38 (October 1994), p. 178.

The advent of scientific forestry was critical in this regard. But the colonial state was also deeply concerned about the assertion of political control – in the remote but economically important Pegu Yoma, for example. These interests did not always coincide with those of capitalist enterprise. Even the twentieth-century predominance of the European firms was as much a reflection of the state's own political interests as it was the result of business influence in government. In the pursuit of those interests, the colonial state drew upon its unique role as a resource manager to enhance control over society and resources.

Since independence in 1948, the Burmese state has sought to restore order in the forests as part of a programme of centralized forest control and exploitation. To be sure, until the early 1970s the power of that state to impose its will over its political opponents was limited outside of central areas – during this era, the Burmese example highlights how a state can be displaced from its role as a resource manager. However, the growing ability of the Burmese state to assert central control over peripheral areas, notably since the advent of the SLORC in 1988, illustrates the 'staying power' of states in the modern era, and the continuing importance of that actor in forest management and politics. Indeed, as the preceding comparative discussion of forest politics in Burma, India, Indonesia and Thailand has illustrated, a common thread in the experiences of these countries is the power of the state to encourage or discourage practices that it deems consonant or otherwise with state interests. Other actors such as transnational corporations and non-governmental organizations have generally assumed a growing importance in Third World forest politics since the Second World War, but this has not been the case everywhere; nor is it to say that the role of the state has been necessarily diminished.[91]

The state in Burma (as elsewhere) is not monolithic. Undoubtedly, colonialism encouraged social cohesion and a particular mind-set that was reflected in the attitudes and actions of European officialdom.[92] But there were also differences of perception and interest which, at times, threatened the internal unity of the colonial state. As noted,

---

[91] Thus, the growth of 'civic politics' (political interaction between actors independent of the state's involvement) does not so much displace the role of the state in the political process as it adds a further dimension to that process. See P. Wapner, 'Politics beyond the State: Environmental Activism and World Civic Politics', *World Politics* 47 (April 1995), pp. 311-40.

[92] George Orwell, *Burmese Days*, Harmondsworth, 1987 [1934]. On the social differentiation of colonial elites, see Ann Laura Stoler, 'Rethinking Colonial Categories: European Communities and the Boundaries of Rule', *Comparative Studies in Society and History* 31 (January 1989), pp. 134-61.

programmatic differences were at the heart of conflict between forest and civil officials in colonial Burma. Such conflict was most intense in the 1870s when the forest service was rapidly expanding its activities, and forest legislation was being debated. It nevertheless persisted throughout the colonial era, albeit at a much reduced level in later years. The expansion of state control in the forest industry after 1948 was the occasion for the development of a new set of differences within the state over forest policy and practice. In the postcolonial era, conflict has occurred between the Forest Department, responsible for conserving commercial forests, and the State Timber Board, the agency created in 1948 to oversee the exploitation of those forests. Yet if these two agencies have differed, at times sharply, over the location and extent of harvesting operations, the SLORC's determination to push ahead with ambitious plans for large-scale development projects (i.e. dams, natural gas pipelines, mining) around the country raises the prospect of greater inter-departmental conflict in the years ahead as conflicting land uses are expressed institutionally. Such conflict is already a noteworthy feature of forest politics in India, Indonesia and Thailand.[93] It is thus important to recognize not only the centrality of state interests, but also the bureaucratic politics that often shapes the determination of those interests.

This book has also demonstrated the ability of everyday forms of peasant resistance to frustrate state forest control. To be sure, there are limits to such resistance. Yet everyday resistance is particularly effective as a means of circumventing access restrictions. Partly, this is because forests provide perfect cover for clandestine action. But its efficacy also derives from the fact that it is in forests that elite control is usually weakest.[94] In a sense, the argument here comes full circle with a point made in Chapter 1. There, it was suggested that the colonial state was anxious to define (or 'imagine') forests because control in these areas was most tenuous. As this book has shown, however, despite the best efforts of forest officials to map, enumerate, demarcate and patrol key reserves, peasants were often able to frustrate their attempts. Given the need to police an extensive area with a limited staff, what is surprising is not that the Forest Department failed to achieve the desired control, but rather that it was able to achieve any control at all.

The civil unrest that disrupted forest management in Burma after

---

[93] Pathak, *Contested Domains*, chap. 2; Philip Hirsch, 'Forests, Forest Reserve, and Forest Land in Thailand', *Geographical Journal* 156 (July 1990), p. 172; Smith, *Politics of Indonesian Rainforests*, p. 21.

[94] James C. Scott, *Domination and the Arts of Resistance: Hidden Transcripts*, New Haven, 1990, p. 189.

1948 largely obviated the need for everyday resistance strategies in insecure areas, and reiterates the point that state forest control can be quite tenuous at times. Yet at the same time the ability of the Burmese state ultimately to defeat its opponents and restore central authority in much of the country's forests by the mid-1990s suggests that the power of the state is not to be gainsaid. Such power is now being applied increasingly to the consolidation of state forest control, but as access restrictions begin to bite, everyday forms of resistance will once more become the norm. In this regard, the record of such resistance in India, Indonesia and Thailand illustrates the likely direction that Burmese forest politics might take in the years to come.

Finally, this book has highlighted the ambiguous relationship between colonialism and the emergence of modern indigenous politics on the one hand, and scientific forestry, access control and conservation on the other. As Chapter 6 noted, Burmese nationalists attacked colonial forest policy in the 1920s and 1930s for not being in the best interests of the Burmese. Whereas peasants were denied access to forest products or land, the urban middle class was deprived of opportunities in government and business. Hence, Burma's forests were not only being run as a 'business concern'. They were, above all, being managed as a European business concern, complete with European doctrines of management (scientific forestry) and economics (capitalism).

Yet the championing of peasant rights and nationalist principles notwithstanding, the Burmese political elite failed to articulate a comprehensive alternative strategy. No effort was made, for example, to suggest how popular forest access was to be balanced with long-term conservancy under indigenous rule. The implications of this lacuna in the nationalist programme became readily apparent after 1937 when the Burmese elite gained additional powers under the last pre-Second World War constitution. Forest management in late colonial Burma came to be associated with political opportunism – the manipulation of forest rules and access for the benefit of the incumbent elite. Forest management was brought under indigenous control, but political expediency became the order of the day.

In 1876 one of the principal architects of state forest control in British India (including Burma), B.H. Baden-Powell, argued that all conservancy measures were '*necessarily disliked...the fact of restriction*, reasonable or not, is what the popular mind feels.'[95] In this view forest conservancy and public opinion were inevitably at odds. Regret-

---

[95] B.H. Baden-Powell, 'Forest Conservancy in its Popular Aspect', *Indian Forester* 2 (July 1876), pp. 3-4.

tably, the subsequent record of forest politics in colonial Burma did little to invalidate this observation.

As this book shows, it could hardly have been otherwise. Given imperial interests, forest conservancy was linked to access restrictions and long-term timber production in such a manner that the interests of Burmese peasants, shifting cultivators and timber traders were neglected. The system of rationalized forest use that was introduced after 1856 was, after all, a colonial creation, and was seen as such by the Burmese. Not surprisingly, then, the advent of partial self-rule marked a new phase in forest politics in which that system was gradually undermined.

In the postcolonial era, Burmese forest politics has been marked by change, notably the Burmanization of the forest bureaucracy and the timber trade. Yet, notwithstanding these changes, what noteworthy about the period since 1948 is in the way in which the Burmese state has sought to restore order in the forests (as part of a broader counter-insurgency programme) in keeping with the basic tenets of scientific forestry. To be sure, the state's emphasis on revenue generation has encouraged a profligate towards Burma's forest resources; timber overharvesting has thus been the norm since the 1970s, if not before. But the emphasis on commercial (as opposed to subsistence) forest use and centralized state forest control by Burma's leaders since 1948 has represented much more than simply a short-term military strategy designed to defeat insurgent groups and enrich the political leadership. Rather, it constitutes a recognition by those leaders of the long-term utility of a system of scientific forest management in which the forests are managed in keeping with the political and economic interests of the state. As elsewhere in Asia, Burma's rulers may have changed, but – at least in the forest sector – the principles underlying that rule have not changed appreciably since the ending of the colonial era.

In this regard Baden-Powell's remarks are as apposite today as they were in 1876. Imperial interests have become 'national' interests (and in the 1990s also 'global' interests), but the tension between forest conservancy and popular opinion remains the same. In Burma, as in other countries in the region, conflict between the state and peasants and shifting cultivators persists, and is rooted in fundamentally different perceptions of what constitutes appropriate forest use. The forest resource continues to be contested but under new political and economic circumstances.

APPENDIX

A NOTE ON FOREST LANDS AND SPECIES

As a result of differing conditions of geology, climate and elevation, Burma's forests are characteristically diverse. From the mangrove swamps of the Irrawaddy delta to the pine groves of the Shan hills, these forests embrace a wide variety of forest types. Scholars have described Burma's forests in detail, but here a more general overview is appropriate.[1] Thus, Burma's forests contain evergreen and deciduous trees, and may be divided into tropical, subtropical and temperate forest types. Temperate forests are located in northern Burma above an altitude of 6,000 feet, while subtropical forests are to be found notably in the Shan States between 3,500 and 7,500 feet. Yet, in this study, it is the tropical forests (under 3,500 feet) that are of principal interest. These forests encompass evergreen rainforests (Tenasserim), mangrove swamps (the Irrawaddy delta), mixed evergreen and deciduous forest (the Pegu Yoma) and dry deciduous and scrub forests (central Dry Zone). Containing some of Burma's most biologically rich forests, this forest type has also been the main focus of forest politics in the country during both colonial and postcolonial times.

From a commercial perspective, the temperate and subtropical forests of the sparsely settled north and north-east are of minimal importance when compared with the tropical forests situated in the more densely populated central and southern regions. In the latter are to be found the key commercial species – teak (*kyun*), *pyinkado, kanyin, thingan, thitkado, padauk, pyinma, in, sha* – that have been the main source of economic exploitation and political conflict.

Above all, it is the tropical forests of the Pegu Yoma that are

[1] There is a fairly extensive literature on the subject. For example, see Sulpice Kurz, *Preliminary Report on the Forest and other Vegetation of Pegu*, Calcutta, 1875; L. Dudley Stamp, *The Vegetation of Burma from an Ecological Standpoint*, Rangoon, 1924; H.G. Champion, 'A Preliminary Survey of the Forest Types of India and Burma', *Indian Forest Records* (n.s.), Silviculture, 1, 1 (1936), pp. 1-286; M.V. Edwards, 'Burma Forest Types (according to Champion's Classification)', *Indian Forest Records* (n.s.), Silviculture, 7, 2 (1950), pp. 135-73; John H. Davis, *The Forests of Burma*, Gainesville, FL., 1960; John Blower *et al.*, 'Burma (Myanmar)' in N. Mark Collins *et al.* (eds), *The Conservation Atlas of Tropical Forests: Asia and the Pacific*, London, 1991, pp. 103-10.

the most valuable. Indeed, this compact range of hills was described in 1931 as 'one of the most valuable forests in the world'.[2] Separating the Irrawaddy and Sittang rivers, the Pegu Yoma begins thirty-five miles north of Rangoon, and runs north for 200 miles until it ends at Yamethin on the edge of the Dry Zone. In terms of forest type, this range of hills is characterized by rainforest in its southern extremity, which gives way to mixed evergreen and deciduous forest, before petering out as dry deciduous forest and scrub in the north. With an average width of only thirty miles, this rectangular-shaped stretch of forest land is about six thousand square miles in area. Yet, it accounted for 50 per cent of the country's total annual teak outturn in the early twentieth century, and about 60 per cent of its total net forest revenue. In recognition of this fact, the Pegu Yoma was largely demarcated as reserved forest by the Forest Department by the end of the nineteenth century. As we show, the region (including the surrounding plains forests) has been traditionally the main battleground of Burmese forest politics.

Conflict has centred on a handful of commercial species.[3] The most important such species is, of course, teak (*kyun*). One of the premier timbers in the world, teak (*Tectona grandis*) has been an important economic resource since precolonial times. Its role in shipbuilding is noted in Chapter 2, but the strength and durability of teak ensured that it has also been in demand for use in the construction of houses, public buildings, *pongyi kaung* (monasteries), furniture, bridges, railway carriages and for conversion into railway sleepers. A tree which can reach a height of 150 feet and a girth of 12-14 feet in the mixed evergreen and deciduous forests that form its favoured habitat, teak is also found in dry deciduous forests. Wherever found, teak rarely comprises naturally more than 10 to 12 per cent of the forest crop, and it is this fact, along with its long commercial maturation (up to 150 years), that has been a key factor in the development of forest policy in Burma.

Such a policy, however, was not always synonymous with teak management. Thus, colonial officials devoted considerable attention in the late nineteenth century to the management of cutch, a water extract of the *sha* tree (*Accacia catechu*) used for tanning and dyeing purposes (Chapter 4). A native of the dry deciduous and scrub forest, *sha* attains a height of only 30 to 40 feet and a girth of 4 to 5 feet, and is thus eminently suited to extraction by small-scale traders.

---

[2] C.W. Scott, 'Lecture on the Forest Geography of Burma', *Indian Forester* 57 (May 1931), p. 245. This paragraph is based on this source.

[3] The following discussion is drawn from Alex Rodger, *A Handbook of the Forest Products of Burma*, Rangoon, 1951 (1921).

Primarily important as the source of cutch, *sha* has also been used for agricultural implements, carts, wheels and fuel.

Next to teak, the key species from a British viewpoint was *pyinkado* (Burmese iron-wood). As its English name, attests, *pyinkado* (*Xylia dolabriformis*) is a tree renowned for its strength and durability. These qualities made it the preferred timber for railway sleepers, but it was also used in bridges and jetties. Growing to 120 feet and a girth of 12 feet, the wood is associated with teak in upper mixed evergreen and deciduous forest, but is frequently found in rainforests that are devoid of teak. In Arakan, it was the preeminent commercial species, and its use was regulated from 1863.

Less well-known than teak and *pyinkado, padauk* (*Pterocarpus macrocarpus*) was valuable to the British primarily for use in gun-carriage wheels. Among the Burmese, however, the wood has been used widely: in cart wheels and axles, boat frames, boxes, furniture, ploughs, house-building and muscial instruments. A tree of medium height (60-80 feet) and girth (5-8 feet), *padauk* is most commonly found in the upper mixed evergreen and deciduous forest, but also grows in dry deciduous forest.

Species without military-strategic and commercial export value to the British (and their Burmese successors) have nevertheless been important in the domestic economy. Promoted by the Forest Department in Europe (Chapter 5), *in (Dipterocarpus tuberculatus)* is a wood that has been used primarily locally in cheap housing, carts, boats and other purposes. A tree between 70 and 110 feet high and 5 to 10 feet in girth, it is found through much of the country, but particularly in the dry deciduous '*indaing*' forests of central Burma. *Kanyin (Dipterocarpus spp.)*, a name applied to various species of *dipterocarpus*, is a wood of inferior quality to *in*, but is used for similar purposes.

Thitka (Pentace burmanica) and *thitkado (Cedrela toona)* are trees of comparable size, range and utility to *in* and *kanyin*. *Thitka* and *thitkado* have been thus in demand for use in boats and houses, as well as for masts and oars; and, as with *in*, were the focus of a sporadic imperial export campaign. It was partly for this reason that these two woods were the first non-teak species reserved by the British in 1873 (Chapter 3).

Thingan (Hopea odorata) is another general purpose timber. Found primarily in the Tenasserim rainforests and the lower mixed evergreen and deciduous forests of Pegu, *thingan* is especially sought after by boat-builders because it is not susceptible to attack by white ants. The wood is also used for masts, piles, carts and furniture. Although *pyinma (Lagerstroemia flos-reginae)* is not immune from attack by white ants, it too is used in the construction of houses and boats. Growing to 100 feet, this tree is found throughout Burma, but prefers flat alluvial ground and stream banks.

If the discussion so far has focused on general purpose construction timbers, it is because these species have been the most valuable. However, Burma's forests have also been the source of a wide variety of other timber and non-timber products. In the mangrove swamp forests, for example, the medium-sized *kanazo* tree (*Heritiera fomes*) became valuable as a source of fuel for Rangoon, and other towns in Lower Burma in the late nineteenth and twentieth century. Such woods as *dahat* (*Tectona hamiltoniana*), *taukkyan* (*Terminalia tomentosa*) and *myaukchaw* (*Homalium tomentosum*) have served as fuelwoods in other parts of the country.

In contrast, the *thitsi* tree (*Melanorrhoea usitata*) is important primarily because it yields the varnish known as *thitsi*. Found in the dry deciduous forests, *thitsi* is tapped for its resin which is used in Burmese lacquer ware. The pine (*tinya*) tree of the Shan States is also tapped for its resin (used for turpentine), but the general inaccessibility of these forests has limited the development of this industry.

The preceding discussion illustrates the economic importance of Burma's tropical forests. Moreover, it gives some indication of why access restrictions have been the source of so much conflict in Burma since the mid-nineteenth century.

BIBLIOGRAPHY

ARCHIVAL SOURCES

Note: All archival material is located in the India Office Library and Records, London, Unless otherwise noted.

Annual Report of the Bombay Burmah Trading Corporation Limited, 1863-1948, Guildhall Library, London.

Atkinson, D.J., 'Situation in 1945 [and 1946]' TMs [1946-7], Oxford Forestry Institute, Oxford.

Blanford, H.R., 'Distribution of Teak Forests', Noted prepared for the Government of Burma, [1936]. MSS Eur. D. 689.

Bruce, Arthur, 'Burma Recollections', MSS Eur. E. 362/3.

Burma Forest Proceedings, 1884-1924.

Burma Office Files (BOF), 1938-47.

Clague Papers, MSS Eur. E. 252/3.

Dawkins Papers, MSS Dur. D. 931.

India Forest Letters, 1867-79.

India Forest Proceedings, 1864-84.

On Gyaw, 'Burma Teak Lease', TMs, [1947], Indian Institute, Oxford.

Progress Report on Forest Administration in Burma, 1863-1940.

Selections from Dispatches to India, 1865-76.

Selections from the Records of the Bengal Government, 1852.

Selections from the Records of the Government of India (Foreign Department), 1855-68.

Selections from the Records of the Government of India (Public Works Department), 1862.

Upper Burma Proceedings, 1886-7.

Working Plans, 1885-1951, Indian Institute, Oxford.

PERIODICALS AND NEWSPAPERS

Note: The following periodicals and newspapers have been cited in the text but are not listed separately below according to article title and author.

Burma, Rangoon, 1952-62.

Burma Weekly Bulletin, Rangoon, 1959.

Burmese Forester, Rangoon, 1951-64.

Far Eastern Economic Review, Hong Kong, 1987-95.

Forests News for Asia and the Pacific, Bangkok, 1977-9.

Forward, Rangoon, 1963-70.

Guardian (newspaper), Rangoon, 1955-9.

Guardian (periodical), Rangoon, 1960-77.

Indian Forester, Dehra Dun, 1876-1954.

Myanmar Forestry, Yangon, 1993-4.
Nation, Rangoon, 1953-61.
Nation, Bangkok, 1990-4.
New Light of Myanmar, Yangon, 1994.
New Times of Burma, Rangoon, 1952.
Working People's Daily, Yangon, 1989-90.

GOVERNMENT DOCUMENTS

Documents relating to forest management

Baden-Powell, B.H., *The Forest System of British Burma*, Calcutta, 1873.
——, *Memorandum on the Supply of Teak and Other Timbers in the Burma Markets*, Calcutta, 1873.
——, 'On the Defects of the Existing Forest Law (Act VII of 1863) and Proposals for a New Forest Act' in B.H. Baden-Powell and J.S. Gamble (eds), *Report of the Proceedings of the Forest Conference, 1873-74*, Calcutta, 1874, pp. 3-30.
——, *A Manual of Jurisprudence for Forest Officers*, Calcutta, 1882.
—— and J.S. Gamble (eds), *Report of the Proceedings of the Forest Conference, 1873-74*, Calcutta, 1874.
Barrington, A.H.M., *Forest Administration in the Arakan Forest Division*, Rangoon, 1918.
Blanford, H.R., 'Regeneration with the Assistance of Taungya in Burma', *Indian Forest Records*, 11, 3 (1925), pp. 81-121.
Brandis, Dietrich, *Rules for the Administration of Forests in the Province of Pegu*, Rangoon, 1859.
——, *Memorandum on the Forest Legislation proposed for British India other than the Presidencies of Madras and Bombay*, Simla, 1875.
——, *Suggestions regarding Forest Administration in British Burma*, Calcutta, 1876.
Burma Forest Act 1881, Rangoon, 1884.
Burma Forest Committee, *Report of the Burma Forest Committee 1925*, Rangoon, 1926.
Burma Forest Department, *Review of Forest Administration in Burma during the five years 1909-10 to 1913-14*, Rangoon, 1916.
——, *Departmental Instructions for Forest Officers in Burma*, Rangoon, 1919.
——, *Manuel of Standing Orders for Forest Subordinates*, Rangoon, 1919.
——, *Working Plans Manual Burma*, 3rd edn, Rangoon, 1948 [1938].
——, 'Empire Forest and the War: Burma' in *Fifth British Empire Forestry Conference: Statements*, n.p., 1947, vol. I, pp. 1-26.
Champion, H.G., *The Problem of the Pure Teak Plantation*, Calcutta, 1932.
——, 'A Preliminary Survey of the Forest Types of India and Burma', *Indian Forest Records* (n.s.), Silviculture, 1, 1 (1936), pp. 1-286.
Chit-Swe, Major-General, Minister for Agriculture and Forests, 'Country Statement to the Twenty-fifth Session of the United Nations FAO Conference', Rome, 1989.

Edwards, M.V., 'Burma Forest Types (according to Champion's Classification)', *Indian Forest Records* (n.s.), Silviculture, 7, 2 (1950), pp. 135-73.

Forest Department, *Forestry Situation in Myanmar*, Yangon, 1989.

——, *Greening Project for the Nine Critical Districts of the Arid Zone of Central Myanmar*, Yangon, 1994.

——, 'Myanmar Country Report', paper presented at the Project Advisory Committee, 26-8 July 1994, Hanoi (Vietnam).

——, 'Myanmar Forest Policy', fourth draft, Yangon, July 1994.

Forest Enquiry Committee, *Report of the Forest Enquiry Committee 1937*, Rangoon, 1937.

Forestal International Limited, *Forest Feasibility Study: Forest Resources*, Rangoon, 1978, vol. I.

Gallant, M.N., *Report to the Government of Burma on the Teakwood Trade*, Rome, 1957.

Government of Burma, *The Burma Forest Manual*, Rangoon, 1922.

Government of India, *Seasoning of Timber by Girdling Previous to Felling*, London, 1868.

——, *Copy of Enclosures of Forests Despatch from the Government of India*, no. 14, Calcutta, 1874.

——, *Code of Instructions for the Conduct of Office Business and for the Regulation of Accounts in the Forest Department*, Calcutta, 1886.

Government of the Union of Myanmar, *Government of the Union of Myanmar Pilot Watershed Management Project for Kinda Dam, Phugyi and Inle Lake*, Yangon, 1992.

Hart, G.S., *Note on a Tour of Inspection in Burma*, Simla, 1914.

——, *Note on a Tour of Inspection in the Forests of Burma*, Simla, 1918.

Hill, H.C., *Memorandum on the Forest Laws in Force in Upper Burma*, Rangoon, 1889.

India Forest Research Institute, *100 Years of Indian Forestry 1861-1961*, Dehra Dun, 1961, vol. I.

Kyaw Myint Than, Than Lwin, Sein Thet and Sann Lwin, 'Watershed Management in Myanmar', unpubl. MS, Ministry of Agriculture and Forests, Yangon, 1990.

Kyaw Tint and Tun Hla, *Forest Cover of Myanmar: The 1989 Appraisal*, Yangon, 1991.

Leete, F.A., *Memorandum on Departmental Extraction v. Cooperation with Traders for the Development of Trade in Burma Hardwoods*, Rangoon, 1923.

Mehm Ko Ko Kyi, Tun Hla, Pe Thein and Saw Win, 'Forest Management in Myanmar', paper prepared for the ESCAP/UNDP regional seminar-cum-study tour, Yangon, 1990.

Ministry of Forestry, Planning and Statistics Department, *An Outline of the Forest Situation and Investment Opportunities in Myanmar*, Yangon, 1993.

Monroy, J.A. von, *Report to the Government of Burma on Integration of Forest and Industries*, Rome, 1952.

Proceedings of the First Burma Forest Conference held at Maymyo between the 13th and 20th June 1910, Rangoon, 1910.

Ribbentrop, B., *Forestry in British India*, Calcutta, 1900.

Rodger, Alex, *Forest Reservation in Burma in the Interests of an Endangered Water-Supply*, Calcutta, 1909.

——, *A Handbook of the Forest Products of Burma*, Rangoon, 1951 (1921).

Scott, C.W., *Measurements of the Damage to Teak Timber by the Beehole Borer Moth*, Rangoon, 1932.

Sindall, R.W., *Report on the Manufacture of Paper and Paper Pulp in Burma*, Rangoon, 1906.

Smith, Conrad F., *Report on the Myanma Forestry Sector*, Yangon, 1991.

——, Memo from Conrad F. Smith to FAO Resident Representative, 1 January 1991, Yangon.

State Law and Order Restoration Council, *The Forest Law*, SLORC Law no. 8/92, Yangon, 3 November 1992.

Thein, *The Fuelwood Situation in Burma*, Rome, 1959.

Troup, R.S., *Burma Padauk*, Calcutta, 1909.

——, *Burmese In Wood*, Calcutta, 1909.

Union of Myanmar, *Brief Notes on the Ministry of Forestry and its Department and Enterprises*, Yangon, n.d.

Watson, H.W.A., *Note on Departmental Extraction of Teak in Prome, Zigon and Tharrawaddy Divisions, Pegu Circle, Lower Burma*, Rangoon, 1917.

——, *A Note on the Position on the Province as Regards the Preparation and Revision of Working Plans*, Rangoon, 1921.

——, *A Note on the Pegu Yoma Forests*, Rangoon, 1923.

——, *A Note on Forest Administration and Policy in the Federated Shan States*, Rangoon, 1929.

Other Government Documents

Aitchison, C.U., *A Collection of Treatises, Engagements and Sanads relating to India and Neighbouring Countries*, Calcutta, 1909, vol. II.

Binns, B.O., *Amherst District Gazetteer*, Rangoon, 1935.

Bribery and Corruption Enquiry Committee, *Report of the Bribery and Corruption Enquiry Committee 1940*, Rangoon, 1941.

Burma Legislative Council Proceedings, Rangoon, 1901-21.

Burma Legislative Council Proceedings, Rangoon, 1923-36.

Burma Legislature, House of Representatives Proceedings, Rangoon, 1937-41.

Burma Legislature, Senate Proceedings, Rangoon, 1937-40.

Burma Ministry of Finance, *Financial and Economic Annual of Burma, July 1943*, Rangoon, 1943.

Burma Reforms Committee, *Report and Appendices*, and *Record of Evidence*, Rangoon, 1922, vol. I-IV.

Burma Retrenchment Committee, *Report of the Burma Retrenchment Committee 1934*, Rangoon, 1934.

Butler, J., *Gazetteer of the Mergui District*, Rangoon, 1884.

Committee on Expenditure on the Public Services, *Reports of the Committee on Expenditure on the Public Services, 1939-40*, Rangoon, 1940, part I.

Craddock, Reginald, *Speeches by Sir Reginald Craddock, Lieutenant-Governor of Burma, 1917-1922*, Rangoon, 1924.

Dawson, G.W., *Bhamo Distruct Gazetteer*, Rangoon, 1912.
Director of Information, *Is Trust Vindicated? A Chronicle of the Various Accomplishments of the Government headed by General Ne Win during the Period of Tenure from November, 1958 to February 6, 1960*, Rangoon, 1960.
Director of Information, *Burma: National Economy*, Rangoon, 1963.
Economic and Social Board, *Pyidawtha: The New Burma*, London, 1954.
Fiscal Committee, *Second Interim Report of the Fiscal Committee 1939*, Rangoon, 1938.
Furnivall, J.S., and W.S. Morrison, *Syriam District Gazetteer*, Rangoon, 1914.
Further Correspondence Relating to Burmah, no. 3, London, 1886.
Government of Burma, *Thayetmyo District Gazetteer*, Rangoon, 1911.
——, *Village Manual*, Rangoon, 1940.
Grantham, S.G., *Tharrawaddy District Gazetteer*, Rangoon, 1920.
Great Britain, *Minutes of Evidence taken before the Royal Commission upon Decentralization in India*, London, 1908, vol. III.
——, Indian Statutory Commission. *Memorandum submitted by the Government of Burma to the Indian Statutory Commission*, London, 1930, vol. XI.
Hardiman, J.P., *Lower Chindwin District Gazetteer*, Rangoon, 1912.
Hertz, W.A., *Myitkyina District Gazetteer*, Rangoon, 1912.
Ministry of Planning and Finance, *Report to the Pyithu Hluttaw on the Financial, Economic and Social Conditions of the Socialist Republic of the Union of Burma for 1985-86*, Rangoon, 1985.
Ministry of National Planning and Economic Development, *Review of the Financial, Economic and Social Conditions for 1993-94*, Yangon, 1994.
National Commission for Environmental Affairs, *Environmental Policy and Legislation for Myanmar*, Yangon, 1993.
——, *The Need for a National Environmental Policy in Myanmar*, Yangon, 1993.
Neild, Ralph, and J.A. Stewart, *Kyaukse District Gazetteer*, Rangoon, 1925.
Owens, F.C., *Pakokku District Gazetteer*, Rangoon, 1913.
Page, A.J., *Pegu District Gazetteer*, Rangoon, 1917.
Proceedings of the Council of the Governor General of India, Calcutta, 1878-81.
Royal Commission on Agriculture in India, *Evidence Taken in Burma*, London, 1928, vol. XII.
Scott, J. George, and J.P. Hardiman, *Gazetteer of Upper Burma and the Shan States*, Rangoon, 1900, vol. II, part I.
Selected Correspondence of Letters Issued from and Received in the Office of the Commissioner, Tenasserim Division for the Years 1825-26 to 1842-43, Rangoon, 1916.
Sindall, R.W., *Report on the Manufacture of Paper and Paper Pulp in Burma*, Rangoon, 1906.
Spearman, H.R., *The British Burma Gazetteer*, Rangoon, 1880, vol. I.
Thailand-Myanmar Joint Commission on Bilateral Cooperation, *Agreed Minutes of the First Meeting of the Thailand-Myanmar Joint Commission on Bilateral Cooperation*, Yangon, 16-18 September 1993.

Thompson, T.S., *Soil Erosion and its Control in the Shan States, Burma*, n.p., 1944.

Two-Year Plan of Economic Development for Burma, Rangoon, 1948.

U.K. Parliament, 'Return of Contract between the Secretary of State for India and the Bombay-Burma Trading Corporation referring to the Teak Forests of Upper Burma, and Correspondence relating thereto', *Sessional Papers* (Commons), *Accounts and Papers* 12, vol. 58, 24 August 1889.

Wilkie, R.S., *Yamethin District Gazetteer*, Rangoon, 1934.

SECONDARY WORKS: BOOKS, ARTICLES, THESES

Adams, W.M., *Green Development: Environment and Sustainability in the Third World*, London, 1990.

Adas, Michael, *The Burma Delta: Economic Development and Social Change on an Asian Rice Frontier, 1852-1941*, Madison, 1974.

——, 'From Avoidance to Confrontation: Peasant Protest in Precolonial and Colonial Southeast Asia', *Comparative Studies in Society and History* 23 (April 1981), pp. 217-47.

——, 'Bandits, Monks, and Pretender Kings: Patterns of Peasant Resistance and Protest in Colonial Burma, 1826-1941' in Robert P. Weller and Scott E. Guggenheim (eds), *Power and Protest in the Countryside: Studies of Rural Unrest in Asia, Europe, and Latin America*, Durham, NC, 1982, pp. 75-105.

——, 'Colonization, Commercial Agriculture, and the Destruction of the Deltaic Rainforests of British Burma in the Late Nineteenth Century' in Richard P. Tucker and J.F. Richards (eds), *Global Deforestation and the Nineteenth-Century World Economy*, Durham, NC, 1983, pp. 95-110.

——, 'From Footdragging to Flight: The Evasive History of Peasant Avoidance Protest in South and South-east Asia', *Journal of Peasant Studies* 13 (January 1986), pp. 64-86.

——, *Machines as the Measure of Men: Science, Technology, and Ideologies of Western Dominance*, Ithaca, 1989.

Ahmad, Nafis, *Economic Resources of the Union of Burma*, Natick, MA, 1971.

Albion, Robert Greenhalgh, *Forests and Sea Power: The Timber Problem of the Royal Navy 1652-1862*, Cambridge, MA, 1926.

Anderson, Benedict R. O'G., *Language and Power: Exploring Political Cultures in Indonesia*, Ithaca, 1990.

——, *Imagined Communities: Reflections on the Origin and Spread of Nationalism*, rev. edn, London, 1991.

Anderson, David, and Richard Grove (eds), *Conservation in Africa: People, Parks and Priorities*, Cambridge, 1987.

Andrews, Ernest, *The Bombay Burmah Trading Corporation Limited in Burmah, Siam and Java*, n.p., 1930-1, vols I-III.

Andrus, J. Russell, *Burmese Economic Life*, Stanford, 1956 [1948].

Arnold, David, and Ramachandra Guha (eds), *Nature, Culture, Imperialism: Essays on the Environmental History of South Asia*, Delhi, 1995.

——, 'Introduction: Themes and Issues in the Environmental History of

South Asia' in David Arnold and Ramachandra Guha (eds), *Nature, Culture, Imperialism: Essays on the Environmental History of South Asia*, Delhi, 1995, pp. 1-20.

Arnold, J.E.M. and W.C. Stewart, *Common Property Resource Management in India*, Tropical Forestry Papers no. 24, Oxford, 1991.

Ashton, Peter S., 'A Question of Sustainable Use', in Julie Sloan Denslow and Christine Padoch (eds), *People of the Tropical Rain Forest*, Berkeley, 1988, pp. 185-96.

Atkinson, D.J., 'Forest and Forestry in Burma', *Journal of the Royal Society of Arts* 96 (1948), pp. 478-91.

Aung San, 'This Burma', *Burma Digest* 2 (15 March 1947), pp. 1-4, 65.

Aung Tin, 'Forest Policy with Reference to Forest Propaganda for the Union of Burma', unpubl. MS., Forestry Institute, Oxford, 1962.

Aung Tun Thet, *Burmese Entrepreneurship: Creative Response in the Colonial Economy*, Stuttgart, 1989.

Ba Maw, *Breakthrough in Burma: Memoirs of a Revolution, 1939-1946*, New Haven, 1968.

Barber, Charles Victor, 'The State, the Environment, and Development: The Genesis and Transformation of Social Forestry Policy in New Order Indonesia', unpubl. Ph.D. thesis, University of California, Berkeley, 1989.

Barker, A.N., 'the Forest Position in Burma – January 1946', *Empire Forestry Review* 25, 1 (1946), pp. 36-41.

Barrington, A.H.M., 'Forest Development in Burma', *Empire Forestry* 4, 2 (1925), pp. 251-60.

Bayly, C.A., 'Indian Society and the Making of the British Empire', *New Cambridge History of India*, Cambridge, 1988, vol. II, part I.

Beinart, William and Peter Coates, *Environment and History: The Taming of Nature in the U.S.A. and South Africa*, London, 1995.

Beresford, Melanie and Lyn Fraser, 'Political Economy of the Environment in Vietnam', *Journal of Contemporary Asia* 22 (January 1992), pp. 3-19.

Blaikie, Piers, *The Political Economy of Soil Erosion in Developing Countries*, London, 1985.

Blaikie, Piers, and Harold Brookfield, *Land Degradation and Society*, London, 1987.

Blanford, H.R., 'Forest Management and Preparation of Working Plans in Burma', *Empire Forestry* 4, 1 (1925), pp. 54-65.

Blower, John, 'Conservation Priorities in Burma', *Oryx* 19 (April 1985), pp. 79-85.

Blower, John and James Paine, with Saw Hahn, Ohn, and Harold Sutter, 'Burma (Myanmar)', in N. Mark Collins, Jeffery A. Sayer, and Timothy C. Whitmore (eds), *The Conservation Atlas of Tropical Forests: Asia and the Pacific*, London, 1991, pp. 103-10.

Boomgaard, Peter, 'Forest Management and Exploitation in Colonial Java, 1677-1897', *Forest and Conservation History* 36 (January 1992), pp. 4-14.

Brandis, Dietrich, 'The Burma Teak Forests', *Garden and Forest* 9 (1895), pp. 1-32.

———, *Indian Forestry*, Woking, 1897.

Braund, H.E.W., *Calling to Mind: Being some account of the First Hundred Years (1870 to 1970) of Steel Brothers and Company Ltd.,* Oxford, 1975.

Brown, Ian, *The Elite and the Economy in Siam, c. 1890- 1920,* Singapore, 1988.

Bryant, Raymond L., 'Political Ecology: An Emerging Research Agenda in Third-World Studies', *Political Geography* 11 (January 1992), pp. 12-36.

——, 'Shifting the Cultivator: The Politics of Teak Regeneration in Colonial Burma', *Modern Asian Studies,* 28 (May 1994), pp. 225-50.

——, 'Forest Problems in Colonial Burma: Historical Vairations on Contemporary Themes', *Global Ecology and Biogeography Letters* 3 (July-November 1993), pp. 123-37.

Bunker, Stephen G., *Underdeveloping the Amazon: Extraction, Unequal Exchange, and the Failure of the Modern State,* Urbana, 1985.

Cady, John, F., *A History of Modern Burma,* Ithaca, 1958.

Champion, Harry and F.C. Osmaston (eds), *E.P. Stebbing's The Forests of India,* London, 1962, vol. IV.

Christian, John LeRoy, *Burma and the Japanese Invader,* Bombay, 1945.

Craddock, Reginald, *The Dilemma in India,* London, 1929.

Crosthwaite, Charles, *The Pacification of Burma,* London, 1912.

Dauvergne, Peter, 'The Politics of Deforestation in Indonesia', *Pacific Affairs* 66 (Winter 1993/4), pp. 497-518.

Davis, John H., *The Forests of Burma,* Gainesville, FL, 1960.

De'Ath, Colin, 'A History of Timber Exports from Thailand with Emphasis on the 1870-1937 Period', *Natural History Bulletin of the Siam Society* 40 (summer 1992), pp. 49-65.

Diokno, Maria Serena I., 'British Firms and the Economy of Burma, with Special Reference to the Rice and Teak Industries, 1917- 1937', unpubl. Ph. D. thesis, University of London, 1983.

Doherty, Faith, and Nyein Han, *Burma: Human Lives for Natural Resources Oil and Natural Gas,* Bangkok, 1994.

Donnison, F.S.V., *Public Administration in Burma: A Study of Development during the British Connexion,* London, 1953.

Dovers, Stephen R., and John W. Handmer, 'Contradictions in Sustainability', *Environmental Conservation* 20 (Autumn 1993), pp. 217-22.

Dunleavy, Patrick, *Democracy, Bureaucracy and Public Choice: Economic Explanations in Political Science,* London, 1991.

—— and Brendan O'Leary, *Theories of the State: The Politics of Liberal Democracy,* New York, 1987.

Elliot, Jenny, 'Environmental Degradation, Soil Conservation and the Colonial and Post-colonial State in Rhodesia/Zimbabwe' in Chris Dixon and Michael J. Hefferman (eds), *Colonialism and Development in the Contemporary World,* London, 1991, pp. 72-91.

Evans, Peter B., Dietrich Rueschemeyer and Theda Skocpol, 'On the Road toward a More Adequate Understanding of the State' in Peter B. Evans, Dietrich Rueschemeyer and Theda Skocpol (eds), *Bringing the State Back In,* Cambridge, 1985, pp. 347-66.

Falkus, Malcolm, 'Early British Business in Thailand' in R.P.T. Davenport-Hines and Geoffrey Jones (eds), *British Business in Asia since 1860*, Cambridge, 1989, pp. 117-56.

Falla, Jonathan, *True Love and Bartholomew: Rebels on the Burmese Border*, Cambridge, 1991.

Feeny, David, 'Agricultural Expansion and Forest Depletion in Thailand, 1900-1975' in John F. Richards and Richard P. Tucker (eds), *World Deforestation in the Twentieth Century*, Durham, NC, 1988, pp. 112-43.

Ferrars, Max, and Bertha Ferrars, *Burma*, London, 1900.

Foucar, E.C.V., *I Lived in Burma*, London, 1956.

Freeman, John F., 'Forest Conservancy in the Alps of Dauphiné, 1287-1870', *Forest and Conservation History* 38 (October 1994), pp. 171-80.

Furnivall, J.S., 'Land as a Free Gift of Nature', *Economic Journal* 19 (1909), pp. 552-62.

——, 'The Fashioning of Leviathan: The Beginnings of British Rule in Burma', *Journal of the Burma Research Society* 29 (April 1939), pp. 3-137, reprint edited by Gehan Wijeyewardene, Canberra, 1991.

——, *Netherlands India: A Study of the Plural Economy*, Cambridge, 1967 [1939].

——, *Colonial Policy and Practice: A Comparative Study of Burma and Netherlands India*, New York, 1956 (1948).

——, 'Safety First: A Study in the Economic History of Burma', *Journal of the Burma Research Society* 40 (June 1957), pp. 24-38.

Gadgil, Madhav, 'India's Deforestation: Patterns and Processes', *Society and Natural Resources* 3, 2 (1990), pp. 131-43.

Gadgil, Madhav and Ramachandra Guha, *This Fissured Land: An Ecological History of India*, Delhi, 1992.

Gadgil, Madhav and Ramachandra Guha, 'Ecological Conflicts and the Environmental Movement in India', *Development and Change* 25 (January 1994), pp. 101-36.

Geary, Grattan, *Burma After the Conquest*, London, 1886.

Geary, Kate, *The Role of Thailand in Forest Destruction along the Thai-Burmese Border 1988-1993*, Bangkok, 1994.

Giddens, Anthony, *Central Problems in Social Theory: Action, Structure and Contradiction in Social Analysis*, London, 1979.

Gilmartin, David, 'Scientific Empire and Imperial Science: Colonialism and Irrigation Technology in the Indus Basin', *Journal of Asian Studies* 53 (August 1994), pp. 1127-49.

Golay, Frank H., Ralph Anspach, M. Ruth Pfanner, and Eliezer B. Ayal, *Underdevelopment and Economic Nationalism in Southeast Asia*, Ithaca, 1969.

Grove, Richard H., 'Colonial Conservation, Ecological Hegemony and Popular Resistance: Towards a Global Synthesis' in John M. MacKenzie (ed.), *Imperialism and the Natural World*, Manchester, 1990, pp. 15-50.

——, 'Conserving Eden: The (European) East India Companies and their Environmental Policies on St. Helena, Mauritius and in Western India, 1660 to 1854', *Comparative Studies in Society and History* 35 (April 1993), pp. 318-51.

Guha, Ramachandra, *The Unquiet Woods: Ecological Change and Peasant Resistance in the Himalaya*, Delhi, 1989.

——, 'Saboteurs in the Forest: Colonialism and Peasant Resistance in the Indian Himalaya' in Forrest D. Colburn (ed.), *Everyday Forms of Peasant Resistance*, London, 1989, pp. 64-92.

——, 'An Early Environmental Debate: The Making of the 1878 Forest Act', *Indian Economic and Social History Review* 27, 1 (1990), pp. 65-84.

Guha, Ramachandra and Madhav Gadgil, 'State Forestry and Social Conflict in British India', *Past and Present* 123 (May 1989), pp. 141-77.

Haeuber, Richard, 'Indian Forestry Policy in Two Eras: Continuity or Change', *Environmental History Review* 17 (spring 1993), pp. 49-76.

Hall, D.G.E. (ed.), *The Dalhousie-Phayre Correspondence 1852- 1856*, London, 1932.

——, *A History of South-East Asia*, 4th edn, London, 1981.

Harbinson, Rod, 'Burma's Forests Fall Victim to War', *The Ecologist* 22 (March/April 1992), pp. 72-3.

Harvey, G.E., *British Rule in Burma, 1824-1942*, London, 1946.

Havill, T.L., 'Social Forces affecting Technical Assistance Programs in Forestry, a Case Study: Burma', unpubl. Ph.D. thesis, Syracuse University, 1966.

Headrick, Daniel R., *The Tools of Empire: Technology and European Imperialism in the Nineteenth Century*, Oxford, 1981.

Helfer, John William, 'Third Report on Tenasserim', *Journal of the Bengal Asiatic Society* 8 (December 1839), pp. 973-1005.

Heller, Michael, 'The Politics of Telecommunications Policy in Mexico', unpubl. D.Phil. thesis, University of Sussex, 1990.

Heske, Franz, *German Forestry*, New Haven, 1938.

Hill, Glen, 'Wildlife Trade in Mergui Tavoy District, Kawthoolei December 1991-April 1993', TRAFFIC Southeast Asia Field Report no. 2, Chiang Mai, 1993.

Hirsch, Philip, 'Deforestation and Development in Thailand', *Singapore Journal of Tropical Geography* 8 (1987), pp. 129-38.

——, *Development Dilemmas in Rural Thailand*, Singapore, 1990.

——, 'Forests, Forest Reserve, and Forest Land in Thailand', *Geographical Journal*, 156 (July 1990), pp. 166-74.

Hirsch, Philip and Larry Lohmann, 'Contemporary Politics of Environment in Thailand', *Asian Suvey* 29 (1989), pp. 439-51.

Hla Pe, *Narrative of the Japanese Occupation of Burma*, recorded by Khin, Cornell University Data Paper no. 41. Ithaca, 1961.

Hong, Evelyne, *Natives of Sarawak: Survival in Borneo's Vanishing Forests*, Penang, 1987.

Horowitz, Michael M., 'Ideology, Policy, and Praxis in Pastoral Livestock Development' in Michael M. Horowitz and T.M. Painter (eds), *Anthropology and Rural Development in West Africa*, Boulder, 1986, pp. 251-72.

Howard, Alexander L., 'Commercial Prospects of Burma Woods', *Asiatic Review*, 19 (July 1923), pp. 396-401.

——, 'The Forests and Timbers of Burma', *Journal of the East India Association* (n.s.) 15 (1924), pp. 139-51.

Htin Aung, *Epistles Written on the Eve of the Anglo-Burmese War*, The Hague, 1968.

Hurrell, Andrew, 'A Crisis of Ecological Viability? Global Environmental Change and the Nation State', *Political Studies*, 42 (1994), pp. 146-65.

Hurst, Philip, *Rainforest Politics: Ecological Destruction in South-East Asia*, London, 1990.

James, N.D.G., *A History of English Forestry*, Oxford, 1981.

Jenkins, Bill and Andrew Gray, 'Bureaucratic Politics and Power: Developments in the Study of Bureaucracy', *Political Studies* 31 (June 1983), pp. 177-93.

Jewitt, Sarah, 'Europe's "Others"? Forestry Policy and Practices in Colonial and Postcolonial India', *Environment and Planning D: Society and Space* 13 (1995), pp. 67-90.

Johnston, R.J., *Environmental Problems: Nature, Economy and State*, London, 1989.

Keeton, Charles Lee III, *King Thebaw and the Ecological Rape of Burma: The Political and Commercial Struggle between British India and French Indo-China in Burma, 1878-1886*, Delhi, 1974.

Kelley, R. Talbot, *Burma: Painted and Described*, London, 1912.

Keyes, Charles F., 'The Karen in Thai History and the History of the Karen in Thailand' in Charles F. Keyes (ed.), *Ethnic Adaptation and Identity: The Karen on the Thai Frontier with Burma*, Philadelphia, 1979, pp. 25-61.

Khin Maung Kyi, 'Western Enterprise and Economic Development in Burma', *Journal of the Burma Research Society* 53 (June 1970), pp. 25-51.

Knappen Tippetts Abbott McCarthy, *Economic and Engineering Development of Burma*, London, 1953, vol. II.

Koeing, William J., *The Burmese Polity, 1752-1819: Politics, Administration, and Social Organization in the Early Kon-baung Period*, Ann Arbor, 1990.

Komkris, Thiem, 'Forestry Aspects of Land Use in Areas of Swidden Cultivation' in Peter Kunstadter, E.C. Chapman and Sanga Sabhasri (eds), *Farmers in the Forest: Economic Development and Marginal Agriculture in Northern Thailand*, Honolulu, 1978, pp. 61-70.

Kunstadter, Peter, 'Hill People of Northern Thailand' in Julie Sloan Denslow and Christine Padoch (eds), *People of the Tropical Rain Forest*, Berkeley, 1988, pp. 93-110.

Kurz, Sulpice, *Preliminary Report on the Forest and other Vegetation of Pegu*, Calcutta, 1875.

Langham-Carter, R.R., 'Burmese Rule on the Toungoo Frontier', *Journal of the Burma Research Society* 27 (1937), pp. 15-32.

Lawson, A.A., *Life in the Burmese Jungle*, Sussex, 1983.

Leach, E.R., *Political Systems of Highland Burma: A Study of Kachin Social Structure*, London, 1986 [1954].

——, 'The Frontiers of "Burma"', *Comparative Studies in Society and History* 3 (1960), pp. 49-68.

Leungaramsri, P., and N. Rajesh, *The Future of People and Forests in Thailand after the Logging Ban*, Bangkok, 1992.

Lewis, Martin W., *Green Delusions: An Environmentalist Critique of Radical Environmentalism*, Durham, NC, 1992.

Lewis, Norman, *Golden Earth: Travels in Burma*, London, 1952.

Lieberman, Victor B., *Burmese Administrative Cycles: Anarchy and Conquest, c. 1580-1760*, Princeton, 1984.

——, 'Secular Trends in Burmese Economic History, c. 1350-1830, and their Implications for State Formation', *Modern Asian Studies*, 25 (February 1991), pp. 1-31.

Linebaugh, Peter, 'Karl Marx, the Theft of Wood, and Working Class Composition: A Contribution to the Current Debate', *Crime and Social Justice* 6 (fall-winter 1976), pp. 5-16.

Lintner, Bertil, *Outrage: Burma's Struggle for Democracy*, London, 1990.

Lohmann, Larry, 'Land, Power and Forest Colonization in Thailand', *Global Ecology and Biogeography Letters* 3 (July-September 1993), pp. 180-91.

——, 'Freedom to Plant: Indonesia and Thailand in a Globalizing Pulp and Paper Industry' in Michael J.G. Parnwell and Raymond L. Bryant (eds), *Environmental Change in South-East Asia: People, Politics and Sustainable Development*, London, 1996, pp. 23-48.

Lowe, R.G., 'Development of Taungya in Nigeria' in Henry L. Gholz (ed.), *Agroforestry: Realities, Possibilities and Potentials*, Dordrecht, 1987, pp. 137-54.

MacGillivray, A.W., 'Forest Use and Conflict in Burma 1750-1990', unpubl. M.Sc. thesis, University of London, 1990.

Mann, Michael, 'The Autonomous Power of the State: Its Origins, Mechanisms and Results' in John A. Hall (ed.), *States in History*, Oxford, 1986, pp. 109-36.

Mannin, Ethel, *Land of the Crested Lion: A Journey through Modern Burma*, London, 1953.

Marshall, Harry I., 'Karen Bronze Drums', *Journal of the Burma Research Society* 19 (April 1929), pp. 1-14.

——, *The Karen People of Burma: A Study in Anthropology and Ethnology*, Columbus, Ohio, 1922.

Mather, Alexander S., *Global Forest Resources*, London, 1990.

Maung Maung, *Burma's Constitution*, 2nd edn, The Hague, 1961.

——, *Burma and General Ne Win*, London 1969.

Maung Maung, 'Nationalist Movements in Burma, 1920-1940: Changing Patterns of Leadership: From Sangha to Laity', M.A. thesis, Australian National University, 1976.

McCrae, Alister, *Scots in Burma: Golden Times in a Golden Land*, Edinburgh, 1990.

Mekvichai, Banasopit, 'The Teak Industry in North Thailand: The Role of a Natural-Resource-Based Export Economy in Regional Development', unpubl. Ph.D. thesis, Cornell University, 1988.

Mills, J.A., 'Burmese Peasant Response to British Provincial Rule 1852-1885', in D.B. Miller (ed.), *Peasants and Politics: Grass Roots Reaction to Change in Asia*, London, 1979, pp. 77-104.

Morehead, F.T., *The Forests of Burma*, London, 1944.

Moscotti, Albert D., *British Policy and the Nationalist Movement in Burma 1917-1937*, Asian Studies at Hawaii, no. 11, Honolulu, 1974.

Murali, Atluri, 'Whose Trees? Forest Practices and Local Communities in Andhra, 1600-1922', in David Arnold and Ramachandra Guha (eds), *Nature, Culture, Imperialism: Essays on the Environmental History of South Asia*, Delhi, 1995, pp. 86-122.

Murphy, Raymond, *Social Closure: The Theory of Monopolization and Exclusion*, Oxford, 1988.

Myo Myint, 'The Politics of Survival in Burma: Diplomacy and Statecraft in the Reign of King Mindon, 1853-1878', unpubl. Ph.D. thesis, Cornell University, 1987.

Nisbet, Hugh, *Experiences of a Jungle-Wallah*, St Albans, Herts, 1936.

Nisbet, John, *Burma under British Rule and Before*, Westminster, 1901, vols I-II.

——, 'The Development and Trade of Burma', *Imperial and Asiatic Quarterly Review* 25 (1908), pp. 73-97.

Ogilvie, G.H., 'A Forestry Officer's Life in Burma', *Sylva* (Edinburgh) 14 (1934), pp. 20-1.

Ooi Jin Bee, 'The Tropical Rain Forest: Patterns of Exploitation and Trade', *Singapore Journal of Tropical Geography* 11 (December 1990), pp. 117-42.

Orwell, George, *Burmese Days*. Harmondsworth, 1987 (1934).

Pathak, Akhileshwar, *Contested Domains: The State, Peasants and Forests in Contemporary India*, London, 1994.

Pearn, B.R., *A History of Rangoon*, Rangoon, 1939.

Peet, Richard and Michael Watts, 'Development Theory and Environment in an Age of Market Triumphalism', *Economic Geography* 69 (July 1993), pp. 227-53.

Peluso, Nancy Lee, *Rich Forests, Poor People: Resource Control and Resistance in Java*, Berkeley, 1992.

——, 'The History of State Forest Management in Colonial Java', *Forest and Conservation History* 35 (April 1991), pp. 65-75.

Pelzer, Karl J., 'Swidden Cultivation in Southeast Asia: Historical, Ecological, and Economic Perspectives' in Peter Kunstadter, E.C. Chapman and Sanga Sabhasri (eds), *Farmers in the Forest: Economic Development and Marginal Agriculture in Northern Thailand*, Honolulu, 1978, pp. 271-86.

Peters, P.E., 'Struggles over Water, Struggles over Meaning: Water and the State in Botswana', *Africa* 54 (1984), pp. 29-49.

Perree, W.F., 'Indian Forest Administration', *Asiatic Review* 23 (April 1927), pp. 241-58.

Poffenberger, Mark, 'The Evolution of Forest Management Systems in Southeast Asia' in Mark Poffenberger (ed.), *Keepers of the Forest: Land Management Alternatives in Southeast Asia*, West Hartford, Conn., 1990, pp. 7-26.

Pointon, A.C., *The Bombay Burmah Trading Corporation Ltd., 1863-1963*, Southampton, 1964.

Pollack, Oliver B., *Empires in Collision: Anglo-Burmese Relations in the Mid-Nineteenth Century*, Westport, CT, 1979.

Potter, Lesley, 'Environmental and Social Aspects of Timber Exploitation in Kalimantan, 1967-1989' in J. Hardjono (ed.), *Indonesia: Resources, Ecology, and Environment*, Singapore, 1991, pp. 177-211.

Pouchepadass, Jacques, 'British Attitudes towards Shifting Cultivation in Colonial South India: A Case Study of South Canara District 1800-1920' in David Arnold and Ramachandra Guha (eds), *Nature, Culture, Imperialism: Essays on the Environmental History of South Asia*, Delhi, 1995, pp. 123-51.

Pragtong, Kamon and David E. Thomas, 'Evolving Management Systems in Thailand' in Mark Poffenberger (ed.), *Keepers of the Forest: Land Management Alternatives in Southeast Asia*, West Hartford, Conn., 1990, pp. 167-86.

Puntasen, Apichai, Somboon Siriprachai and Chaiyuth Punyasavatsut, 'Political Economy of Eucalyptus: Business, Bureaucracy and the Thai Government', *Journal of Contemporary Asia* 22 (1992), pp. 187-206.

Rangarajan, Mahesh, 'Imperial Agendas and India's Forests: The Early History of Indian Forestry, 1800-1878', *Indian Economic and Social History Review* 31 (April-June 1994), pp. 147-67.

Rawat, Ajay S. (ed.), *History of Forestry in India*, New Delhi, 1991.

Redclift, Michael, *Sustainable Development: Exploring the Contradictions*, London, 1987.

Repetto, Robert and Malcolm Gillis (eds), *Public Policies and the Misuse of Forest Resources*, Cambridge, 1988.

Ricardo, David, *The Principles of Political Economy and Taxation*, London, 1821 (1817).

Richards, John F. and Richard P. Tucker (eds), *World Deforestation in the Twentieth Century*, Durham, NC, 1988.

Richards, Paul, *Indigenous Agricultural Revolution: Ecology and Food Production in West Africa*, London, 1985.

Robinson, Richard, *Indonesia: The Rise of Capital*, Sydney, 1986.

Rueschemeyer, Dietrich and Peter B. Evans, 'The State and Economic Transformation: Toward an Analysis of the Conditions Underlying Effective Intervention' in Peter B. Evans, Dietrich Rueschemeyer and Theda Skocpol (eds), *Bringing the State Back In*, Cambridge, 1985, pp. 44-77.

Rush James, *The Last Tree: Reclaiming the Environment in Tropical Asia*, New York, 1991.

Said, Edward, *Orientalism*, London, 1978.

Saldanha, Indra Munshi, 'The Political Ecology of Traditional Farming Practices in Thana District, Maharashtra (India)', *Journal of Peasant Studies* 17 (April 1990), pp. 433-43.

Scott, C.W., 'Forestry in Burma', *Journal Oxford University Forest Society*, 3rd ser. 1 (1946), pp. 24-34.

Scott, James C., *The Moral Economy of the Peasant: Rebellion and Subsistence in Southeast Asia*, New Haven, 1976.

——, *Weapons of the Weak: Everyday Forms of Peasant Resistance*, New Haven, 1985.

——, *Domination and the Arts of Resistance: Hidden Transcripts*, New Haven, 1990.

Shein, *Burma's Transport and Foreign Trade 1885-1914*, Rangoon, 1964.

244 *Bibliography*

Shein, Myint Myint Thant and Tin Tin Sein, ' "Provincial Contract System" of British Indian Empire, in Relation to Burma: A Case of Fiscal Exploitation', *Journal of the Burma Research Society* 52 (December 1969), pp. 1-27.
Shirley, G.S., 'Growing of Timber so far as Forest Villages and Taungyas are Concerned (Burma)', *Third British Empire Forestry Conference Papers* (1928), pp. 612-15.
Shiva, Vandana, *Ecology and the Politics of Survival: Conflicts over Natural Resources in India*, London, 1991.
Shway Yoe (J. George Scott), *The Burma: His Life and Notions*, Edinburgh, 1989 (1882).
Silberman, Bernard S., *Cages of Reason: The Rise of the Rational State in France, Japan, the United States and Great Britain*, Chicago, 1993.
Silva, Eduardo, 'Thinking Politically about Sustainable Development in the Tropical Forests of Latin America', *Development and Change* 25 (October 1994), pp. 697-721.
Simmonds, P.L., 'The Teak Forests of India and the East, and Our British Imports of Teak', *Journal of the Society of Arts* 33 (February 1885), pp. 345-55.
Skocpol, Theda, 'Bringing the State Back In: Strategies of Analysis in Current Research', in Peter B. Evans, Dietrich Rueschemeyer and Theda Skocpol (eds), *Bringing the State Back In*, Cambridge, 1985, pp. 3-37.
Slym, M.J., *Memorandum on Jungle Fires*, Maulmain, 1876.
Smeaton, Donald Mackenzie, *The Loyal Karens of Burma*, London, 1887.
Smil, Vaclav, *The Bad Earth: Environmental Degradation in China*, Armonk, NY, 1984.
Smith, Adam, *An Inquiry into the Nature and Causes of the Wealth of Nations*, edited by R.H. Campbell and A.S. Skinner, Oxford, 1976 (1776), vols I-II.
Smith, Martin, *Burma: Insurgency and the Politics of Ethnicity*, London, 1991.
——, *Ethnic Groups in Burma: Development, Democracy and Human Rights*, London, 1994.
——, *Paradise Lost? The Suppression of Environmental Rights and Freedom of Expression in Burma*, London, 1994.
Smith, Shannon L., *The Politics of Indonesian Rainforests*, Monash University Centre of Southeast Asian Studies Working Paper 76, Clayton, 1992.
Spencer, J.E., *Shifting Cultivation in Southeastern Asia*, Berkeley, 1966.
Stamp, L. Dudley, *The Vegetation of Burma from an Ecological Standpoint*, Rangoon, 1924.
Stebbing, E.P., *The Forests of India*, London, 1922-6, vols I-III.
——, 'The Teak Forests of Burma', *Nature* 160 (13 December 1947), pp. 818-20.
Steinberg, David I., *Burma's Road Toward Development: Growth and Ideology under Military Rule*, Boulder, CO, 1981.
Steinberg, David Joel, David P. Chandler, William R. Roff, John R.W. Smail, Robert H. Taylor, Alexander Woodside and David K. Wyatt, *In Search of Southeast Asia: A Modern History*, rev. edn, Sydney, 1987.
Stoler, Ann Laura, 'Rethinking Colonial Categories: European Communities

and the Boundaries of Rule', *Comparative Studies in Society and History* 31 (January 1989), pp. 134-61.

Taylor, Robert H., *Foreign and Domestic Consequences of the KMT Intervention in Burma*, Ithaca, 1973.

——, 'Politics in Late Colonial Burma: The Case of U Saw', *Modern Asian Studies* 10 (April 1976), pp. 161-93.

——, 'Perceptions of Ethnicity in the Politics of Burma', *Southeast Asian Journal of Social Science* 10, 1 (1982), pp. 7-22.

——, *An Undeveloped State: The Study of Modern Burma's Politics*, Centre of Southeast Asian Studies Working Paper no. 28, Melbourne, 1983.

——, *The State in Burma*, London, 1987.

Thomas, Keith, *Man and the Natural World: Changing Attitudes in England, 1500-1800*, Harmondsworth, 1983.

Thompson, E.P., *Whigs and Hunters: The Origin of the Black Act*, London, 1975.

Tinker, Hugh, *The Union of Burma: A Study of the First Years of Independence*, London, 1957.

Toke Gale, *Burmese Timber Elephant*, Rangoon, 1974.

Trager, Frank N., *Toward a Welfare State in Burma: Economic Reconstruction and Development, 1948-1954*, New York, 1954.

——, *Burma: From Kingdom to Independence: A Historical and Political Analysis*, London, 1966.

—— and William J. Koenig, *Burmese Sit-tans, 1764-1826: Records of Rural Life and Administration*, Tucson, AZ, 1979.

Troup, R.S., 'Forestry in India', *Calcutta Review* 273 (July 1913), pp. 305-15.

——, *The Silviculture of Indian Trees*, Oxford, 1921, vol. II.

Tucker, Richard P., 'The British Colonial System and the Forests of the Western Himalayas, 1815-1914' in Richard P. Tucker and J.F. Richards (eds), *Global Deforestation and the Nineteenth- Century World Economy*, Durham, NC, 1983, pp. 146-66.

——, 'The British Empire and India's Forest Resources: The Timberlands of Assam and Kumaon, 1914-1950' in John F. Richards and Richard P. Tucker (eds), *World Deforestation in the Twentieth Century*, Durham, NC, 1988, pp. 91-111.

Tucker, Richard P. and J.F. Richards (eds), *Global Deforestation and the Nineteenth-Century World Economy*, Durham, NC, 1983.

Vandergeest, Peter and Nancy Lee Peluso, 'Territorialization and State Power in Thailand', *Theory and Society* 24 (1995), pp. 385-426.

Walinsky, Louis J., *Economic Development in Burma, 1951-1960*, New York, 1962.

Walker, K.J., 'The State in Environmental Management: The Ecological Dimension', *Political Studies* 37 (March 1989), pp. 25-38.

Walker, R.B.J., *Inside Outside: International Relations as Political Theory*, Cambridge, 1993.

Wapner, Paul, 'Politics beyond the State: Environmental Activism and World Civic Politics', *World Politics* 47 (April 1995), pp. 311-40.

Weber, Max, *Economy and Society*, edited by Guenther Roth and Claus Wittich, New York, 1968, vols I-III.

Wellner, P., 'A Pipeline Killing Field: Exploitation of Burma's Natural Gas', *The Ecologist* 24 (September/October 1994), pp. 189-93.

Williams, J.H., *Elephant Bill*, London, 1950.

——, *Bandoola*, London, 1953.

Williams, Susan, *Elephant Boy*, London, 1963.

Wilson, Geoff A., *The Urge to Clear the 'Bush': A Study of Native Forest Clearance on Farms in the Catlins District of New Zealand, 1861-1990*, Christchurch, 1992.

Winichakul, Thongchai, *Siam Mapped: A History of the Geo-Body of a Nation*, Honolulu, 1994.

Winters, Robert K., *The Forest and Man*, New York, 1974.

Won Zoon Yoon, 'Japan's Occupation of Burma, 1941-45', unpubl. Ph.D. thesis, New York University, 1971.

INDEX

247

6

Forest Secretary, 132
Forest Settlement Officer, 61, 74, 84, 85, 119
forest settlements, 87
forest subordinate unions, 148
forest villages, 112
forestry: 19, 145, 158, 159, 160; imperial, 128, 136; Karen, 167; *laissez-faire*, 18, 23-36, 212; precolonial, 39-41, 78; social, 182, 219; socialist, 168-77, 214; SLORC, 177-92; *see also* scientific forestry
Forests and Mines, Ministry, 134
Forests Minister, 131, 132, 133, 144, 145, 146
forests, tropical: 226-7, 229; afforestation, 13, 161-2, 163, 183-4; deforestation, 5, 12, 13, 20, 52, 53, 78, 79, 92, 93, 95, 115, 118, 161, 163, 183, 189, 191, 192, 198, 202, 210; deltaic, 8, 52, 118; plains, 52, 59, 117; reforestation, 5, 70-1; social and ecological significance, 6, 72
forests, types of, 226-7
Foucar and Company, 64, 101
Foucar, Ferdinand, 64
Framework Convention on Climate Change, 190
France, 7, 18, 47, 203, 205, 220
Fryer, Frederick, Chief Commissioner, 95
fuel, fuelwood, 118, 119, 161, 162, 183, 186, 217, 229
fuel reserves, 54, 119
Furnivall, J.S., 13

General Council of Buddhist Associations (GCBA), 130, 131, 136, 138
General Council of Sangha Sammeggi (GCSS), 136
Germany, German, 7, 18, 46, 47, 48, 203, 205, 208, 220
Giddens, Anthony, 9
Gillis, Malcolm, 12
Gladstone Wyllie, 63
Global Environmental Facility, 190

Goldenburg, John, 64
Government Forests, 54
Government of Burma Act (1935), 133
Government of India Act (1991), 129
Great Depression, 113, 124, 140, 144, 151, 204
green teak scandal, 101, 102; *see also* BBTCL
greening project, 183-4, 187
Grove, Richard, 36
Gudem hills, 199
Guha, Ramachandra, 10, 11, 57, 196
Guthrie, Superintendent, 31, 34

Hainan Island, 134
Hanthawaddy district, 119
Hauxwell, T.A., Conservator, 119
Helfer, John, 33, 34
Henzada district, 86, 117
High Court, Burma, 169
Hill, Harry, Conservator, 78, 83
Hla Pe, U, Forests Minister, 134
Hman, U, Chief Conservator, 162
Hodgkinson, G.J.S., Commissioner, 86
Hsaya San, 138, 139
Hsaya San rebellion, 138-9, 141, 158, 196
Htoon Aung Gyaw, U, 154
Hume, A.O., 59

improvement fellings, 107, 113, 158
in 72, 109, 228
India, Indian: 4, 11, 23, 26, 27, 36, 45, 46, 50, 57, 58, 65, 105, 109, 129, 133, 139, 143, 146, 154, 196; 215-17; conflict over forests, 198-200; forest officials, 199-200, 211; government of, 4, 24, 30, 31, 33, 35, 45, 46, 50, 54, 57, 61, 65, 66, 102, 114, 115, 126, 210-11; medical surgeons, 32, 36; scientific forestry, 215-17
Indian Forest Act (1865), 46, 56, 198
Indian Forest Act (1878), 56, 57, 58, 60, 210
Indian Forest Department, 46, 50, 198, 209-11, 215
Indian Mutiny (1857-8), 45